Locating Migration

Locating Migration

Rescaling Cities and Migrants

Edited by Nina Glick Schiller and Ayşe Çağlar

Cornell University Press
Ithaca and London

Copyright © 2011 by Cornell University

All rights reserved. Except for brief quotations in a review, this
book, or parts thereof, must not be reproduced in any form without permission in writing from the publisher. For information,
address Cornell University Press, Sage House, 512 East State
Street, Ithaca, New York 14850.

First published 2011 by Cornell University Press
First printing, Cornell Paperbacks, 2011
Printed in the United States of America

Library of Congress Cataloging-in-Publication Data

Locating migration : rescaling cities and migrants / [edited by]
Nina Click Schiller and Ayşe Çağlar
        p. cm.
   Includes bibliographical references and index.
   ISBN 978-0-8014-4952-9 (cloth : alk. paper)
   ISBN 978-0-8014-7687-7 (pbk. : alk. paper)
   1. Emigration and immigration—Social aspects.   2. Cities and
towns—Social aspects.   3. Urban policy—Social aspects.
4. Transnationalism—Social aspects.   I. Schiller, Nina Glick.
II. Simsek-Çağlar, Ayşe.   III. Title.
JV6225.L64   2011
307.2—dc22   2010022723

Cornell University Press strives to use environmentally responsible suppliers and materials to the fullest extent possible in the
publishing of its books. Such materials include vegetable-based,
low-VOC inks and acid-free papers that are recycled, totally
chlorine-free, or partly composed of nonwood fibers. For further
information, visit our website at www.cornellpress.cornell.edu.

Cloth printing   10 9 8 7 6 5 4 3 2 1
Paperback printing   10 9 8 7 6 5 4 3 2 1

To Leyla and Sinan
—*Ayşe Çağlar*

With love and gratitude to my multilocal,
transnational family: mother Evelyn Barnett, daughters
Rachel and Naomi Schiller, husband and partner
Stephen Reyna and our Reyna children, Braden, Damon,
and Zander, and all our grandchildren, Lexus, Ellie,
Isobel, Cameron, Chase, and William.
—*Nina Glick Schiller*

Contents

Acknowledgments

Our profound thanks to Professor Günther Schlee, director of the Max Planck Institute for Social Anthropology, and to Professor Burt Feintuch, director of the Center of the Humanities, University of New Hampshire, and the James H. Hayes and Claire Short Hayes New Hampshire History, Culture, and Government Chair in the Humanities for the support that made this book possible. We also thank and acknowledge the thoughtful contributions of Devan Aptekar (proofing), Caitriona Devery (indexing), and Darien Jane Rozentals (copyediting).

Locating Migration

Chapter 1

Introduction

Migrants *and* Cities

AYŞE ÇAĞLAR AND NINA GLICK SCHILLER

When we began to study migration in two seemingly different but relatively impoverished cities, one in the northeastern United States and the
other in the "postsocialist" region of Germany, we were surprised by what
we found. Migrants' experiences in these two cities were in some ways
hauntingly similar to each other and significantly different from what we
had observed in New York and Berlin. We were immediately confronted by
the realization that locality matters in migration research in a more differentiated way than it has been acknowledged in migration scholarship. Moreover,
research that compared cities with different relationships to migrants could
yield new insights. These realizations led us to ask why these rather obvious
points should seem so surprising. Why wasn't it apparent to us from the start
that migrant settlement and transnational connection in denigrated provincial cities would differ from that in urban centers with worldwide reputations as desirable places to live? To answer these questions we organized a
workshop that brought together scholars from two different strands of urban
research that usually don't talk to each other. Scholars immersed in debates
on concepts of urban sociospatiality and the neoliberal restructuring of cities
met collaboratively with ethnographers whose work focused on migrants'
settlement and transnationality. This book is the result of insights produced
from that interchange.

The book explores the varying pathways that migrants of different occupational, class, cultural, racialized, or religious backgrounds have established in a range of cities in the United States and Europe that are differently
positioned within globalization processes. It builds on insights and on debates developed over the past few years about the mutual constitution of the

global, national, and local migrants' contributions to the transnationality of cities, and concepts of scale and neoliberal rescaling. It also asks why critics as well as scholars of migration so often fail to address variations between cities and the differential outcomes of urban restructuring. Why are the roles of migrants in urban restructuring rarely discussed and even less frequently made the topic of comparative research?

Locating Migration responds to the need to think beyond existing scholarships and established paradigms when discussing and studying the relationship between cities and migration. There is a growing literature on migration that reflects fierce debate about the impact of immigrants on nation-states. For the most part, policy discussions of immigrants and the city have been framed by calls for integration and social cohesion (especially in Europe), or they focus on problem areas such as criminality, drugs, poverty, and violence. Migration scholars, meanwhile—whether they are debating assimilation, integration, transnationalism, or diversity—seldom move beyond the framework established by policymakers.

Within the migration literature there are many studies of migration *to* cities and the life of migrants *in* cities but very little about the relationship of migrants *and* cities. However, in most of this scholarship cities figure merely as containers providing spaces in which migrants settle and make a living. Despite the vast migration scholarship on what are labeled ethnic, transnational, or diasporic communities in specific cities, we still know very little about how migrants actively contribute to the restructuring and repositioning of either their cities of settlement or those to which they are transnationally connected.

When it comes to urban studies, the robust literature on the neoliberal remaking, reimagining, and competitive marketing of cities is strangely silent about migration. At best, migrants appear as members of ethnic communities, as a component of the urban labor force, or as a group of actors who influence housing markets and processes of neighborhood redevelopment. In urban policy circles, migrants and people of migrant background are generally approached through the lens of social problems for the city. Increasingly, however, international migrants have become significant actors in the reconstitution of the daily life, economics, and politics of cities throughout the world. The transnationality of their social and cultural worlds helps shape—as well as respond to and fuel movements against—the growing social and economic disparities that currently accompany urban regeneration.

This, therefore, is a book for those concerned with migration as well as with cities. Cities everywhere are affected by global competition for investment, new-economy industries, and changing market pressures, including those that favor gentrification and urban regeneration. These pressures lead city leaders and developers around the world to promote their city as a global "brand." Migration, when considered locally, is a part of this global restructuring and reimagining of urban life. However, because cities differ in how they participate in and are affected by these global trends, the impact of migration varies and must be assessed in relationship to specific localities.

Consequently, to examine the relationship between migrants and cities is to think comparatively within the intersection of migration and urban studies. Various research projects and edited volumes increasingly compare cities, but the parameters of comparison are not clearly defined or theorized. This book builds toward a form of comparative method that Charles Tilly (1984, 82) called "variation-finding" in "comparing big structures and large processes." This method of comparison establishes principles "of variation in the character or intensity of a phenomenon by examining systematic difference amongst instances." In this introduction we explore principles of systematic variation in migrants' relationship to cities as these are shaped by the positionality of cities within economic, political, and cultural fields of power. In no case, in a variation-finding form of comparison, is everything held to be similar. What we hold to be similar instances are the relative positionings of cities within power hierarchies that are globally rather than only nationally constituted. Even as their pathways of incorporation in and transnational connection to cities differ in ways that reflect the varying positionality of these cities, migrants actively shape and sometimes transform relative urban scalar positioning.

By linking different pathways of migrant incorporation to the varying scalar positioning of the cities in which they are embedded, researchers can usefully investigate varying relationships between migrants and cities, beyond the general understanding of "city as context." Through their varying forms and trajectories of incorporation, migrants respond to the differential opportunities provided by the positioning of cities. These opportunities include variations in regulatory regimes, local infrastructures and possibilities for entrepreneurial activities, employment, education, housing, and entrance into local political and cultural life. In the remainder of this introduction we draw on the work of the contributing authors to make a series of points that move us toward a new comparative perspective on migration, urban restructuring and global repositioning, and what we call "city scale."

Locating Migration approaches migrants as residents of cities and actors within and across space rather than as aggregated ethnic "communities." Through case studies of cities in the United States, Europe, and Africa, we can begin to see migrants' transnational social fields being shaped by (and part of) the restructuring, connecting, and global repositioning of particular cities—and particular places and institutions within those cities. We also see globe-spanning processes that are part and parcel of the daily experience of urban life and to which cities as structures of the organization of social life contribute. Migrants of various class backgrounds appear in these narratives as actors within and across space.

If it is necessary to situate migrants within specific locations and as agents and subjects of the global processes that reposition those localities, it is also important to consider the dimension of time. The role of migrants as actors within a city changes over time. Migrants respond to and contribute to each city's historical and institutional legacies, even as they are part of the continuing reconstitution of global processes that are substantiated locally. The authors in this book approach the dimension of time in different but ultimately complementary ways. Most provide a synchronic view of migrants as actors within the neoliberal restructuring of cities, while others (Bela Feldman-Bianco and Judith Goode especially) choose more long-term historical trajectories, addressing the ongoing repositioning of cities over time.

Working Definitions

The conceptual framework that we propose for the study of migrants and cities builds from several foundational terms: "neoliberalism," "scale," "restructuring," "rescaling," and "city scale." Neoliberalism can be approached as a series of projects to reorganize capital accumulation, which include both legitimation narratives and sets of practices (Leitner, Peck, and Sheppard 2007). Fostered by corporate, governmental, and intellectual actors, these projects began in the 1970s in the wake of the collapse of the Bretton Woods system for regulating the international monetary order. Whether they will survive or be strengthened by the global economic crisis of 2008–9 remains to be seen.

Neoliberalism cannot be reduced to a fixed set of attributes and policies that have produced the same predetermined outcome everywhere. Rather, it must be seen as specific projects that have drawn on a "global assemblage" of technologies of governance with variable results (Ong 2006; 2007, 5). This assemblage has facilitated a logic of accumulation that is selectively applied in diverse political contexts and within specific places. Neoliberal projects have included the reduction in state services and benefits, the disinvestment of states in urban economies, the diversion of public monies and resources to develop private service-oriented industries from health care to housing (sometimes in arrangements called public-private partnerships), and the relentless push toward global production through the elimination of state intervention in a host of economic issues from tariffs to workers' rights. Each of these aspects of neoliberalism has had a discrete impact on a particular urban area, but together they all have affected the relationship between migrants and cities of settlement.

As is the case with every historic turn in capitalism as a form of the accumulation of wealth and power, neoliberal projects have included efforts to restructure the social relations of production, including work, property, institutions, mechanisms of governance, the deployment of military power, definitions of citizenship, and individuals' sense of self. As David Harvey (2006) has pointed out, these restructuring processes have spatial dimensions. In other words, despite the narratives of unfettered flows of capital and cyberspace networks of communication, capital at its core continues to be based on sets of unequal social relations that occur between specific people who interact from specific locations. All social relations are situated in time and space. The construction and destruction of localized investment, produced by these social relations, is one of the dynamics of capitalism.

Geographers have contributed an important body of scholarship on the neoliberal restructuring and rescaling of cities and the transnational social movements that have been stimulated by, resisted, or aspire to move beyond neoliberal projects (see, for example, Brenner and Theodore 2002b; England and Ward 2007; Leitner, Peck, and Sheppard 2007). These projects include such globe-spanning institutions as the World Bank and the World Trade Organization, regional institutions such as the European Union, and local efforts to dispossess the urban poor through urban restructuring. All these developments have disrupted fixed notions of territorially bounded political units. The result has been a qualitative transformation of the hierarchy of authority and power of a set of relationships geographers refer to as scalar. No longer can urban, regional, national, and global scales be easily understood as a nested set of institutional relationships. Instead, cities now have to negotiate directly with regional or globally connected financial institutions and regulatory regimes, a process described by some theorists as "jumping scale" (Smith 2003; Swyngedouw 1992).

The need to theorize transformations in governance that reorganize spatial orders and the relationships between power-wielding political and administrative institutions has led to debates about the concepts of scale and discussions of rescaling. Meanwhile, we've seen a host of new terms coined to describe the relationship between global processes of neoliberal forms of capital accumulation and urban space: "global city," "world city," "ordinary city," "globalizing city," "nested city," and "transnational urbanism" (Abu-Lughod 1999; Amin and Graham 1997; Friedmann 1995; Hill 2004; Marcuse and van Kempen 2000; Robinson 2006; Sassen 1991; Smith 2001). We address the emergence of these terms and our discomfort with some aspects of the literature on the relationship between the urban and the global in chapter 4.

For now, let us just say that from our perspective all cities today are global in the sense that they have been affected by the globe-spanning processes of neoliberal restructuring and rescaling. As Peter Marcuse and Ronald Van Kempen (2000, xvii) have noted, globalization is "a process that affects all cities in the world, if to varying degrees and varying ways, not only those at the top of the 'global hierarchy.'"

In a similar vein but using the idioms of critical geographers, Neil Brenner comments in chapter 2 that "the urban scale operates as a localized node within globally organized circuits of capital accumulation, whereas the global scale is in turn constituted through networks of interlinked cities and city-regions." That is to say, to some degree all cities have been restructured and rescaled by processes in which the global and local are more than intertwined; they are part and parcel of the same ongoing processes of reconstructing and reimagining place. However, because the degree of engagement in these processes varies from city to city, as a result of local circumstances, histories, and resistance, not all cities end up in the same place, so to speak.

Therefore, we need a way to describe the differential structural repositioning of cities.

· · ·

The first section of this book consists of three chapters, each of which offers a different perspective on the terms "scale" and "rescaling" and on their utility in developing a conceptual framework that we can use to analyze the relationship between migration and cities. Each of the chapters offers a different approach to conceptualizing sociospatiality within globe-spanning processes of neoliberal restructuring, but one thing is clear: taken together these chapters present new lines of theorization, which can contribute to a new dialogue about migration and cities.

Brenner in chapter 2 joins with geographers who distinguish questions of scale from those of space, place, territory, or networks. He argues that "the churning, polymorphic geographies of urban restructuring and migration processes cannot be conceptualized exclusively in scalar terms." However, he insists that scalar concepts have indeed become essential tools for deciphering some of the key dimensions of contemporary urban transformations, including those associated with migration flows. Preferring to speak of scalar processes rather than scale, he associates "scale questions" with "those associated with the hierarchical differentiation and redifferentiation of sociospatial relations." He reserves the term "scale" for the task of conceptualizing the vertical integration of territorial units, separating this form of linkage from other forms of interconnection that he conceptualizes as networks.

In chapter 3, Michael Samers has no use for the term "scale" and proposes instead the term "sociospatial unit." He argues that "territoriality has 'effectivity' (that is, it exercises power) only through the performance of particular institutions that are shaped and reshaped by social networks and the complex power relationships between actor networks, institutions, and structures." Despite a different choice of terminology, Samers, through his interest in labor regimes, shares with Brenner and with us a commitment to capturing the unstable and mutating constellations of neoliberal practices and political regimes that have been transforming cities.

Neither approach seems to us capable of fully encompassing the dynamic processes that scholars have been trying to highlight when they deploy the term "scale" and its cognates, "scaling" and "rescaling." This is because the various concepts to which we apply the term—city, city-region, nation-state, world region, globe, as well as previous scalar concepts of city-state, league, colony, and empire—are simultaneously about spatial relationships, power, governance, and narrative.

As Samers notes, discussions of the repositioning of cities in the context of global neoliberal processes often leave the terms "scale," "scaling," and "rescaling" undefined. In chapter 4, we suggest that scaling refers to the ordering of sociospatial units within multiple hierarchies of power. Rescaling refers to a reordering of these relationships. Taken together the terms scaling and rescaling serve as a conceptual shorthand that allows us to speak of the intersection between two processes: restructuring, including movements of various forms of capital, and the reorganization of the relationships of power between specific sociospatial units of governance. The term "scalar positioning" refers to the intersection of restructuring and rescaling processes at a particular moment of time.

The reordering of sociospatial units within hierarchies of governing power over territory, persons, and resources (as well as within distributions of social and cultural capital) did not begin with neoliberalism. These processes are as old as cities. Neoliberalism has been just the latest historical conjuncture of rescaling processes. This conjuncture rearranged governance so that cities became directly positioned as global competitors.

Where does this leave the term "scale"? It is not the goal of this book to resolve the debates among geographers about the overall utility of concepts of scale, but most of the authors in this book approach city scale as a useful concept for facilitating comparisons among cities. We define city scale as the differential positioning of a city, which reflects both (1) flows of political, cultural, and economic capital within regions and state-based and globe-spanning institutions, and (2) the shaping of these flows and institutional forces by local histories and capacities. From this perspective, city scale is a relative position operating on a field of power, rather than a measure of the density of new-economy connections such as the indexes that have been posited by world cities researchers (Beaverstock, Smith, and Taylor 2000).

Proximity to other urban centers and the emergence of city-regions also must be considered in scalar assessment (Harding 1997). The approach to city scale we advocate allows us to examine hierarchies of different forms of power, which include migrants as social actors who both are shaped by and participate in these forms of power. In our view, in comparative research, the size of the population of the city is useful not as an absolute measure but as a possible indicator of regional, national, and global relationships. (For different understandings of the important of size, see Günther Schlee's afterword.)

It is important to emphasize that an analysis of the scalar positioning of cities facilitates a comparative dynamic explanatory framework; this approach does not justify simple causal statements. Neoliberal programs of capitalist restructuring have been shaped by existing political and institutional contexts, which are themselves the product of earlier regulatory regimes, institutional arrangements, and political configurations between different social forces (Leitner, Peck, and Sheppard 2007). Thus, neoliberal urbanism has unfolded in close interaction with the historical, structural, and contentious legacies of each city. For example, despite their similar characteristics and regional proximity, the Italian cities of Ravenna and Rimini (described by Ruba Salih and Bruno Riccio in chapter 7) have different trajectories and forms of contestation. Senegalese street peddlers, who became local entrepreneurs, were welcomed in Ravenna, while migrants of the same background and occupation have faced strong anti-immigrant sentiments and resentment in Rimini.

The two cities' different modes of receiving and incorporating migrants into the local economy, public life, and services can be traced back to their different histories of economic development. This includes the differing roles played by tourism and past alliances made between local political sectors in each city and the Italian state. Urban social forces—including the participation of migrants in social movements—take shape within specific local legacies and are influenced by past political compromises and alliances. Even when cities experience similar scaling/rescaling processes, the historical and institutional background of a particular city plays a crucial role in the way restructuring processes are implemented, challenged, experienced, and negotiated by local actors.

However, although historical circumstances have an impact on the repositioning of cities, each city is not unique. Therefore it is possible to utilize the concept of city scale and the relative scalar positioning of cities to compare relationships between migrants and cities. Cities' relationships to migrants can usefully be compared in terms of each city's degree of success or failure in restructuring and repositioning itself to compete globally.

For years scholars have been searching for a conceptual framework that can encompass both global processes and local histories. However, by framing the global and local as discrete processes, even as they call for analyses that bring the global to bear on the local, they preclude insights into the constitution of the global as grounded processes of social relations. As a result, over the decades urban studies has tended to swing back and forth between an interest in the global and the local. Currently, there is growing support for studying the particularities of each city and dismissing comparative projects.

Neil Brenner's useful reading of the history of urban studies (chapter 2) traces debates on the appropriate analytical frameworks for the study of urban life back to the 1972 call by Manuel Castells to reconsider "the urban question." For Castells, the city played a central role in the constitution of capital, various forms of industrialization, and accompanying processes of social and cultural change. Cities were portrayed as a specific system of capitalist relations that could be studied, in Brenner's words, "as a determinate structure within the capitalist mode of production." Brenner contrasts Castells's approach to the contemporary work in urban studies upon which *Locating Migration* builds. In this more recent approach the tendency to reify city scale recedes as the urban is situated in relationship to its mutual constitution of other sites of organized power.

Yet some scholars—including several in this book—still fear that any concept of city scale may reify the city and neglect disparities within it, including the uneven effect of globalizing processes on residents of different classes, neighborhoods, hot spots, and social networks. Consequently they either delimit what is meant by city scale or focus on internal divisions within the "spatial order" of the city (Brenner, chapter 2; Marcuse and Van Kempen 2000; van Dijk, chapter 6). Some theorists of space are now calling for the study of a range of space-constructing processes including "place-making" and networks of spatial connectivity (Jessop, Brenner, and Jones 2008; Smith 2001, 2005). We see the weaknesses as well as the strengths of this return to a multiplicity of terms to theorize the ways in which global processes are related to spatialization. Focusing on local contestations in specific places is an important research agenda, but it is different from the task we set for ourselves here—to develop a comparative conceptual framework that makes sense of migrant relationships to cities.

If scholarship on place-making now focuses on specific local places and networks, migration scholarship remains entangled with the national scale. In migration studies, migrants are often reduced to unitary actors within the nation-state who can only be understood to exercise the options of loyalty, voice, or exit (Hirschmann 1970). This perspective reflects and reinforces a linear understanding of migration process in which transnational connectivity is read as an imperfection of migrant incorporation. It also fails to address the variable forms of incorporation in relationship to the scalar positioning of the city of settlement and transnational connection. The approach to migration and cities developed in this book seeks to move beyond methodological nationalism—that is, an intellectual orientation that not only takes the nation-state as the unit of analysis but also confines discussions of social processes within national boundaries (Beck 2000b; Wimmer and Glick Schiller 2002).

Efforts to move beyond methodological nationalism and toward a comparative perspective of the relationship between migration and cities can build on two themes that emerge from the case studies presented in this book: (1) multiple pathways of migrant incorporation and transnational connection and the scalar positioning of cities and (2) migrants as scale makers. The remainder of this introduction explores these themes, the first briefly and the second in some depth. In chapter 4, we explore further the disparate trajectories of migration and urban studies as a step toward developing a comparative analytical framework for studying the relationship between neoliberal restructuring and rescaling and migrant settlement and transnational connection.

It is important to note here why, despite significant caveats, we think that the term "migrants" is a useful analytical category for the specific challenge of this book. Those ascribed to the category "migrants" play different roles in urban restructuring in terms of their education, class, occupation, national identities, gender, religion, and generation. Differentiation by generation makes the category of migrant even more problematic. Various authors in this book (Feldman Bianco, Caroline Brettell, Salih and Riccio, and Monika Salzbrunn) include in their analysis persons of migrant background (second generation and beyond) *if* they participate in networks organized around ancestral origins. None the less, by speaking about "migrants" this book is able to situate these groups of people as active participants in the daily activities and legitimization processes that are restructuring and reimagining cities all around the world.

In the United Kingdom and elsewhere in Europe, persons of migrant background often rightly reject the term "migrant" because it casts them as foreigners despite their legal and social citizenship. However, despite the fact that many people of migrant background see their country of residency as the center of their lives, current anti-immigrant polemics subject people of migrant background to racialization, stereotyping, and social distancing. Responding to the intense anti-immigrant rhetoric that contemporary politicians all around the world encourage and endorse, *Locating Migration* emphasizes the multiple roles that people of migrant background play as local actors rather than as threats to the body politic. The concept of migrant as it is deployed here takes into account the legal and discursive power of the institutions of a nation-state to define individuals as foreign in status, culture, or religion—even when they were born in the country and have full residency rights or legal citizenship. At the same time, by using the term migrant to refer to international migrants this book acknowledges the power of states to discursively differentiate the native from foreign means that in many but not all countries of the world internal migration is discounted or taken for granted. *Locating Migration* focuses on the relationship between cities and those people whose categorization as migrants obscures their identification with, and agency in, local urban transformations and struggles.

Multiple Pathways and the Scalar Positioning of Cities

Most migration literature focuses on how immigrants organize their neighborhoods, businesses, religious activities, and politics around ethnic identities. By contrast, the authors in this book demonstrate that ethnic incorporation is *only one* of the multiple pathways of migrant incorporation. Migrants also settle by forming social relations with people they are connected to through non-ethnic professional, neighborhood, political, religious, and economic relationships. The multiple and diverse pathways of incorporation traced in the pages of this book must be seen alongside (indeed, as part of) the struggle of urban leaderships to reposition their cities within national and global scales.

The perspective on migrant settlement illustrated here builds on and sharpens the analysis of a small but important strand of migration scholarship (especially evident in Europe) about differing opportunity structures. This body of work moves migration scholarship beyond a culturalist framework and enables the introduction of a political-economy analysis. Most of this literature, however, links modes of migrant incorporation to opportunity structures—citizenship laws, public policies, and relationships between government and organized religion—that operate at the level of the nation-state. National variation such as the different acceptance of public displays of religion in the United States and France are important to consider, as illustrated in Monika Salzmann's description of the different reception accorded the Murid brotherhood in New York and Paris (chapter 9). Also crucial to the story, however, are the local variations between cities that form the basis for city leaderships and local populations to counter anti-immigrant national policies. Such variations reflect relationships of power including processes of the production and destruction of fixed capital such as machinery, human capital, such as the utility of certain skills, and cultural capital including the reputation of cities. It is through these historic processes that the local is regionally, nationally, and globally constructed, grounded, reconfigured, and challenged.

In both chapter 4 and chapter 10 we emphasize the need to move migration scholarship beyond studies based on gateway cities to consider cities of different scale. The relative positioning of a city within hierarchical fields of power may well lay the groundwork for the differential lifechances and incorporation opportunities of migrants locally and transnationally. It is likely that migrants enter into urban life in different ways and have a differential impact in the restructuring trajectories of cities, depending on the city's scalar positioning. By examining the various ways that cities have experienced neoliberal restructuring and rescaling processes, migration scholars can more readily compare the different local urban dynamics that migrants confront and participate in. Such an approach will also allow researchers to investigate situations in which migrants' agency may contribute to the efforts of a city to reposition itself globally or to maintain its position of dominance.

Chapter 10 describes the non-ethnically organized pathways of migrant incorporation and transnationalism in two cities, Manchester, New Hampshire, and Halle in eastern Germany. Despite their many differences, both cities must confront limitations on opportunity structures imposed by neoliberal restructuring and rescaling. Unlike the long-standing gateway city of New York (Salzbrunn, chapter 9) or more recent gateways such as Amsterdam (van Dijk, chapter 6) and Dallas-Fort Worth (Brettell, chapter 5), cities that are downscaled are often unable to provide public or corporate support for ethnically based community organization. Nor do they provide opportunities for economic mobility for migrants or support for migrant professionals, who are often central actors in local ethnic politics and successful diasporic organizations found in global cities such as New York or Paris. In downscaled cities there are also fewer possibilities for migrants to become crucial agents of restructuring and bids for rescaling, a role they have been able to play in Dallas with its upscale positioning or in Philadelphia, which is striving to regain its previous upscale status.

The importance of locality in shaping migrant incorporation also emerges in Rijk Van Dijk's comparison of The Hague and Amsterdam (chapter 6). Because of their different positioning in relationship to the Dutch state and transnational institutions, Amsterdam and The Hague present Ghanaian migrants with different conditions of housing, a different job market, and contrasting levels of police surveillance. The Hague, a bureaucratic city, which serves as headquarters to various international organizations, offers different kinds of opportunities to Ghanaian migrants than does the commercial economy of Amsterdam. Consequently, despite their common national background, Ghanaian migrants in Amsterdam and The Hague find different pathways of economic, religious, and political incorporation.

Migrants as Scale Makers

The case studies in this book show that migrants find multiple ways to contribute to the competitive repositioning of their adopted cities as those cities participate in urban and regional restructuring. We indicate this constitutive role by referring to migrants as "scale makers." Migrants become scale makers as they labor, produce wealth, raise families, and create and reproduce social institutions, thereby contributing to the economic, social, cultural, and political life of their cities. The case studies reveal several different ways that migrants become active agents in the neoliberal transformation of cities: (1) as part of the labor force upon which the cities build their competitiveness; (2) as historical agents; (3) as agents of neoliberal urban restructuring who contribute to or contest the changing status and positioning of neighborhoods and cities; (4) by facilitating privatization and neoliberal subjectivities; and (5) by offering alternative social visions.

Part of the Labor Force

Migrant labor plays a crucial and varied role in making cities competitive regionally, nationally, and globally. As we see in chapters 5 and 8, powerful actors in the Dallas-Fort Worth area and in Philadelphia look to highly skilled migrant labor in their efforts to position their cities globally. Dallas-Fort Worth, an upscale migration gateway metroplex, has built a knowledge economy on companies like Texas Instruments and large health care facilities. Caroline Brettell demonstrates that these industries work together with and support Indian ethnic organizations in order to recruit and retain professional or high-tech workers from India and from among U.S.-educated Indian migrants. Transnational immigrant organizations make possible an adequate supply of the technical talent needed to maintain not only the power and wealth of these corporations but also the relative global positioning of the city in which the corporations are located.

Having lost its industrial base, Philadelphia is less competitively positioned than Dallas-Fort Worth. The city's leadership has made its medical-education complex central to an urban regeneration strategy, striving to reposition Philadelphia globally as a center of knowledge. Given its national reputation as a rather downtrodden city, Philadelphia has become reliant on migrant professionals, their transnational networks, and persons of migrant background (second-generation migrants) to sufficiently staff these knowledge-based industries. The city approaches these migrants not as ethnics contributing cultural difference but as "talent" and "knowledge workers." The high-powered universities, which rely on a supply of these workers, attract the investment of corporate capital. The hospitals and universities look to low-paid migrants as well as native workers to maintain these facilities.

In chapter 7, Ruba Salih and Bruno Riccio demonstrate that unskilled migrants in northern Italy can serve as scale makers at the regional as well as city level. Unable to match low-wage industries elsewhere in the wake of the neoliberal restructuring of Italy's trade and tariff policies, the towns of the Emilia Romagna region faced industrial collapse and severe demographic decline. Industries such as ceramics, survived a wave of deindustrialization and depopulation, maintained their local presence and stayed competitive through the hiring of low-wage and more flexible migrant labor. By changing the parameters of this region's interconnectedness to national and global markets and its position within national and regional hierarchies, migrant labor in Emilia Romagna played an important role in the rescaling of this region.

Historical Agents

Periods of economic and political growth have been shaped in part by the role that migrants have played in the positioning of cities within national and global hierarchies of power. In turn local histories shape the nature of alliances that migrants can make with city leaders, finance capitalists, or the urban poor in contesting and facilitating the restructuring of the cities of their settlement. We see this in Bela Feldman-Bianco's chapter on New Bedford, Massachusetts. With its origins in fishing and whaling industries, New Bedford was for many decades a significant site of commerce and the generation of capital. The city's ability to attract immigrant labor contributed to its transnational positioning as a major center of textile production in the nineteenth century. A historical scalar perspective reminds us that so often, in Europe as in the United States, successful industrial cities have been the products of immigrant incorporation within transnational commercial and financial connections. Feldman-Bianco's account also illustrates that within a particular city the leadership's willingness to embrace a migrant diaspora as an agent of urban restructuring and rescaling may be shaped by the city's past transnational history. The fact that transnational connections figure prominently in New Bedford's historical memory and self-portrait contributes to the propensity of its leadership to look to Portuguese transnational capital in its efforts to leave behind its current downscaled position.

Judith Goode's account of Philadelphia also highlights the importance of a historical scalar perspective. Philadelphia's legacy of racial polarization, which was resolved through the incorporation of an African American stratum into the city's political leadership, became an important contextual factor in the insertion of both highly skilled and entrepreneurial migrant sectors into the reinvention of Philadelphia. The racial politics of the city's political structure undercut the opposition of working-class and poor African Americans to neoliberal restructuring and gentrification. The absence of nativism against migrants in other neighborhoods also seems to have been facilitated by a vital collective memory of the city's immigrant past.

Agents of Neoliberal Urban Restructuring

"Gentrification" is a term used to signal the displacement of poor and working-class people from central city neighborhoods and housing stocks as wealthy people increasingly live, shop, and socialize in these locations (N. Smith 1999). Originally described as a North American and European phenomenon, this form of revaluing property and the desirability of place has become a significant aspect of the neoliberal development of cities in many countries of the world. Developers and political leaders often see gentrification processes as central to the implementation of urban regeneration policies. These are designed to transform cities by ensuring that they attract a new mix of investment and economic activities, including leisure, consumption, and tourism.

Gentrification can be differentiated from the historic urban process of sequential displacement, in which migrants who are unskilled workers or small entrepreneurs change the composition of poor and working-class neighborhoods. However, in the context of neoliberal restructuring, the settlement processes of working-class migrants, to the extent that they revitalize neighborhoods, sometimes pave the way for gentrification of those neighborhoods and in other cases contribute to urban regeneration efforts. For this reason, scholarship on gentrification recognizes that the process involves multiple actors with various class backgrounds (Atkinson and Bridges 2005).

Several of our authors demonstrate that to understand the relationship between migrants' neighborhood development, broader restructuring including gentrification, and urban regeneration, it is necessary to address the relative and changing global positioning of the city (and sometimes the city-region). The chapters that describe the relationship between migrants and the cities of Manchester, New Hampshire (chapter 10); New Bedford, Massachusetts (chapter 11); Philadelphia (chapter 8); and Paris and New York (chapter 9) describe neighborhood redevelopment in which migrants who are workers or owners of small businesses play important roles. Their investments help preserve and revalue aging residential areas and revitalize declining or moribund business districts. However, the significance of this redevelopment, its relationship to gentrification, and its effects on the regeneration of other places in the city and the region vary greatly, depending on and at the same time contributing to the ongoing rescaling of the city.

In downscaled cities migrants who establish small businesses may be agents of development in the city center. This has been the case in Manchester and Halle/Saale. This example demonstrates that gentrification processes are not necessarily indicators of rescaling. Despite the fact that these migrants are agents of change, urban development has still not been able to alter the cities' positioning. However, in a city with more possibilities of new-economy industries, such as Philadelphia, different synergies are possible. In Philadelphia, wealthy migrants who arrived as professionals, knowledge workers, and students desiring an urbane quality of life have been the forces of gentrification in inner-city neighborhoods. In search of affordable housing and small-business opportunities, working-class migrants have contributed to the city leadership's regeneration project by developing other neighborhoods. However, the possibility that this restructuring will be successful in globally repositioning the city is far from clear. Moreover, as elsewhere, there has been a contest between various social forces, including poor and working-class migrants, to see who will reap the benefits of the rescaling efforts

In cities with little else to promote besides tourism and culture industries, certain sectors of an immigrant population may play a significant part not only in the redevelopment of a neighborhood but also in the city as a whole. Their impact may in fact be regional. As Feldman-Bianco demonstrates, Portuguese migrants have been playing this role in New Bedford. In contrast, in cities such as New York, which are capable of attracting larger-scale capital investments, migrant entrepreneurs may play significant roles only in fringe or slum neighborhoods rather than the city center. However, as Monika Salzbrunn's research with Senegalese Murids in Harlem indicates, migrants' businesses, institutions, and flows of capital through transnational networks may initiate gentrification.

There are also instances, such as the Parisian one described by Salzbrunn, where local residents can resist urban developers by marketing themselves as a migrant neighborhood filled with multicultural diversity. Such diversity is proving vital to the competitive positioning of cities in a global tourist landscape. Salzbrunn also indicates the fragility of such victories, as successful neighborhood redevelopment attracts wealthier people, initiating gentrification processes. But the degree to which urban regeneration projects can contribute to a city's developing or maintaining a position of global importance varies. The relationship of migrants to a city reflects and contributes to these variations.

When we examine the relationship between cities and migrants, it becomes apparent that the redevelopment of neighborhoods, urban regeneration, and the rescaling capacities of cities are shaped by subjective assessments, as well as objective factors such as capital flows or corporate headquarters. As Salzbrunn's examples from New York and Paris and van Dijk's from Amsterdam and The Hague show, migrants' changing evaluations of localities within transnational fields reallocate prestige to newly emerging "spiritual centers" or hot spots. Migrants evaluate cities and neighborhoods, developing their own hierarchies of places based on the value and prestige of localities within migrant transnational fields.

Neighborhoods and cities that are seen by migrants as desirable settlement destinations may attract further flows of migrants, who contribute to the cultural diversity desired by urban promoters and developers, as well as flows of investments from within migrant transnational social fields. Thus the migrants' subjective rescaling of places is not just a question of their granting certain localities symbolic value; this form of rescaling has concrete economic consequences. It can contribute to the political and economic repositioning of these places locally and globally.

Facilitating Privatization and Neoliberal Subjectivity

As the case studies in this book document, migrants also become scale makers through their facilitation of the neoliberal agenda, including the abrogation of public responsibilities for social services and the privatization of public service programs. Migrants are implicated in these transformations in complex, multidirectional ways. They respond to neoliberal urbanism as do other urban residents by accepting certain "reforms" while actively contesting particular initiatives, as Salzbrunn's description of the Sainte Marthe neighborhood campaign makes clear in chapter 9. However, they play a specific role in facilitating the reduction or privatization of local public services in their localities of both settlement and departure.

In this regard, migrants' entanglements with the urban restructuring are twofold. First, migrant labor is strategically positioned so that in some cases it enables the state to cease providing public services. Second, migrants contribute to neoliberal governance by encouraging a form of subjectivity that reinforces the ethos of the self-reliant, enterprising individual. For example, as Salzbrunn demonstrates (chapter 9) migrants' self-reliance is upheld within polemics that celebrate neoliberal subjectivities and target impoverished African Americans.

Salih and Riccio's account of the growing dependence of the Emilia Romagna region of Italy on the domestic labor of eastern European migrant women provides a striking example of how the strategic location of migrant labor eases the state's withdrawal from public services without fueling much unrest in the society. This region has not only the lowest birth rate and the highest elderly population in Italy but also a higher rate of native-born women in the labor force. The migrant women, who provide their labor as domestic and care workers to the middle- and lower-income groups, enable the state's withdrawal from welfare provisions like child care and elderly care without disrupting native women's diverse placement in the labor process. Migrant domestic workers become strategic in the context of erosion of welfare services. In Manchester and Halle, in the absence of social services, migrants organized church networks that extended social and emotional support not only to migrants but also to natives.

Migrants may also facilitate neoliberal restructuring through their support of localities or institutions in their countries of origin. One example of this is seen in Brettell's description of the efforts of Indian organizations in Dallas-Fort Worth to provide financial support to the Indian Institute of Technology

(IIT) when public monies for the budget of the institute were cut. In order not to jeopardize the competitiveness of their IIT degrees, Indian migrants compensated for the budgetary cuts in higher education necessitated by the neoliberal policies in India.

Neoliberalism is about governing not only spaces but subjects. Neoliberal policies have been geared toward fostering self-enterprising and self-managing subjects who must rely on their own efforts to replace activities and services formerly understood to be public and social responsibilities. Communitarian thinking and voluntary networks of trust have become part of the governmental technologies that help to construct neoliberal subjectivities (Leitner, Peck, and Sheppard 2007, 4). The chapters by van Dijk, Salzbrunn, Goode, Brettell, and Nina Glick Schiller and Ayşe Çağlar all provide examples in which local authorities upheld migrants as models of self-reliant survival without support from state services and programs. For example, in Amsterdam and The Hague, the self-sufficiency and self-reliance of civic life of the Ghanaian community immersed within a Pentecostal civic life implicated them in efforts to discount the need for supportive social services.

Offering Alternative Social Visions

Migrants not only facilitate neoliberal governance, they also participate in social movements that contest neoliberal restructuring or the power of the central state to deny rights and services to migrants and other residents of cities and regions. Finding their agency in the city denied and at the same time being subject to neoliberal disparities, migrants may turn to alternative social visions. The quest for alternative visions may lead migrants and natives to the fundamentalist projects of global religions or various movements for social justice. While the transformative role of migrants cannot be seen as uniformly contributing to struggles for social justice, the potential is there and needs to be acknowledged.

In chapter 8, Goode shows the ambivalent positioning of migrants within the local community-based organizations and vis-à-vis local authorities in Philadelphia. She documents a case in which migrant petty vendors became politically active against the gentrification efforts of the university in partnership with the city government, which was displacing and "developing" neighborhoods. However, while resisting one kind of public-private partnership, the migrants became part of community organizations that were in league with the very authorities they were contesting. The Philadelphia case highlights the simultaneous multiple and contradictory alliances of migrants in urban rescaling. Goode's material resonates with Salzbrunn's description of the ambivalent and tension-ridden relations between Senegalese migrants and African Americans and their implication in contesting and participating in neoliberal partnerships in Harlem. Ultimately we see the difficulty of labeling migrants as either victims or beneficiaries of these processes.

Through their presence and participation in the restructuring of the local economy, migrants may contribute to the efforts of local governments to "jump scale," contesting or even seizing powers formally held by the national government. The new regional law in Emilia Romagna, bypassing the national law, gave migrants access to certain local services such as public housing and opposed the central government's anti-immigrant stance. That this defiance of the national state reflected an actual reorganization of the power hierarchy was made clear when the actions of Emilia Romagna were brought to the Italian constitutional court. The court ruled in favor of the regional government's independent immigration policies. Similarly, New Bedford, Massachusetts, which relies on undocumented migrants to provide a cheap labor source for sweatshops, has become one of a number of U.S. cities where local officials have opposed federal immigration policies. In that case there has been no readjustment of legal authority.

Rescaling efforts, which stimulate local governments to stand with their migrant populations and against national populations, illustrate the contradictions and potentials for struggle that have been generated as part of neoliberal restructuring (Purcell 2003a). Moreover, as the examples from Philadelphia, Paris, Manchester, and Halle demonstrate, neoliberal measures that restructure urban spaces and economies have increased the precariousness of life. Contemporary aspirational movements can be seen as a response to and a critique of the growing inequalities and disempowerment that have accompanied the implementation of neoliberal agendas. At the same time these movements are a response to the denial to most residents of the city—native or migrant alike—of the capacity to participate in the decisions and institutions that shape their daily life and future.

These transformations may engender a local repertoire of experiences and sensibilities that are shared by those who are considered natives and those of migrant background. The experiences that these poor and working-class people have in common and their identification with a city provide saliency to social and religious movements. Pentecostal Christianity, local neighborhood struggles, or efforts to oppose urban regeneration can move beyond a migrant-foreigner divide that locates migrants and natives in different registers of humanity and rights. Using very disparate forms of discourse, these forms of social action can be understood as claims to a "right to the city" (Lefebvre 2006). However, movements that claim local rights to the city stall without an acknowledgement of the mutual constitution of the local and the global. It is important that both scholars and activists recognize that cities are themselves global terrains. As such they are sites of the substantiation and contestation of hierarchies of globe-spanning power.

• • •

This book calls for a new approach to the study of migrant settlement and transnational connection in which cities rather than nation-states, ethnic groups, or transnational communities serve as the starting point for comparative analysis. We argue for a theory-inspired comparative agenda that will advance conceptual and empirical knowledge on urban and migrant dynamics. Those who engage in the comparative study of cities must clarify why specific cities are being compared and explain the basis of their comparison. This book takes a step toward developing a comparative urban scholarship by approaching cities not as containers but as fluid and historically differentiated entry points from which to explore urban restructuring and migrants' integral role in these processes. This approach can advance our knowledge about the different pathways of migrant incorporation and transnationalism in cities of different scale. *Locating Migration* demonstrates that migrants are residents of cities and actors within them, understanding that to be a resident of a city is to live within, contribute to, and contest globe-spanning processes that shape urban economy, politics, and culture.

Part I

Migration and Cities

Reframing the Topic

Chapter 2

The Urban Question and the Scale Question

Some Conceptual Clarifications

NEIL BRENNER

Since the early 1990s, there has been an unprecedented explosion of social-scientific interest in the dual problematic of scale and rescaling. First, it is now widely recognized that the scalar constitution of modern capitalism—its differentiation among local, regional, national, transnational, and global geographical units—is not a preexisting feature of social life but is, rather, historically produced, reorganized, and contested (Swyngedouw 1997b; Smith 1995). Second, building upon this theoretical proposition, key contributions to geopolitical economy, state theory, urban and regional studies, social movement studies, and environmental geography have drawn attention to diverse forms of contemporary scalar transformation, or rescaling, in which inherited scalar arrangements are being challenged and reworked (Keil and Mahon 2009; Marston 2000; Sayre 2008, 2005; Sheppard and McMaster 2004). Whereas the social sciences have long contained implicit assumptions regarding the scalar constitution of political-economic processes, these more recent interdisciplinary developments indicate that the "scale question" is now being confronted with an unprecedented methodological reflexivity.

In this chapter, I draw upon this newly consolidated literature on the scale question in order to conceptualize the changing character of what has come to be known as the "urban question." The urban question has a complex lineage within the twentieth-century social sciences (Saunders 1986), but it was first labeled as such in the early 1970s by Manuel Castells ([1972] 1977); it has subsequently been debated extensively by urbanists and social theorists alike (Katznelson 1993; Merrifield 2002a, 2002b; Sassen 2000c). I argue below that post-1980s scalar transformations have fundamentally rewoven the geographical and institutional terrain on which the worldwide process of urban development is unfolding. Thus the urban question and the scale question are today intertwined in ways that require sustained theoretical, methodological, and empirical scrutiny.

As argued programatically by the editors of this book, the contemporary rescaling of urban space and the development of scale-attuned approaches to sociospatial analysis present researchers with an opportunity to reinvigorate their understanding of the nexus between cities and migration (Çağlar and Glick Schiller, chapter 1). As many of the chapters in this book demonstrate, migration networks are themselves being significantly rescaled in conjunction with the consolidation of new transnational social spaces. These rescaled migration networks are, the contributors argue, closely articulated with rescaled urban spaces. Consequently, as Ayşe Çağlar and Nina Glick Schiller propose, a scale-attuned approach has the potential to generate new perspectives on the urban dimensions of rescaled migration processes and on the role of migration in the ongoing rescaling of urban spaces.

While affirming the general usefulness of "the lexicon of geographical scale" (Smith 1992) in urban studies and critical geopolitical economy, this chapter also underscores the "limits to scale" (Brenner 2001). Specifically, I advocate a conceptual narrowing of scale questions to those associated with the hierarchical differentiation and redifferentiation of sociospatial relations. Concepts of scale, I argue, should not be conflated with those of space, place, territory, or networks. Concomitantly, the churning, polymorphic geographies of urban restructuring and migration processes cannot be conceptualized exclusively in scalar terms. I argue, nonetheless, that scalar concepts have indeed become essential tools for deciphering *some* of the key dimensions of contemporary urban transformations, including those associated with migration flows. More generally, this chapter advocates a shift from discussions of scale as such to the analysis of scalar *processes*—for instance, the scaling and rescaling of urbanization, state regulation, migration, and so forth. As we shall see, this proposition has some potentially significant implications for the study of the socio-institutional interfaces between cities and migration.

I develop these arguments, first, through some theoretical remarks on the evolution of spatialized approaches to the urban question since the rise of radical urban theory in the late 1960s. I argue that contemporary patterns of geo-economic and geopolitical restructuring are profoundly transforming the scalar configuration of urban processes under modern capitalism. Subsequent sections underscore the methodological usefulness of a scalar perspective on contemporary capitalism but underscore the persistent difficulty of defining its distinctive analytical content. I confront this problem by offering a series of general propositions intended to specify the determinate conceptual parameters of scale questions and, by implication, rescaling processes. The chapter concludes by outlining several methodological consequences that flow from the preceding discussion, with specific reference to the questions about cities and migration around which this book is framed.

Space, Scale, and the Urban Question

Since the early 1970s, debates on the urban question have centered closely around the conceptualization of space in research on cities (Gottdiener 1985). However, in their efforts to conceptualize urban spatiality, urban theorists have necessarily introduced diverse assumptions concerning the distinctiveness of the urban scale of sociospatial organization (as opposed to, for instance, the regional, the national, or the global scales). To unpack this assertion and its implications for contemporary urban theory, I reconstruct briefly some of the scalar assumptions upon which previous rounds of debate on the urban question have been grounded.

In his classic work *The Urban Question* ([1972] 1977), Manuel Castells attacked the Chicago school of urban sociology for its failure to grasp the historical specificity of the urban form under capitalism. Against this universalistic "urban ideology," Castells set out to delimit the role of the "urban system" as a determinate structure within the capitalist mode of production. In so doing, he implicitly distinguished two basic dimensions of the urban, which for present purposes can be termed its scalar and its functional aspects. The scalar aspect of the urban concerned the materiality of social processes organized on the urban scale as opposed to supra-urban scales. In Castells' terminology, scales are understood as the differentiated "spatial units" of which the capitalist system is composed (445–50). The functional aspect of the urban, his most explicit focus in *The Urban Question*, concerned not merely the geographical setting or territorial scope of social processes but their functional role or "social content" (89, 235). According to Castells' famous argument, the specificity of the urban spatial unit could not be delimited theoretically with reference to its ideological, its political-juridical, or its production functions but only in terms of its role as a site for the reproduction of labor-power (235–37, 445). The essence of Castells' position, then, was the attempt to define geographical scale in terms of its social function. He repeatedly acknowledged the existence of multiple social processes within capitalist cities but argued that only collective consumption was *functionally specific* to the urban scale. Castells' attempt to spatialize Althusserian structuralism was thus premised upon an understanding of geographical scales as spatial expressions of social functions.

Castells (1976) began to modify this position almost immediately after the publication of *The Urban Question*, but the earlier work continued to exercise a strong influence upon conceptualizations of geographical scale within urban studies. Peter Saunders' (1986) critique of Castells' early work usefully illustrates the extent of this influence. The core of that critique was a rejection of the notion that any of the social processes located within cities are, in a necessary sense, functionally specific to that geographical scale. This observation led Saunders to view urban spatial organization as a merely contingent effect and thus as a flawed conceptual basis for confronting the urban question. However, in reaching this conclusion, he implicitly embraced Castells' own criterion of functional specificity as the theoretical linchpin to the urban question. It was this underlying assumption that enabled Saunders to invoke the supra-urban character of the social processes located within cities as grounds for dismissing the possibility of a coherent spatial definition of the urban. His alternative proposal to define urban sociology as the study of consumption processes preserved the label "urban" only as a "matter of convention." Saunders thereby rendered the urban dimension of urban sociology entirely accidental, a random choice of geographical scale.

Despite their opposed conclusions, both positions in the Castells/Saunders debate were premised on two shared assumptions regarding the role of geographical scale in the urban question. First, both authors viewed the urban scale as the self-evident empirical centerpiece of the urban question. Because of their overarching concern with the functional content of the urban, Castells and Saunders reduced its scalar aspect, the existence of distinctively urbanized spatial units within an unevenly developed global capitalist system, to a prexisting empirical fact rather than conceptualizing it as a theoretical problem in its own right. Consequently, neither author could explicitly analyze the ways in which the urban scale is itself socially produced or, most crucially from the vantage point of the post-1980s period, the possibility of its historical transformation. Second, the arguments of both Castells and Saunders were grounded on what might be termed a "zero-sum" conception of geographical scale—the notion that scales operate as mutually exclusive rather than as co-constitutive frameworks for social relations. On this basis, both Castells and Saunders implied that supra-urban geographical scales were merely external parameters for the urban question. By contrast, as we shall see shortly, the interlinkages between urban and supra-urban scales are today generally considered intrinsic to the very content of the urban question.

Various alternatives to Castells' early work were elaborated during the late 1970s and early 1980s, as many urban scholars attempted to redefine the specificity of the urban. The key task from this perspective was to delineate social processes that were tied intrinsically, but not exclusively, to the urban scale. Thus cities were now analyzed as multidimensional geographical sites in which, for instance, industrial production, local labor markets, infrastructural configurations, interfirm relations, urban land-use systems, and consumption processes were clustered together. From David Harvey's (1989) capital-theoretic account of urban built environments and Allen J. Scott's (1980) neo-Ricardian theorization of the urban land nexus to Michael Storper and Richard Walker's (1989) post-Weberian analysis of industrial agglomeration and territorial development, these approaches replaced Castells' criterion of functional specificity with that of scale specificity (for overviews of these discussions, see Soja 2000). The analytical core of the urban question was no longer the functional unity of the urban process but rather the role of the urban scale as a multifaceted geographical materialization of capitalist social relations. In effect, Castells' early position was inverted. Against his conception of scales as the spatial expressions of social functions, the social relations of capitalism were now analyzed in terms of their distinctive patterns of agglomeration and territorialization on the urban scale.

These multifaceted analyses of urban spatiality soon flowed into broader explorations of the production of space and spatial configuration under capitalism. David Harvey's (1989, 1982) historical-geographical materialist conceptualization of the spatial fix exemplified this tendency. In his writings of the 1980s, Harvey continued to view the urban scale as a key geographical foundation for the accumulation process and elaborated a periodization of capitalist development focused on successive historical forms of urbanization. At the same time, Harvey began more explicitly to conceptualize the role of supra-urban spaces and processes—for instance, regional divisions of labor, national institutional constellations, supranational regimes of accumulation, and world market conditions—as central geographical preconditions for each historical spatial fix under capitalism. Closely analogous methodological strategies were also elaborated by other scholars such as Doreen Massey, Neil Smith, and Edward Soja, who now embedded a discussion of the urban question within an account of capitalist spatiality on supra-urban scales, whether with reference to changing spatial divisions of labor, patterns of uneven spatial development, or forms of crisis-induced restructuring.

Three aspects of these debates deserve emphasis here. First, insofar as these analyses of urban spatiality flowed directly into a wide range of supra-urban questions—the regional question, the problematic of uneven development, the core-periphery debate, and so forth—the coherence of the urban question was severely unsettled (Soja 1989, 94–117). Whereas explorations of the urban question had contributed crucially to this broader spatialization of Marxian political economy, the latter trend now appeared to be supplanting the urban question itself, relegating urban space to a mere subtopic within the more general issue of capitalism's uneven historical geographies. Second, these analyses introduced more multidimensional conceptions of geographical scale than had previously been deployed. Scales were no longer equated with unitary social functions but were viewed increasingly as crystallizations of diverse, overlapping political-economic processes. Third, despite this methodological advance, the historicity of geographical scales was recognized only in a relatively limited sense. Capital was said to jump continually between the urban, regional, national, and global scales in pursuit of new sources of surplus value, but the possibility that entrenched scalar hierarchies and interscalar relations might themselves undergo restructuring was not systematically explored. It was not until the early 1990s, with the proliferation of research on the urban dimensions of economic globalization, that more historically dynamic conceptualizations of geographical scale and interscalar configurations were elaborated within critical urban studies.

The Urban Question as a Scale Question?

The urban question has continued to provoke intense debate since the 1990s, but its meaning has been redefined in conjunction with ongoing debates on worldwide processes of urban and regional restructuring. In contrast to previous conceptions of the urban as a relatively self-evident scalar entity, contemporary urban researchers have been confronted with major transformations in the institutional and geographical organization not only of the urban scale, but also of the worldwide scalar hierarchies and interscalar networks in which cities are embedded. Under these circumstances, they have begun to reconceptualize the urban question with direct reference to diverse supra-urban rescaling processes.

This methodological reorientation can be illustrated with reference to several strands of contemporary urban and regional research. First, global city theorists and industrial geographers have emphasized the enhanced strategic importance of place-specific social relations, localization, and territorial concentration as basic geographical preconditions for global economic transactions (Knox and Taylor 1995). From this perspective, the urban scale operates as a localized node within globally organized circuits of capital accumulation, whereas the global scale is in turn constituted through networks of interlinked cities and city-regions. Second, many authors have analyzed dramatic shifts in both the vertical and horizontal relations among cities, as manifested, for instance, in the consolidation of new global urban hierarchies; in accelerated informational, financial, and migratory flows among cities; in the construction of new planetary interurban telecommunications infrastructures; in intensified interurban competition; and in countervailing forms of interurban cooperation and coordination (Graham 1997; Taylor 2004). From this perspective, the urban is not only a nested level within supra-urban political-economic hierarchies but also the product of dense interscalar networks linking dispersed locations across the world system. Third, recent regulationist-inspired analyses have linked processes of urban restructuring to various ongoing transformations of state spatial organization that are depriveleging the national regulatory level and giving new importance to both supranational and subnational forms of governance (Brenner 2004; Jessop 2002). From this perspective, the urban scale is not only a localized arena for global capital accumulation but also a strategic regulatory coordinate in which a multiscalar restructuring of (national) state spatiality is currently unfolding.

The appropriate interpretation of contemporary urban transformations remains open to considerable debate, but three core propositions appear to underpin significant strands of the aforementioned research traditions:

1. *Nationalized scalar fixes are being destabilized.* The nationalized formation of capital accumulation, state regulation, urbanization, and sociopolitical struggle that prevailed throughout the older capitalist world during the Fordist-Keynesian-Bandung period has been destabilized since the mid-1970s. Under contemporary conditions, therefore, the "institutional arrangements that at one time were congruent at the national level are now more dispersed at multiple spatial levels"; meanwhile, a "multifaceted causality runs in virtually all directions among the various levels of society: nations, sectors, free trade zones, international regimes, supranational

regions, large cities and even small but well-specialized localities" (Boyer and Hollingsworth 1997, 472, 470).

2. *Strategies to reorganize inherited scalar arrangements are proliferating.* Following the crisis of North Atlantic Fordism, diverse sociopolitical strategies have been mobilized to reorganize inherited interscalar configurations in key realms of political-economic organization and everyday life, including urbanization (Swyngedouw 1997b). Both within and beyond cities, these rescaling strategies are widely viewed as a means to displace or resolve crisis tendencies, to manage regulatory problems, to recalibrate power relations, and to establish a new geographical basis for capitalist development and political-economic governance. In this context, cities and city-regions have become increasingly strategic sites of regulatory experimentation, institutional innovation, and sociopolitical contestation (Scott 1998).

3. *A relativization of scales is occurring.* The medium- and long-term consequences of such rescaling strategies for urban development patterns still remain relatively inchoate, but they do appear to herald the formation of new interscalar configurations in which the national scale of political-economic organization has been significantly reconstituted. This situation has been aptly described by Jessop (2000) as a "relativization of scale." From this point of view, contemporary spatial transformations have not generated a unidirectional process of globalization, triadization, Europeanization, decentralization, regionalization, or localization, in which a single scale—be it global, triadic, European, regional or local—is replacing the national scale as the primary level of political-economic coordination. What we are witnessing, rather, is a situation of "scalar flux"—a wide-ranging, contested recalibration of inherited scalar hierarchies and interscalar relations throughout global capitalism as a whole.

In sum, as indicated by the proliferation of terms and phrases such as the "local-global interplay," the "local-global nexus," "glocalization," and "glurbanization," many urban researchers have begun to conceptualize the current round of geo-economic restructuring as a complex rearticulation of interscalar organization. The problematic of geographical scale—its spatial organization, its social production, its political contestation, and its historical reconfiguration—has thus been inserted into the very heart of the urban question. Whereas the urban question had previously assumed the form of debates on the functional specificity or scale-specificity of the urban within relatively stable interscalar hierarchies, since the 1990s the urban question has been widely rearticulated in the form of a *scale question.*

Methodological Challenges and Pitfalls of Scalar Analysis

The task of deciphering the tangled scalar hierarchies, mosaics, and networks that have been emerging in the wake of contemporary geo-economic and geopolitical transformations is still in its embryonic stages, but it is now being confronted by a growing number of scholars, including those within critical urban and regional studies (Sheppard and McMaster 2004) as well as within migration studies (Çağlar and Glick Schiller, chapter 4; Samers, chapter 3). But even as urbanists mobilize scalar concepts with increasing reflexivity, significant methodological challenges are associated with the tasks of (1) deciphering the role of cities within contemporary rescaling processes, (2) understanding the implications of such processes for the dynamics of urban development, and (3) theorizing the nature of rescaling processes themselves.

An essential precondition for confronting these challenges is to construct an appropriate conceptual grammar for representing the processual, dynamic, and politically contested character of geographical scale and interscalar institutional arrangements. A reification of scale appears to be built into everyday scalar terms (local, urban, regional, national, global, and so forth) insofar as they represent distinctive sociospatial processes (such as localization, urbanization, regionalization, nationalization, transnationalization, globalization, etc.) as if they were frozen permanently within geographical space as self-enclosed, coherently bounded entities.

Moreover, existing scalar vocabularies are poorly equipped to grasp the complex, perpetually changing historical interconnections and interdependencies among geographical scales. Insofar as terms such as "local," "urban," "regional," "national," and "transnational" are used to demarcate purportedly separate territorial "islands" of social relations, they obfuscate the profound mutual imbrication of all scales and the tangled interscalar networks through which the latter are constituted. These difficulties are exacerbated still further by the circumstance that much of the social-scientific division of labor is still organized according to distinctive scalar foci—for instance, urban studies, regional studies, comparative politics, international relations, and so forth—which tend to obstruct efforts to explore the dynamics of interscalar relations and transformations.

Finally, even among those who are concerned to develop a reflexively scale-attuned approach to geopolitical economy, the theorization of scale itself has become increasingly contentious. Theorists differ, for instance, on how best to delineate the essential properties of scale, on the appropriate analytical and empirical scope of the concept, on its relation to other key sociospatial concepts, and on its application to the study of concrete social processes and relations (see, for instance, Amin 2003; Bulkeley 2005; Collinge 2006; Escobar 2007; Jonas 2006; Howitt 1998; Sheppard and McMaster 2004; Sayre 2005). Clarification of such questions awaits further theoretical debate, methodological experimentation, and concrete investigation by scale-attuned researchers both within and beyond the field of urban studies.

For present purposes, I shall not attempt to review these ongoing theoretical debates, which advance diverse theoretical agendas and are oriented toward a broad range of concrete inquiries. Instead I offer a cursory statement of the key elements within my own conceptualization, which emerged in conjunction with an inquiry into the geographies of urban governance restructuring in post-1960s western Europe (Brenner 2004). The proposed approach is at odds with several prominent methodological tendencies in contemporary sociospatial theory, including (1) the treatment of scale as a general metaphor for sociospatiality as such (Marston 2000); (2) the equation of scale with territorialist understandings of space (Amin 2002, 2003); (3) calls to abandon scalar concepts in favor of topological modes of analysis (Amin 2002; Marston, Jones, and Woodward 2005); and (4) the construction of sociospatial theory on the basis of transhistorical or ontological claims regarding the nature of social life as such (Collinge 2006; Escobar 2007). My goal here, however, is not to outline my differences with such positions but rather to specify a conceptualization of scale that may be useful for deciphering contemporary patterns of urban and regional restructuring as well as the rapidly changing transnational social fields in which migration processes are situated (see Çağlar and Glick Schiller, chapter 4; Samers, chapter 3).

While the following propositions initially deploy the term "scale," they quickly transcend this problematic discursive convention and elaborate a reformulated conceptual grammar based on processual notions of scaling and rescaling. Scales, in this framework, are no more than the temporarily stabilized *effects* of diverse sociospatial processes, which must be theorized and investigated on their own terms. It is, in short, *processes* of scaling and rescaling, rather than scales themselves, that must be the main analytical focus for approaches to the scale question (Swyngedouw 1997b). This conceptualization is intended to provide a basis for further inquiry into contemporary rescaling processes, whether of urbanization, state regulation, migration, or other sociospatial relations. I begin with epistemological foundations before turning to problems of conceptualization and analysis.

Eight Propositions on Rescaling

1. *Scale is a 'real abstraction' of historically and geographically specific social relations.* What are the conditions of possibility for describing the social world as being differentiated among distinct, relatively coherent geographical scales? I rely here upon a critical realist epistemology (Sayer 1992) in which the intelligibility of scalar categories is understood to be derived from a prior state of affairs: namely, the internal differentiation of specific social processes among variegated yet interconnected scalar levels, which in turn structure perceptions, understandings, and representations within everyday life and social-scientific inquiry. Whatever they might signify—and, as indicated, this is a matter of considerable disagreement—scalar concepts are not simply categories of analysis imposed by the researcher ("conceptual abstractions," in Max Weber's sense). Rather, as understood here, the lexicon of geographical scale (Smith 1995) emerges as a "real abstraction" of structures, strategies, and transformations within the social world (on the

latter term, see Sayer 1992). Under late modern capitalism, therefore, the intellectual necessity of the scale question is linked intrinsically to the changing organizational and spatial configuration of this historically specific social formation. While versions of a scale question may well have arisen under earlier configurations of capitalist development, their conditions of possibility and therefore their conceptual foundations would have differed qualitatively from those associated with the current, post-1980s conjuncture of uneven global capitalist development (for a radically opposed, ontological starting point, see Marston, Jones, and Woodward 2005).

2. *Scales result from the vertical differentiation and redifferentiation of social relations.* But what is the concrete reference point for scalar categories? What distinguishes scalar concepts from other discourses used to describe forms of sociospatial organization under capitalism? As conceived here, the differentiation of social relations by scale results from the "vertical ordering" (Collinge 1999) or spatial hierarchization of social formations. For, in addition to the "horizontal" or areal differentiation of social practices across geographical space, there is also a "vertical" differentiation in which social relations are hierarchically articulated among—for example—global, supranational, national, regional, metropolitan, and local levels. The spatialities of scale cannot be understood entirely in terms of this vertical, hierarchical dimension (see below). However, I am proposing here the strong claim that the *differentia specifica* of scalar organization lies in the vertical differentiation and redifferentiation of social relations. Scale thus necessarily (that is, on a definitional level) presupposes the hierarchical structuration of sociospatial relations. Only in the complete absence of such vertical structuration could the ascalar vision of a "flat ontology" postulated by Marston, Jones, and Woodward (2005) become plausible.[1]

3. *Scales exist because social processes are scaled.* Geographical scales—the discrete tiers or levels within interscalar hierarchies—are not static, fixed, or permanent properties of political-economic institutions or of social spatiality as such. They are best understood, rather, as socially produced, and therefore malleable, dimensions of particular social processes—such as capitalist production, social reproduction, state regulation, and sociopolitical struggle. Insofar as any social, political, or economic process or institutional form is internally differentiated into a vertical hierarchy of relatively discrete spatial units, the problem of its scalar organization arises. It is more precise, therefore, to speak of the scaling (scale differentiation) and rescaling (scale redifferentiation) of particular types of social processes and institutional forms than of scales per se. Or, to formulate the point differently: scales are the provisionally stabilized *outcomes* of scaling and rescaling *processes;* the former can be grasped only through an analysis of the latter.

4. *Scales can only be grasped relationally.* Scales cannot be construed adequately as fixed units within a system of nested territorial containers defined by

absolute geographic size (a "Russian dolls" model of scale). The institutional configuration, function(s), histories, and dynamics of any one geographical scale can only be grasped relationally, in terms of its upward, downward, and transversal links to other geographical scales situated within the broader interscalar configuration in which it is embedded. Consequently, the significance of scalar terms such as "global," "national," "regional," "urban," and "local" is likely to differ qualitatively depending on the historically specific scalar morphologies associated with the distinctive social processes or institutional forms to which they refer. From this point of view, it is analytically imprecise to speak of scale in singular terms—as, for instance, in discourses about "the" urban, "the" regional, "the" national, or "the" global. Such substantialist formulations misleadingly imply that individual scales contain a coherence in and of themselves and thus bypass the essential task of analyzing their relational co-constitution in and through multiscalar structuration processes.

5. *Forms of interscalar organization represent mosaics, not pyramids.* The institutional landscape of capitalism is not characterized by a single, all-encompassing scalar pyramid into which all social processes and institutional forms are neatly enfolded. Every social process or institutional form may be associated with distinctive patterns of scalar differentiation. The pattern of scalar differentiation associated with national states, for instance, may only partially correspond to that of national urban hierarchies, which may in turn only tendentially correspond to that of nationalized patterns of financial circulation or commodity exchange. Consequently, the scalar architecture of capitalism as a whole is composed of a mosaic of superimposed, tangled, crosscutting, and unevenly overlapping interscalar hierarchies whose units are rarely coextensive or isomorphic.

6. *Interscalar configurations are embedded within polymorphic geographies.* Processes of scaling and rescaling occur in close conjunction with other forms of sociospatial structuration, such as territorialization (enclosure, bounding), place-making (agglomeration, clustering), and network formation (the construction of interspatial connectivity). The scalar differentiation of any given social process or institutional form is therefore only one among many potentially significant dimensions of its geographical configuration: scale is only one facet of sociospatial relations (Brenner 2009b). For this reason, studies of scaling and rescaling must avoid the pitfall of "scale-centrism" in which the scalar attributes of social processes or institutional forms are privileged to the neglect of their other sociospatial dimensions.

7. *Rescaling processes are frequently path-dependent.* To date, the bulk of the literature on scale production, with its empirical focus on the tumultuous post-1970s period, has emphasized the cataclysmic forms of scalar transformation that ensue during phases of systemic crisis. Under these conditions, extant scalar configurations are dismantled and rejigged; and following

intense sociopolitical struggles, radically new hierarchies of scale may be established. However, scalar configurations are not infinitely malleable, even during phases of intensified and accelerated restructuring. Moreover, processes of rescaling do not entail the simple replacement of one interscalar configuration by another, fully formed one or the total disappearance of some scales as others supersede them. Rather, rescaling processes generally occur through the path-dependent, mutually transformative interaction of inherited interscalar arrangements with emergent strategies to recalibrate the latter. This means that even in the midst of intense pressures to restructure a given interscalar order, inherited scalar configurations may close off certain pathways of rescaling by circumscribing the production of new scales within determinate institutional and geographical parameters. The differential modalities of scalar restructuring—from the incremental and the systemic to the cataclysmic—arguably deserve much more extensive theoretical and empirical investigation among analysts of rescaling processes.

8. *Rescaling processes rework the positionalities of sociospatial formations and thus recalibrate the geographies and choreographies of power relations.* The scaling and rescaling of social processes mediates, and is in turn mediated by, asymmetrical and thus conflict-laden social power relations (Berndt 2000; Castree 2000; Herod 1997; Smith 1993; Swyngedouw 1997b). On the one hand, the establishment and reorganization of scalar hierarchies create geographies and choreographies of inclusion/exclusion and domination/subordination that empower some actors, alliances, and organizations at the expense of others, according to criteria such as class, gender, race/ethnicity, and nationality. In this manner, rescaling processes can modify the positionalities of particular sociospatial forms, that is, their relational position within the broader system of uneven spatial development of global capitalism (Sheppard 2002). On the other hand, scalar hierarchies may operate not merely as arenas of social power struggles but also as their very *objects* insofar as they are challenged and unsettled in the course of sociopolitical struggles and conflicts over positionality. In Neil Smith's (1993, 101) concise formulation, "The scale of struggle and the struggle over scale are two sides of the same coin." The specification of the particular historical-geographical conditions under which scalar hierarchies may become stakes rather than mere settings of social struggles over positionality is a task that awaits more systematic investigation.

It is worth reiterating one central, if apparently paradoxical, analytical conclusion that flows from the foregoing propositions: *scales do not exist as such.* Given my emphasis on (1) the pluralized, polymorphic, and heterogeneous character of sociospatiality; (2) the inherent relationality of each tier within interscalar hierarchies; and (3) the profoundly dynamic, processual character of interscalar configurations, the rather static, monodimensional language of scale appears increasingly inadequate. As indicated above, we are dealing not with a political economy of fixed, discrete, singular, and nested scales, but rather with a multiplicity of *scaled political economies* that are implicated in, and are in turn productive of, diverse, tangled patterns of scale differentiation and scale redifferentiation.

The task, therefore, is not merely to recognize the scale-differentiated character of political-economic life but, more generally, (1) to explore the diverse social dynamics in and through which scaled political-economic configurations are actively produced and continuously transformed during the course of capitalist geohistorical development; and (2) to trace the ways in which such scaled political-economic orders structure (i.e. at once constrain *and* enable) social relations of power, domination, exploitation, and struggle. From this point of view, the phrase "new political economy of scale" (Keil and Mahon 2009) should be understood as no more than a shorthand reference to recent efforts to decipher the continuous scaling and rescaling of political-economic life under capitalism. The notion of "scaled political economy" arguably provides a more precise label for the theoretical approach proposed here, for it underscores that the focal points for scalar inquiry are not scales in themselves but rather the *processes* of scaling (scale differentiation) and rescaling (scale redifferentiation) that underpin the dynamics of institutional evolution and sociopolitical struggle under late modern capitalism.

The Limits to Rescaling?

While the preceding propositions may need further refinement in conjunction with concrete research on urban and regional restructuring, I believe they offer a productive alternative to recent writings that blunt or overextend scalar concepts (Marston 2000) as well as to deconstructive proposals to abolish or abandon scalar concepts entirely (Collinge 2006; Marston, Jones, and Woodward 2005). Moreover, the preceding discussion explodes any approach to the urban question that conceives its object as a self-enclosed local or even regional space. Clearly, further studies are required in order to grapple with the key analytical tasks that flow from this process-based, multiscalar conceptualization. Most urgent among these are (1) theorizing the mechanisms through which contemporary urbanization processes are scaled and rescaled; (2) exploring the specific conditions under which apparently stabilized interscalar configurations of urbanization are shaken up, rejigged, and transformed; (3) analyzing the contextually variable pathways and trajectories through which urban configurations are being rescaled; (4) deciphering the diverse political strategies, social forces, and territorial alliances that mobilize around, or against, particular strategies to rescale urbanization processes; and (5) examining the interplay between processes of scaling/rescaling and other processes of sociospatial restructuring (such as place-making, territorialization, and networking) during the geohistory of capitalist urbanization.

The proliferation of explicit debates on geographical scale and rescaling during the 1990s can be understood as an important extension and fine-tuning of the spatialized approaches to urban and regional political economy that had been developed during the preceding decade, provoked in no small measure by the post-1970s shaking up of the scalar hierarchies and interdependencies associated with organized capitalism. Subsequently, and not only within urban and regional studies, discussions of the scale question have provided a more precise conceptual grammar for analyzing the continual, hierarchical redifferentiation of sociospatial relations during a particularly volatile period in the geohistory of capitalism. Whereas a sophisticated analytical vocabulary had already been developed in the 1980s for grasping key dimensions of capitalist spatiality, the new lexicon of geographical scale has provided urban researchers with a powerful means to denaturalize, historicize, and critically interrogate the very spatial units and hierarchies in which social relations are configured. Consequently, recent debates on the scale question have provided urbanists and other critical geopolitical economists with an important analytical lens through which to begin to decipher the geographies of contemporary restructuring processes.

On my reading, recent contributions to the analysis of scale production and scale transformation have particularly massive implications for the field of urban studies, whose unit of analysis remains deeply ambiguous even after nearly a century of debate regarding the nature of the urban question. However, as the propositions enumerated above indicate, I would caution against the tendency to overextend scalar concepts in urban studies or in any other branch of sociospatial analysis. This is because *scalar structurations* of social space (based upon relations of hierarchization among vertically differentiated units) are analytically distinct from other forms of sociospatial structuration, such as place-making, localization, territorialization, and networking (Brenner 2009b; Jessop, Brenner, and Jones 2008). The lexicon of geographical scale is most powerful, I have suggested, when its analytical limits are explicitly understood (Brenner 2001). Parodoxically, an analytically narrower conceptualization of scale facilitates a much broader but more precise application of this concept to the vicissitudes of worldwide capitalist restructuring.

Scaling Migration Studies?

In their introduction to this book, Çağlar and Glick Schiller suggest that attention to scalar questions can provide a fruitful methodological basis for investigating the reworked transnational fields of power within which both cities and migration processes are situated. Their call for a scalar turn within migration studies stems, in part, from a sustained critique of the various forms of methodological nationalism that underpinned earlier work in this vibrant research field (Wimmer and Glick Schiller 2002). Scalar concepts are viewed as a methodological basis for migration research that does not presuppose nation-states or national populations as the natural units of social life. The city—or, as they term it, city scale—is their proposed focal point for pursuing this wide-reaching methodological agenda.

Çağlar and Glick Schiller are not simply advocating an urban focus for migration studies, however. This would replace methodological nationalism with an equally problematic methodological localism (Brenner 2009a). Rather, their proposal entails nothing less than a reconceptualization of the object of migration studies in reflexively scalar terms. This means that none of the spaces of migration—urban, regional, national, transnational—can be viewed as pre-existing or static frames for social life, as mere arenas within which social relations are positioned or enclosed. Instead, all such spaces are seen as being produced and coproduced through the very social relations under investigation. It is in this context that Çağlar and Glick Schiller propose to view cities as strategically crucial sites for scale-attuned investigations of migration processes. In their reflexively scale-attuned conceptualization, cities are to be understood not simply as arenas within which migration happens, or as localized niches within nationally anchored political-economic spaces. Instead, as the above discussion of urban debates indicates, a scalar perspective entails conceiving cities as relationally evolving sociospatial nodes within transnational fields of power.

In sum, then, the methodological agenda of this book appears to cut in at least two major directions. On the one hand, the editors and contributors strive to rethink the cities/migration nexus by adopting a scalar perspective on *cities*. Once cities are conceived as differentially positioned spaces within transnational scalar hierarchies, it is possible to explore their roles as strategic sites for migration processes in potentially illuminating ways. In this sense, the research presented here advances and extends the scale-attuned approaches to critical urban theory that were reviewed and evaluated above. On the other hand, the contributors are also concerned with reconceptualizing the spatialities of *migration processes*. Of course, much recent work in migration studies has grappled with the implications of transnationalism as a basis for understanding diasporic flows and communities (Wimmer and Glick Schiller 2002). The scalar perspective proposed by Çağlar and Glick Schiller is intended to offer a more nuanced, differentiated mapping of the rapidly evolving social geographies associated with transnational migration patterns. In this sense, the following chapters contribute to the ongoing project of reconceptualizing the object of migration studies in the context of contemporary forms of geo-economic and geopolitical restructuring.

These are exciting, productive agendas, and the empirical studies presented in this book illustrate some of their possible applications in diverse spatiotemporal contexts and with reference to a broad range of migrant social formations in Europe, North America, and beyond. By way of conclusion, I raise four questions associated with the project of "scaling" migration studies.

1. *Theorizing scale.* As indicated above, this issue is highly contested in the literatures on urban studies and sociospatial theory, and it is equally subject to debate in this book. Indeed, most of the following chapters adopt a much broader conceptualization of scale than the relatively circumscribed one proposed in this chapter. Moreover, the concept of scale serves a variety of analytical functions across the different types of investigation presented here. Particularly in the early stages of applying any methodological innovation, conceptual heterogeneity can be quite fruitful, as it enables researchers to rethink their object(s) of inquiry, to access inherited questions in new ways, and to open up entirely new types of questions, without being excessively constrained by predetermined definitional boundaries. At some point, however, the use of polysemic concepts may engender methodological and empirical confusion: the very concepts that inspired new lines of research may be blunted or rendered chaotic as a consequence of their diverse, often mutually opposed, modes of application. The field of migration studies is only beginning to grapple reflexively with scalar concepts, and it will be exciting to see how the latter are deployed, and toward what interpretive and empirical ends, in the years ahead. But it will be equally important, in the course of this research, for scholars to specify as precisely as possible how they understand concepts such as scale, scaling, and rescaling. If the latter are not to become all-purpose spatial metaphors or to become synonymous with other sociospatial concepts—space and place, for example—such definitional precision will be increasingly essential. I view this as a key methodological question for scale-attuned analysts of migration: What *is* scale, and how are migration processes being scaled and rescaled in relation to other contemporary forms of sociospatial transformation?

2. *Rescaling/restructuring.* This set of issues is equally acute with regard to the concept of rescaling. In several of the chapters below, the concept of rescaling is used as a general descriptor for the transformed global context within which cities are currently situated. This general conceptualization of rescaling is surely well justified, both theoretically and empirically: cities are being repositioned through a series of worldwide and national political-economic transformations, and this repositioning has significant ramifications for diasporic flows and for urban migrants. But here, too, there are dangers of conceptual blunting or overstretch. As argued above with reference to debates on the urban question, rescaling represents only one among several dimensions of contemporary sociospatial transformation—others include the remaking of places, territorialization and reterritorialization processes, and the rearticulation of social networks. There is, therefore, a need for precise analytical attention to the polymorphic character of sociospatial restructuring; the notion of rescaling should not be treated as a universal metaphor for sociospatiality as such (Brenner 2009b; Jessop, Brenner, and Jones 2008). Yet there is still a further ambiguity in this concept: many references to restructuring in this book are focused less on the rearticulation of local/

national/global relations or the worldwide repositioning of cities than on other, more specific processes of political-economic transformation—for instance, neoliberalization, patterns of capital investment and disinvestment, or the reorganization of labor markets. While each of the latter processes may well have scalar dimensions and may also be undergoing some form of rescaling, these issues do not always seem to be analytically central to the substantive arguments being advanced about them. Thus emerges a second key question for scale-attuned analyses of migration and cities: In what sense, if any, does the *rescaled* context of contemporary urbanization—as opposed to some other aspect of urban restructuring and/or worldwide sociospatial restructuring—help explain or contextualize the migration flows and/or migrant social formations under investigation?

3. *The object of migration studies.* One of the most provocative contributions of the following chapters is their emphasis on the sociospatial contexts of migration processes and migrant social formations—and thus, more generally, on the object of migration studies as a distinctive research field. Rather than presupposing that migration occurs within some fixed, given sociospatial frame—be it a neighborhood, a city, or a national state—the contributors to this book begin to explore how such spatial units are themselves produced and transformed through social relations. This methodological move arguably represents a significant advance not only on the various forms of methodological nationalism that defined inherited approaches to migration studies but also on more recent work on transnationalism, with its productive but rather generic emphasis on the worldwide character of diasporic flows and communities. Yet there are some methodological tensions and challenges within the emergent project of developing scale-attuned approaches to migration studies. In some of the following chapters, specific cities or regions are presented as the empirical context for the various transformations under investigation. While these spaces are in no way taken for granted, they are nonetheless described as relatively straightforward contextual milieus—Philadelphia, Dallas, Emilia Romagna, and so forth. Thus understood, it is the *relation* between these relatively bounded urban milieus and the transnational spaces of capitalism that is being rearticulated; the milieus as such remain relatively stable and can be labeled and analyzed accordingly with reference to their official jurisdictional names. This relatively concrete, empirical understanding of a research site is surely defensible on a pragmatic level—migration has to take place *somewhere*, and we need labels for describing such locations that do not carry excessive theoretical baggage. Other chapters, however, begin to push beyond such concrete or empirical understandings of the research site and the object of investigation within migration studies. For them, the task is not only to explore the impacts of geo-economic and geopolitical rescaling upon the (localized) contexts within which migration processes are embedded. Just as important, they also attempt to reconceptualize the very nature of those

contexts—that is, their tendential character *as* distinctive "milieux," "arenas," "sites" and so forth. How should we label such rescaled spaces of migration, and how can we conceptualize their conditions of emergence, reproduction, and transformation? To some degree, earlier work on diaspora has begun to confront this challenge through the introduction of neologisms such as "translocality" and "ethnoscape" (Appadurai 1996). To what degree does the scalar lexicon introduced in this book provide new openings for other, perhaps more precise labelings and/or alternative conceptualizations? I view this as a third essential conceptual challenge that is opened up in this book. To what extent, and in what ways, can the very object of migration studies be redefined in scalar—or at least scale-attuned—ways?

4. *Scale and political strategies.* As discussed above, theorists of scale have emphasized the role of scalar configurations in articulating and reproducing forms of social power, exclusion, and marginalization. Concomitantly, contributors to the scale literature have emphasized the strategic importance of scale in struggles against established modes of political-economic domination. Especially in recent times, rescaling has frequently served as a political strategy through which marginalized social actors and organizations have mobilized to undermine or even supersede extant institutional arrangements. This book contains rich examples of strategic uses of rescaling by diverse migrant actors and organizations. Some of these examples illustrate how migrants have actively contested contemporary processes of neoliberalization and other policy trends that intensify exclusion, marginalization, and inequality. Interestingly, however, other chapters show how the activities of migrants and migrant organizations have, often unwittingly, reinforced or even accelerated neoliberal or exclusionary modes of urban policy. These examples suggest the importance of distinguishing the substantive *content* of migrant political mobilizations from the strategic institutional and/or spatial *means* through which that content is to be realized. In some cases, no doubt, the politics of scale will be central—the goal of struggle and the scale of struggle will be, to return to Smith's (1993, 101) formulation, two sides of the same coin. Yet there may also be instances in which the scaling of migration politics remains relatively incidental to the stakes involved—whether because such struggles involve a more direct contestation of other dimensions of sociospatiality (for instance, place or territory) or because they do not contest any dimension of sociospatial organization. We thus arrive at a final conceptual challenge for scale-attuned investigations of migration. How can we conceptualize the spatial politics mobilized by migrants and migrant organizations? To what extent, and under what circumstances, do such mobilizations involve a politics of scale (which contest established scalar configurations) and/or a politics of rescaling (which aim to construct alternative scalings of political-economic life)?

The preceding considerations are intended not as criticisms of the adventurous, exploratory work presented in this book but rather as a provocation to further reflection and debate regarding the theoretical and empirical implications of scale questions within the field of migration studies. The following chapters exemplify a variety of ways in which the city/migration nexus can be investigated through diverse appropriations and applications of scalar discourse. Rather than attempting to discipline these emergent efforts according to any particular conceptual framework, this chapter has attempted to contextualize them in relation to previous engagements with scalar questions within the fields of urban studies and critical sociospatial theory.

Will scale-attuned migration scholars revisit or reinvent some of the same methodological aporias that have emerged in recent debates on scale within critical sociospatial theory and urban studies? Or will they find creative ways of transcending such aporias—whether through the deployment of more precise concepts of scale; by confronting systematically some of the methodological challenges enumerated above; or, perhaps, through the elaboration of alternative conceptualizations that circumvent such dilemmas entirely? Answers to these questions can be pursued only through continued, theoretically reflexive engagement with the very types of research questions pursued in this book. This is a prospect that should be welcomed by spatially reflexive scholars both within and beyond the field of migration studies.

Note

1. My intention, in emphasizing the verticality of scalar relations, is not to deny the importance of horizontal forms of interscalar interaction and interdependence—for instance, networks of relations between actors and organizations located within geographically dispersed cities, regions, and territories. I argue, however, that geographical scales and networks of spatial connectivity are mutually constitutive rather than mutually exclusive aspects of social spatiality. Networks of spatial connectivity are directly structured by scaling processes insofar as the latter serve to demarcate (1) the specific, if often rather amorphous, spatial *units* between which the networks in question are interconnected; and (2) the spatial *orbits* of the networks in question. While geographical scale may structure such relations of horizontal connectivity, scalar categories hardly provide a full description of the multidimensional spatialities inherent in these relations.

Chapter 3

The Socioterritoriality of Cities

A Framework for Understanding the Incorporation of Migrants in Urban Labor Markets

MICHAEL SAMERS

All cities are global.... [A]ny idea of "non-global" cities needs to be banished.
—Peter J. Taylor, *World City Network: A Global Urban Analysis*

Introduction

In this chapter, I will focus on a hitherto underdeveloped area of research in the context of Europe and North America—that is, the explicit relationship between (city) scale and the incorporation of migrants in urban labor markets.[1] Let me first discuss each of these issues briefly in turn. In the most rudimentary of understandings, "city scale" might refer to the size of cities (let us say in terms of population, surface area, or—in the case of so-called global cities—their putative economic importance). Understood in the context of our concerns here, large cities and world or global cities would supposedly involve *unique* labor markets and hence a specific relationship to migrant incorporation. A second understanding of scale—in human geography at least—emerged in the late 1980s and had as its focus fixed scales such as the local, regional, national, and international. This was designed to capture what many perceived as an almost epochal rescaling of social relations—upward, downward, and outward from the scale of the nation-state. Here, scale sometimes meant the *spatial extent* of social processes (and as a consequence scale as territory and scale as spatial extent were conflated). In any case, this literature argued that the processes involved in the construction of labor markets extended across such scales and were therefore shaped by them. Later debates (that is, from the latter half of the 1990s onward) abandoned this essentialist notion of fixed scales to encompass a more fluid inductive approach where the process under investigation determines the scale and not the other way around. The problem, however, is that the term "scale" (or "scalar") is rarely defined, and I argue in this chapter then that scale remains a deeply troubled concept in human geography and the social sciences more broadly.

A second problematic in explorations of the relationship between cities and the labor market incorporation of migrants has been a lack of critical reflection over the last decade on the theories and concepts deployed to understand such incorporation. With few exceptions, a "human capital theory" or a social-occupational division of labor (or sociospatial division of labor) approach is the mode of analysis de rigueur in North America. In Europe, existing studies rely on either a similar social-occupational (spatial) division of labor analysis or an inadequate and unsophisticated conception of labor market segmentation (often of the "dual labor market hypothesis" type), sometimes "reading off" the types of jobs that immigrants perform from arguments associated with Saskia Sassen's (1991) "global city hypothesis."

To respond to these two problems above, I draw on a literature—mainly from human geography—to ask what is meant by scale. After an abbreviated review of the scale literature, I jettison (no doubt heretically and against the grain of this book) the notion of scale in favor of what I will call simply "socioterritoriality." I then show how the notion of socioterritoriality may be welded to what I call "international labor market segmentation" (ILMS) in the context of low-paid labor in European cities.[2] In that sense, my analysis concerns only wage labor rather than immigrant entrepreneurship. Nonetheless, in drawing out this conceptual pairing between socioterritoriality and international labor market segmentation I question whether the preoccupation with the global cities hypothesis in particular leads us down an erroneous route, where somehow it is the size or economic importance of a city that renders it necessarily distinct in terms of the labor market incorporation of migrants. In this chapter, then, I am proposing a framework that analyzes labor market incorporation from the perspective that all cities are global cities (see Robinson 2002; Taylor 2004) in the sense that they are shaped by flows from around the world, although some cities' labor markets may be more similar than others.

From the Question of Scale to the Socioterritoriality of Cities

What Is Scale?

A lively and explicit debate about scale—at least among critical human geographers—has raged since the mid-1990s. Much of this debate has thrown up a barrage of (perhaps intentionally) slippery terms that seem to create more heat than light (see also Marston, Jones, and Woodward 2005 for a similar perspective). A definition of scale is rare in the scale literature, although the latter seems to rely on David Delaney and Helga Leitner's (1997, 93) idea of scale as a "nested hierarchy of bounded spaces of differing size" or on John Agnew's (1997, 100) notion of scale as "the level of geographical resolution at which a given phenomenon is thought of, acted on or studied" (cited in Brenner 2001, 609 n.3).[3]

Where scale is not defined, or defined poorly, critical geographers do not hesitate to resort to an analysis of scale as object—for example, the restructuring of scale (Smith and Dennis 1987); the production of scale, scaled politics, and rescaling (Herod 1991; Swyngedouw 1997a); the politics of scale (Smith 1992); the social construction of scale (Marston 2000); scale processes[4]; scalar structuration (Brenner 2001, 2004); and scalar dimensions of practices (Mansfield 2005). In sum, scale by itself is rarely defined (though again, that a definition has proved elusive may be purposeful since an ontology of scale is generally rejected—e.g., Jones 1998). An exception is Nina Glick Schiller and Ayşe Çağlar's definition in the introduction to this book, where they approach scale processually and in relationship to the neoliberal reordering of space and related flows of various forms of capital. They use the terms "scale" and "rescaling" as a conceptual shorthand to speak of the intersection of two processes of restructuring and repositioning:

> We suggest that scaling refers to the ordering of sociospatial units within multiple hierarchies of power. Rescaling refers to a reordering of these relationships. Taken together the terms scaling and rescaling serve as a conceptual shorthand that allows us to speak of the intersection between two processes: restructuring, including movements of various forms of capital, and the reorganization of the relationships of power between specific sociospatial units of governance. The term "scalar positioning" refers to the intersection of restructuring and rescaling processes at a particular moment of time.

But such a definition remains unique. Thus the attention of some scholars is turned instead toward the search for processes that produce scale, while for others, such as Becky Mansfield (2005), the point is to somehow start with scalar (processes) rather than some fixed notion of scale. In this sense, then, "scalar" seems to be an adjective in search of a noun.

The literature may be suffering from an inability to agree on or even arrive at a clear definition of scale (Leitner and Miller 2007), but it has no doubt matured in its disavowal of fixed scales entailing a crude vertical metaphor of the local, regional, national, supranational, and global, as well as a rigid conceptualization of globalization-driven downscaling, outscaling, and upscaling. Instead, the literature espouses a more relational conception of a scale "scaffolding" (Brenner 2001, 2004; Leitner and Miller 2007; Mansfield 2005; Marston, Jones, and Woodward 2005). As Mansfield (2005) put it, what is interesting is "to ask about the ways (i.e., through what processes and for what reasons) different scales are produced and given significance at any particular time and/or place. This complexity is not captured in the idea of rescaling, but rather in the idea of scales as *dimensions* of particular events and processes" (468).

In fact, Mansfield argues, for example, that "the national is not a level, arena or even orientation, but is a dimension of social practice and the production of space" (ibid.). This is why she prefers to talk not of rescaling but of "scalar dimensions of practices" instead of "practices occurring at different scales" (ibid.). Again, this seems to echo earlier acknowledgments of the process-based or structurationist conception of scale (in which scale seems to be akin to spatial extent). Yet Mansfield's discussion seems to replicate some of the circular, tautological, and confusing character of much of the scale debate. Indeed, she seems to reject scale as territory but accepts it as spatial extent that somehow disavows territoriality. It is perhaps this very confusion that has partly spawned a rejection of scale altogether.

Working without Scale?

The easy and more tempting alternative is to start with a horizontal topology—that is, with networks rather than scale. Yet immediately two problems emerge. First, a network topology is inadequate since networks themselves are shaped through territories, and second, a network topology does not necessarily imply a particular conception of power. (I discuss these problems in more depth subsequently.) Another tempting route is a Derridean or post-structuralist dismissal of scale itself—a position forcefully, if not always convincingly, argued by Sallie Marston, John Paul Jones, and Keith Woodward (2005).[5] They do agree that there is a politics of scale, but they argue that human geography can and should do without scale: "[W]e elect to expurgate scale from the geographic vocabulary" (422). In its place, they call for a "flat ontology"—a kind of "onto-genesis"—that is comprised of three mechanisms: first, "an analytics of composition and decomposition," which avoids the common tendency to envision the world as a series of uninterrupted flows; second, an "attention to differential relations" that generate the "driving forces" of this material composition, which also avoids the common tendency to "stratify and classify geographic objects"; and third, an emphasis on "localized and non-localized emergent events of differential relations actualized as temporary—often mobile—'sites' in which the 'social' unfolds" (423).

These three dimensions constitute their flat ontology, which itself entails a site ontology, without doubt another slippery concept that I have insufficient space here to elaborate upon. Nonetheless, their main contribution in this regard seems to be an argument for sites as provisional constellations—events that bring together different provisional social relations. But whether this site ontology is not itself a spatial metaphor that smacks of scale begs for more than just cursory reflection. This gargantuan problem aside, what is important about Marston et al.'s article are its theoretical insights—that is, its focus on process rather than on scale as some sort of fixed scaffolding and their contention that one tends to find what one is searching for through the vertical apparatus of scale. Indeed, a major aim of the article is to echo the work of the feminist geographers Kathy Gibson and Julie Graham (Gibson-Graham 1996, 2002) in their dismissal of the global (or globalization) as some kind of scale that operates *on* people to disempower them.

The Limits of Working without Scale

My sense is that while Marston and her colleagues (2005) offer some useful insights on the scale debate, they not only misrepresent the scale literature in their disproportionate focus on the "fixity" dimension of scale but do not escape the quandary concerning the operation of power relations through different spaces, places, or territories with their metaphors of site and ontology of site (for criticisms of Marston et al. but a defense of scale see Jonas 2006; Hoefle 2006; Leitner and Miller 2007). Indeed, one anthropologist (Hoefle 2006) has even criticized their conception as "too anthropological," one that threatens to "kill the goose [the discipline of geography] that laid the golden egg [the concept of scale]." Whatever the objection of scale-inclined anthropologists, I am certainly sympathetic to Marston et al.'s post-structuralist/deconstructive argument, but it still raises the question as to how social forces such as urban labor market segmentation are set in motion. In other words, how and where is power wielded, and what are the scope and extent of these power relations?

From Scale to Socioterritoriality

Again I share Marston and her colleagues' reservations about scale, though it does force us to confront the nature of sociospatial relations in alternative ways. At the same time, I agree with Neil Brenner (2004), in his definition of scale above, that territories or "territorial units" are important prisms through which to understand social relations. And I do agree that nationally oriented territories, for example, are important insofar as they exercise real economic, political, and social power though the practice of legal, fiscal, and other institutions (for example, what Torpey 1998, in the context of migration, has called the "monopoly over the legitimate means of circulation"). Yet I remain less than convinced about the necessity of the term "scale" and cautiously accepting of the vertical differentiation and/or nested hierarchical scaffolding that many theorists of scale advocate.

Certainly, some legal, fiscal, and related institutions associated with territories such as the European Union (EU) may *in practice* be more powerful than the legal and fiscal institutions associated with territories inscribed by putatively sovereign nationally oriented states, which in turn may be *in practice* more powerful than the governments and polities of cities, and so forth. But this vertical understanding of territory need not necessarily entail a nested hierarchy.[6] And it is true that some social relations may have wider social scope and spatial extent than others that we might want to call scale (though this may be very difficult to determine sometimes). But then there is the risk of conflating scale as the social scope and spatial extent of those social relations and scale as force (that which produces certain kinds of social relations). In any case, the idea that scales have force may represent just another form of "spatial fetishism"—a reification of spatial relations.

Indeed, as Brenner well knows through his structurationist perspective, even the legal, fiscal, and other institutions of these acknowledged territorial hierarchies need to be reproduced—or if you will, performed—by agents bound up within these institutions. And the actors involved are shaped and reproduced by territorial configurations (with their respective institutions and agents) other than in those in which they perform these institutions. In short, economic, social, and political processes transcend territories, whether these territories are supranational (e.g., the EU), national (e.g., France), regional (e.g., the Ile de France), metropolitan (e.g., Agglomération de Paris), urban (e.g., the city of Paris), or suburban (e.g., the nineteenth arrondissement. Thus our task is to tease out the messy relations of structures, institutions, and social networks. In this respect, I peddle a perhaps dialectical and rhizomic view that we need to analyze the moments of territorial fixity within the moments of extraterritorial flows and their social networks (this does not mean these flows and social networks exist outside territories). Such flows can include people, commodities, money (capital), laws, customs, rules, and regulations, conjoined with their respective social networks. The moments of flows and social networks construct territoriality, which in turn constructs the extraterritorial flows and social networks. But these are certainly not just any old flows and networks; rather, they are connections defined by class power, bound up with other axes of power (e.g., racial, patriarchal, heteronormative, and so forth) that shape and are shaped by territories (see especially Harvey 2001 but also Balibar and Wallerstein 1991 and the vast literature on the governmentality of migration).

My argument, then, is that territoriality has "effectivity" (that is, it exercises power) only through the performance of particular institutions that are shaped and reshaped by social networks and the complex power relationships between actor networks, institutions, and structures.[7] I will call this socioterritoriality to be simple. Such a conception is designed to move beyond the often hackneyed dichotomy of global and local that has become pervasive across the social sciences and the popular media. In some respects, my understanding of socioterritoriality is similar, though not identical, to Martin Albrow's (1996) more phenomenological notion of "sociospheres" and the emerging idea of "assemblages" (Escobar 2007; Ong and Collier 2004). In fact, there is no reason that these three concepts could not be fruitfully conjoined, and I have no intention of providing an exclusive spatial master concept that employs an uncompromisingly rigid ontology, as Helga Leitner,

Eric Sheppard, and Kristin Sziarto (2008) warn against. Nonetheless, my notion seems to place more emphasis on the capacity of traditional entities such as "political territories" (from urban municipalities to national states) to exercise power. With such thinking in hand, I now want to shift focus by offering some critical comments on existing understandings of labor market incorporation with respect to migrants. This will in turn serve as a springboard for showing the usefulness of the notion of socioterritoriality.

Migrant Incorporation in Urban Labor Markets: A Review and Critique of the Literature

Research on the labor market incorporation from a non-neoclassical economic perspective involves studies where either space is not accorded any explicit treatment or spatial considerations are overt. The former is a vast body of work that includes studies in the vein of the "dual labor market hypothesis" (Piore 1979) and its more sophisticated offspring—labor market segmentation theory (e.g., Peck 1996). The occupational or sectoral division of labor literature fits between the spatially vague and the spatially overt literature. While the more spatially vague studies (the bulk of this body of work) suffer from an uncritical methodological nationalism (for critiques see Beck 2000b; Glick Schiller, Çağlar, and Guldbrandsen 2006; Peck 1996; Wimmer and Glick Schiller 2003), other research involves a more explicit spatial treatment but remains problematic in its evocation of the dichotomous global processes and local restructuring.

Concerning the more explicitly spatial literature, we can include the work surrounding the global city hypothesis (Samers 2002; Sassen 1991); studies by anthropologists of labor migration and the city (for reviews see Bretell 2003, Kearney 1986, Xiang 2007) research by economic geographers and economic sociologists on the sociospatial division of labor (Ellis, Wright, and Parks 2007) or by urban sociologists on the transnational dimensions of this division of labor (Smith 2001); work across the social sciences on ethnic enclaves, immigrant enclaves, or immigrant entrepreneurship (Rath and Kloosterman 2000 offer a review); and studies into the spatial practices of workers (a vast literature in anthropology, sociology, and labor geography). There are also bodies of work that address the spatial dimensions of labor market segmentation (e.g., Bauder 2006; Hanson and Pratt 1995; Morrison 1990; Peck 1996), including accounts of hiring practices (Waldinger and Lichter 2003), as well as the "embodied" character of labor markets and the importance of "cultural capital" to employment (Bauder 2006; McDowell, Batnitsky, and Dyer 2007). Given my exegesis on the importance of socioterritoriality, it is with this latter spatial literature that I will be concerned here. The aim is to eventually connect these fruitful yet flawed or incomplete approaches to the idea of socioterritoriality and international labor market segmentation. In the sections that follow I review and critique three broad strands of work that are more spatially inflected—namely, the "global cities hypothesis," what I call the "sociospatial division of labor literature," and labor market segmentation theory.[8]

The Global Cities Hypothesis and the Labor Market Incorporation of Migrants

The global city hypothesis (Sassen 1991) is a conceptual model whose over-arching argument is that economic globalization has created a set of cities (global cities) that have more in common with each other in their economic and social characteristics than they do with other cities in their respective national boundaries (see also Glick Schiller and Çağlar, chapter 4). I review her arguments with respect to immigration in more depth elsewhere (Samers 2002), but in brief, Sassen claims that global cities represent the locus of low-paid migrant workers, largely from the "global south," who work (often informally) at the bottom end of labor markets (in cleaning, restaurants, "downgraded manufacturing," "downgraded mass consumer services," and non-mass consumer services). The latter involve providing services to afflu-ent customers in the gentrifying centers and neighborhoods of these new global cities. These affluent customers are the highly–skilled, highly paid migrant and citizen workers, working mostly in more formalized employ-ment in producer services (accountancy, finance, insurance, and so forth). There is a certain logic of demand at work here. Global cities seem to precede the existence of migration (cf. Sassen 1988, 1996), and the dualistic structure of the labor market creates a specific demand for migrant workers at the low and high end. In her article "New Employment Regimes in Cities" (1996), however, Sassen seems to lean toward a supply-side argument, in which mi-gration drives the restructuring of these cities (see also the introduction to this book). In short, the economic and labor market structure of global cities both shapes and is shaped by this global circulation of people.

Sassen's arguments have endured endless scrutiny (see, e.g., Benton-Short, Price, and Friedman 2005; Jones 2002; McCann 2004; Robinson 2002; Short and Kim 1999; White 1998; Yeoh 1999). First and foremost, the global city hy-pothesis may harbor a strong dose of tautological thinking. In other words, it is an analytical mistake to identify global cities a priori and then evaluate their characteristics in order to proclaim their "global city-ness." Rather, I argue that the task should be more inductive, aiming to define what is unique (if anything) about those cities deemed global and indeed what might be unique about the labor markets associated with them (Samers 2002). Second, in Sassen's (1996) revision of the hypothesis, global city labor markets are the product of global economic forces and local (economic) processes.[9] For some, then, this might be a perfect illustration of how the global and local scale come together in cities. In light of my lengthy critique of scale above, it should be clear why this is unsatisfactory—namely, because migrant workers and their respective urban labor markets shape and are shaped by overlapping and fluid socioterritorialities that cannot be captured by this kind of scale meta-phor, a fixed notion of global and local (see also, e.g., Ley 2004). Indeed, a third significant problem is that Sassen employs an ethnocentric and econo-mistic reading of cities and labor market restructuring (White 1998). It there-fore ignores the roles of national and local (welfare) states and the way in which they mediate the ravages of global restructuring in terms of putatively global city labor markets outside the United States (Hamnett 1994, 1996; cf. May et al. 2007).

A fourth issue is whether the labor market inequality or polarization that Sassen and related scholars describe is similar across these global cities. In fact, Sassen is not alone in espousing these polarization arguments. The vast but not uncontested literature on neoliberalism has pointed to an era of un-precedented inequality in at least the wealthier countries since the Gilded Age. This has prompted other thinkers, such as Ulrich Beck, to speak of the "Brazilianization" of economies and of labor markets (2000a); that is, of a polarized income structure based partly on polarized jobs. What is striking here is the resemblance of these polarization arguments to dual labor market theory, especially because the labor market segmentation theory of the 1980s and 1990s sought to dispel Michael Piore's simplistic reasoning. Migrant workers are not simply confined to the low end and high end of urban labor markets; they perform jobs across a range of sectors, including welfare sec-tors, which may have the effect of sustaining the urban health care systems in European countries (e.g., with respect to the EU, see e.g. Kryiakides and Virdee 2003; May et al. 2007; Raghuram and Kofman 2002; Yeates 2004).

Fifth, even if there may be something called global city labor markets, with their concentration of particular jobs and stark divisions, the question remains whether these characteristics (and the processes that create them) are unique to cities such as Amsterdam, Brussels, London, or Paris and whether these labor markets are found elsewhere in smaller (but arguably no less global) cities such as Manchester, Milan, or Munich. The problem is that we do not have the empirical evidence—particularly with respect to European cities—to support or refute these claims. This is part of a much wider empiri-cal task that lies ahead for those seeking to understand migrants' working lives and the development of cities.

The Sociospatial Division of Labor Literature

There is now a substantial literature by economic sociologists and a handful of economic geographers and economists that investigates the occupational/sectoral division of labor, particularly in North America but also increasingly in the EU. Such work explores the presence of immigrants in particular sec-tors by connecting human capital variables with labor market performance in a national context, though this approach entails many weaknesses.[10] In contrast, other work (such as Ellis, Wright, and Parks 2007; Mattingly 1999; Wright and Ellis 2000a; Wright et al. 2000) is more promising and sophisti-cated. For example, Richard Wright and Mark Ellis (2000a) and Wright and his colleagues (2000) investigate the relationship between "social capital" (associated with particular nationalities or ethnicities), immigration policy, and immigrants' performance in the labor market, usually reflected in earnings and/or occupational position. This work also has the advantage of an explicit focus on gender, place of birth, and time of arrival with (at least some attention to) economic restructuring associated with politically defined or officially inscribed urban territories (central cities or other census-defined entities).

Other work in the context of immigration is more attentive to the relationship between place of employment, place of residence, and social reproduction (Mattingly 1999). Building upon this now well-developed tradition of research, Mark Ellis, Richard Wright, and Virginia Parks (2007) argue that the residential location of immigrants matters to the concentration of immigrants in particular jobs. In other words, the spatial access to jobs may be as important as the social access. Their focus on the fine-grained intrametropolitan sociospatial division of labor highlights not only the interrelated nature of production and social reproduction (a connection to which I will return later) but also the multiple territorialities that shape labor markets.

And yet here, too, there are limitations to such research. Data and methodological problems aside (including the conundrum of how to account for undocumented migrants and informal employment), there are at least four conceptual problems with this body of work. First, it employs a dichotomous (and static separation) between citizen and noncitizen, rather than focusing on the gradations of citizenship created by the vicissitudes of immigration policies. In other words, it matters whether one has residency but no right to work or the right to work but for only so many hours (and I discuss this point in further depth in a subsequent section). Despite the time-of-arrival variable relating to immigration policy, then, the result is a depoliticization of labor markets, in which the relevance of policy becomes largely invisible. This is particularly important in the context of undocumented migrant workers whose varied citizenship statuses shape their working opportunities.

Second, the literature on sociospatial divisions of labor "naturalizes" group distinctions in labor markets (Hanson and Pratt 1991, 1995) as a proxy for social capital (e.g., the use of a priori national or ethnic categories such as Black African, Kurdish, or North African) rather than exploring how such groups are formed and mobilized in the practice of hiring, firing, promotion, and so on. Indeed, Jouin's (2006) study of the Paris construction industry shows how the social bonds of same-nationality migrants are reinforced through stereotypes and hiring practices of the temporary firms involved. In any case, the uncritical mobilization of national groups in this literature is curious at best (since some of the literature recognizes how some jobs become gendered over time), and at worst it entails the peddling of racial or ethnic constructions that ignore multiple identities produced through the intersection of territory, class, race, gender, and other axes of differentiation.

A third problem with this literature is that it fails to explore the territory or space within individual firms and how these figure in the segmentation of migrant labor.[11] Labor is segmented not simply by occupation or type of job but also by job category, with the particular pay, benefits, hours, and other regulations that such categories involve.

A fourth limitation is that it completely ignores any of the insights of the scale literature, and where it does speak of space, it does so either in isolation (countries or cities are isolated from other territorialities) or through the typical hackneyed distinctions between globalization processes and local effects that I noted above.

Labor Market Segmentation Theory

In order to move to a discussion of what I call international labor market segmentation, it will be necessary to just say a few things about labor market segmentation theory. Michael Reich, David Gordon, and Richard Edwards (1973) coined the term "segmentation" to explain how different sectors within the labor market were governed by different rules of operation (this is especially germane if certain sectors are occupied predominantly by immigrants). Labor market segmentation theory sought to move beyond both the limitations of the dual labor market hypothesis and the problems of human capital theory. Again, like dual labor market theory, the segmentation literature never really departs from its nationally oriented framing. Building on the conceptual and spatial poverty of labor market segmentation research, Jamie Peck (1996) offers one of the most comprehensively synthetic conceptualizations of labor market segmentation to date. He proposes a "fourth generation" of research, in which labor market segmentation can be explained by the intersection of "production imperatives" (in conventional terms, labor demand factors), "processes of social reproduction" (labor supply factors), and "forces of regulation" (the role of the state, and other non- or quasi-state actors as well). His fourth-generation approach moves the debate further by focusing on the role of geographic or spatial contingency and in particular the nature of local labor markets. Peck's treatment of labor market segmentation is a remarkable achievement, but it is not without limitations—namely, that it emphasizes the supposed local nature of labor markets, at the expense of what I call their international character. With this in mind, below I outline how we might combine socioterritoriality with what I referred to in the introduction as the concept of international labor market segmentation.

Socioterritoriality and the Incorporation of Migrants in Urban Labor Markets

What Is International Labor Market Segmentation?

Employing Peck's tripartite schema, I argue below that the incorporation of migrants in urban labor markets can be understood through the prism of international labor market segmentation (Samers 2008). However, it is certainly not meant to capture *all* the dimensions of a migrant's working experience, from the mobilization and resistance strategies of workers, to immigrant entrepreneurship or other more phenomenological and identitarian concerns that have preoccupied many anthropologists and sociologists.[12] In fact, my approach remains rather top-down, incorporating a more centered notion of power than might be favored by after-scale theorists such as Arturo Escobar (2007) or Marston et al. (2005), but I believe this is not unwarranted given the relative lack of mobilization and resistance among migrant workers in European cities. Again, my aim is to develop a framework for understanding how particular workers are segmented into certain kinds of jobs and the obstacles they face in urban labor markets. The emphasis is on an inductive approach, in which the character of migrant labor market incorporation is privileged analytically over an approach that "typologizes" cities (such as the global cities hypothesis) and then draws inferences about the incorporation of migrant labor (see Glick Schiller and Çağlar, chapter 4; 2009; Grillo 2000; Low 1996, 1997).

My conception of ILMS involves three intersecting socioterritorialities. These should *not* be seen as somehow fixed scales. Thus it concerns first the sorting of labor drawn from around the world by national governments (in the country of both origin and destination) and to some extent supranational entities (such as the European Union) according to a set of desirable characteristics (skill, cultural proximity with respect to the imagined national community of the destination country, and so on). When I use the word "international" in this context, I am referring to international *actors* that produce segmentation by shaping the supply of migrant labor. But this should also be distinguished from the international *outcomes* of this segmentation (I discuss this latter point in greater detail below). This notion of segmentation is different from what is usually understood by labor market segmentation. I am not analyzing the mobility (or the lack of it) between clearly defined labor market sectors (Samers 2008) but rather how different people are situated within different sectors on the basis of their specific countries of origin.

Second, the same immigration policies then result in a sorting of labor *within* economies delimited by national governments, so that migrants are segmented (according to national origin or other ascribed characteristics such as gender) into specific sectors and jobs, with their own particular rules of operation. Such segmentation entails both social and spatial dimensions. The social dimension is exemplified in the employment precariousness (through visa restrictions for example) that may force certain nationalities into sectors or occupations where migrants work routinely without the correct papers, such as in home care, domestic labor, construction, and catering in and around most European cities. This is sometimes captured by the literature on sociospatial divisions of labor discussed above. The spatial dimension is reflected in the extent to which a specific nationality may be constrained to live in particular regions of European countries (Samers 2008). We have seen this for example, in the twentieth-century practice of pseudo-"pass laws" in

France, which provide migrant workers with visas that tie them to both particular sectors or industries and specific regions, reflecting the spatial concentration of those industries themselves (Grillo 1985). Many asylum seekers in Germany, such as Eritreans, are prevented from working in the eastern *Länder* of Germany but are also kept from moving (Edin, Fredriksson, and Åslund 2004; Koser 2007; see also Mendoza 2001 on Spain).

Third, international labor market segmentation also involves the segmentation of migrant workers *within* firms or organizations. This reflects a more conventional understanding of labor market segmentation. However, I would emphasize the significance of organizations as well as firms, since many migrants work, for example, in the hospitals of national health care systems of European cities, where immigration regulations also shape their segmentation. The segmentation of migrants by employers occurs through assumptions about their worthiness based on such ascribed characteristics as country of origin, ethnicity, gender, skin color, or their cultural preferences and capital (manner of dress, language ability, etc.) (Bauder 2006; McDowell, Batnitsky, and Dyer 2007; Waldinger and Lichter 2003). This kind of segmentation is well documented in European cities (for more recent studies, see Grzymala-Kazlowska 2005; Holgate 2005; Jouin 2006). However, white indigenous employers do not produce this. Even in the "super-diverse" cities of Europe and the United States, immigrant employers also entertain such racialized hierarchies and cultural judgments (e.g., Grzymala-Kazlowska 2005; Vertovec 2007.

However, my approach differs from existing labor market segmentation theory and the sociospatial division of labor literature in that I assume that workers are segmented on the basis not only of citizenship but on the basis of their "denizenship" status (Hammar 1990). Denizenship refers to the gradations, or shades, of migrants' legal status. At the same time that one's legal status may be restricted (limited in its term, for example) or precarious (as when one is awaiting regularization or refugee status), migrants may also be violating certain dimensions of their residence status (e.g., by working when they have no right to work, or by working for more hours than are permitted). And they may move between different statuses, a situation that Liza Schuster (2005), relying on fieldwork in Italy, calls "status mobility." Moving beyond the notion of simple illegality, then, Martin Ruhs and Bridget Anderson (2006) argue that one should speak of "semicompliance" (on a continuum between full and noncompliance—the latter more familiarly called illegal status).

While countless studies have shown that being clandestine or without proper papers (noncompliance), creates vulnerabilities for migrants in the labor market, Ruhs and Anderson argue that semicompliance shapes the jobs they perform, either because the migrants themselves choose only certain jobs that reflect their precarious statuses, or perhaps more rarely because employers recognize their vulnerability[13] (see also Anderson and Rogaly 2005; Kogan 2004; Mendoza 2001; Reyneri 2001; Ruhs and Anderson 2006; Schuster

2005). In Italy, for example, employers often give migrants jobs just before their residence permits are about to expire. Evidence of an official job enables the Italian authorities to extend the migrant's residence permit. But just as the permit is granted, the employer switches to a more informal arrangement with the migrant in order to avoid paying taxes or insurance. However, most cases in Italy differ from this example because, since work and residence permits are now combined, migrants' vulnerability increases as the expiration date of their permit approaches (Schuster 2005).

The Strength of International Labor Market Segmentation

We can identify at least three major strengths of ILMS vis-à-vis Peck's (1996) analysis. First, it builds on an existing emphasis in labor market segmentation—that is, the focus on racial discrimination. However, in most of the earlier segmentation research, those who were discriminated against on the grounds of the color of their skin were *citizens*. Indeed, it is striking that no study of immigration and labor market segmentation has ever pointed out this distinction between the earlier work and studies of migrants in particular. In contrast, ILMS allows us to incorporate the relationship between labor market segmentation and the production of denizenship and semicompliance, as noted above. Second and similarly, ILMS allows us to focus on how employers might segment migrants on the basis of the countries from which they originate. A third strength of ILMS is that it allows us to account for the conditions of social reproduction in the country of origin, not just the country of immigration. While anthropologists have long discussed the relationship between the "here" and the "there" in terms of migrants' experiences (Bretell 2007), the question of social reproduction is either insufficiently or unevenly discussed in Peck's (1996) analysis (see Samers 2008). Following a more general literature in migration studies on social reproduction, the concept of ILMS maintains that reproduction occurs across various territorial boundaries, not least through the international, transnational, or interstate transfers of remittances, forms of capital pooling, social transfers, and other forms of nonpecuniary assistance and care. To take one example, agricultural contract workers in France pay social charges at the French rate, but their family allowances and pensions that they receive in their home countries are five times lower than the French rate (Council of Europe/Parliamentary Assembly 2003). These types of state-sanctioned remittances serve to structure the migrant's individual budget in the country of immigration and his or her family budget in the country of origin and as a consequence may determine—in complex ways—what wages, working conditions, and working hours the migrant will accept in the country of immigration. In short, the international character of these processes shapes the supply of labor and the conditions under which workers are willing to be employed (Kofman 2005b; Yeates 2004).

Furthermore, labor is mobilized not just in relative proximity to the job available but, for example, through international smuggling and trafficking networks. In other words, immigration policy shapes the entrance of migrants into the urban labor market and in many cases the jobs they perform, the conditions under which they work, and the very supply of workers in particular nationally oriented territories. In sum, conceptualizing the processes of social reproduction as occurring through various socioterritorialities allows us to overcome the problem in labor market segmentation theory of the eclipse of neoclassical "methodological individualism" by "methodological nationalism" (Peck 1996, 86 n.10).

The Relationship between ILMS, Socioterritoriality, and the Development of Cities

As a way of explaining the labor market incorporation of migrants in cities, ILMS needs to be understood through the prism of socioterritoriality, since production, social reproduction, and regulation are shaped through multiple territorialities and complex social networks. Our theoretical and empirical task should *not* consist of specifying global cities beforehand in some taxonomic exercise in order to examine the nexus of cities and migration. Rather, we should ask how the socioterritoriality of urban firms and organizations creates specific kinds of labor market demand and intrafirm segmentation practices and how this in turn shapes migration and migrant practices within different cities. Second, ILMS impels us to explore how forces of regulation figure in the functioning of labor markets and the availability of migrant workers. This might include exclusionary, discriminatory, or selective EU, national, and substate immigration policies, national and substate welfare and employment policies, municipal fiscal and housing policies, and firm or organizational rules and regulations. But we also have to ask other international (or transnational) questions about social reproduction. For example, what is the relationship between the country of origin and the country (or countries) of immigration? How do remittances shape household budgets, reinforce social networks, and reproduce migration practices? It is in answering these questions that we can develop a more sophisticated means of exploring the incorporation of migrants within urban labor markets. How does the fact that socioterritoriality and the labor market segmentation of migrants are intertwined shape the economic, political, and social development of European cities, for example? It would be a mistake to assume that we can gauge the political and social mobilization of migrants from their position in labor markets. However, I maintain that their experience *as workers* connects them psychologically, symbolically, and materially not only to particular workplaces, cities, and certain areas or neighborhoods within cities but also to wider movements (social movement unionism, contentious politics, and so forth) that in turn have the effect of transforming cities.

• • •

To help us understand the relationship between the multiple pathways of labor market incorporation and migrants in cities, I have promulgated two conceptual revisions. First, I maintain that the use of the term "scale" involves definitional imprecision, conflation, and obfuscation. In its place, I argue for "socioterritoriality." This is a dialectical and rhizomic concept that entails a mutually constitutive relationship between territories, institutions, actors, and material and immaterial flows. These in turn are shaped by class and other axes of differentiation and power (e.g., racial, patriarchal, and heteronormative practices). At the same time, I use but also remain critical of the insights of the global cities hypothesis, the sociospatial division of labor approach, and fourth-generation labor market segmentation theory. I have called, therefore, for the concept of international labor market segmentation. I show how we might better understand the interaction between labor markets, migrants, and cities by soldering these two concepts together. ILMS is only a framework and does not demonstrate empirically what might be either unique or common about the way in which low-paid migrants toil in Europe's cities, but we should probably avoid the temptation to create Weberian ideal types of cities that are denuded of both the dynamism of social processes and the temporal specificity of these processes, including migrations, employment relations, and urban transformations. Rather, the task should be to identify the temporality of the principal sociospatial processes that shape migrants' working lives in cities across the world, how migrants experience these processes, and how they in turn shape the economic, political, and social development of cities.

How might we approach this methodologically? One response, which emanated from the symposium on which this book is based, is to begin with the concept of "methodological urbanism" rather than individualism, collectivism, nationalism, or globalism. Presumably such a methodology would begin with the premise that each city is unique with its own specific labor markets and immigration patterns and thus working experiences. This *may* be one potential avenue, but it does not answer the question of how different migrants can have working experiences that may be decidedly different, even within the same city. We would therefore be driven to lower our methodological resolution to the analytical unit of, let us say, the neighborhood—and call it methodological "neighborhoodism," until we reach the resolution of the workplace, the household, or even the body. It should be clear, then, that methodological urbanism alone may not be the tidy answer for which some of us had hoped.

I therefore propose that we might begin with a "methodological socioterritoriality," which is decidedly loose about both the territoriality involved in the construction of social processes and the human experiences bound up within them. To be loose is certainly no answer either, but it does keep multiple paths open for a project whose beginnings I have only begun to sketch here.

Notes

1. By labor market incorporation, I am referring to two processes: obtaining waged employment, whatever its formal or informal character, and obtaining promotion, whether this position involves higher pay, higher status, or some other characteristic deemed desirable by a migrant worker.

2. My concern here is with primarily low-paid labor, although some of my comments refer to the relevance of relatively higher-paid migrant labor (such as nurses) in welfare sectors.

3. See also Brenner (2001, 2004), Leitner and Miller (2007), Leitner, Sheppard, and Sziarto (2008), Mansfield (2005), Marston (2000), Marston, Jones, and Woodward (2005), and McMaster and Sheppard (2004) for a short review of definitions and an overview of this scale literature.

4. Defined by Brenner as "the hierarchical differentiation and (re)ordering of geographical scales" (2001, 593).

5. Earlier, Marston herself (2000) argued in favor of the concept of scale.

6. As Ivan Light (2004) observes, even cities shape national immigration regulations (for an idea how, see Samers 2002), though it is unclear what agency and social processes he associates with cities. In any case, Helga Leitner and Byron Miller (2007) note that the scale literature, and especially the work of Marston et al. (2005), seems to conflate verticality with hierarchy.

7. My understanding of power relations draws from both John Allen (2004), who sees power as spatially contingent, relational, and visible by its effects, and Andrew Sayer (2004), who critiques Allen's work for his disavowal of the "container theory of power." In other words, I assume that employers and various arms of the state, for example, all have the capacity to exercise control over migrants, despite the latter's sometimes successful mobilizations against the exercise of such power.

8. I do not discuss the literature on spatial practices of workers here because its aims are generally different from those of the labor market segmentation literature. However, they are related in at least two ways. First, the early labor market segmentation theorists focused on resistance by workers within firms and on the implications of this resistance for workers' segmentation (e.g., Edwards 1979; Friedman 1977). Second, the spatial practices literature includes work on the nexus of scale and trade unionism, social movement unionism, and so on (e.g., Castree 2000; Herod 2001; Moody 1997; Sadler 2000; Wills 2000). These wider social movements are important to how cities evolve, and I therefore briefly mention their relevance toward the end of the chapter.

9. However, it is unclear how far Sassen privileges her local, entrepreneurship-centered, bottom-up argument.

10. I do not have the space here to offer a critique of the human capital approach. See Peck (1996) for a general critique and Samers (2008) for a critique with respect to migrant labor.

11. I conceive the space of the firm as a territory, in much the same way that Marston argued that the home is a scale. Certainly, firms and organizations are situated within various socioterritorialities, but they may also be considered territories in themselves, since they involve particular structures, institutions, and agents—that is, forms of human organization. They must also be distinguished from other forms of territoriality, such as national states and supranational organizations that clearly involve a different or much wider range of identities cultural practices and economic activities.

12. As mentioned at the outset of this chapter, formal and informal immigrant entrepreneurship is a significant dimension of economic activity associated with immigrants in European cities. Part of the myopia of segmentation theorists with respect to understanding the economic incorporation of migrants has been the neglect of the importance of entrepreneurship in cities (Logan et al. 2000). In general, the segmentation, entrepreneurship, day laboring (Valenzuela 2001), and "ethnic niche" literatures have tended to ignore each other (Schrover, van der Leun, and Quispel 2007), but both wage labor and immigrant entrepreneurship

should be considered together in the conceptualization of urban labor markets. However, as stated earlier, an analysis of immigrant entrepreneurship and cities lies beyond the scope of this chapter.

13. Anderson et al. (2006) point out that it is unclear whether employers are always aware of migrants' denizenship status, especially when false papers are involved.

Chapter 4

Locality and Globality

Building a Comparative Analytical Framework in Migration and Urban Studies

NINA GLICK SCHILLER & AYŞE ÇAĞLAR

In this chapter, we review the literature on migrants in cities and on neo-liberalism and cities as a step towards building a comparative analytical framework on the relationship between migrants and urban restructuring and rescaling. We explore the reasons for the failure to study migrants as agents of the restructuring and rescaling of localities in ways that adequately address the global aspects of urban restructuring. In addition, we suggest that the debates among urban geographers about the utility of an analysis of the neo-liberalism and the rescaling of city can enrich migration studies. In building on these debates we note that those scholars who have developed a global perspective on the spaces of "actually existing neoliberalism" don't analyze the role of migrants in the remaking of cities (Brenner and Theodore 2002a). The purpose of our critique of migration and urban studies is twofold. We wish to challenge migration scholars to think comparatively about the neo-liberal restructuring of locality and roles of migrants within these globe spanning processes. We also hope that urban scholars will begin to examine the role of migrants as scale makers who actively participate in the reconstitution and repositioning of cities. The chapter consists of four sections. The first addresses the ways in which the methodological nationalism of the migration literature has impeded the theorization of locality. The second and third examine debates over neo-liberal restructuring and rescaling including the role of various forms of contestation. In the conclusion, we briefly reiterate the analytical perspective developed from our critique of the literature.

At present, locality for many migration scholars is no more than the place from which people depart, the neighborhood in which immigrants settle, or the places that migrants connect through transnational networks. Those few researchers who have developed the concept of locality generally explore the specific institutional structure and historical context of a particular city with little or no reference to globe spanning connections that cities may share (Waldinger 1986a; Foner 2000). The differential placement of cities within processes of urban restructuring that are global in their reach while local in their realization is rarely referenced and has yet to be theorized in migration scholarship. Aside from the global cities researchers, there is a parallel omission among most urban scholars who have addressed the postindustrial city or urban neoliberal rescaling and restructuring. They may mention migration, but migrants are not conceptualized as active agents who not only reflect but also contribute to the restructuring of various cities (Brenner and Theodore 2002b; Fainstein and Campbell 2002; Marcuse and van Kempen 2000; Scott and Soja 1996; Smith and Feagin 1987; M.G. Smith 2002).

However, this absence of a comparative and global perspective on the relationship between migration and cities may not be apparent for several reasons. First of all, a great deal of research about migration has been done in a relative handful of cities—New York, London, Los Angeles, Singapore, Berlin—that seem almost synonymous with migration. Second, there is an impressive literature on immigrant communities and histories within certain cities. Moreover, at various points in urban anthropology and urban studies, researchers seemed to be specifically suggesting that the relationship between migrants and cities should be studied. They spoke of the "city as context," suggesting that research about an "immigrant community" must be situated within the institutional structure and path-determined history of a specific city of settlement (Brettell 2003; Çağlar 2001; Ellis 2001; Glick Schiller and Fouron 1999; Goode and Schneider 1994; Leeds 1994; Soysal 2001; Straßburger, Ubehan, and Yalçin-Heckmann 2000; Yalçin-Heckmann 1997). In the third place, there is a scholarship of migrants as labor—faceless or talented—or entrepreneurs within specific urban economies (Light, Bernard, and Kim 1999; Rath 2000; Wilson and Portes 1980).

Some of this literature contains promising insights for building a comparative global perspective on locally significant variations. We can find provocative statements that seem to begin to theorize the relationship among migrant settlement, transnational networks, and differences between cities. Peter Taylor and Robert Lang (2005, 2), for example, have observed that "cities with large concentrations of immigrants can have strong global connections due to the ebb and flow of both people and money back to countries of origin." By the 1990s, a handful of migration researchers in Europe had begun to trace relationships between the size, significance, and political configuration of particular cities in which migrants were settling and the pattern of incorporation of these migrants (Bommes and Radke 1996; Koopmans and Stratham 2000; Rex 1996; Schmitter Heisler 1998). This work complemented the increasing number of ethnographies, especially in the United States, that describe migrants settling in suburban, rural, or non-gateway cities (Brettell 2005a, 2005b; Holtzmann 2000; Koltyk 1997; Lamphere 1992; Mahler 1995).

Yet this scholarship, with its promising insights, hypotheses, and contextual analyses, has not produced an analytical framework that allows us to comparatively explore cities as localities that are shaped by and shape migrant settlement and transnational connection.

Most of these studies have not examined the relationship between migrant incorporation and dynamic restructuring of capital that has heightened the competition between cities. Yet there are important synergies between the processes through which financial, political, and cultural capital is accumulated and the way in which migrants are differentially positioned in and contribute to the restructuring and repositioning of cities. To date, only a handful of scholars have examined the multiple and varying ways in which migrants actively contribute to the globe-spanning neoliberal processes that are grounded within acts of contemporary urban place-making (Garbaye 2005; Mitchell 2003; Smith 2001). Even much of this pathbreaking work has separated the study of place from the processes of uneven neoliberal globalization, which rapidly intensified sociospatial disparities within and across cities, regions, and nation-states.

The comparative framework that we believe is needed builds on but departs from debates in geography about the way in which territory is experienced and understood in relationship to social networks, institutions, labor processes, contestations, and cultural and social reproduction that are simultaneously embedded in and across space (Amin and Graham 1997; Cox 1997; Leitner, Peck, and Sheppard 2007; Massey 2005; Smith 2001). For example, in perhaps the most comprehensive effort to date to theorize migration and urbanism, Michael Peter Smith (2001, 5) has argued for a concept of "transnational urbanism," which he offers as a "cultural rather than a strictly geographic metaphor." In taking a radical social constructionist approach to place-making, Smith derided analyses of neoliberal globalization, which he saw as an economic reductionism devoid of cultural processes. He specifically rejected David Harvey's analysis of the locally situated global differentiation and reconstitution of capital. Harvey (2005, 2006), building on Marx, has highlighted the significance of the "creative destruction" of capital in the remaking of contemporary cities.

We find Harvey's contribution more useful for migration scholars because, together with other urban geographers of neoliberalism, he has highlighted the recent reconstitution of cities through efforts to implement, contest, and reformulate globe-spanning neoliberal agendas (2005, 2006; see also Smith 2002; Brenner and Theodore 2002a). Such an approach allows us to move toward an explanatory framework that can analyze variations in migrants' pathways of local and transnational incorporation. However, Harvey has not sufficiently addressed the differential outcomes of the processes of capital accumulation that he outlines on people's strategies and actions. A comparative approach to the relationship between migrants and cities is necessary and desirable. Exploring these relationships comparatively allow us to examine the mutual constitution of global processes and the local economic, political, and cultural contexts as they are acted upon and actively shape the lives of migrants. That is to say, a city's relationship to migrants needs to be understood within a theory of locality that addresses several processes. These include the globally connected but locally based ongoing processes of capital formation, destruction, and restructuring; the positioning of localities within hierarchies of political, economic, and cultural power that extend within and across nation-states; and the active role of migrants as place makers and scale makers shaping neoliberal restructuring and rescaling through their multiple social positions within and across space.

Although our specific concern is the relationship between migration and cities, the comparative framework we advocate is more generally applicable to the concept of locality, understood as the sociospatial dimension of human experience (Massey 2005). Cities are only one of a range of places that need to be theorized in relationship to migration. Depending on the context, locality could refer to a village, a neighborhood, a city, a metroplex, or a region. We speak of a theory of locality in order to highlight the processes of the restructuring and rescaling of capital production that we think must be addressed in examining migrants' processes of settlement and transnational connection. These processes literally always "take place." They occur and connect within specific spaces and are shaped by, as well as shape, the history as well as particular local practices and representations of those spaces. At the same time we stress that in our understanding, capital is always an unequal social relationship situated within normatively endorsed, disparately represented, and institutionally maintained regimes.

While acknowledging that migration scholars need to develop an analytical framework through which to approach locality, we argue for the salience of cities within a broader process of theory building. From our perspective, cities cannot be understood as bounded units of territory but, as with all human spaces of habitation and usage, as spaces of social relationships that happen in and across territory. To this extent, we agree with those place theorists who "emphasize how places are heterogeneously constituted through the polyvalent inter-connectivities linking them, rather than as having distinctive essential characteristics that emerged behind the boundaries separating them from the rest of the world" (Leitner, Sheppard, and Sziarto 2008, 161; see also Massey 2005).

However, a focus on the multiple-connectedness of cities should not detract from the fact that cities are also units of governance and representation, with functions such as regulation, taxation, and service provision, which make them useful starting points from which to examine the role of hierarchies of power in place-making. Cities' powers of governance and self-representation make their territorial aspects significant in the local constitution of territorially based construction and deconstruction of capital. In migration studies, if approached comparatively and within a global perspective, cities can serve as important instances in the exploration of the interface between migrants' pathways of incorporation and the materialization of broader processes of restructuring and rescaling in space. As units of governance with powers of taxation and local development, cities have been playing prominent roles in neoliberal agendas. They have been constituted as globally recognized brands directly competing for investment and global talent.

Migration Scholarship and Methodological Nationalism

Most migration scholars, even those who trace the dynamics of "transnational communities," have been unable to theorize the mutuality of the global and local because of deep-seated methodological nationalism. Methodological nationalism is an orientation that approaches the study of social and histori-cal processes as if they were contained within the borders of individual na-tion-states (Beck 2000b; Martins 1974; Smith 1983; Wimmer and Glick Schiller 2002, 2003). Nation-states are conflated with societies. The term "method-ological nationalism" emphasizes the political implications of the container notion of society. The very problematic of migration studies is shaped by the conflation of the nation-state with society. Much of migration scholarship has developed to address the threat that migrants are believed to bring to their new country of settlement, which is defined as "the host society."

Because the nation-state is equated with society for methodological na-tionalists, the social fabric and the integrity of social institutions and the cul-tural norms that support them are seen as contained within state borders. Through this logic, the fundamental social division becomes the opposition between natives, who are assumed to uniformly share common social norms, and foreigners. Coming from what are thought of not only as distinctively different states but also as different societies, foreigners are portrayed as car-rying with them the particular distinctive common national norms. In this paradigm, migrants are intruders on the shared and homogenous cultural and social space contained within the borders of the nation-state in which they are settling. Much of mainstream migration theory consistently disre-gards both the social and cultural divisions within each nation-state and the experiences, norms, and values migrants and natives share because they are embedded in social, economic, and political processes, networks, movement, and institutions that extend across state borders (Gordon 1964).

Of course, not all currents of social science theory reflect the orientation of methodological nationalism; Marxist, world system, and world society theorists have argued differently. However, it was not until the 1990s with the growth of globalization studies that mainstream social science systemati-cally acknowledged the significance of globe-spanning flows of capital, labor, ideas, forms of media, and formal and informal networks. The word "glo-balization" took on many meanings and represented both a paradigmatic change in the units of analysis in many disciplines and a particular narrative on world history. At the heart of the new scholarship was a concern for a process of global economic and institutional restructuring that began in the

1970s and had implications for people's lives everywhere. Of central importance in this restructuring was the emergence of flexible processes of capital accumulation that were less dependent on national economic structures
(Harvey 1989). Not surprisingly, given that the basic paradigm of migration
scholarship was rooted in methodological nationalism, most scholars studying migrant settlement in European or U.S. cities did no more than give lip
service to the new globalization studies. One exception was the growth of the
research on transnational migration. But even these researchers did not address the local/global nexus in ways that contributed to a theory of locality
and its contemporary transformations.

The Ethnic Lens

Beginning with Fredrick Barth's (1969) emphasis on the social constitution
of ethnic boundaries, there is a voluminous historical and ethnographic
literature that details the constructed nature of ethnic identities (Brubaker
2004; Hill 1989; Glick Schiller 1977; Gonzalez 1988; Rath and Kloosterman
2000; Sollors 1989). Furthermore, even authors who accept the framing of
their research within the paradigm of ethnic community often provide descriptions of divisions based on class, religions, region of origin, or politics
among members of the same group. However, despite this understanding
of the problematic nature of ethnic groups as a unit of analysis and object
of study and the calls for "writing against culture," (Abu-Lughod 1991), the
ethnic lens predominates in migration studies. Its persistence is one aspect
of the continuing methodological nationalism of migration studies—namely,
the tendency to deploy a homogenized concept of culture based on national
historical narratives of differentiation in the framing of research problems
and strategies.

Beginning with an ethnic lens, migration researchers often assume that
migrants from a particular nation-state or region constitute an ethnic group
before their identity, actions, social relations, and beliefs are studied. Making
an ethnic lens central to a research design prioritizes one form of identification, subjectivity, basis for social interaction, and source of social capital over
all others (Glick Schiller 2005a, 2005b, 2009; Glick Schiller and Çağlar 2008a,
2008b; Glick Schiller, Çağlar, and Guldbrandsen 2006). The use of the word
"community" as synonymous with the term "ethnic group" compounds the
problem because it contributes to defining a particular mode of settlement
and identification before the research has been conducted. The possibility
of assessing the actual degree of heterogeneity in migrants' identities, practices, and social ties is at best made more difficult and at worst forestalled.
The research design itself precludes the study of migrants' non-ethnic ties,
which inform their practices within urban and national spaces and transnationally (Çağlar 1997).

The research on migrant economic incorporation through small business
ownership or employment provides an example of the ways in which the

widespread use of the ethnic group as a unit of analysis hinders our under-standing of how migrants contribute to and are shaped by the reconstitu-tion and rescaling of cities. There is a rich and valuable literature on migrant economy, migrant business, and entrepreneurialism (Bonacich and Modell 1980; Light 1972; Waldinger 1986a, 1986b; Wilson and Portes 1980). However, such research has too readily been framed in terms of "the ethnic economy" and "ethnic entrepreneurs." Having reduced the study of the relationship of migrants to the ethnic community, researchers debated the centrality of the ethnocultural characteristics of the migrant groups in the analysis of their economic activity and incorporation. The debate was framed by precluding from the research the larger factors that shape locality and all entrepreneurial activities within it. Those researchers who emphasized ethnocultural charac-teristics emphasized factors such as the historical business experience of each ethnic group settling in the city and the cultural resources they were able to bring to their entrepreneurial activities. Such an approach led investigators to examine the compatibility of migrants' cultural and religious beliefs and practices with entrepreneurial activities, as well as their ability to organize themselves on the basis of ethnic social networks and trust relations particu-larly suitable for small business.

Viewing entrepreneurship through an ethnic lens, researchers have com-pared, for example, Southeast Asians and the Afro-Caribbean migrants in London; Moroccan, Surinamese, and Turkish migrants in Amsterdam; and Vietnamese and North African migrants in Paris. In general the activities of immigrant businesspeople have been assessed only in terms of their contri-butions to the growth of ethnic enclaves, the relations between ethnic groups, or the discrimination faced by an ethnic group. Too little has been said about the contextual and historical structuring of these world cities, which shaped the dynamics of business growth and expansion of local economic activities and opportunities.

A growing number of researchers of ethnic businesses have critiqued the use and conceptualization of ethnic categories and moved beyond them (Pé-coud 2000; Rath and Kloosterman 2000). These studies correctly ask what makes migrant economic practices and migrant entrepreneurs ethnic. Is it the ethnic origin of the entrepreneurs and the owners of the business place? Is it the characteristics of migrants' networks and their use of strategies in conducting business? Those who advocate a critical position urge scholars to pay more attention to the general economic, sociological, and geographic contexts of these economic activities and to consider the migrant entrepre-neurs primarily as socially embedded economic actors in the Schumpeterian sense (Light, Bernard, and Kim 1999; Portes 1995; Rath 2000; Waldinger and Bozorgmehr 1996). These scholars plead for concentrating on the economic environment and on the institutional context of migrant business practices.

However, despite the relevant questions about the ownership and control in migrant business activities and the critique of the criteria used to differ-entiate the ethnic and the non-ethnic bases of business activity in particular places, most of these researchers have not developed a comparative perspective on locality or moved their research beyond globally significant cities. Their discussions have remained at the level of national welfare states and the opportunities this form of governmentality provides to migrant business and entrepreneurs at that scale. Little attention is paid to the fact that migrants as economic actors share the possibilities of economic opportunities and constraints with other entrepreneurs in the economy of a particular locality as it experiences and acts within globe-spanning processes of restructuring. Nothing is said about the possibility that migrants through their local and transnational connections may contribute to local opportunity structures. Migration scholars rarely study migrants' non-ethnic forms of economic incorporation or explore a variety of relationships that extend beyond ethnically based migrant communities (Jacobs, Phalet, and Swyngedouw 2004).

As a consequence of their ethnic lens, researchers have represented a particular pathway of migrant incorporation and form of business organization as characteristic of the ethnic group's incorporation into an entire nation-state. They have left little conceptual space open in which to examine variations between cities in forms of migrant incorporation. Yet these variations may contribute to and reflect ways in which migrants and nonmigrants form relationships within and between places. While a few scholars have compared migrant incorporation within the different economic and political configurations of different cities in the same nation-state, they have not gone on to develop a comparative analytical framework (Betz 1996; Koopmans and Stratham 1999; Itzigsohn 2000; Itzigsohn and Saucedo 2002; Rex and Samad 1996).

New approaches to migrants in cities continue to be filtered through the ethnic lens. For example, the recent work on "superdiversity" in British cities acknowledges the internal divisions within ethnic groups in terms of language, place of origin, legal status, and stratification and the challenges this situation poses to the service providers (Vertovec 2006). However, despite underlining the problems involved in using ethnic categories for analysis and as the basis for policy suggestions, this perspective continues to rely primarily on the classification of migrants according to ethnic categories. The sources of superdiversity are said to lie mainly in the proliferation of migrants with different ethnic origins rather than in the actual practices of migrants that reflect and contribute to the heterogeneity of the city. Moreover, researchers have most often associated global cities such as London with this kind of diversity, without paying sufficient attention to the ways diversity is signaled, organized, and configured differently in cities of different scalar positioning. Yet migrants in different cities, even within the same ethnic group, may differ by labor market incorporation and may play varying roles in terms of their roles as mediators in a city's insertion in the global/local processes of restructuring and re-representing urban space (Hiebert 1999).

The role of locality in shaping migrant subjectivities and pathways of incorporation is also obviated by those scholars of diaspora and transnational migration who assume that those who share an ancestry and history of dispersal also share an identity and form of communal relations as they migrate and settle. These scholars and the migration scholarship they have criticized share a common ground. Much of diaspora research has been built on the axis of ethnic belonging and ethnically based social ties (Soysal 2000). The ethnic lens when used as the optic for transnational migration studies has impeded researchers' ability to note, adequately document, and theorize the fact that migrants also build non-ethnic transnational social fields based on religious, political, professional ideological, and economic networks.

The networks of migrants that actually link people in specific and multiple localities are transformed through an ethnic lens into a bounded transnational community that stretches between a homeland and a new land. As a result, much transnational migration research disregards broader restructuring processes that are grounded unevenly in territory and therefore fails to theorize the processes that are transforming localities. Even scholars of transnational migration, who have addressed uneven globalization, have highlighted the transnational formation of ethnic identities and long-distance nationalism. They have routinely ignored a range of non-ethnic modes of incorporation that reflect and contribute to the restructuring of localities (Basch, Glick Schiller, and Szanton Blanc 1994; Glick Schiller and Fouron 2001). As a result, the sending and the receiving states have been approached as if there were equality and homogeneity between regions and localities within a national territory. State policies and the related opportunity structures are often assumed to have the same effect on migrant settlement in all localities within a nation-state. Similarly, the sending state's activities with regard to migrants have rarely been researched in terms of the sociospatial characteristics of localities of departure (Çağlar 2006). Yet unless we link the opportunity structures available to migrants to the repositioning of their localities of departure, settlement, and connection, we cannot adequately develop an analysis of migrants and their relationship to place-making within and across nation-states.

Building Theories about Migrant Settlement and Transnational Connection from Paradigmatic Cities

Cities within one national territory have been treated as interchangeable in many migration studies. The members of a particular ethnic background are studied in one urban context—usually a city in which they have a dense concentration—but the contextual factors shaping the practices and social ties of migrants in that specific locality are implicitly assumed to be similar throughout the nation-state. In theories about ethnic segregation, enclaves, or diasporic networks, for example, Turks in Berlin, Pakistanis in Manchester, or Cubans in Miami become the study of Turks in Germany, Pakistanis in Britain, or Cubans in the United States (Çağlar 1995; Heckmann 2003; Mandel 1990; Stepick and Portes 1993; White 1999; Werbner 1990, 2002). This kind of spatial indifference to other than the national scale in migration scholarship extends into comparative studies. The study of migrant settlement in particular cities has been utilized to compare settlement processes and social ties of migrants in different states. Studies of Turkish migrants in specific cities—namely, Berlin and Paris—have entered the literature as representing differences between the Turkish experiences in the entire nation-states of Germany and France (Amiraux 2001; Kastoryano 2002).

In fact, researchers have identified a set of cities, commonly designated as "gateways," that are differentiated from other cities because they share a combination of historical and opportunity factors that attract large proportions of new migrants (Clark 2004; Ley 2003). Yet, paradoxically, these same researchers often regard gateway cities as paradigmatic of migration processes throughout the nation-state in which these cities are located. They disregard the unique factors that make these cities gateways. For example, Berlin acquired a stable place within the debates about the integration of migrants in Germany (Baumann et al. 2004; Kaya 2002; Soysal 2001). The way migrants organized their lives and their economic, religious, and cultural activities and practices in Berlin became the model by which to conceptualize migrant economic, religious, and cultural incorporation in Germany.

Sometimes gateway cities are the same cities that other researchers have called global—London, Paris, New York, and Los Angeles. When using data from these cities, migration scholars have studiously ignored the argument that global cities have been relatively disarticulated from the nation-state in which they are geographically located. Occasionally research on specific forms of incorporation in a city that is designated gateway by some and global by others, such as New York, has been compared to a smaller scale locality, such as the U.S. city of Providence, Rhode Island (Itzigsohn 2000; Itzigsohn and Saucedo 2002). But even in these instances, the researchers did not develop their observations of differences in pathways of incorporation in the two localities into a theory of locality and migration.

In all these studies, locality is first highlighted and then put aside in matters of theory. Yet unless we link the opportunity structures available to migrants to the positioning of localities of departure and settlement within multiple hierarchies of power, we cannot adequately analyze migrant practices, their patterns of organization, and their strategies of participation. The nature of the neoliberal transformations of particular localities shapes the formation and dynamics of the migrant transnational social fields that link those places.

Confining Discussion of Neoliberal Restructuring and Repositioning to Global Cities

One body of work, founded on what some have called the global cities hypothesis, has consistently offered a global perspective on the relationship between urban restructuring and migration (Samers 2002). The contributors to this literature confined their analysis of the global restructuring and re-positioning of cities to a small set of cities that they postulated were entangled more with each other than with the other localities of the nation-states in which they were located (Abu-Lughod 1995; Eade 1997; Friedmann and Wolff 1982; Friedmann 1986; King 1991; Sassen 1991, 2000a; Taylor 1995). The global cities hypothesis and the literature it generated had many strengths and weaknesses, and it is not our purpose here to add to the debate about the utility of the concept (Samers 2002). Instead, we assess those aspects of the analysis that are useful in the study of the relationship between global processes and all contemporary cities.

Global cities scholars hypothesized that the growing disjuncture between geographical and social spaces and the changing landscape of social, economic, and cultural proximities were all outcomes of the uneven spatiality of globalization. They made the discontinuity of spaces within the nation-state the focal point of their analysis and argued that despite their different national contexts, certain metropoles occupied a particular and shared positioning within the hierarchies of power and the circuits of global capital flow. As a consequence, certain cities, which they designated as global or world cities, resembled each other in terms of their socioeconomic and financial structures, functions, and institutional capabilities and were thus closer to each other than to other cities within the same national territory.

The global cities perspective had its roots in research conducted in the 1980s on the international division of labor, the mobility of labor and capital in response to the global dynamics of industrial financing, and the growth of an informal sector of urban employment (Nash and Fernandez Kelly 1983; Sassen-Koob 1984). From this base, scholars turned to the study of migrant settlement and transnational connection within the restructured labor markets of global cities (Sassen 1988). They noted the growth of an hourglass urban economy with an affluent set of businesses based on the facilitation of knowledge, fashion, culture, marketing, and financial industries and a low-wage sector of nonunionized service workers and small sweatshops. The low-wage sector, it was generally agreed, attracted and depended on immigrant labor.

The global cities hypothesis offered a different entry point into global process than did two equally unsustainable premises of the first wave of globalization scholars. In one approach, global flows of capital, media, ideas, technology, and people transformed the local into a single homogenous worldwide domain (Friedman 2000). In the other, local factors shaped the penetration of global forces so that the outcome produced only a multitude of heterogeneous local responses rather than any global trends (Appadurai 1996; Hannerz 1992). Disrupting this flattened local-global view, the global cities hypothesis stressed that the intensification of flexible capital accumulation was accompanied by the continuation and heightening of the uneven and localized character of capitalist investment. By emphasizing the uneven spatialization of global capitalism, the global cities perspective made clear that much more was at stake than a diversity of experiences of the local. This perspective highlighted the restructuring of nation-states' relationships to territory and facilitated discussions of the ways the global production of economic disparity was experienced locally.

In short, according to global cities scholars, global forces take particular forms in particular places and affect the dynamic configuration of specific localities, including processes of migrant settlement and transnational connection. However, the perspective that these researchers brought to the study of spatialization and the configuration of localities was never extended to other urban contexts, including the many cities worldwide that were marginalized and forced to fiercely compete for capital investment on a very uneven playing field. Many scholars assumed that global cities were the only ones that were increasingly decoupled from the nation-state and experienced a consequent altered relationship to their respective states.

Consequently, despite its contributions, global cities research impeded the systematic development of a theory of locality in migration studies and a comparative perspective on migrant incorporation in cities. In fact, when urban researchers in the 1990s initiated a discourse about capital and industrial restructuring, they failed to connect the changes that they acknowledged were taking place in cities in relationship to global forces to an analysis of modes of migrant incorporation. Certain cities were called "postindustrial" (Waldinger 1996b, 4), "cities of high finance" (Waldinger and Bozorgmehr 1996), "post-Fordist/post modern metropolis" (Scott and Soja 1996, viii), or "capitalist" (Smith and Feagin 1987). The labels had little analytical comparative value and have not proved useful in understanding the variable positioning of cities within global processes of localization.

The Missing Scalar Dimension

In an attempt to develop the analytical tools necessary to address "cities and the geographies of 'actually existing neoliberalism'" (Brenner and Theodore 2002a), a group of urban geographers built on the global cities scholarship but moved beyond it to focus on the more general phenomenon of the global rescaling of cities and states (Brenner and Theodore 2002b, 2; see also Brenner 1998, 1999a, 1999b; Brenner 2004; Brenner et al. 2003; MacLeod and Goodwin 1999; Smith 1995; Swyngedouw 1992, 1997b). Their analysis of neoliberal restructuring allows scholars to address the differential impacts of global processes on different localities. The state is not neglected in this literature, nor are global processes reduced to an analysis of political economy. These theorists draw attention to the fact that the hierarchies and structural positioning of cities cannot be assumed to be nested in interstate or national-regional hierarchies but must be understood as situated within global fields of power. Hence the positioning of cities reflects their relationship to global, national, and regional circuits of capital. Global political, economic, and cultural processes are fundamentally part of and are shaped by the histories of specific cities and states (Massey 2005).

This analysis led to a reevaluation of the concept of scale and rescaling and the development of a scalar perspective. A scalar perspective is not a top-down analysis or one that separates the local, national and the global but one that allows us to trace their mutual constitution. In utilizing and developing this perspective we approach scale not as fixed nested sociospatial units of territory or governance but as dynamic and relative and fluid repositionings of territorially based forms of organization within globe-spanning hierarchies of power.

More specifically, a scalar perspective on locality takes note of the ways in which all cities were forced to compete for investments in new industries for which culture and knowledge have become prized commodities. Rather than just categorizing cities as postindustrial or global, scholars have highlighted the implications of the globe-spanning restructuring processes for urban labor forces, housing stocks, entrepreneurial strategies, infrastructure development, and the tax polices of cities that were no longer based on industrial production. Scale theorists noted that cities now marketed themselves globally in an effort to attract flows of investment and a mix of new-economy industries and clients and customers that would sustain growth.

New-economy industries were ones that produced services demanded within the global economy, including tourism. To attract new industries such as computer-related technologies required that the city offers a mix of human capital, higher-education facilities, and cultural and recreational facilities. In the age of heavy industry, cities fared differently depending on such factors as access to harbors, railroads, or highways. Now new-economy industries require lifestyle facilities and urban cultural profiles capable of attracting and maintaining a highly skilled workforce.

Scholars arguing for a scalar approach have underlined the changing relationship not only between localities in the context of globalization but also between localities and states. According to these theorists, state activity is rescaled in the context of emergent neoliberal market-oriented restructuring projects. State intervention and activity are institutionally and geographically differentiated (Brenner et al. 2003; Jessop 2001). Thus it is not possible to assume that intervention is equal and homogenous throughout the state. However, this does not mean that states lose their role as active players; on the contrary, they contribute actively to the development of uneven geographies of urbanization and territorial inequalities within the national territory. They shape this restructuring process through their spatially selective interventions.

States reorganize their socioeconomic activity to increase the competitiveness of certain cities and zones. Through the provision of state subsidies or contracts and support for key infrastructural facilities and public services in particular zones—such as airports or research facilities—they remain important actors in shaping the new patterns of uneven spatial development. Of course the organization of state subsidies has historically differed between the European states, with their range of welfare and public interventions, and the United States, where intervention has been more indirect in the form of military and police expenditures, contracts, and urban block grants. In this context, the competition among cities to attract global capital is entangled with their competition to attract forms of state support.

However, among those geographers concerned with neoliberal processes of restructuring, there has been significant debate about the concept of scale, the utility of a scalar perspective as an overall framework, and the degree to which a comparative approach to urban restructuring and rescaling is feasible and desirable. Some researchers, especially those concerned with the agency of social movements and contestation, have critiqued top-down analysis and asserted the need to examine local path dependencies, histories, and conditions (Leitner, Peck, and Sheppard 2007).

Concerned with delineating the ways in which urban space has been redeveloped, marketed, and branded and the differential effects of urban makeovers on neighborhoods and their populations, scale theorists have paid almost no attention to immigrants except as forms of mobile labor. However, although they have said little about migrant incorporation and transnational connection, it is evident that their perspective provides important theoretical openings with which to approach the significance of locality in migrant incorporation. The relative positioning of a city within hierarchical fields of power may well lay the ground for the life chances and incorporation opportunities of migrants locally and transnationally. In order to understand the different modes and dynamics of migrant incorporation and transnationalism, we need to address the broader rescaling processes affecting the cities in which migrants are settling. A scalar perspective can bring into the analysis of migrant incorporation the missing spatial aspects of socioeconomic power, which is exercised differently in different localities.

In placing migrant incorporation within scale theory, we need to address public discourses about the representation and marketing of the city. Urban resources, including the skills and qualities of their migrants, acquire a new value and become assets in the global competition between cities. Migrants and their "cultural diversity" become marketable assets for the cultural industries of the cities in which they settle (Zukin 1995).

However, as we stressed in chapter 1, migrants' roles in cities are not confined to either labor or culture. They can be seen as scale makers who in their multiple positionings within urban life contribute actively to facilitating, legitimizing, and contesting neoliberal restructuring and its local constitution of global processes. It is important to stress that it is not only the so-called global cities that compete on a global terrain. All cities, including those that are failing, engage in global competition, and localities that experience marginalization are part of the same processes that shape the cities acknowledged to be global. The place and role of migrants in this competition might differ depending on the scalar positioning of these cities. Drawing from the literature on urban rescaling, we argue that we can better differentiate and understand migrant incorporation and transnationalism in different cities, if we relate them to the processes of restructuring political, economic, and cultural space within the context of hierarchies of power, including the social relations of capital. That is to say, our understanding of rescaling of cities entails the reordering of the scope and power of social networks of all urban actors.

In recent years and despite the fruitfulness of the literature on neoliberal restructuring and rescaling of cities and state, many geographers have become uncomfortable with the concept of scale (Brenner, chapter 2; Marston, 2000; Marston, Jones, and Woodward, 2005) Samers, chapter 3). Agreeing with Hoefle (2006:238) that the geographer's critique of scale tended to "kill the goose that laid the golden egg," we argue for its use as an integrative term that allows us to conceptualize the simultaneity of multiple networks that serve to constantly construct, delimit, and reconstitute spatialized relationships. Capitalist restructuring has been shaped by the existing political and institutional contexts and contestations, which are themselves the products of earlier regulatory regimes, institutional arrangements, and political configurations between different social forces (Çağlar and Schiller, chapter 1).

We therefore find the term "city scale" useful in developing a comparative framework for urban analysis. We define city scale as the differential positioning of a city, which reflects both its articulation of flows of political, cultural, and economic capital within regions, state-based, and globe-spanning institutions and the shaping of these flows and institutional forces by local histories and capacities. From this perspective, city scale is a relational position operating on a field of power. It is not an absolute measure such as the indices of the density of capital flow, corporate headquarters, or of new-economy connections that have been posited by world-cities researchers. It is important to note that the scalar positioning of cities is dynamic and processional.

We believe that this concept of city scale facilitates the ability of migration researchers to conceptualize the different pathways of migrant incorporation and transnational connection in relationship to forms of past and contemporary forms of interurban competition. A scalar perspective allows us to analyze the dynamics of locality in interaction with power hierarchies. For this reason it enables us to incorporate the uneven character of globalization into our analysis. The concept of scale offers us a framework with which to analyze the structures and dynamics of cities or urban zones in close relations to processes of capital accumulation that are not necessarily confined within the states yet interact with states' regulatory regimes controlling very different degrees of wealth and power.

Placing Migrants: The Globality of Cities and Social Forces in a Comparative Perspective

As the literature on the neoliberal restructuring of the city grew, it stimulated countercurrents and critiques. Some scholars rejected all concepts of scale;

others responded to what they felt to be a too structural argument by emphasizing the countervailing currents of social movements in their local and transnational networks of connection. These alternative theorists noted that those concerned with the global effect of neoliberalism within urban spaces had done little to address the specific "globality" of all cities and the contribution of either social movements or local forces to urban restructuring. A group of urban scholars challenged the global city researchers' analysis of urban development in relation to global structures. Critiquing what they saw as a restricted and homogenized understanding of globality, these scholars provided useful insights with which to address migrants' variant incorporation in cities of differential positioning. For our purposes here, we concentrate only on those critiques that challenge the boundary of the category of global cities.

A growing number of scholars responded to the global cities hypothesis by refusing to see globalization as a fixed state; for them it was a process affecting all cities in the world, though not in a uniform way. These researchers questioned the utility of building global hierarchies of cities according to their financial and control functions and then using these criteria to exclude as not global most of the cities of the world. Criticizing global city researchers' structural analysis of space with its reliance on macrofactors, Peter Marcuse and Ronald van Kampen (2000) suggested that all cities are "globalizing" in that they participate in globalization, though not in a linear fashion, and definitely not in ways determined solely by structural factors. They argued that the impact of globalization on different cities depends on a number of contingencies, of which the position of the city, though important, is only one.

While correctly challenging the limitations of the global city approach, most of these scholars threw the baby out with the bathwater. For example, by offering a concept of multiple contingencies, without a hierarchy among them, Marcus and van Kampen provide little basis for developing a comparative analysis of migrant incorporation in cities of different globality, significance, and reach. From this perspective all cities become "ordinary" (Amin and Graham 1997; Robinson 2006). Global cities lose their specificity vis-à-vis other cities in terms of their positioning within the hierarchies of power and capital flows. In extending the boundaries of globality to encompass all other cities, the crucial aspects of the global city perspective—namely, the uneven spatialization of global capital restructuring—is lost. By arguing for the primacy of each city's unique and specific cultural ambience, historical trajectories, and ways of being global, this literature has flattened the unevenness of globalization and consequently lost the basis for a comparative analysis of the interplay between globalization, urban development, and differential specialization.

However, not all critiques of the global city have denied global urban hierarchies and the possibility of a comparative perspective. In order to provide a nuanced reading of the relationship between globalization and the city that can accommodate the local distinctiveness and the capacities of the state, Richard Hill (2004) has proposed a lens of "nested hierarchies." Hill has used nestedness in a more complex way—as the multidirectional relationships referring to global niche, regional formation, national development model, and local historical context. Rather than approaching a city's structural position within the global as a whole, Hill finds it more productive to examine the multilevel configurations in which the city is nested. In this way, he acknowledges the globality of all cities but establishes the basis for a hierarchy and consequently a comparative view of cities. He argues that "global variables are not the decisive determinants of urban form and functioning. The relationship between globalization and a city's economic base, social structure and spatial organization...depends upon the whole multilevel configuration in which the city is nested" (10).

Hill's insights are useful, but his terms are problematic. The concept of nestedness is commonly used within the literature on geographic scale to designate a fixed relationship between administrative units and territory viewed as named places. In this sense, cities have been seen as embedded or nested in regions of countries and nation states. The emphasis Hill places on national development models limits his ability to shed the methodological nationalism that the concept of nestedness implies. If we view the urban, the regional, and the national scales as a nested set of relationships that mediate global dynamics, we can too easily disregard the neoliberal dynamics that have been transforming state spatiality. This transformation has been highlighted by scale theorists who have worked to describe and theorize the disruption of such relations.

The critiques of the global cities research and the scalar approach to neoliberal restructuring have also been important in initiating explorations of local social forces, including migrants, and of political struggles in the production of all globalized urban spaces. These explorations have sparked research that situates the agency of social movements within multilevel urban processes. Scholars such as Helga Leitner (Leitner, Sheppard, and Sziarto 2008) have highlighted the complex and changing matrix of global, national, economic, and political forces that shape urban development and transformation. They have underscored networked relations and multiple spatial connectivities rather than focusing on global hierarchies determined by top-down structural analysis.

Contrary to the majority of urban scholarship—in which migrants' agency is invisible except as labor, differentiated into global talent and the unskilled—the urban social movements literature, which has traced the relationship among social movements, place-making, and neoliberalism, recognizes migrants as social and political actors in urban movements (Leitner, Peck, and Sheppard 2007; Smith 2001). This literature, which acknowledges the agency of migrants as political actors, most often has focused on the claim-making processes of the undocumented migrants (*sans papier*), asylum seekers, and nonstatus refugees in a particular city. It explores the challenges these mobilizations pose to the existing rights and citizenship regimes in a particular national context (Nyers 2003; McNevin 2006; Varsanyi 2006). One variant of the social movement literature highlights transnational activism, but much of this work has not been anchored in the differential contributions made by cities of different scalar positionings (Tarrow 2005). Moreover, research on transnational migrants as activists has generally been conducted through an ethnic lens, tracing these transnational networks only in instances of long-distance nationalism or ethnoreligious nationalist movements such as the migrants who built Kurdish political organizational networks (Østergaard-Nielsen 2003).

Building on the literature of social movements and contentious politics, the scholars of urban struggles go beyond these studies by situating the social movements and the social and political agency of migrants within the broader dynamics of neoliberal urban restructuring and place-making processes. However, paradoxically, those theorists of urban renewal and place-making who address migrants do so in ways that reject the possibility of comparative analysis of urban restructuring by using a scalar perspective. For example, Leitner and her coauthors place contentious urban politics within the complex spatialities of such politics, which they believe cannot be reduced to vertical, interscalar relations but rather entail horizontal and multiple spatialities (Leitner et al. 2007; Leitner, Sheppard, and Sziarto 2008). Arguing for the necessity of including diverse spatial politics, such as place-making, networking, sociospatial positionality, and mobility across space, these scholars note that "while scale does matter to contentious politics, it is *one* of a variety of co-implicated spatialities whose complex intertwining cannot adequately be captured through a scalar lens" (Leitner, Sheppard, and Sziarto 2008, 161, our emphasis).

We recognize the impact of local and transnational networks and the place-making processes that are implicated in the positioning of migrants as social and political agents in urban restructuring, as well as in urban contentious politics. However, we argue that in order to develop a comparative perspective on migrants' multiple locations within urban development and politics, we must avoid a flat ontology of co-implicated diverse networks and spatialities. These networks and their spatial realization are the substantiation of social relations that reorder power hierarchies as they evolve and reshape diverse spaces. Ruba Salih and Bruno Riccio's contribution to this book illustrates this point (chapter 7). They demonstrate clearly how different spatialized networks in a particular region of Italy were reordered through the regional restructuring of capital. The existing local and transnational incorporation opportunities of migrants (including their diverse translocal networks) in the Emilia Romagna region and the migrants' locations within the politics and economy of the region were reorganized in relation to the national and global repositioning of this region. At the same time the migrants' networks contributed to this restructuring and repositioning.

The "right to the city" literature has also stressed the saliency and agency of local social movements within the context of neoliberal restructuring (Harvey 2003, 2008; Mitchell 2003; Lopes de Souza 2001; Wastl-Walter, Straeheli and Dowler 2005). However, while the original formulation by Lefebvre (1996) was specifically situated in class struggle and in the inequalities among classes within the dynamics of capitalist accumulation, in more recent iterations the concept of a right to the city has been expanded to social positions encompassing diversity in ethnicity, race, religion, gender, age, and neighborhood. The right to the city has become a general frame to describe some of the social movements that challenge the failures of democracy, which have been accentuated by neoliberal restructuring (UNESCO-UN-HABITAT-ISS 2005).

The perspective we advocate here contributes to the ongoing discussion of Lefebvre by examining variations in the types of claims that migrants make in relation to their different positioning in specific cities. We move from an abstract concept of "the city" to examine migrants as constitutive agents in the relative positioning of different cities.

Migrants construe their rights under certain conditions and in relationship to their different situations, class, gender, race, and ethnicity, which are entangled with the scalar positioning of these cities. Migrants make claims in many cities, but their success varies. It varies in relationship to the opportunities provided by the positioning of these cities, which is shaped by but not solely determined by each city's historical and institutional legacies and its local and shifting alignments of power. Through their ethnographies, many of the authors in this book document the various ways in which migrants' transnational ties, activated as part of the differential positioning of these cities, facilitate and promote their assertion of their rights. Depending on the situation, migrants' claims to rights lead them to contest, legitimate, or reinforce neoliberal restructuring.

In making their claims, migrants' assert their multiple forms of agency. Scholars of urban movements have begun to examine certain aspects of the multiple roles migrants play. Michael Peter Smith (2001), for example, recognizes migrants as transnational agents in urban politics with multiple class positions. In point of fact, as we argue in chapter 1, migrants in their role as scale makers contribute to the competitive repositioning of cities in multiple ways that have yet to be systematically addressed. In relationship to the neoliberal transformation of cities migrants have: (1) acted as historical agents, (2) constituted a vital part of the labor force upon which the cities build their competitiveness, (3) served neoliberal gentrifiers and the reevaluators of neighborhoods and cities, (4) justified the neoliberal devolution of state powers and the formation of neoliberal subjectivity, and (5) offered alternative social visions (Glick Schiller and Çağlar and Schiller, chapter 1).

• • •

The chapter suggests that in order for migration scholars to theorize locality, they must do much more than acknowledge the social construction of space or the broad forces of neoliberal globalization that engendered new migrations (Smith 2001; Castles and Miller 2003). Researchers must address the ways in which unequal global processes including migration have been transforming economies, institutions of power, and the patterning of social life in specific places and pay attention to how specific localities are differently affected. There is much that can be learned both from the global cities literature and from its critics. The literature reminds us that the spatialization of capital is unequal and uneven. Those who have responded with a scholarship that celebrates ordinary cities and multiple spatializations offer migration scholars a way to enter into dialogues about globality and its variants in cities around the world. By providing an analysis of urban restructuring that moves beyond cities not categorized as global and gateway, they have laid the groundwork for a comparative analysis of the incorporation and transnational connection of migrants in cities of different scalar positioning. However, they themselves have chosen not to follow this path. Meanwhile, migration scholars generally have stood apart from the debates, without fully realizing the potential of the scholarship produced within the global cities hypothesis or by its critics.

Moreover, to understand the contexts of settlement and transnational connection, migration scholars must not only examine how each locality is situated within rapid flows of capital and changing hierarchies of power but also explore the ways in which migrants and cities remake each other as they themselves become part of networks of capital, organizations, institutions, families, and informal interpersonal relations mediated through particular places.

To develop a global perspective on migrants in cities is to ask new questions and begin to provide new answers about variation and similarity across time and space. It is crucial from this perspective to remember that power is exercised differently in different times and places. If we forget that globalization is an uneven and unequal process of differentiation, we are unable to develop a comparative analytical framework capable of addressing the differing roles of migrants in various cities and the variations that exist in migrant insertions and transnational connection in those cities. Consequently, in this chapter we have called for a dialogue between migration scholars and scholars of urban restructuring that can explore the mutually constitutive relationship between the migrants and urban economies, politics, and development.

We have also suggested the elements of a comparative perspective that would build on the intersection of migration studies and the scholarship of scale. Despite the transnational and urban turn in migration research, the comparative analysis of migrant incorporation in cities still remains nested in discussions of national regimes and their differing immigration policies and resultant opportunity structures. The significance of the different localities for migration, settlement, and transnational connection must be addressed. Attention to the scalar positioning of different cities becomes more necessary and possible for migration scholars as increasingly migrants are settling in cities of different scalar dimensions and a growing number of migration scholars are working in these cities. Similarly, scholars of urban scale have the possibility of examining migration and city scale in a situation of the dispersion of migrant settlement. We have suggested that it would be fruitful for them to address comparatively the synergies between variations in migrant settlement and the global/local dynamics that are transforming specific localities of departure, settlement, and connection.

The locality-specific opportunity structures and transnational connections that may shape migrants' insertions in diverse networks very often remain veiled by the methodological nationalism of migration scholarship. The ways in which a specific locality may shape relationships beyond the national (sometimes in disjunctive ways) have been neglected to a great extent. Furthermore, the ethnic lens, when used as the optic for transnational migration studies, has impeded researchers' ability to note, adequately document, and theorize the fact that migrants also build non-ethnic transnational social fields based on religious, political, professional, ideological, and economic networks (Glick Schiller and Çağlar 2008b; Glick Schiller, Çağlar, and Guldbrandsen 2006). The diversity and the scope of migrants' relationships to their place of settlement and *to other localities* around the world remain understudied. Yet there is increasing evidence that the nature of the neoliberal transformations of particular localities shape the formation, dynamics, and reach of the migrant transnational social fields that link places across borders unevenly (see chapters 5, 7, 9, and 11 of this book).

However, no matter on what basis a comparative framework is designed, it will be important to note that neoliberal rescaling projects trigger social processes, social resistance, and new forms of power struggles and articulations of interests among the existing social groups, including migrants in the localities in which they are grounded. No matter how similar cities are in terms of scale, their complex layers of social history and social structure result in differential localizations of these projects with different representations, legacies, and expectations. Thus the nature of migrants' agency, which is simultaneously shaped by and constitutive of the positioning of a specific locality, is by no means a given in its form and representations. By paying attention to the place of migrants within the social fabric of specific cities, scholars of scale may be better able to explore the differential outcomes of rescaling processes even in places of similar scale. Migrants' agency is located at the intersection between the historical path dependency of each locality and its relationship to the global forces that shape the city's scalar positioning.

If globalization is both a localization process and one that profits from uneven spatiality, migration studies must acknowledge and analyze these processes in relationship to variation in migrant incorporation. Migrants are part of the social fabric of the cities in which they settle. Migrant ties, activities, and practices—in short, migrants as forces of integration as well as fragmentation—are parts of the changing urban politics and new geographies of urban governance and representation. Consequently, any analysis of the restructuring of this social fabric will be incomplete without considering the impact of migration. At the same time, migration scholarship cannot be separated from an analysis of the past and present restructuring of the localities from and in which migrants depart and settle.

The interplay between global forces that are restructuring cities and the active role of migrants is not confined to global cities but is observable in cities positioned differently within global capital flows and power hierarchies. Migrants, whose location in urban economics, culture, and politics is shaped by the neoliberal restructuring of each particular city, are themselves constitutive of the very repositioning and rescaling struggles of these cities. To approach migrants as scale makers is to acknowledge their contribution to the contemporary reinvention of urban life.

Note

This chapter was developed during Nina Glick Schiller's tenure as Willy Brandt Visiting Professor at Malmö University and James and Claire Hayes Chair of the Center for Humanities of the University of New Hampshire. An earlier version was presented at the MIGRINTER Conference, "Twenty Years of Research on International Migration," in Poitier, France, July 5, 2006, and served as an initial framework for the 2009 article "Towards a Comparative Theory of Locality in Migration Studies: Migrant Incorporation and City Scale," *Journal of Ethnic and Migration Studies* 35 (2): 177–202. Our special thanks to Mohamed Kamel Dorai, Bert Feintuch, Maja Povrzanović Frykman, Jenney Mooney, and Russell King for support and encouragement in the development of this work.

Part II

Migrants as Scale Makers

Rescaling Urban Neighborhoods, Cities, and Their Regions

Chapter 5

Scalar Positioning and Immigrant Organizations

Asian Indians and the Dynamics of Place

CAROLINE B. BRETTELL

On March 13, 2006, the *Dallas Morning News* published an article (Sanchez 2006) that focused on a bill introduced in the state of Kansas to repeal legislation allowing the children of illegal immigrants to pay in-state college tuition rates. While the bill did not make it out of committee, one Kansas representative commented, "Until something is addressed at the federal level, we and other states are just floundering." A Utah representative, commenting on similar challenges in his state, noted, "We're caught between a rock and a hard place. Immigration is a federal issue, but now that people keep coming, it's a state problem." These comments, by two frustrated state legislators, reflect a problem of scale in the United States with respect to immigration (Ellis 2006). While the formulation of immigration policy occurs at the national level, immigrant incorporation occurs at the local level, within states, regions, cities, neighborhoods, and even households.[1]

In this chapter I draw on research in the Dallas-Fort Worth metropolitan area (DFW) to address the issue of scale.[2] I explore a developing synergy between a particular type of postindustrial economy associated with the scalar positioning of Dallas, the attraction to the area of highly skilled immigrants from India, the settlement of these immigrants in the suburbs, and the formation of organizations that not only facilitate immigrant social, economic, and political incorporation but also allow immigrants to jump scales, operating simultaneously in local, regional, national, and transborder arenas.

Erik Swyngedouw (1997b) uses the term "glocalization" to refer to the mutual constitution of the global and the local but argues that other scales (including the regional and the national) are also deeply implicated in local processes. Kimberly Holton (2005, 8) suggests that the term captures relationships of people to territory that are "influenced *both* by grounded face-to-face encounters *and* by transnational flows of capital, media, resources, products, information, and populations." Further, some feminist geographers (Rankin 2003, 722) have observed that many theories of globalization overlook "the economic, political, and cultural practices taking place within households and communities." The implication of all this work is that only research at more microscales can capture how the global (including the global transfer of population) meets the local or, more precisely, how the global and the national flow through the local (or regional) and hence are experienced and shaped by local populations, including immigrants.

The city is one such microscale, something that Michael Smith (2001) captures in his concept of "transnational urbanism." But what is "the city," and are all cities alike? Clearly the answer to the latter question is no. Not only do cities have different histories, including different histories of experience with the foreign-born, but they are also positioned differently in relation to global forces. These are dimensions of the broader issue of cities as contexts for different processes of immigrant incorporation (Brettell 2003; Foner 1987; Lamphere 1992; Waldinger 1996a). One outcome of this more place-based "city as context" approach is a different model than that offered by the Chicago School of Sociology in relation to the incorporation of third-wave immigrants who entered the United States between 1880 and 1924. This model described the settlement of first-generation immigrants in inner cities and the gradual move to the suburbs as the second and particularly the third generation grew to maturity. It was a model associated with the political economies of cities that developed during the Industrial Revolution. Jobs, cheap housing, and retail businesses were located close to the urban core. Public transportation, used by the majority of the working population in a preautomobile age, moved people around the urban core. Immigrant enclaves characteristic of New York and Chicago developed, shaped by these aspects of political economy as well as by patterns of segregation and discrimination. In New York City in 1890 more than half of the Italian population lived in three wards that bordered Canal Street (Foner 2000, 39). Even today a large Chinese immigrant population is concentrated in the Lower East Side of Manhattan (Kwong 1996), while Dominicans are concentrated in Washington Heights, Russians in the "Little Odessa" of Brooklyn's Brighton Beach, and Koreans in Flushing (Min 1996).

Such enclaves have been part of the fabric of postwar gateway cities of immigration such as Los Angeles and Miami—the latter the locus of "Little Havana" (Portes and Stepick 1993). Yet something else also occurred in U.S. cities with the spread of the automobile and the transformation to a service- and knowledge-based economy in the mid- to late twentieth century. Despite having immigrant enclaves, Los Angeles has become a "polymorphic and centrifugal metropolis" made up of a "galaxy of suburbs" (Soja 1992, 27). These suburbs have themselves become diversified; they are the new frontiers where the global confronts the local.[3] Geographer Wei Li (1998, 481) has coined the term "ethnoburb" to describe suburbs that are multiethnic yet often dominated by a single ethnic minority group and that have developed "under the influence of international geopolitical and global economic restructuring, changing national immigration and trade policies, and local demographic, economic and political contexts." Yet not all cities have ethnoburbs, particularly if—as in Washington, D.C., for example—no single ethnic minority group or immigrant population dominates.

This said, the diversification of the suburbs and the more dispersed patterns of settlement by comparison with first-generation third-wave immigrants are characteristic of newer cities of immigration, the so-called emerging gateways (for example, Atlanta, Dallas, Phoenix, and Washington, D.C.) that have witnessed a rapid explosion in their foreign-born populations during the 1990s.[4] These are large metropolitan regions with multiple centers of economic, social, and political activity and a scalar positioning that is different from more identifiable global cities such as New York, Los Angeles, and London. How are immigrants incorporated in these postindustrial suburban places where sometimes no single immigrant population dominates and where immigrant households are often residentially dispersed? In the absence of the kind of ward politics that emerged within the clustered ethnic enclaves of older gateway cities of immigration like New York and Chicago, how do immigrants in these new suburban metropolises become politically incorporated and develop a political voice? And at what scale does this political voice operate? Finally, how do immigrants develop the kind of social capital that has always been important to social incorporation? I argue here that to answer these questions we must look at the organizations that emerge among immigrant populations in particular urban contexts and, further, that any discussion of these organizations must be attentive to the scalar positioning of the city. I develop this argument through an analysis of the Dallas-Fort Worth area and its experience with post-1965 immigrants.

The Place: Growth and Transformation in a Sunbelt Metropolis, 1970–2000

The Dallas metropolitan area is a sprawling postwar sunbelt metropolis that developed with the automobile and white flight to the suburbs. In 1940, the city covered 114 square miles and had a population of 295,000 residents. Twenty years later both the resident population (680,000) and the geographical area (three hundred square miles) had more than doubled. By 1970, Dallas, with a population of 844,000, was highly segregated. Although 74 percent of the population was white (including 7.6 percent classified as Hispanic) and 25 percent black, nineteen census tracts were 95–100 percent black; nine more were 90 percent black, and twelve were 75 percent black (Achor 1978). In that year, just over 2 percent of the population was foreign-born. Ten years later, as the suburbs expanded and as a new wave of Mexican immigrants began to arrive in the area, the ethnic composition of the population in the city of Dallas began to change (table 1).

By 2000, Dallas had become the eighth largest metropolitan area in the United States (with 3.5 million residents);[5] the proportion of this population that was foreign-born increased from 8.8 percent in 1990 to 16.8 percent in 2000. In 2000, 33.9 percent of the population of the Dallas central city was Hispanic, as was 15.3 percent of the suburban population. The Asian population had also grown to 4 percent of the total in the city and 5 percent in the suburbs. While these are figures by "racial" category and hence include the native-born as well as the foreign-born, they offer some hint of the changes that were taking place demographically and spatially. In 2005, according to U.S. Census American Community Survey data, 12.4 percent of the population of metropolitan Dallas was foreign-born. Fifty-eight percent of the foreign-born were from Mexico and 5 percent from El Salvador. Immigrants from India and Vietnam each made up 4 percent of the total foreign-born population, while Korea, the Philippines, and China (excluding Hong Kong and Taiwan) each made up 2 percent. Finally, immigrants from Pakistan, Guatemala, Honduras, Canada, the United Kingdom, Iran, Nigeria, and Peru each made up 1 percent of the foreign-born (15 percent diverse others).

Demographic growth and change were fueled by an economic boom that began in the late 1970s and was spurred by the completion of DFW International Airport, making the region an important transportation hub. By the mid-1980s, the metroplex (a term formulated in 1971 to describe the cities

TABLE 1
Racial/ethnic composition of population as percentage of total, Dallas primary metropolitan statistical areas (PMSA), central city, and suburbs, 1980–2000

	Dallas PMSA	Dallas central city	Dallas PMSA suburbs
White, non-Hispanic	1980—73.4%	1980—61.5%	1980—87.2%
	1990—67.6	1990—52.3	1990—80.6
	2000—56.2	2000—38.3	2000—69.0
Black, non-Hispanic	1980—16.1	1980—25.4	1980—5.3
	1990—15.5	1990—25.1	1990—7.3
	2000—15.2	2000—23.1	2000—9.7
Asian	1980—0.9	1980—0.9	1980—0.9
	1990—2.5	1990—2.5	1990—2.5
	2000—4.6	2000—4.0	2000—5.0
Hispanic (all races)	1980—8.9	1980—11.4	1980—5.9
	1990—14.0	1990—19.7	1990—9.2
	2000—23.0	2000—33.9	2000—15.3
Foreign-born	1980—4.5	1980—6.1	1980—3.0
	1990—8.8	1990—12.5	1990—5.8
	2000—16.8	2000—24.4	2000—11.7

Source: U.S. Census, 2000.
Note For the 2000 data, only those persons identifying themselves as "White alone" and "Black or African American alone" are categorized as "White, non-Hispanic" and "Black, non-Hispanic," respectively. "

of Dallas and Fort Worth and the urban/suburban areas surrounding them) "ranked third behind New York and Chicago as headquarters for companies with more than $1 million in assets" (Payne 2000, 423). The Dallas area offers a good example of the shift from rust belt to sunbelt that Kevin Cox (1997, 1) has identified as a process of change at a regional scale parallel to that occurring at the global scale, a process that has created new peripheries and new technological and industrial spaces. In other words, just as global spaces have been restructured by the penetration of global capital, so too have regional (within a single nation-state) spaces.

Despite the financial setback of the later 1980s, the boom was restored by the 1990s, and Dallas quite forthrightly began to position itself as a "world-class international city." In 1990, it was well connected to Washington, D.C. with George Herbert Walker Bush in the White House and his son, George W. Bush, residing in the city before moving to Austin to serve as governor of Texas. A decade later, George W. Bush was elected president, enhancing the political capital of the city and tightening its links with the White House. Key individuals in Dallas were named to critical national and international positions: for example, an ambassador to Hungary and an ambassador to the Organization for Economic Cooperation and Development in Paris; a White House assistant to the president for personnel who later moved to the position of deputy director for management of the Office of Management and the Budget; a White House counsel who had previously served on the Dallas City Council; and the Secretary of Housing and Urban Development, who had served as the president and CEO of the Housing Authority of Dallas between 1989 and 1996.

According to the Greater Dallas Chamber of Commerce, DFW ranked first in the nation for employment growth in the 1990s—760,600 new jobs were created. The local economy was growing at 4.2 percent annually, outpacing the national average. The economy was also becoming more diversified, and several corporate headquarters moved to the area, including J.C. Penney and Exxon-Mobil. In the suburbs north of the city a telecom corridor developed, driven by the expansion of Texas Instruments and companies such as Alcatel, Nortel, and Ericsson. Another high-tech corridor was developed to the west in the suburb of Irving with companies such as Nokia and Verizon. Just prior to the post-9/11 downturn, Dallas had more information-sector jobs than all but two other cities in the United States. This knowledge-based economy was enhanced by the rapid growth of two branches of the University of Texas in the DFW area—the University of Texas at Dallas (known for its STEM—science, technology, engineering, and math—expertise) and the University of Texas at Arlington. The Cox School of Business at Southern Methodist University, also in Dallas, moved into the top twenty business schools in the nation, and UT-Southwestern, from its small beginnings, became a premier medical school and research center with several Nobel Prize winners on its faculty. By 2006 the DFW area had twenty-two companies on the Fortune 500 list, moving DFW "into fifth place among US Metros with Fortune 500 companies located within a region" (Greater Dallas Chamber 2006).

TABLE 2
Foreign-born in Dallas PMSA and three primary counties in 2000
(percentage of total in each place)

	Dallas PMSA	Collin County	Dallas County	Denton County	Total number in 3 counties
Total foreign-born	591,169	65,279	463,574	40,591	569,444
Mexican	58.5%	26.8%	63.85	39.3%	329,096
Vietnamese	3.7%	4.1%	3.6%	5.0%	21,647
Indian	4.3%	8.8%	3.4%	7.2%	24,694
Korean	1.9%	3.4%	1.6%	4.3%	11,362
Chinese	3.1%	13.7%	1.7%	3.5%	18,336

Source: U.S. Census, 2000.
Note: Chinese includes those from Hong Kong and Taiwan as well as mainland China.

This economic and research climate was attractive both to immigrants with high human capital (highly skilled, well-educated) who were drawn to the area by the telecommunications, health, and financial industries and to those with low human capital who found employment in construction, manufacturing, or unskilled services. Mexican nationals, many of whom came with little education, were the largest group to respond to the rescaling, making up 58 percent of the foreign-born population that had settled in the Dallas metropolitan area by 2000. While the foreign-born population of Dallas County increased from 10.6 percent of the total population in 1990 to 20.1 percent in 2000, perhaps of more significance is what happened north of the city, in suburban Collin County, and to the northwest, in Denton County. In Collin County the proportion of the population that was foreign-born increased by 318 percent between 1990 and 2000; the comparable figure for Denton County was 176 percent. While Mexicans contributed to this suburban growth in the foreign-born, of equal importance were increases in Asian populations—Vietnamese, Indian, Chinese, and Korean in particular. In Collin County, the four largest Asian immigrant populations constituted a larger percentage of the foreign-born than did Mexicans. In Denton County they were one-fifth of the foreign-born population (table 2).

Asian Indians in the Dallas Metropolitan Area

Asian Indians have been one of the fastest-growing immigrant populations in the United States. Although individuals from the Indian subcontinent have been in the United States since the nineteenth century (Leonard 1997), their numbers have remained small. Only in 1980 did the U.S. census officially break them out as a separate group. In that year 387,223 were counted nationwide. By 2000, just over one million foreign-born from India were counted in the United States, representing 3.3 percent of the U.S. foreign-born population. While the largest areas of settlement for Asian Indians are in the states of New York, New Jersey, California, and Illinois, they have also contributed to the growth of the foreign-born populations in Greater Washington, D.C., Atlanta, Phoenix, Houston, and Dallas.

In the Dallas metropolitan area, a small number of Indians arrived in the early 1960s to take up jobs in scientific and technical fields at local universities and with companies such as Texas Instruments. With the expansion of high-tech industries and the growth of the city, including the growth in the health sector, the number of Asian Indians also increased, especially after 1980. As some of this first wave of Indians became citizens, they began to sponsor relatives, some of whom did not have the same level of education. The second wave of immigrants found employment as small business owners, providing a range of services in restaurants, motels, grocery and convenience stores, and jewelry and sari shops. The new boom in technology in the 1990s, coupled with the expansion of the H1B highly skilled worker visa category, resulted in a new wave of young and well-educated Indians, many of them software engineers. Therefore, despite some class diversity, the DFW area, because of its scalar position and its employment profile, has attracted a large number of new-economy professionals who are extremely prosperous.

In Dallas County, Indians first settled in the inner-ring suburb of Richardson, where the public school system was strong and where some of the early high-tech companies set up offices. The population doubled during each decade and with this growth expanded north into the communities of Collin County, especially Plano, west into the community of Irving, and northwest into communities such as Carrollton and Lewisville in Denton County. By 2000, the census enumerated 25,207 foreign-born Indians in the Dallas Primary Metropolitan Statistical Area. More recent data from the American Community Survey indicates that despite new restriction on immigration after 9/11 this population has continued to grow in the area during the first decade of the twenty-first century.

As in some other metropolitan areas of new Asian Indian settlement (Friesen, Murphy, and Kearns 2005; Skop 2002; Skop and Li 2003), Asian Indians in Dallas are residentially dispersed, and their spatial incorporation is largely suburban because it is in these suburbs that the corporate and research engines of the new economy have built their headquarters. This "heterolocal" (Zelinsky and Lee 1998) pattern of settlement has led to the development of nodes of activity, largely through organizations and commercial centers, that bring Asian Indians together not only for common cultural/ethnic purposes but, more important, for common interests that operate at multiple scales.[6] Geographer Susan Hardwick has recently noted that Zelinsky (2001), in his effort to clarify the concept of heterolocalism, as well as to respond to a critique emerging from geographers Richard Wright and Mark Ellis (2000b), "expanded his discussion of applying this new model to a variety of scales.... In contrast to other models of sociospatial behavior...the deterritorialized web of connections that maintains heterolocalism exists at both metropolitan and nonmetropolitan scales and may even find expression at transnational or global scale" (Hardwick 2006, 215–16). Heterolocalism, in other words, is a model that takes place, scale, and networks into account.

In the remainder of this chapter I explore some of the organizations that have emerged among Asian Indians in the Dallas metropolitan area in relation to the spatial, scalar, and network dimensions of heterolocalism. In a previous discussion of some these organizations (Brettell 2005b), I referred to Agarwal's (1991, 73) description of a Los Angeles Indian population that was not particularly united and not very politically active. Agarwal linked these characteristics to a traditional Indian distaste for politics and volunteerism— "the average Indian feels a strong sense of responsibility toward his family, but not necessarily toward his community." By contrast, I have found the Dallas area Indian community to be quite different, with a powerful commitment to volunteerism and among some an interest in promoting the voice of Asian Indians both regionally and nationally. These attitudes and actions are manifested and operationalized in the organizations they have created to position themselves in a city that is itself strongly positioned within the region, powerfully linked to Washington, and through its new economy vitally positioned globally.

The size of the Indian community in the Dallas metropolitan area (neither too big nor too small) and its selectivity (more high-tech and professional immigrants than convenience store/gas station owners, although the latter, as noted above, have come as part of the second wave of sponsored relatives— see Brettell 2005a) may explain some of the differences between Los Angeles and Dallas. It also underscores the importance of assessing the impact of place on institution building in immigrant communities and on the process of immigrant incorporation more generally. This speaks directly to the question of scalar positioning, the "differential positioning of cities determined by the flow and control of capital and structures of power as they are constituted within regions, states, and the globe" (Glick Schiller, Çağlar and Guldbrandsen 2006, 615). Thus, my discussion of some of the organizations that have been developed by Asian Indians in the Dallas metropolitan area is mindful of the opportunities offered by the scalar position of the city-region itself, which make it possible for Asian Indians to be incorporated in their daily life at multiple scales, establishing and maintaining grounded face-to-face interactions on the one hand and jumping scales on the other to reach into national or global arenas. With slightly different terms, this is precisely the argument that James (2005, 194) makes when he states that "globalization works differently at different levels and in different spheres of human activity" and that globalization theory itself must take into account "the contradictory and uneven layering of different practices and subjectivities across all social relations."

Asian Indians in Workplace and Professional Organizations

Workplaces are the spaces within cities where the foreign-born and native-born interact most extensively. In some of these spaces organizations that serve immigrant populations have sometimes emerged, reflecting the way that corporate America has responded to increasing diversity. The fact that such organizations exist and are vibrant in Dallas has much to do with the scalar positioning of this metropolitan area in a broader global context. DFW is the locus for important national and multinational corporate headquarters.

Two examples in the DFW area are American Airlines and Texas Instruments (TI). At each of these companies there are special groups of Indian employees—the American Airlines Indian Employees Resource Group and Texas Instruments Indian Diversity Initiative.[7] The TI group, one of several nation-based initiatives at the company, was founded in 1994 to provide a career advancement forum for Indian-origin employees. In addition, this group helps TI to recruit and retain top Indian talent as well as to facilitate their settlement in the area; in other words, incorporation is a clear mission of the organization. It is quite common for TI to recruit a family from India and then for the company's human resources department to contact the Indian Diversity Initiative to talk to the family about "mainstreaming," to explain the company benefits to them, and to help the family with general social integration. Information about the initiative is included in the recruitment package.

This organization maintains its own e-mail list and sponsors two business seminars, one cultural event, and a personal interest seminar each year. According to a past chair of the initiative, in a company as large as TI, these events offer important opportunities for networking. The Indian Initiative also funds the activities of some nonprofit organizations in the area that support Indian causes (like ASHA for Education or Pratham).[8] TI has set aside a budget for each nation-based initiative that has been formed. Clearly the benefits are mutually reinforcing to the company, which aspires to be global and to attract global talent, and to Asian Indian immigrants, who are seeking the best working opportunities they can find in the global marketplace. A company like TI, with great historical depth locally and with a worldwide reputation, fosters this synergy.

American Airlines has a similar organization—the Indian Employees Resource Group, founded in 1998 and distinct from an Asian group (composed primarily of north Asians) that already existed. Initially it was established to help with immigration issues, but when the Sabre system (a computer reservation system developed by American Airlines) was split off, the focus turned to the cultural education of coworkers as part of the company's diversity program. Thus in collaboration with the Muslim group and the Asian group, the Indian Employees Resource Group sponsors an Asia Day once a year during the lunch hour. The members collect money for Indian causes, sponsor speakers, promote mentoring activities, and lend support to charity events sponsored by the India Association of North Texas. A past co-chair reported one misstep in their history—when they organized a Diwali banquet. A Muslim employee rightly observed that Diwali is a Hindu festival, not an Indian festival. The co-chair commented that she was forced to think about what she could do at a different scale of cultural identity, to submerge a politics of difference at one level (religious) to achieve a politics of collaboration at another.

There are also professionally based organizations that operate outside corporate America but foster networks and facilitate incorporation at multiple scales. One of the more active of these is the DFW Indian Nurses Association. In the United States, there is a vibrant recruitment effort for nurses from the state of Kerala in southern India.[9] One woman in the DFW area has started a business placing Indian nurses in the United States. Her father, who is in Bombay, works with her in a transborder enterprise. A former diplomat in the United States, he supervises the training in India, including teaching about living in other cultures, and she makes the contacts with local hospitals and sets up the interviews for individual nurses. The DFW Indian Nurses Association was launched in 1995 to help nurses who were traveling to the United States alone and often faced problems of adjustment. Today the nurses who come already have family in the United States, so this activity is not as important as it once was. The emphasis has therefore turned to networking, finding solutions to common problems, continuing education so that Indian nurses can develop their professional competencies and keep abreast of technological changes, lobbying on health policy issues, and charity work.

The DFW Indian Nurses Association has over two hundred Indian nurses as members who pay $20 in annual dues and receive a yearly publication. The organization has its own board of directors (president, vice president, secretary, treasurer, several committee chairs, and a few at-large seats) but is also affiliated with a national organization of Indian nurses as well as with an organization in India—thus promoting activities at multiple scales. In addition to sponsoring one Indian nurse each year for her studies, the DFW Indian Nurses Association holds an annual Nurses Day Banquet and throws a New Year's party—activities that serve to sustain community and to bring the dispersed population together. Clearly, this organization exists because of the global movement of health care professionals on the one hand and, on the other, a local economy like that in DFW that is large enough and rich enough to attract these foreign-born professionals and support their incorporation.

Another professional organization with a slightly different mission is TIPS, the Texas Indian Physicians Association. TIPS draws on the disposable charitable income of Indian physicians in the Dallas region to engage in both local and transborder activities; the national scale is skipped. The organization supports several clinics in India and sponsors a volunteer health clinic in the Dallas area that provides free consultation and medications to immigrants who have no health insurance. Many clients are elderly parents who are visiting children here and have no access to health care. Others are those working in jobs without insurance or those who have been laid off and lost their insurance—something that happened with greater frequency after 9/11 and the high-tech bust. Ninety-nine percent of the clients are Indians, although the physicians volunteering for TIPS exclude no one. Such an organization can thrive only in a metropolitan area with a significant health care industry that has drawn a critical mass of immigrants with medical training.

Furthermore, it fills a gap in a state where public services are less emphasized than in other high immigration states such as California and New York.

Finally, one of the most active professional organizations in the DFW area is the alumni association for the various campuses of the Indian Institute of Technology (IIT), the premier technology university in India. A national IIT alumni organization, as the umbrella to the individual campus organizations, was founded in the 1996 in response to Indian government cutbacks in funding for the IIT campuses. The alumni were concerned that if these institutions lost their status, their own degrees would be devalued. To prevent this, they raised a good deal of money, particularly in the United States. The IIT Bombay Heritage Fund, which became a 501(c)(3) charitable organization in 1997 and set itself a goal of raising $2–5 million dollars yearly to remit to India, raised close to $20 million in the late 1990s. The Indian government, realizing that donors from abroad who were using an American model to support Indian institutions were beginning to dictate what should happen at these universities, reinitiated their support for the IIT campuses in India. Further, IIT became aware of how important it was to stay in touch with alumni—something U.S. institutions depend on.

Although IIT graduates have been in the DFW area since the 1960s, they were few in number. The DFW chapter of IIT alumni was started in 1998–99, facilitated by the power of e-mail and the Web to find people and keep them connected. While other cities on the East and West Coast have alumni organizations for the separate Indian campuses of IIT (which are competitive and to some extent hierarchical in terms of prestige in India), in Dallas, a city with a different scalar position from Los Angeles, and in DFW, a region with a different scalar position from Silicon Valley, there are not enough people to sustain separate IIT alumni groups. As a result, all IIT alums in the area have come together in a single organization. A former president of the DFW area association IIT noted initial reluctance to do this because there is a lot of pride in the individual campuses, but everyone realized that nothing would work if they did not join forces. At first there were informal and irregular gatherings, but eventually a more formal organization emerged with structured programming, including monthly lunches and regular monthly happy hours. In the spring of 2004 this organization sponsored a conference on outsourcing that was attended by 160 people, including many mainstream individuals. They used radio programs, flyers, their e-mail list, and word of mouth to promote it. In addition their members participated in national conferences—in 2002 Bill Gates was the main speaker. A second DFW-area conference was held in the fall of 2005—the theme was the new knowledge economy and how it is being impacted by an increasingly globalized (aka "flat") world.

The mission of the organization in DFW is twofold: to serve the IITs in India by providing financial and other resources and to promote the brand— that is, to raise the profile of IIT graduates and hence promote their success in the American workplace. It is, said one past president, "enlightened self-interest." The bonds among this group of people already exist. Many have known one another for some time and work for the same companies—TI, I2 Technologies (an Indian company in the United States), and American Airlines. Others are entrepreneurs. The DFW chapter has about 150 paid members (membership is $50 annually) and about 150 additional people on a mailing list for events. The organization is now incorporated and operates strictly on a volunteer basis with a small board of directors and a larger executive committee.

Organizations like the IIT alumni association are viable in a metropolitan area such as Dallas that offers career opportunities to Asian Indian management and engineering professionals. This organization, like other workplace and professional organizations discussed here, facilitates networking as it promotes professional expertise. These immigrant-based professional associations offer arenas for economic claims making, and sometimes this in turn is leveraged for political purposes at multiple scales. Taking on the criticism of outsourcing is a reflection of these political and economic dimensions as well as an indication of the impact of global activities on local lives. Efforts to brand the IIT degree through collective organizational activities position members to compete locally, nationally, and globally. Finally, by raising funds to develop and strengthen the IIT campuses in India, nonresident Indians are empowered to shape the actions of the Indian state itself in relation to some of its most important educational institutions.

Scales of Activity and Empowerment: The Role of Ethnic Organizations

Up to this point I have emphasized the relationship between the scalar positioning of DFW and various workplace and professional organizations that emerge both from within and outside a particular immigrant population. Scale can also be approached in relationship to the positioning of immigrant actors and the local, national, and transnational networks they establish through their organizational activities. Here I take my inspiration from Andrew Herod and Melissa Wright (2002, 2)—who, in a discussion of "placing scale" and "geographies of power," ask "how social actors go about attempting to scale their own activities in ways that allow them to exercise power,"—as well as from Paul James (2005, 196–97), who emphasizes the "embodied" integration that links people to local places in the context of the more disembodied processes "associated with the crossing of spatial and temporal boundaries." I begin by describing one Indian immigrant whom I will call Sunil.

Sunil has been in the United States for more than twenty-five years and works for a technology company. He began his community involvement by participating in the local DFW Hindu temple. He was involved in organizing the *Seva* (a Sanskrit word for selfless service) activities of the

Fig. 1. Corporations located in the Dallas-Fort Worth area facilitated the flourishing of Indian organizations as well as migrant transnational ties to their Indian alma mater institutions. Indian organizations increasingly participated in local, state, national, and transnational politics. Here Louisiana governor Bobby Jindal, the first U.S. Indian American governor, addresses the Texas chapter of the Indian American Friendship Council in Dallas in 2006. IAFC banquet, Dallas, 2006. Photo by Mahendra Yajni.

temple—providing food to homeless shelters, furnishing a neighboring school with food supplies, and responding to various disasters in the United States and abroad. Once established within his religious community, he became actively engaged with the India Association of North Texas (IANT), a local pan-Indian organization that serves the entire North Texas Indian community (see Brettell 2005b) and eventually rose to the office of president. During his term in office, he began to reach out to the national level; for example, he invited Congressman Frank Pallone, the founder of the India caucus in the U.S. Congress, to speak at one of the two annual events sponsored by IANT for the entire community. After stepping down as president, Sunil threw his energies into establishing the Texas chapter of the Indian American Friendship Council (IAFC), a national-level organization founded by an Indian-born resident of California.

IAFC operates nationally, but its mission is transborder—to promote better ties between India and the United States. In the three years that Sunil served as the Texas coordinator he invited prominent Indian-Americans to the annual banquets: Iowa state assemblywoman Swati Dandekar; New Jersey state assemblyman Upendra Chivukala; South Carolina House representative Nikki Randhana Haley; Minnesota state senator Satveer Choudary;

managing editor of the *India Tribune*, J.L. Rao; managing editor of *India Abroad*, Aziz Haniffa; and Congressman Bobby Jindal of Louisiana.[10]

Various non-Indian local and state-level politicians have also been in attendance, including Texas congresswoman Eddie Bernice Johnson. Each year at these annual banquets a check is presented to one or two mainstream charitable organizations such as the American Red Cross, Meals on Wheels, Boy Scouts, Girl Scouts, and the American Cancer Society—an important gesture, in Sunil's view, of participation and integration. The themes of the banquets appear to reflect a broadening focus: "Connecting the Communities, Making a Difference" (2004), "Democracy Leads to Freedom Leads to Opportunity" (2005), and "Strategy, Stability and Security" (2006). At the 2006 banquet President George W. Bush's trip to India and his discussions about nuclear weapons with Indian prime minister Manmohan Singh were mentioned several times by those who believed that India had achieved a new stature in the global arena and should claim its "rightful place" on the UN National Security Council.

The local activities of the Texas chapter of a national organization with international goals situate and empower the Indian community in the Dallas region in relation to mainstream organizations in the metropolitan area as well as in relation to power brokers in Texas and other states. It is through organizations such as IAFC that interurban and interstate networks are created that link places and people. Furthermore, many of these people come together in a single physical space once a year when IAFC holds its national convention in Washington, D.C. At that meeting power brokers from the halls of Congress show up in full force, recognizing by virtue of their attendance the progressive empowerment of Asian Indians in the United States and the growing and significant relationship between the "world's oldest democracy and the world's largest democracy" (a phrase used repeatedly by Asian Indian research participants). That the Texas chapter of the IAFC has grown and is thriving in such a short time is partly due to Sunil's efforts, but it is also because during the first decade of the twenty-first century Texas and Dallas have been densely networked to Washington, D.C. The IAFC offers a good example of an organization that is simultaneously about local empowerment (Sunil is a recognized community leader), about a voice at the level of the nation-state, and about efforts to help position India vis-à-vis the United States.

Sunil's trajectory of community involvement is a perfect example of scalar changes in civic engagement over the life course of an immigrant who becomes progressively more incorporated locally, regionally, and nationally through participation in immigrant community organizations. Indeed, it was as another informant described this process more generally to me that Sunil, whom I have known for some time, came to mind as a perfect (although clearly not the only) example of the process by which Indians in Dallas build and operate within multiscalar networks: "[Community participation] is a process. First people get involved in their religious organizations. Then they get involved in the Indian community organizations. Then they move to the next level outside the community with chambers, school boards, mainstream organizations. One is a stepping-stone to the next. This is the path for the first generation."

This informant went on to note that there are immigrants who come to the United States who are "nothing in terms of education and affluence," and they use the organizations to move themselves up; in the process they also expand their business because they build connections. Power, in other words, is political, social, and economic and can be effectively and strategically garnered at different scales, even by small business owners who are not part of the knowledge-based high-tech economy that drives the Dallas engine. The key question here is whether this process occurs with greater frequency and more success in a city such as Dallas because of its economic and political positioning. Another informant, a woman, had this to say about the process of the changing and progressive scale of community involvement that she had noticed among Indian immigrants in the DFW area: "When people first come they are not involved. It is a struggle to survive. You are on an F1 or H1 visa and it is hard to get beyond all your own needs and requirements. When you are older and more settled that is when you get involved. You might start with the Lions Club, and then the India Association, and then you might begin to get more involved in politics. Politicians are realizing the potential of Indians and soliciting them from both parties. This is fine. This is the system. But it is all a process of growing political awareness."

These comments from Indian research participants, together with the example of Sunil, illustrate what Elzbieta Gozdziak and Susan Martin (2005, 264) emphasize in quoting from Michael Walzer's book *What It Means to Be an American*: "that Americans first acquire political competence within their ethnic, cultural and religious associations." It is within these local associations that they learn leadership skills upon which they can build if and when they choose to operate in broader regional and national arenas and to jump from one scale to another as they become more civically involved.

However, introducing the concept of city scale raises the question of whether this process happens in all places and at all times. Surely not! Associations like the IAFC are themselves worthy of close examination for what they tell us about scalar positioning. But we can also learn much from Sunil's experience because his multiple levels of involvement would not be possible in cities that lack the national and even global political and economic weight of Dallas and the DFW region. Likewise, those people who "are nothing in terms of education and affluence" would not have the same opportunities elsewhere that they have in Dallas. In short, the scalar positioning of Dallas facilitates the life course trajectory of incorporation of first-generation immigrants like Sunil. Further, the DFW case itself suggests that Gozdziak and Martin's more general statement about how immigrants become American and become civically engaged needs to be mindful of the context within which this process takes place and the scalar opportunities provided by this context.

The scalar positioning of the DFW metropolitan area offers a context within which the more than eighty organizations founded by Asian Indians who have settled in the area can thrive. Many of these are regional (for example, Kerala Association, Bengali Association, Gujarati Association, Goan/East Indian/Mangalorean Association, Telugu Association) or religious (Hindu, Jain, Swaminarayan, and Sikh temples, a Chinmaya mission, various mosques, Marthomite and other Christian churches) organizations that reflect not only the diversity of this immigrant population but also the localized identities that they bring with them to the United States. Nina Glick Schiller, Ayşe Çağlar, and Thaddeus Guldbrandsen (2006) suggest that non-ethnic Christian pathways of local and global incorporation may occur with greater facility in weakly positioned cities such as Manchester, New Hampshire, and Halle, Germany, than in more globally positioned cities such as Dallas, where religious incorporation in more ethnically based institutions is possible because the city and the immigrant populations can sustain them, both economically and demographically.

Many of these localized religious organizations and some of the regional associations as well are linked to national and sometimes transnational organizations. Priests for the Marthoma Church, for example, arrive from southern India for three-year terms. The Chinmaya mission in Dallas has its own local and relatively autonomous board of directors, but it is also part of Chinmaya West, a regional organization to which dues are paid, and it is ultimately governed by a swami in India. Links to the website of the Dallas Chinmaya mission can be found on both the Chinmaya West website and that of Chinmaya India. By contrast, while the DFW Hindu temple invites gurus from India to speak, it is relatively autonomous organizationally and has developed its own set of practices, including its building program, in the United States (Brettell 2005b).

There are also numerous cultural organizations in the area—musical, dance, and literary societies, a few political organizations such as IAFC, and organizations whose primary mission is charitable (such as ASHA or Pratham, described in note 8) or to serve the community in some way (for example, the various Indian Lions Clubs). Some of these, like Chetna,[11] operate only on a local scale, while others are linked to regional counterparts (Pratham Dallas and Pratham Houston have shared entertainers at their fund-raising galas), national counterparts, or "mother" organizations based in India. Still others are pan-Indian organizations, such as the India Association of North Texas, founded in 1963, or pan-Asian, such as the DFW Asian Chamber of Commerce. Some individuals participate in only one or two of these organizations, while others, like Sunil, participate in the activities of several either simultaneously or progressively. Some serve as liaisons between a group in their own community and one in another—for example, the individual who acts as the representative for the India Association of North Texas to the DFW Asian American Citizens Council.

• • •

The nature of an urban metropolitan area such as DFW with its knowledge economy based on dispersed high-tech firms, large and complex health care facilities, and major universities attracts Asian Indians with appropriate skills and interests and contributes to the forms of settlement and organization in which they participate or that they have established. While South Asians, and particularly Indians, have recently been identified as new cosmopolitans (Rajan and Sharma 2006, 2) who "blur the edges of home and abroad by continuously moving physically, culturally, and socially," not enough has been said about the localities of settlement that make multiple connectivity possible. It is not the size of the metropolis alone but the types of opportunities it offers for settlement and interconnection that need to occupy our attention. A metroplex such as DFW, with companies that recruit and facilitate settlement, leads not to a clustered enclave but to a dispersed pattern of residence, generally in the suburbs where Indian immigrants can find high-quality and affordable housing as well as good schools. This pattern in the context of a locality that concentrates economic and political power shapes the organizations that are possible and the ability of immigrants to build myriad forms of social capital that combine ties to the mainstream economy with various forms of ethnic-based organizing. Not only do these organizations overcome the absence of territorial propinquity, but they also allow for multiple scalar relationships. These in turn facilitate the further building of social capital that eases economic incorporation locally, nationally, and sometimes globally. Furthermore, social capital networks provide the foundation for collective activities that sometimes involve civic engagement and hence enhance political incorporation. These processes of incorporation occur at different scales, and the scalar emphasis varies from one organization to another. Some organizations are largely focused on the local context and local activities; thus the DFW Hindu temple serves the local Indian population. Others facilitate political activity at the national scale; for example, the Indian American Friendship Council aims to influence U.S. foreign policy with regard to India. Still others jump the national scale to focus on the transborder connection with India; we see this in charitable organizations such as Pratham that raise significant funds to support schools in urban neighborhoods and villages. Some organizations operate at multiple scales.

In this chapter I have suggested that the scale and scalar positioning of the city of Dallas and the DFW region are also important to consider because they provide the political and economic context within which a host of organizations can emerge and thrive. The high-tech industries and high levels of employment offer a kind of economic and political power to the city and its immigrant residents that is not necessarily available in other urban contexts that have smaller economies and are less well positioned globally. Indian immigrants in Dallas, through the organizations they develop, become social actors who scale their activities to take advantage of these local opportunities to make themselves visible. Within the workplace and professional organizations that I have described here, they can position themselves at multiple scales from the local to the global to exercise influence. The multiple scales in which they operate reflect their multiple identities, their changing aspirations for themselves and for their communities, and the complexities of the process of incorporation.

The analysis here makes it evident, as Swyngedouw (1989, 31) has suggested, that locality must be resurrected in our analyses of immigrant incorporation because it is at this level (in cities and neighborhoods) that we can document how immigrants are making place, claiming space, reembedding themselves, reterritorializing themselves, and practicing citizenship. From this local foundation, they also move out into national and transborder spheres. Their transnational activities, many of which take place in the context of the local organizations they create in the cities where they have settled, do not obviate incorporation; rather, they facilitate it. This is one of the ways in which the global meets the local.

Notes

1. For further discussion of local legislation across the United States see Singer, Hardwick, and Brettell (2008).

2. Dallas area research began in 2001, funded by the National Science Foundation (BCS 003938). Any opinions, findings, and conclusions or recommendations expressed in this chapter are those of the author and do not necessarily reflect the views of the National Science Foundation.

3. William Frey (2001) notes that minorities accounted for most of the suburban growth during the 1990s in 65 of the 102 largest metropolitan areas. More than half of Asian Americans in large metropolitan areas reside in the suburbs, as do half of Hispanics, but only 39 percent of blacks live there(5). Not all individuals classified as belonging to these minority groups are immigrants.

4. This term was first formulated by Audrey Singer (2004), who distinguishes between "continuing gateways," "postwar gateways," "emerging gateways," and "pre-emerging gateways."

5. The 2000 figures are for the Dallas Primary Metropolitan Statistical Area (PMSA), which includes the following counties: Collin, Dallas, Denton, Ellis, Henderson, Hunt, Kaufmann, and Rockwall. The Consolidated Metropolitan Area includes the Fort Worth-Arlington PMSA and four additional counties: Hood, Johnson, Parker, and Tarrant.

6. See Brettell (2008) for a discussion of how commercial centers become central places for a heterolocal population.

7. There are similar groups for other foreign-born populations, but I interviewed only Indian-born individuals about the organizations with which they were involved.

8. ASHA for Education (*asha* is the Hindi word for hope) promotes basic education for underprivileged children in India. Pratham also has an educational mission. It was launched in 1994 in Mumbai slums by an Indian who had made his money in the United States and then returned to India to help advance his country. A global organization, Pratham has chapters in the United States, United Kingdom, and the Middle East.

9. For further discussion of Indian nurses in the United States see George (2005) and DiCicco-Bloom (2004).

10. The *India Tribune* is published in Chicago, while *India Abroad* is published in New York City. Many Indian households in the Dallas area subscribe to one of these newspapers. They are a source for local and national news about Indian American communities as well as news about India. U.S. national news is presented from an Indian perspective. See Bhalla (2006) for further discussion. Jindal was later elected governor of Louisiana and Nikki Randhana Haley announced a bit for the governorship of South Carolina in the fall of 2009.

11. Chetna focuses on domestic violence within immigrant families. For further discussion of domestic violence among South Asians in the United States see Abraham (2000). There are several "Indian" Lions Clubs in the DFW area. See Brettell and Reed-Danahay (2008) for further discussion.

Chapter 6

Cities and the Social Construction of Hot Spots

Rescaling, Ghanaian Migrants, and the Fragmentation of Urban Spaces

RIJK VAN DIJK

In moving toward a cultural understanding of globalization, many scholars have overlooked the compression of time and distance highlighted by the trajectories of tourists visiting global cities (Abrahamson 2004; Krause and Petro 2003; Sassen 1991, 2000b). Tourists compress time and space between specific sites independently of the global rescaling of these cities. They do not experience an entire city but only particular parts of it, challenging us to more carefully examine specific locations within a city rather than treating the urban unit as a single, undifferentiated space. The phenomenon of global tourism thus challenges us to examine the way various actors rework experiences of spatiality through their networks. Migrations and the transnational connections of migrants must also be included in our discussions of the rescaling of cities. Most of the cities portrayed as global, including Amsterdam, function as gateways in processes of transnational migration. We need to move beyond the conception of global cities portrayed as a global network that is developing more rapidly than nation-states through incorporation into the worldwide economic system (Sassen 1998).[1] Cities and various spaces within them are not always classified as global and as gateways connected to distant places.

Most of these cities, including Amsterdam, function as gateways in transnational movements of migration. As Nina Glick Schiller, Ayşe Çağlar, and Thaddeus Guldbrandsen (2006) have argued, while in the past at the level of the nation-state a range of cities may have been situated within a national hierarchy of places, cities of varying degrees of power and prominence are being rescaled at a global level, and migrant networks may be shaped by and contribute to this rescaling.[2] These scholars propose that to understand migration flows and the incorporation and transnational connections of migrants, we must address the relative positioning or scale of the city.

Michael Samers (chapter 3) has also expanded on the scalar perspective on cities by noting that all cities can be global. This position complements Glick Schiller and Çağlar's argument (chapters 1 and 4) that migration must be taken into account in assessing the forces that shape the globality of cities. Yet their approach is hindered by their retention of a unitary and monolithic understanding of the city and their failure to use a scalar conceptualization of space to apprehend the city's internal diversity. Exclusively emphasizing the scalar positioning of the city as a unified whole obscures the fact that in transnational flows, only specific sections and sectors predominate in the process of global rescaling. Tourists and migrants are drawn only toward the specific places within larger cities that serve as hot spots in their mobile endeavors.

In cultural terms, certain inner-city spaces are more connected globally than others, thus complicating the notion of an integrated global city—a problematic that I call "methodological urbanism."[3] According to this perspective, a global city such as Amsterdam cannot stand in for the nation-state as a whole where processes of migration and mobility are concerned, and a city is not a totality (Glick Schiller 2005b). Particular inner-city hot spots within Amsterdam may not be representative of the entire city, and other differentially positioned cities within the nation-state may also be transnationally connected. A hot spot in Amsterdam may have a lot in common with a hot spot in a differently positioned city, but it may differ from the points of gravitation and their local embeddedness in another global city such as London. We need to know more about the global connections between hot spots before we can declare an entire city to be part of a process of global rescaling.

Such a perspective highlighting urban gateway fragmentation is useful when analyzing migration to cities that belong to various scales of global or national interaction. Following this approach, this chapter focuses on migration from Ghana to the Netherlands—primarily to Amsterdam, but also to other cities such as The Hague and Rotterdam. Ghanaian immigration has centered on, and in the process generated, certain hot spots in the Netherlands that must be considered in an explanation of the local incorporation, however limited, of the Ghanaian diaspora. The crucial question, following Henri Lefebvre (1991) and Neil Smith (1990), is, what defines these hot spots? Rather than use an objectifying logic to explain the existence of a hot spot, I argue for a more nuanced, subjective understanding of why a certain area or set of social relations is designated a hot spot. An analysis of hot spots that incorporates an interrogation of their subjective understandings moves away from the literature on urban segmentation that conceives of processes of ghettoization as forms of socioeconomic exclusion that can be measured in objective terms (see Çağlar 2001; Pattillo 2003). Though they cannot be quantified, intersubjective processes involving sensibilities of space and place can be evaluated. Such an approach allows those studying urban spatiality to understand how a hot spot is ontologically defined through the migrants' own perceptions.

In the Ghanaian migrant context, the intersubjective definition of hot spots is intimately connected to a specific form of popular and transnational Christianity known as Pentecostalism (Van Dijk 2002a, 2002b, 2002c). In locally embedded migrant communities, the place and position of Pentecostalism appears to be influential in the social construction of hot spots. This differential fragmentation and the linking of hot spots, to which Ghanaian migrants originating in urban centers as Accra and Kumasi gravitate, are the subjects of this chapter. My goal in analyzing this fragmentation in the global rescaling of hot spots and comparing The Hague and Amsterdam is to sensitize scholars of both cities and migration to the subjective aspects of scalar positioning. What makes hot spots in these cities? Why are they considered "hot"? Why and how does this sensibility play a role in the way these spaces become connected?

Bifurcating Hot Spots

This section discusses the gateway hot spots of cities such as Amsterdam and The Hague, demonstrating the relevance of a fragmented city perspective to an inquiry into the relationship between migration and city scale. I pursue the Marston-versus-Brenner debate on the utility of a scalar perspective, which engages with different levels of interaction. At issue is whether a scalar perspective allows researchers to trace the trajectories through which power is generated or reduced—economically, politically, and religiously. Neil Brenner criticizes Sallie Marston (Brenner 2001; Marston 2000; Marston and Smith 2001) in what Mark Purcell (2003b) calls a nondebate, for not acknowledging how groups and economic formations acquire power by engaging in higher scales of interaction. Yet the strength of Marston's analysis is precisely her attention to the "atomic" unit the household represents (Marston 2000).[4] She focuses on how the incorporation of the household in present-day capitalism is affected by city scale and facilitates an appreciation of the fragmentation of the city within a scalar perspective (see also Buzar, Ogden, and Hall 2005).

In Amsterdam the most immediate migrant gateway is a suburban area known as the Bijlmer. Located at a considerable distance from the city center and middle- and upper-class residential areas, it acquired a ghettoized image soon after it was developed as a postwar reconstruction area. Rather than attracting the Dutch baby-boom generation originally intended to live in the suburb's overdesigned low-cost housing, the Bijlmer was settled by labor migrants drawn by the booming Dutch economy of the 1950s and 1960s. These included large groups of Turks and Moroccans and thousands of migrants from the former Dutch colonies of Surinam and the Antilles who arrived in the 1970s and 1980s. It was in this multicultural district that many smaller clusters of Africans also found a place to settle, among them Ghanaians, who were beginning to arrive in the early 1980s.

The arrival of Ghanaians in the Netherlands was part of a larger pattern of out-migration from Ghana during this time, as more than 15 percent of the Ghanaian population emigrated as a result of the country's deteriorating economy and political instability (Peil 1995). The Bijlmer became a focal point for African immigration, and the direct links between Accra and Kumasi in Ghana and this area multiplied and deepened (Nimako 1993; Smith 2007). With more than one million inhabitants, Amsterdam rapidly became the largest city in the Netherlands; the Bijlmer likewise grew as house prices skyrocketed, leaving immigrants with few other residential options. The Bijlmer today is home to a still-increasing but unknown number of Ghanaians and is perceived by the authorities as a hot spot, largely because of its large population of undocumented immigrants. Estimates suggest that between ten and twenty thousand Ghanaian immigrants live in the area, accounting for half of the entire Ghanaian population in the Netherlands. While the area became known for police investigations that futilely attempted to curb undocumented immigration in the early 1990s, the suburb's problems escalated in 1992 when an Israeli plane crashed into an apartment building in the area. The precise number of casualties of the ensuing fire remained murky, although the authorities estimated forty-three deaths. The accident sparked an investigation into the scale and nature of undocumented immigration among Ghanaians that reached the Dutch parliament, where it catalyzed the introduction of laws to curb unregulated immigration into the Netherlands. Among these measures was the Problem Countries Circular Letter of April 1996 in which five countries were specifically named for their fraudulent identity documents; Ghana was at the top of the list. Consequently, the so-called *Koppelingswet* law was introduced, permitting the exchange of information between various government and nongovernment databases regarding the identity of citizens and foreigners living in the Netherlands (Van Dijk 2004).

Despite the increased attention of the authorities, the police, the media, and social work and welfare organizations, Ghanaians in the Bijlmer continued along a bifurcated road of both incorporation and community building while maintaining transnational connections. One element of this strategy was the establishment, dating from the early 1980s, of "internal" structures and organizations—some of which were based on ethnic identities—such as hometown associations (known as *kuo*), burial societies, and diaspora chieftaincies. Setting up chiefly "stools" (seats of traditional authority) in areas such as the Bijlmer was seen by members of ethnic groups as the pinnacle of success within the Ghanaian migrant community.

The second type of organization that emerged was from the start much more focused on integration as a strategy. Although aspiring to become umbrella structures that would bring together the various ethnic organizations, these organizations adopted the dominant Dutch political discourse, expressing concerns about the Ghanaian community in the Bijlmer to the municipal

authorities. These discussions addressed the complexity of the local settlement that included forms of mediation between migrants and Dutch society.
These included Ghanaian shops, companies, and associations that could provide for community daily needs including food, clothing, leisure, and social
connections as well as gainful employment. In talking to representatives of
the umbrella organization RECOGIN (Representative Council of Ghanaians
in the Netherlands), I learned that their conversations with the authorities
were motivated by a fear of ghettoization; they were eager to help eliminate the obstacles that impeded the wider exposure of Ghanaians to Dutch
society. For this reason they engaged in talks with the ministries of Internal
Affairs (*Binnenlandse Zaken*) and City Development (*Grote Stedenbeleid*) about
the position of the so-called small minorities (as opposed to the larger minority groups from Morocco and Turkey), specifically in regard to labor, education, health-care, and crime prevention policies.

RECOGIN acted on behalf of the Ghanaian community when organizing
visits by Ghanaian celebrities such as Kofi Annan or the Ashanti paramount
chief in Ghana, the Asantehene. At the same time it supported studies of the
position of Ghanaians that demonstrated that through self-reliance the community had become upwardly mobile in Dutch society (see Nimako 2000).
These reports saw the Ghanaian minority as a shining example of indepen-
dence through self-determination and as a community that did not depend
on Dutch welfare and social-security systems. The researchers demonstrated
that many Ghanaians were perfectly capable of finding their own way in the
Dutch labor market, starting small-scale businesses, obtaining suitable housing, and coping with criminality in their own circles. The message was one
of liberalism and noninterference. These reports responded to early 1990s
police attention in the Bijlmer and its reputed high levels of undocumented
immigration, fraudulent documents, criminal networks, and illegal activities. RECOGIN also pursued a path of integration in the realm of public culture by producing newsletters and magazines and running a radio station
for which it received municipal support. Rather than maintaining a distinct
Ghanaian cultural life in the diaspora, these Ghanaian representative organizations were creating their own niche within the larger structure of Dutch society. The pinnacle of this project of greater acceptance in the public domain
was the appointment of a young Ghanaian woman as a representative of
the Labour Party (PvdA) on the local city council in Amsterdam. Yet despite
RECOGIN's efforts, the complexity of Amsterdam itself makes it unlikely
that the Ghanaian community will have any real impact on the positioning or
power of the city as a whole by pursuing a strategy of incorporation.

While the Bijlmer as a hot spot became the focus of attention by authorities
and civil associations, the area was becoming hot in quite another sense—
with respect to the rise of Ghanaian Pentecostal churches in the area's underground parking garages (Oomen and Palm 1994; Ter Haar 1998). Most of these
garages had secluded areas that otherwise would have been used as storage
rooms or small community halls or would have hosted small enterprises.

During the late 1980s and early 1990s, dozens of new independent Pentecostal churches held their services in these parking lots; these churches were totally unconnected to any other formal organization and lacked access to an alternative space to conduct their activities. They emerged partly as satellites of churches with headquarters in Ghana or other cities around the world (Hamburg, Frankfurt, London, and New York) and partly as unaffiliated churches that sprang up in this particular community. In some cases these Biljmer branches have established satellites in Ghana or elsewhere (see Gifford 1998, 2004 on the emergence of Pentecostalism as the most popular form of Christianity in Ghana as well as in its diaspora).

Most of these churches were and today still are led by Ghanaians; their pastors address audiences in English or Twi, one of Ghana's major languages (usually with simultaneous translation). The average church membership is 250 adults, the majority of whom are Ghanaian (of various ethnic backgrounds); other members include English-speaking—mostly West African—nationalities, particularly Nigerians. The churches have few members from Dutch autochthonous communities, partly because of the language barrier. Although their interaction with the Dutch community in the Bijlmer, in Amsterdam, or beyond has remained limited, these churches are connected to international networks of Pentecostal churches and have formed nodes through which a transnational exchange of Pentecostal pastors, preachers, booklets, videos, and other material operates.

In addition, these churches have begun to play an increasingly important role in the arrangement of marriages, funerals, and ceremonies relating to birth that take place between Ghana and the Ghanaian diaspora (Van Dijk 2004). The location of the church and the reputation of pastors as trustworthy partners in arranging these matters internationally have become crucial in the eyes of followers. Arranging such events is time-consuming and expensive, since much effort is devoted to organizing religious ceremonies for an individual or couple simultaneously in Amsterdam and Ghana as well as elsewhere in the diaspora. The transnational celebration of rituals offers prestige to the person or family organizing them. Operating from underground parking garages, the churches have become important partners in the transnationalization as well as the pentecostalization of these ritual forms.

As these Ghanaian migrants have produced a transnational ritual world of global interaction on their own terms, they have linked hot spots in different cities of the world in ways that have consequences for the scalar relations of the urban spaces that are being connected. Large meetings can be held with Pentecostal preachers flown in from all around the world. Festivities and ceremonies such as funerals, marriages, or name-giving ceremonies (*dinto*) and dedications (namegiving in church) can be organized in the presence of thousands of guests from the Netherlands or neighboring countries. While most guests are Ghanaian, these connections span global Pentecostal networks, involving church websites and other media to announce and report these and similar events.

It is important to note that none of these organizations—from RECOGIN to the ethnic hometown-based associations to the plethora of churches—have ever managed to gain an overarching moral authority over all Ghanaians in the Bijlmer. RECOGIN's focus on integration did not correspond with the transnational interests of the Pentecostal churches or with the emphasis on cultural authenticity of the ethnically based associations, and vice versa. Questions of spatiality are involved here. The size, density, and social complexity of the Bijlmer have simply been too large to unify the Ghanaian community under the rubric of a clear-cut moral authority. The Bijlmer was becoming too hot for some Ghanaians as they felt too much was happening in the absence of any kind of overarching moral regime. They began to leave the area for the quieter city of The Hague, where it has been easier to create a local sense of morality. The Hague is attractive as a place of high status within global political and legal networks, and it also provides a range of employment and entrepreneurial opportunities.

Holland Spoor Connection

Since the arrival of the first migrants from Ghana in the late 1970s, life for Ghanaian residents of The Hague has centered around one location: a railway station. Holland Spoor station in an area called the Schilderswijk became the gateway to The Hague, with Ghanaian settlement concentrated in nearby low-cost housing areas. Ghanaians began settling in the many small streets around this station among other migrant communities from Morocco, Turkey, Somalia, Surinam, and India, all of which found easy access to low-cost accommodations. During the 1980s several thousand Ghanaians established their first contacts near this station, and the first Ghanaian entrepreneurial activities, such as small shops and trading companies, took root in its immediate vicinity. Holland Spoor became deeply connected to the Ghanaian settlement and its characteristic flow. For Ghanaian migrants Holland Spoor also became the pinnacle of the city's internal hierarchy of spaces—the center from which a web of connections was established and the geographical marker that anchored the Ghanaian mental mapping and social experience of the city. It was only toward the end of the 1980s and in the early 1990s that Ghanaians began moving out of the Holland Spoor vicinity to settle in a larger suburban residential area in the southeastern part of the city. However, today the social life of the Ghanaian migrant population is still to a large extent concentrated around Holland Spoor station in well-known multiethnic quarters of the Schilderswijk such as Hoefkade, Hobbemastraat, and along all their interconnecting streets.

Holland Spoor became a place of interest to many Ghanaian migrants because of the access it offered to the local job market. The first groups of African migrants in the 1980s were able to find unskilled and semiskilled jobs in the legal formal employment sector and with even greater frequency in the informal sector that was off the books and outside any formal system of taxation. In addition to being the seat of government and the home of the International Court of Justice and institutes for higher learning, Holland Spoor was also a site where labor in the fishing and meat-production industries and in office cleaning and waste removal was recruited and organized.

The area also was a point of access to greenhouses in the Westland area south of the city that demanded high levels of unskilled, manual labor. Early each morning, small vans would transport laborers to the greenhouses in the Westland. Reports in the 1980s listed the horticultural sector as one of the sectors with the highest levels of undocumented employment. By the late 1980s and early 1990s the Westland had become notorious because of police raids seeking to round up and deport undocumented laborers. Consequently, Ghanaians came to feel that working in greenhouses without the required papers was no longer a viable opportunity because they were literally too visible. Whether or not they had work permits, Ghanaians in The Hague soon ceased to consider the greenhouse sector as a source of employment.

Instead, they turned to the cleaning and hygiene business, seeing it as a sector less prone to police inspection. The Hague is a city with a large number of offices—government buildings and national and international organizations all need cleaning. The position of the city as a center of government, law, and learning was linked to the possibilities it presented to Ghanaians for a mode of incorporation into the city. Almost every Ghanaian I contacted had been, or still was, active in this sector, usually in a second or third job. It is safe to say that the cleaning profession continues to be of great importance to the economic positioning, social status, and survival strategies of the Ghanaian community. The sector is serviced by a large number of commercial employment agencies. Uncertainty is high, and working for one employer for a prolonged period is rare, but work is always available; as a result, frequent circulation among agencies and employers is common.

Cleaning jobs commonly require working at night and on weekends, leaving room for other jobs during normal office hours. Jobs are passed on from one person to another if somebody needs support in difficult times. This sector is important for Ghanaians because of its inherent invisibility, the limited opportunities it allows for the police to check identities, and the relative certainty of year-round work that it provides. However, for Ghanaians with educational qualifications, work in this sector is only temporary, as (for men in particular) a failure to achieve upward social mobility and secure work of a more permanent character can be a source of embarrassment.

To the east and north of The Hague, industrial, trading, and commercial sites have developed where semiskilled work is needed in meat production, in transport companies, on the assembly lines of small electronics factories, in floral and horticultural businesses, and in wholesale companies that assemble and transport goods to supermarkets. These labor sectors are less fluid than those mentioned above, and Ghanaians who have been able to find employment here usually have longer-term contracts or even permanent positions.

The status of Ghanaians working in these sites is usually legal because they have resided in the Netherlands for a longer period than have laborers in the other sectors mentioned above.

Ghanaians also contribute to The Hague through the shops they have established. Located mainly in the Schilderswijk, these businesses trade in clothing, African foods and agricultural products, dried fish, and even luxury items from Ghana such as soap, perfume, cosmetics, and audiovisual equipment. Other Ghanaian companies offer services related to the shipment of goods and secondhand cars, clothes, and spare parts to Ghana and West Africa as a whole. These shops and companies play an important role in the consumptive styles and appetites not only of Ghanaians but also of a wider population of African migrants that they serve. The Ghanaian shop owners describe themselves as latecomers on the scene, as they have found most of the available spaces in the open-air markets taken by other ethnic minorities. For Ghanaians, however, these small businesses contribute to a strong sense of self-sufficiency and community.

Much of the cultural life in the Ghanaian community revolves around their shops, which are seen as meeting places where news and gossip are exchanged, jobs can be found, festivities and celebrations are announced, and Ghanaian delicacies can be purchased. Shops and shipping agencies announce their Ghanaian background by hanging out Ghanaian flags or by painting Ghana's national colors on their windows. Through their Ghanaian connections these businesses have been successful in gaining dominance in the market for African produce and the transportation of goods to and from West Africa. Shop owners and shipping agents tend to have legal status in Dutch society and therefore do not worry about visibility. Other African groups in The Hague, such as Zairians, Nigerians, and Liberians, have not been able to make inroads in this domain and depend on Ghanaian shops and agencies for the goods they want from Africa. Many meals in the African community in The Hague are cooked with foodstuffs purchased from Ghanaian shops. Particularly in Ghanaian homes, there exists a sense of pride at not being dependent on the Netherlands for all aspects of everyday life.

Ghanaians have also moved into the door-to-door distribution of newspapers and advertising material. The major advantage of this sector is that work permits and other documents are never demanded; distribution usually takes place in the early morning or in the evening and therefore escapes public scrutiny. Ghanaians tend to view this sector as one of the very last niches in the socioeconomic structure where initiative is possible and interference from official bodies is absent. It is likely that they moved into this sector in response to a tightening of Dutch immigration laws and the increasing enforcement of work permits even for work at a low income level.

Holland Spoor serves not only as a site in which Ghanaians have built and contribute to the local and African economy but also as a religious hot spot. It is here that the first Ghanaian Pentecostal groups in The Hague emerged. The rise of Pentecostalism in The Hague began later than in Amsterdam, where the first Ghanaian Pentecostal churches began to appear in the Bijlmer in 1984 (Ter Haar 1998). A small group—a "prayer warrior fellowship," as some interlocutors used to call it—began meeting in The Hague in 1988 and 1989.[5] A few years later, a branch of the Church of Pentecost was established in the Hague, partly as a result of the influx of some its members from Amsterdam. Around the same time, with the movement of Ghanaians from Germany to The Hague, a branch of the Christian Mission Outreach Church was established, although its headquarters remained in Hamburg.

Soon other Ghanaian Pentecostal churches were established near Holland Spoor,[6] and a number of "house fellowships" started to operate in The Hague. Although initially small with unstable memberships, these fellowships soon developed into churches with regular meetings and a fixed leadership. While some churches opened as satellites of churches in Ghana, others developed by seceding from established congregations. In any case, the rapid increase in the number of churches in a relatively small community since 1990 has surprised many, including Ghanaians themselves. These churches and their role in the Ghanaian community in The Hague have not been the subject of intensive study, as have those in Amsterdam.[7] However, it has become clear that these Pentecostal churches have formed the de facto legitimate moral authority within the Ghanaian community. They are able to offer a more coherent organization of communal life than those located in the Bijlmer (Van Dijk 2004, 2005a) and can frame the Holland Spoor neighborhood as a Ghanaian hot spot linked transnationally to spaces in cities elsewhere around the world.

Comparing The Hague and Amsterdam: Issues of Linking and Fragmentation

There are notable similarities between The Hague and Amsterdam in the way that Ghanaian migrants are gravitating toward a limited number of city hot spots. The underlying dynamic of this fragmentation of the city may be familiar: it revolves around the availability of jobs, housing, contacts, and other opportunities for migrants aspiring to improve their lives. Amsterdam is the only Dutch city that can be considered a global city; The Hague and Holland Spoor are not judged to play a pivotal role in the global economy by comparison with Amsterdam and the Bijlmer. However, Ghanaian migrants see the situation differently. They organize transnational connections in The Hague without seeing Amsterdam's role as pivotal. In other words, to Ghanaian migrants, The Hague's linking hot spots are not premised upon the existence of Amsterdam's hot spots.

A central question that follows from this situation is how Amsterdam as the gateway city of The Netherlands is being bypassed by nodal points in The Hague. A second and related question is that if the smaller city is creating linking spots of a different scale and nature (namely religious), what does this mean for the migrants' incorporation in this city? Is the nature of these processes in Holland Spoor different from those occurring in the much larger Bijlmer? To return to the first question, let us consider the following.

Prophetess Auntie M. and the Abirem Prayer Camp

In October 1997, prophetess Auntie M. paid a visit to her followers in The Hague, an event that had been announced well in advance among the Pentecostal churches in the city. Auntie M. was the seventy-year-old leader of the Abirem Pentecostal Prayer Camp located in the Zongo Abirem near Kumasi in Ghana; among the members of the various churches in the Hague, this camp, its leader, and its healing and protective powers were well regarded. Her arrival in The Hague signaled for many the start of a "good time" of healing, deliverance from the powers of Satan, and a tackling of the problems faced by Ghanaians in everyday life in Dutch society. A "crusade" of several nights was planned, at which Auntie M. would meet all those who had visited her camp in the past and all who had benefited from her prayers and miracles before they left Ghana for Holland. Large revivals were held in her honor at which she, in her frail voice, asked people to come forward if they needed prayers for problems related to childbirth, marriage, employment, and "making papers" (identity documents and residence permits). At this invitation, huge crowds usually pushed forward—all seeking to be touched by the prophetess in the hope that benevolent spiritual forces would solve their "paper problems."

In an interview, Auntie M. explained that the Abirem Pentecostal Prayer Camp had begun in 1987 when she was fifty-eight. The prophetess hails from Tepa-Suponsô; raised in a family of cocoa farmers, she never went to school and engaged in the family occupation of cultivating cocoa. In 1986 she had a vision instructing her to give up her farm and travel to Abirem, where there was no water, no rivers were flowing, and people were facing a hard time. She was allowed to start a camp on an abandoned cocoa farm in this area. In her view, the dryness of the area was caused by the presence of four shrines and their priests (*akomfo*) in Abirem: the shrines of Akonodi from Larteh, Subono from the north, and Tingwa and Atakwama from Benin (following their migration from there in search of land). Confronting the power of these akomfo, Auntie M. cured a number of sick people through prayers and fasting. From then on people started coming to her camp in greater numbers instead of going to the akomfo and wanted to settle near her. The success of the *akomfo* waned, and eventually the *Akonodi* priests decided to leave the area and return to Larteh. This success, together with the healing miracles she performed, became widely known within Ghana and the churches. As many of her followers happened to live in The Hague, this assembly decided to invite her to tour the Netherlands.

The first notable element of this account is the direct linking of hot spots that bypass global cities (Amsterdam and Accra) yet are tremendously important for understanding the scale and intensity of interaction. The Hague and Kumasi are the connected cities; their smaller demographic size may not reflect their positioning within national and global scales of various economic, political, or cultural relationships or that of very specific hot spots within these cities.[8] Transnational relations constituted through this prophetess link what are known as the "stranger" quarters (the *zongo*) of the Ashanti Empire's cities with the Holland Spoor area in The Hague, spaces that are apparently hot because of intense religious activity. The zongo have a long record of harboring spiritual powers (De Bruijn, Van Dijk, and Van Dijk 2001). Since they are spaces inhabited by the proverbial stranger (commonly migrants from the northern part of Ghana), the source of their spiritual power is extraneous, capable of crossing borders and boundaries and therefore more powerful than even that of the established priesthood or other forms of political authority (Van Dijk 1997, 2003). However, the city as a whole is not considered the seat of an extraordinary extraneous power—the zongo embody.

The prophetess's power is capable of surpassing the established powers in the area; her Pentecostal prayer camp in Ghana is known for its spiritual powers and the mysterious power to provide people with the identity papers (passports, visas, etc.) they require to cross borders (Meyer 1998; Van Dijk 1997, 2001). Auntie M. was able to open a similar zongo-like space in The Hague. As she positioned herself near Holland Spoor, Ghanaians arrived from all over the country (including the Bijlmer) to be touched by spiritual powers, especially those that would provide them with identity documents and residence permits. It was through the prophetess that the "power in the blood of Jesus" was channeled to the believer, allowing her to bring about miracles of healing and prosperity.

The second important aspect of the scalar positioning of The Hague and its hot spot that emerges from this example is that the city became rescaled in religious terms, however temporarily, because of this event. Obviously, this rescaling was based on a cultural understanding of the meaning of gateway by the people concerned and of the terms by which certain forms of activity turn a hot spot into a gateway linkage. In this case, the role of Holland Spoor as a gateway was grounded in its offer of spiritual access within a transnational world rather than its economic or political relevance for the city or the Ghanaian community.

In contextualizing this case I am emphasizing that the changing subjectivities of the migrants (in terms of religious convictions and spirituality) reflect the changing scalar positioning of localities of departure (Kumasi, Accra) and settlement (The Hague)—not in general, unspecific terms but in very precise religious terms. The scalar subjective repositioning of Accra and Kumasi occurred on the basis of the changing positioning of religion—from the regionalized spiritual protection of the zongo style to that of Pentecostal churches operating transnationally. While sites like the prayer camps of prophetess Auntie M. can superficially be explained in terms of a locally significant religious social fabric, they should also been seen as new phenomena. What has changed is the repositioning of such religious activity on a global and transnational scale, offering a global scale of (religious) identity formation.

This rescaling is also constituted by the extensive pentecostalization of the public domain that took place in Ghana and has become dramatically and extensively visible in Accra and Kumasi since the 1980s (Meyer 2004, 2007). This process entails a public presence in the form of crusades, evangelistic rallies, and the construction of megachurches; in media outlets such as Pentecostal radio stations, television channels, and phone-in programs at night; and, finally, in political speech (see De Witte 2005; Meyer 1995, 2004, 2007).

The events in The Hague should also be interpreted in light of this rescaling and its underlying religious-political agenda—namely, the move toward a pentecostalization of the public domain that the Ghanaian community has created for itself (Van Dijk 2004, 2005a). There is an important difference here between these scalar repositionings. While in Accra and Kumasi—as in The Hague and Amsterdam—transnational Pentecostalism has captured the imagination of city dwellers and created a religious urbanity, the processes by which the different scalar positions of the Ghanaian cities manifest themselves within religious domains may be distinct. Actors such as well-known Pentecostal leaders from urban centers around the world who journey to these cities contribute to the scope of such transnational ties. Through their presence, these cities become part of a globe-spanning Pentecostal circuit. However, the churches in The Hague are not part of this circuit: they bring Auntie M. to the Netherlands but may not invite the Billy Grahams, Reinhard Bonnkes, or Benny Hinns of this world. Unlike the influence of these globe-circling figures, whose presence in many cities reflects and contributes to Pentecostal global and transnational rescaling, the impact of religious events in The Hague, such as the arrival of Auntie M., remains limited to the immediate Ghanaian or West African circle of migrants. Nevertheless, the prophetess's arrival represents the creation of transnational access for African migrants by promising successful border crossing for members and clients through spiritual inspiration and the working of prayers.

Does the kind of transnational religious rescaling produced by these encounters in The Hague differ from that produced in Amsterdam, where there are occasional visits by well-known Pentecostal preachers introducing "Holy Ghost fire" into local Pentecostal congregations? If so, why? Do the meetings in The Hague have implications for the city's scalar positioning in religious terms? To answer these questions, a detailed comparison between the positions of Ghanaians in Amsterdam and those in The Hague is needed. What difference does city scale make in terms of its positioning and of the religious hot spots that produce a specific kind of rescaling? And, subsequently, what role do Pentecostal activities play in those differing positionings?

An important indicator of the relevance of city scale to the way these locations link up with migration and place-making in the host society is that Holland Spoor is increasingly attractive for Ghanaian migrants. They are drawn by the site's tranquility—its "quiet," as some Ghanaians would say—as well as its prestige. Some informants explained that they had relocated from Amsterdam to The Hague largely because of the relative quiet in the latter. The Bijlmer had become too hot for them because of the size of the immigrant community there, and the proliferation of unconnected representative bodies for Ghanaian migrants led them to feel that there was a moral lacuna in that locality. A structured authority was missing; resultant problems included frequent police investigations and numerous internal conflicts within the Ghanaian migrant community as a whole.

After the Bijlmer plane crash in 1992, the police apparently became much more active in checking identity papers, visas, and work permits within the Amsterdam agglomeration. Outside this area, a sense of supervision was less acute, and the Ghanaian migrant community maintained its invisibility vis-à-vis the local authorities. Occasional conflicts arose within the community in the Bijlmer and even in the meeting places of certain Ghanaian Pentecostal churches. This promoted a sense that the Bijlmer was a "wild place"; internal strife and rivalries had not surfaced in The Hague to such an extent.[9] In the case of the Bijlmer, the size of the city and the community became inversely related to the ability of its internal organizations to provide effectively for security or links with the social environment. News of the "hotness" of the Bijlmer traveled to Ghana and other places around the world where Ghanaian migrant communities exist. As a prominent gateway, the Biljmer has in a way become a victim of its own success.

Another attraction of The Hague lies in the city's international prestige and image; its cosmopolitan aspects are even recognized in social life in urban Ghana. For instance, in the Accra township of Kotobabi people gather, have a drink, and chat at a site called The Hague Spot. The name "The Hague" connotes international judicial protection, international representation, high morality (certainly compared with Amsterdam), and a high level of interaction with international circles. Living in The Hague is seen as more expensive than living in Amsterdam (although this is difficult to confirm), and this reputation enhances the status of its Ghanaian residents.

Most important, Pentecostal churches in The Hague have been able to create a greater and more effective moral authority than their counterparts in Amsterdam, not only because of their number and the relatively small size of the Ghanaian community but also because of a lack of other organizations contending to represent the migrants. Although in the early 1990s a small body called Ghanatta began providing a platform of exchange between migrants and the city authorities, it never wielded the level of social, moral, or spiritual authority exercised by church leaders. Each of The Hague's Pentecostal churches serves an average adult membership of 250 persons, indicating that the churches are in direct contact with over

Fig. 2. A neighborhood sign in Accra, Ghana, reads Den Haag Spot (The Hague Spot). Migrants' subjective assessments of locations within Accra and The Hague connect hot spots in both cities and influence migrant settlement patterns in ways that contribute to the restructuring and scalar repositioning of both localities. Photo by Rijk van Dijk.

three-quarters of The Hague's estimated total Ghanaian population of approximately 3,000 to 4,000 persons (including undocumented residents). Pentecostal leaders enjoy far more influence than they ever did in Amsterdam (Van Dijk 2004).

The churches in The Hague have effectively created an alternative civic domain with high levels of commitment to and involvement in church activities, which prevent members from participating extensively in other activities in the public domain. The dominance of church life has paradoxically created a kind of invisibility for the community vis-à-vis the broader public and civic domain in The Hague. For example, when the city ran a program called *Stedelijke Adviesraad Multiculturele Stad* (SAM) to address minorities' issues and problems, Ghanaians or representatives of Ghanaian organizations rarely participated. One reason for their absence was that most city council initiatives abide by an implicit mantra that fosters a separation between state and religion; authorities contacted Ghanatta but found it difficult to engage with the important Pentecostal churches. The churches in turn have very few incentives to pursue involvement in city council organizations, as Ghanaians seek to convey that they are capable of handling their own affairs and are wary of any form of external interference.

The absence and invisibility of Ghanaians in official projects aimed at enhancing interaction between minorities and Dutch society at large are apparent in other sectors, such as in social work and employment schemes set up by official bodies. Ghanaians largely do not participate in language courses and other council initiatives such as mother and child care programs or social neighborhood programs, which are meant to encourage the integration of migrants into Dutch society. Social workers employed by the city council in The Hague have repeatedly expressed their amazement at the self-reliance and self-sufficiency of the Ghanaian minority in comparison with other minority groups (Choenni 2002). Part of the explanation for this lies in the role of the Pentecostal leadership and its self-understood function of catering to the needs of the Ghanaian stranger. Public officials have not realized that the majority of the Ghanaians in The Hague have jumped scale; like the international organizations based in The Hague, their integration is transnational—their religious networks have a global, rather than merely Ghanaian, referent (Van Dijk 2005b).

The relative invisibility and self-reliance of Ghanaian Pentecostals has had ramifications beyond this community's non-engagement with the city council's social programs. For instance, there exist virtually no identifiable groups of Ghanaian members of established Dutch Roman Catholic, Presbyterian, or other Protestant churches. Aside from isolated instances of occasional attendance, Ghanaians have not formed a recognizable proportion of Dutch church membership. No close relationships have developed between Ghanaian and Dutch Pentecostal groups such as that of the well-known Johan Maasbach Wereldzending, although Ghanaian Pentecostals do occasionally attend the meetings of Dutch groups. The language barrier is one of the primary reasons for this relative separation. Many Ghanaians do not speak Dutch and do not wish to, preferring to stick to English and Twi; many send their children back to Ghana to receive their schooling in English. Although many of the Ghanaian migrants who have settled in The Hague are not upper-middle-class (by Ghanaian or Dutch standards), they aspire to participation in a cosmopolitan world where knowledge of English is vital. Another factor explaining the separation between Ghanaian and Dutch Pentecostal groups is a difference in culture, in the sense of community expectations regarding the social functions of the church in marriages, funerals, and at times of sickness and crisis in individuals' lives.

Though churches in The Hague exert moral authority within the Ghanaian community, this authority has rarely been used to encourage members to become more engaged with issues of integration. Integration is simply not on the agenda for these churches, and thus their leaders do not invest time and energy in supporting the activities of Ghanatta. Nor is pursuing greater contact with other aspects of Dutch society (which is often considered too permissive) a goal of Pentecostal churches in The Hague. While maintaining a Ghanaian lifestyle in The Hague is difficult because the neighborhood, its shops, and places of leisure cannot be said to constitute a Ghanaian diasporic enclave, the churches have not used their powers to seek greater exposure to Dutch society or to pursue incorporation.

At the same time, these churches cannot be considered the guardians of Ghanaian culture in the diaspora, even though in The Hague they create a hot spot that interacts with a different scale of religious exchange. The processes by which Pentecostalism negotiates a critical distance from local culture and its traditions in Ghana are reproduced in the diaspora (see Van Dijk 2001, 2002c). The churches in The Hague tend to criticize Ghanatta whenever it organizes festivities that celebrate elements of Ghanaian—mostly Ashanti—cultural traditions, rejecting these practices as heathen and full of superstitious backward beliefs. These Pentecostal churches have effectively used their transnational relations to further their critical distancing from Ghanaian traditions, and they selectively determine which traditions can be maintained or Christianized and which are unfit for ceremonial use in The Hague. They have grounded their moral authority in The Hague in transnational circles, in visits by Pentecostal preachers from abroad, and in books, magazines, and tapes in which they find inspiration and legitimacy for their views.

The Hague as a linking spot has thus acquired a different meaning than the Bijlmer for Ghanaian migrants. While Pentecostal churches in the Bijlmer have little control over the local hot spot, churches in The Hague appear to be effective in determining how Ghanaian life, its celebrations and festivities, and its connections to Ghana and other parts of the world are, or should be, organized. Holy Ghost fire made the Holland Spoor area a hot spot in spiritual terms, including a Ghanaian Pentecostalized civic domain (Van Dijk 2004). Its transnational features have spilled over into transcultural practices in church networks that arrange marriages and funerals, which include other African nationals, for whom they offer religious services including healing, spiritual protection, and counseling. The Hague's Pentecostalized civic domain, which operates parallel to the dominant civic domain of the state, has therefore acquired a transnational existence in symbolic and religious terms and in scalar interaction.

• • •

City scale can affect the positioning of migrants in unexpected ways; apprehending the complexity of this significant phenomenon is possible only within a perspective that allows for urban fragmentation. From such a vantage point, it is clear that some inner-city spaces are more globally, transnationally, and transculturally connected than others, thus explaining how and why certain immigrant groups in particular cities are or are not incorporated or integrated into a city's larger economic, political, or sociocultural environments. In both Amsterdam and The Hague, inner-city linking hot spots cannot a priori be perceived as conducive to migrants' integration. The Bijlmer is so large that it allows for the continuation of a Ghanaian lifestyle requiring a minimum of exposure to Amsterdam society more broadly but also fosters institutions and a leadership that advocate for integration. In contrast, Holland Spoor is characterized by the dominance of transnational Pentecostal churches that do not pursue integration in the host society at all. By providing a hot spot, these churches in The Hague allow Ghanaian and other African Christians to become integrated in a transnational experience of Pentecostalism on a different scale of interaction. The Bijlmer is marked by a strong associational life among the Ghanaian community, largely under the umbrella of RECOGIN, and therefore harbors groups that pursue policies of integration and incorporation, if to limited success. On the other hand, Holland Spoor is smaller in size and sited in a city of smaller scalar positioning, which are factors that might suggest a greater incorporation of the Ghanaian migrant community. However, Ghanaian settlement there is marked by a distinct lack of integration. The conclusion that emerges is that while city scale is important, the scale of a specific hot spot and its scale of transnational interaction and appeal appear to be more significant determinants of migrant incorporation.

This chapter has also asked on whose terms scale is constructed. Most authors, such as Brenner (2001) and Marston (2000), have not made allowance for a subjective understanding of geographic notions of scale and scalar repositioning. However, I have examined transnational Pentecostalism as a form of socioreligious scalar repositioning that interlocks with these geographical notions and have shown that the scalar positioning of hot spots has to be explored at the level of a particular simultaneity. Objectified dimensions of urban fragmentation and the criteria of status, class, and identity that mark the privileged positioning of a city space capable of linking directly with a global scale should be considered through a lens emphasizing their subjective realization. In the case of The Hague, these dimensions turn religion into a domain of identity formation that bypasses similar levels of interaction.

This chapter can be read as a critique of Brenner, who has rightly argued for a relational understanding of scale yet has allowed only for an objectivist and objectifying position. A subjectifying position, however, opens up an inquiry into how, and on what terms, this relationality must be understood and investigated. In my examination of transnational Ghanaian Pentecostalism, I have shown that according to the second approach, religious scale is an important determinant of the relationship between religion and migration. A thorough anthropological understanding of the meaning and significance of scalar repositioning necessitates a consideration of both objectifying and subjectifying perspectives.

I thank the editors, Nina Glick Schiller and Ayşe Çağlar, for their invaluable comments and suggestions on a preliminary draft of this chapter.

Notes

1. Based on the foundational work of Henri Lefebvre (1991) and Neil Smith (1990), a literature has developed that conceptualizes a scalar perspective to investigate the relative positioning of cities, states, and the world vis-à-vis their placement in hierarchies of power (see Brenner 1997, 2000, 2001; Smith 1992; Swyngedouw 1997b; Marston 2000).

2. Sassen (2000a, 146) perceives this process as informing a new research agenda:

Cities emerge as one territorial or scalar moment in a trans-urban dynamic. This is however, not the city as a bounded unit, but the city as a node in a grid of cross-boundary processes. Further, this type of city cannot be located simply in a scalar hierarchy that places it beneath the national, regional and global. It is one of the spaces of the global, and it engages the global directly, often by-passing the national.... Pivoting theorization and research on the city might be a fruitful way of cutting across embedded statism and capturing the rescaling of some major social, economic and political processes at the level of the city.

3. I was inspired to use the term "methodological urbanism" by Andreas Wimmer and Nina Glick Schiller's (2002) explication of the concept of "methodological nationalism," referring to the naturalization of the nation-state as a social and political form that is linked to the conflation of "culture" or "ethnicity" with the "nation" and/or the state (see James Scott 1999; for Africa see Malkki 1995).

4. In this sense I disagree with Helga Leitner and Byron Miller (2007), who accuse Marston of discounting human agency by representing the social construction of scale as producing only new structures. Agency should not be mistaken to mean "methodological individualism" and is not tied only to the prototypical "actor." It may also relate to institutions, such as the household, and the way they negotiate structures (for an Africanist perspective on agency, see De Bruijn, Van Dijk, and Gewald 2007).

5. This became known as the Boekhorststraat Fellowship, named after one of the streets near Holland Spoor. The term "prayer warrior" is found globally in Pentecostal networks.

6. These included the Acts Revival Church, Christian Mission Outreach Church, Christian Revival Outreach Church, Church of Pentecost, Holy Ghost Ministries International, and Rhema Gospel Church International.

7. The only study is by Mirjam Krabbenborg (1995) on the position of women in the Acts Revival Church. A later study looked at what it termed the "societal payoff" of migrant churches in The Hague and included a number of Ghanaian-led churches (Van der Sar and Visser 2006).

8. Kumasi is the seat of the Asantehene, the paramount chief of the largest ethnic community in Ghana, the Ashanti.

9. Mar Oomen and Jos Palm (1994) provide a detailed description of a Ghanaian musician moving from Amsterdam to The Hague for this reason.

Chapter 7

Transnational Migration and Rescaling Processes

The Incorporation of Migrant Labor

RUBA SALIH AND BRUNO RICCIO

Sassuolo (Modena), July 2005: The police evacuate the Casbah, a building located in the Braida neighborhood that is inhabited mainly by migrant singles and families in a quite brutal manner. The neighborhood has become a ghetto and home to drug sellers and widespread petty crime. In an interview, the porter of the building, a man from Togo, states that he and the migrants living in the building were the first to call the police for help against the pushers: "Whenever I saw the drug sellers approaching the area I would call the police and the *carabinieri* and they would reply: 'We have no patrols available.' However, when it came to evacuating the building they sent a lot of cars and even a helicopter; look at how many policemen are here today.... The mayor said that the police feared the drug sellers, should I believe that? When it comes to throwing women and children onto the streets there is no problem, and they have even beaten a boy." Following the event a demonstration is organized in solidarity with the migrants, with more than a thousand participants, including locals and migrants.

Sassuolo, February 2006: A woman calls the police saying that a man is harming her. The man, a north African "illegal" migrant, is well known in the Braida neighborhood for sleeping in the building as a squatter. When the police report is made following the incident, the man is said to have been drunk and to have threatened the woman with a broken glass. After the police arrive, they immobilize the man and start beating him, jumping violently on his by then sluggish body as he lies on the floor. Some young migrants happen to be watching the scene and try to intervene to defend their fellow countryman. One of them, a twenty-seven-year-old Moroccan worker in the ceramics industry, documents the beating with his mobile phone. Subsequently the

Fig. 3. This demonstration in the main square in Sassuolo for the right to housing for migrants is evidence of support for migrants' rights in the towns of Emilia Romagna. To remain competitive globally, local industries needed migrant workers; migrant women's housework allowed middle-class women to participate in the workforce. July 2005. Photo by Leonardo Tancredi.

video is handed to the local branch of the Giovani Musulmani d'Italia organization (the young Muslims of Italy) and appears on their website for a few hours before the leaders of the organization withdraw it and deliver the footage to the local police. Their concern is to avoid reinforcing the many voices that, at both local and national levels, are trying to form a divide between migrants and Italian locals. However, the media exposure of the video fosters an ambivalent reaction among the local population and administrators. Some suggest that those directly responsible for the beating should face some penalty but still express their support for the police force. Most of the local people, however, convey their deep solidarity with the police. These people state that the police face the daily intense pressure of increased criminality and need to control a potentially explosive situation. A few days later Sassuolo is once again at the center of the national headlines and becomes a crucial topic within the context of the national electoral campaign. For the next month, Sassuolo is the destination of several ministries and members of parliament, who portray the city as a symbol of the insecurity that both locals and the police are experiencing as a result of bad local policies that gloss over the needs of the local population in the name of "multicultural tolerance."

Fig. 4. The Braida building in Sassuolo, inhabited by migrant workers and families, was locally thought of as the "ghetto." Migrants may be physically marginalized, even as their settlement is supported, in small-scale towns such as Sassuolo, which are experiencing a process of global economic restructuring and rescaling. Photo by Leonardo Tancredi.

Introduction

The term "superdiversity" has been employed, in the British context, to describe the emergence of "new, small and scattered, multiple-origin, transnationally connected, socioeconomically differentiated, and legally stratified immigrants who have arrived over the last decade." This phenomenon, it is argued, "surpasses anything Great Britain has previously experienced" (Vertovec 2006, 1). Such diversity, whenever it is found within immigrant populations, according to Steven Vertovec, has enormous implications for citizenship policies, social provisions, and the general understanding of the whole migration process. We argue that superdiversity has characterized migration to Italy and Emilia Romagna, the specific region we are analyzing in this chapter, ever since migration has become a visible phenomenon. Diversity and dispersion are significant aspects of the Emilia Romagna region and must be linked to our understanding of the rescaling that accompanies neoliberal capitalism.

Italy has generally been seen as a weak nation as a result of its deep internal historical, cultural, economic, and social differences. Indeed, Italian society has been profoundly crosscut by regional (notably south/north), cultural, and political differences (Catholicism coexisting with a historically strong Communist Party). As Jeff Pratt (2002) has insightfully noted, these and other differences characterizing Italian society are important if we are to understand the ways in which migrants have been inserted into the various local contexts. Indeed, policies toward migrants have tended to vary widely, reflecting the larger regional differences in terms of resources, histories, and political cultures.[1] Local differences also affect migrants' settlement and their insertion into the labor market. Agricultural activities are confined mainly to southern and central regions; employment within a post-Fordist industrial sector is concentrated in the north, where migrant women and men are also increasingly participating in a growing service sector. Meanwhile, employment of unskilled labor in construction is prevalent in north and northeastern regions. As a result of the extremely superdiverse, varied, composite, and particularized nature of migrant communities across the country, the very local dynamics and dimension of migration have been the focus of most research in Italy. Scholars of migration in Italy have examined local contexts within large and even small cities in predominantly rural areas (CNEL 1995), as well as major urban centers or global cities such as Milan or Rome (Caponio 2002; Ires Piemonte 1994). Very often this type of research has provided detailed studies on the local processes of incorporation of migrants and the local policies of reception.

However, the focus on local contexts in Italian migration studies has not produced a better understanding of the relationships between the positioning of specific small-scale cities and broader domains of financial, political, and cultural power and the trajectories of migrant departure and settlement (Glick Schiller and Çağlar, chapter 10). Moreover, by generally failing to take the transnational dimension of migration into account, studies of local contexts have not provided deep analyses of the relationship between migrants' incorporation into a new place and global economic restructuring. What these studies have suggested, however, is that locality in Italy is of great importance. In this sense, Italy represents a good case in point to study the effects of rescaling processes—that is, the reorganization of the processes of vertical reordering of socio-spatial units (Glick Schiller and Çağlar chapter 4; 2009) at the intersection with migration and migrants' transnational forms of incorporation.

This chapter explores how migrants' incorporation in the Emilia Romagna region, where we conducted most of our research over the last ten years (Riccio 2000, 2001; Salih 2003), is affected by the concomitant effect of rescaling and restructuring, a dynamic intersection that Nina Glick Schiller and Ayşe Çağlar have defined in this book as a process of scalar positioning. We illustrate how transnational migration was shaped by both the specific histories of various localities and the contemporary restructuring and rescaling affecting local receiving contexts and the region as a whole.

While these localities can hardly be considered "global cities," they have witnessed significant processes of restructuring, which have led to the privatization of welfare provisions and the reshaping of labor market conditions. These transformations paralleled a contested dynamic of rescaling, in a context of a wider reorganization of the relationship between localities, regions, nation-states, and global institutions. As regions and cities strive to become global economic competitors, they also claim a new role in the governance of migration. However, the effects of these developments are complex; political decentralization and restructuring of social policies have produced varied outcomes in different local contexts in Italy, sometimes reinforcing already existing inequalities between regions (Ranci 2005).

The chapter is structured as follows. We begin by introducing the main characteristics of the Emilia Romagna region within the contemporary globalized economy. We then move on to consider an example of the renegotiation of hierarchical power between two institutions, the region and the state, by looking at the process of differentiation in immigration laws at the regional and national levels. There are also important variations within the region itself. We will assess this variability by comparing two neighboring provinces, their economic and political histories, and their different relationships with migrants' transnational projects. We then conclude by taking into account the dispersed presence of migrants' settlement in Emilia Romagna. Their dispersal illustrates the consequences of the differential positioning of cities—shaped by institutions of political, cultural, and economic power—within regions, states, and global urban hierarchies.

Rescaling Processes and Migration in Emilia Romagna

Italy has only quite recently become an important country in terms of immigration. Migrants in Italy represent today 5 percent of the population, and the number of migrants has grown from 500,000 at the end of the 1990s to 2,800,000 in 2005 (Caritas Migrantes 2005). Italy, together with Spain, is now third in the European Union in terms of the number of migrants, ranked after the United Kingdom and Germany. A remarkable percentage of migrants reside in the wealthier northern part of the country, which is home to 59 percent of the total migrant population but to only 44 percent of the national population.

In comparison to the industrial expansion of the 1950s and the 1960s in France and other European countries, contemporary international migration flows to Italy occurred within a framework of changing socioeconomic conditions.[2] While European industrial societies in the postwar period were characterized by a high level of recruitment within an expanding Fordist industrial sector, in the 1990s the importance of the tertiary sector increased. Contrary to the industrial growth characteristic of the traditional immigration countries during the 1950s and 1960s, the Italian labor market manifested a high level of segmentation and flexibility (although this varied within different regions), with the consequent expansion of the demand for temporary and precarious jobs that were not satisfied by the local labor supply (Ambrosini 2001; Pugliese 2000).

Emilia Romagna is one of the most flourishing economic regions in Italy with the peculiarity of having been historically governed by the political Left. As a result, the region received a consistently high investment in welfare services. Immigration to this region has been described as stable, characterized by the presence of a large number of legal migrants and family reunions. Emilia Romagna's economic development, however, has never been based exclusively on a Fordist industrial system. The regional economy has historically been characterized by the success of highly specialized small and medium-sized enterprises. Global restructuring and a very severe demographic decline of the local population are important processes affecting the cities of the region. Emilia Romagna is also considered a leading region in the enactment of social policies toward migrants: measures to foster their integration through reception and health centers, housing, professional training, cultural initiatives, support in education, and immigration councils (Barbagli and Colombo 2004; Riccio 2000; Salih 2002).

Approximately 284,500 migrants reside regularly in the region (10 percent of the total at the national level). At the beginning of 2005, migrants in Emilia Romagna represented 6.2 percent of the total population, in comparison with the national average of 5 percent. Emilia Romagna is ranked fourth, after Lombardia, Lazio, and Veneto, in the number of migrants. The percentage of schoolchildren with non-Italian backgrounds is the highest in the country, highlighting the fact that many families settle, despite maintaining substantial transnational links with their countries of origin. Twenty percent of the total births in the region are to migrant women, a substantial proportion in a context characterized by one of the lowest birth rates in the world.

From a historical point of view we may recall that the region conflated the two Italian models of migratory flows: in the 1950s and 1960s it was a context of internal migration in the northwest of the country but also of emigration to the south of Italy. In the mid-1970s it became a migration destination, and in the 1980s it was a receiving context in terms of international migratory flows. Although the number of immigrant workers in permanent and stable jobs increased over time, especially in small and medium-sized industries (SMEs), the number of irregular (*in nero*) or cash-in-hand workers among immigrants also greatly increased (Motturra 2000). The high level of economic development within the region was a consequence of its peculiar organization into industrial districts (*distretti industriali*), which function through the cooperation and integration of different small and medium-sized industries, usually operating within the same territory, around the same productive cycle. Local authorities played an important role in the development of the economic system of the region as they supplied various services (training, information, etc.) to the citizens, which not only increased the latter's feeling of belonging to the local community but also reduced costs that would otherwise have fallen on the small industries.

Since the late 1980s, changes have occurred at both demographic and economic levels. There has been an increasing need for migrant labor, which should be read against the background of restructuring processes affecting the small industries of the region and the demographic decline of the local population. The Italian population, particularly in Emilia Romagna, is becoming older. It has been estimated that by the next decade there will be a deficit of a hundred thousand workers, especially in the industrial and technical job sector. Two interrelated factors are responsible for this complex situation: the opening up of new markets at the international level and the devaluation of the national currency. On the one hand, export-oriented industries, which can attach considerable added value to their final products (since all phases of production, from research to finance and marketing, are under their control) and can thus control the commercialization of those products, benefited from these changes. On the other hand, industries that produce for an internal market and are mainly involved in the production of semi-manufactured products found themselves under heavy constraints since they were not able to compete with imported products because of higher internal labor costs. This affected a large section of the local economy. Local authorities were under contrasting pressures as a result of this complex situation, which threatened the region's economic system.

The diverse outcomes of globalization have created contrasting needs between these two economic sectors in the local economy: while the former requires more services, infrastructure, and highly qualified personnel, industries belonging to the second group look primarily for a reduction of labor costs and fiscal pressure. In this context, industries of the second group have increasingly turned toward the employment of foreign low-wage manpower, or if they could, have shifted their production to eastern European countries. In addition to traditionally low-wage sectors such as agriculture and the building industry, migrants are now mainly employed in small manufacturing industries, in production of handicrafts, and in the metallurgical and mechanical industries.

Although the majority are unskilled laborers (mechanics, laborers in small and medium-sized firms), one also finds a vast number of skilled and educated migrants who work below their skill level. Many migrants actively participate in the training offered by trade unions and local authorities to enhance their opportunities in the labor market. Although sometimes training may lead to frustrating outcomes in terms of trainees' expectations, many deploy this economic capital back home directly or indirectly. For instance, there are some cases in which dependent workers, after years of participating in training and developing friendships with Italian bosses, become their informal agents by selling the surplus of annual products when they return home. However, these are exceptions. As Neil Brenner and Nik Theodore (2002a, 2; 158) remind us, "actually existing neoliberalism" works through the dialectic between partial destruction and constructed different social "sites of regulation." On the one hand, one must note the general diffused tendency toward cutting labor costs and enhancing labor exploitation; on the other hand, migrants try to grasp other opportunities to reshape transnational strategies of incorporation.

Rescaling and Migration

The rate of local women's participation within the labor market in Emilia Romagna is much higher than the national rate. However, the increasing participation of indigenous women in the labor market has not brought about changes in the traditional division of roles within Italian families. Migrant women are taking on the homemaking domestic roles of local women. The region is experiencing what Jacqueline Andall (2000, 139–40) calls "the racialization of the live-in sphere." This is a situation in which "an old system could be perpetuated with a new supply of labor." Migrant women are mainly employed within the domestic, caring, and cleaning sectors, often without a regular contract (*in nero*), and, in very few cases, in small industries (Alemani 1994; De Fillippo 1994; Vicarelli 1994; Andall and Sarti 2004). The rapid aging of the local population and the growth in women's employment outside the home are two of the main explanations for the insertion of migrant women into the domestic sector at the regional level.

A recent survey showed that families employing migrant women for care and domestic-related jobs in the region are very varied in terms of class and origin. The influx of migrant domestic workers, who take care of the elderly while most local women are working away from home, is transforming the customary social, cultural, and spatial landscapes of not only middle- and upper-middle-class families in major cities but also of middle- and lower-class families living in villages in the mountains and countryside.

Local policies toward migrants are the product of a complex process of interplay between different scales: local, regional, national, and European. Migrant women are inscribed in the rescaling and restructuring of national social provisions in a twofold way: as providers of services in a context of the erosion of the welfare state and also as recipients of increasingly privatized social provisions. In this regard, we are witnessing not only a growing devolution of social welfare functions to lower levels of government but also the transfer of responsibilities to the private sector. Despite the uncontested primacy of Emilia Romagna in the field of avant garde social and migration policies, the number and types of private actors providing welfare-related services and provisions have enormously increased in the region. A study conducted in four different cities in the region showed that 66 percent of the services provided to migrant women were supplied by private actors such as voluntary associations or social cooperatives that offered aid, legal advice, labor orientation, or vocational training; only 26 percent were public (Sgrignuoli 2002).

There are consequential advantages and disadvantages when voluntary third sector organizations become substitutes for the state. We do not deny the importance and potential role that this expanding sector can play. However, we point to the risks that the state's withdrawal from certain areas engenders for particularly disadvantaged subjects who, unlike citizens, do not enjoy formal political and civil rights and who, as a consequence, could become the first targets of cyclical cuts or retreats during particularly harsh economic crises. The regional budget for social policies comes from different sources: local, national, and European. Indeed, most local initiatives in the region are supported by EU funds. Antiracist initiatives and vocational training programs are examples of programs that benefit from these funds. The latter programs are held every year, managed by the regional government, and implemented by the province and some private organizations.

Migrant women's strategies of incorporation also reflect and induce a scalar repositioning of localities. A woman tends to leave her family behind with the intention of spending six months to one year with one family as a domestic or care worker, after which she is replaced by one of her female relatives from her village or city of origin. Here again, we stress the dialectic of destruction and construction of actual neoliberalism. On the one hand, this kind of migratory pattern represents a formidable opportunity for the local and national governments. They are able to use migrant women's labor to contain the social conflicts that may result from the lack of state-subsidized services, while at the same time casting the costs of maintenance of the migrant families left behind onto the country of origin. On the other hand, there are benefits to migrant families. This could be seen as a strategy of "transnational moving while staying at home," by which women alternate in cyclical, short-term migratory shifts, maximizing their economic gains in Italy while keeping up crucial roles in their reproductive spheres back home. This recruitment process also sees women as active agents in a process of time-space compression since, paradoxically, a woman who resides permanently in the local context may find it harder to find a job than a relative of a transnational domestic worker.

To grasp migrants' predicaments in Emilia Romagna, we need to understand that government, services, employment, labor markets, and household dynamics all exist within fields of action that engage within multiple, simultaneous scales of relationships. It is therefore necessary to approach the issue of scale both in terms of the multiple relations in which migrants are engaged across spaces and in terms of the political economy within which these relations are embedded. Within the dynamics of rescaling, however, it is not an easy task to define "migrants' incorporation." When analyzed from a political economy perspective, it is evident that migrants' insertion into the labor market is highly functional to rescaling processes induced by global economic restructuring but is experienced locally. Similarly, migrants may enjoy certain social and cultural rights at local or regional levels, such as the right to health, to schooling, or to "cultural difference," but they are often excluded from political rights by virtue of their nonnational status.

However, while migrants adapt to specific local cultures, economies, and policies, they simultaneously resist them. For example, the transnational dimension of migrants' lives affects (and is affected by) not only their insertion in the local yet globalized labor markets and economies but also their potential to participate within local and community life. While the transnationality (meaning affiliations and identifications but also practices) of migrants' lives in certain cases may be not only acknowledged but also promoted by certain local contexts, as will be illustrated by the material below on Senegalese migrants in Ravenna, in other cases it may be discouraged or seen as threatening the symbolic order of "sedentarism" and belonging to the local context (cf. Malkki 1997).

The Regional versus the National

As Glick Schiller and Çağlar argue in chapter 4 of this book, "Scholars arguing for a scalar approach underlined the changing relationship not only between localities in the context of globalization but also between localities and states." This section provides a view of the shifts in the region policies of migration, ultimately showing how rescaling and restructuring dynamics have had implications for the previous hierarchical institutional connections between national, regional, and local powers. These connections have been reconfigured in favor of a major and new role for local and regional bodies in the governance of migration.

In the last decade not only has there been an acknowledgment of the gendered dynamics and patterns of migration, given the high number of domestic servants that shape the relations and landscapes of even the most remote villages and households, but transnationalism itself is recognized as a key feature of contemporary migration at both national and local levels. After ten years of reports that focused exclusively on male migrants' experiences of integration and their living conditions seen through the exclusive lens of the receiving context, national reports and statistics on migration have begun to focus on the transnational dimension and to note the presence of women migrants within the transnational flows of labor. In its 2004 issue, the Caritas national report, which is one of the most comprehensive annual statistical surveys in Italy recognized transnationalism as an institutional phenomenon, defining contemporary migration as imprinted on a model of "nomadismo migratorio" (nomadic migratory patterns).

This major shift in the way in which institutions understand the contemporary features of migration has been accompanied by the rescaling of its management. Regional policies have prevailed, and the nation-state is no longer the central political actor in the management of migration. In 2004 the regional law was reworked with the goal of overcoming the "multiculturalist" imprint of national politics, which for several years had tended to focus exclusively on "cultural difference." The national law had marginalized the issue of migrants' political rights by producing and reinforcing an image of migrants not as subjects of rights but as fragile and culturally disempowered individuals needing different kinds of help. In contrast to this approach, the region has tried to address problems such as housing. Housing is the most problematic aspect for migrants in Emilia Romagna. The region has tried to promote local policies by countering the actions of private landlords and estate agencies who reluctantly rent to migrants or who require unaffordable rates for very low quality properties (Bernardotti 2001).

To legitimize discrimination in the housing market, property owners speak of the devaluation of their property as a result of an inherent disposition of migrants to overcrowding (Riccio 2000). This discourse had been complimented by a culturalist reading of difference that permitted the segregation, or ghettoization, of migrants' accommodations.

In a rather dramatic move, the 2004 regional law introduced universalistic principles by declaring the end of ethnically differentiated housing services. The new law insured that migrants could have access public housing on the same basis as locals. Furthermore, the region expanded migrants' right to vote in local elections, suggesting that all possible means should be used to expand their citizenship rights. To legitimate this, it invoked European laws and international conventions, completely bypassing the nation-state. These regional actions can be seen as examples of scalar repositioning in which the region, as opposed to the nation-state, claims to have a legitimate right to govern migration, not in terms of flows, but in the domain terms of citizenship rights and the politics and procedures of incorporation.

The conflict between region and nation-state became a national issue when the presidency of the Council of Ministry (under the Berlusconi government that ended in the year 2006) challenged the 2004 regional law on migration in the national Constitutional Court. The national government claimed that the law was not compatible with constitutional principles and that the region was taking too active a role in the management of migration, overcoming and interfering with the state's prerogatives. Indeed, the Bossi-Fini national law, approved during the former Berlusconi government, but still in effect at the time of the court case, had taken an altogether different approach to migration. It had introduce the *contratto di soggiorno* (resident contract). Rather than allocating migrants citizenship rights, this law tied a migrant's residence permit to a job contract; unemployment for more than six months led to expulsion from the country. The court eventually rejected the nation-state's claim, arguing for the full right of the region to rule on migration matters.

This case was not the only one of its kind. Conflicts between the state, the regions, and localities were quite common in between 2002 and 2006. There have been increasing instances where regions (notably Friuli Venezia Giulia and Emilia Romagna) and cities (Torino and Ancona) have formulated new policies of citizenship and incorporation that have been contested by the

Italian state on the basis that they were against the constitution (in that they went beyond the power attributed to these regions by the national law). In Turin and Ancona, two cities ruled by Center-Left coalitions, the mayors approved decrees that extended the right to vote to migrants in local elections, thus bypassing the national law. Both decrees were blocked by the national government, again on the basis that the cities were extending their power to legislate on matters over which only the national state had authority. Of course, here the conflict was not only between regional and national bodies but also between two different political cultures. However, it must be noted that other localities or regions (e.g., Veneto), despite sharing the political position of the national (Berlusconi) government, have contested the latter's politics of migration, especially concerning the management of flows.

Rimini and Ravenna: Two Different Migration Contexts

One aspect specific to the Romagna subregion is the tourist coast, which has provided more precarious employment than the rest of the region and which saw the arrival of numerous street sellers at the end of the 1990s. The Senegalese are among the most numerous foreign communities in Ravenna and Rimini and Senegalese are the majority of these sellers but they have also entered the formal labor market. Working as masons and factory workers, they have encountered exploitation but have also met with some success. However, many prefer the informal labor market, engaging in the street selling that provides flexibility from which they benefit spiritually as well as materially (Riccio 2001). Street selling can function either as temporary employment while a migrant is waiting to find a better job in the labor market or as a seasonal job in settings in which there is a well-established network of vendors, such as in the coast of Emilia Romagna.

Despite the fact that both Ravenna and Rimini are situated on the same coast and have similar characteristics, each city also displays some striking differences in economic structure and in the reception of migrants. These are connected to different historical trajectories.

Although Rimini was a holiday resort in the eighteenth century, its tourism-based economy did not emerge until the beginning of the twentieth century. Its first impressive infrastructural transformation occurred during the Fascist era when the process of urbanization led to an expansion of the residential area and the population grew from forty-seven thousand to sixty-seven thousand. The number of hotels and shops increased accordingly, along with the building industry that was connected with tourism. Consequently, local policies supported tourist activity and tourist-oriented micro-entrepreneurship. Local institutions became important actors in this stage, both as brokers with the state and as distributors of resources within the locality. After the war there was a second economic boom, and Rimini strengthened the development of service-sector industries. Socially, the city also underwent a profound transformation: the decline of the landlord class was more evident than in other provinces of Romagna and a new urban bourgeoisie developed following the growth of mass tourism (Tomasetti 1983). In the transition from an agro-tourist to a fully tertiary-tourist economy, the local authorities played a key role by giving their political support and incentive to this process of tertiarization. This historical cooperation was the basis of political proposals to fight irregular trade and immigration that characterized the province throughout the 1990s.

Although this provincial "fun factory" has been successfully geared toward tourist activity for a long time, the end of the early 1990s was a critical period of economic stagnation because of the pollution caused by algal bloom in the Adriatic Sea. Moreover, as a typical product of the creative destruction of "actually existing neoliberalism" (Brenner and Theodore 2002a, 2), the uneven development of numerous big stores and wholesaler centers started to weaken the economic power of small shopkeepers. Together with the development of shopping centers, the transformation of tourism, which made tourists' visits more intermittent, adversely affected many shopkeepers. Some of them were unable to sell their businesses because they would have lost too much by the sale. Those Italian citizens who felt particularly threatened by the country's rescaling processes and the consequent shifts tended to project this anxiety onto the migrant community. Indeed, this period witnessed the first racist demonstrations by shopkeepers against migrant street sellers. The focus on irregular trade and its connection with migration in public discourses may also have legitimized the associations of traders and shopkeepers (Riccio 1999).

However, research on informal trade in the subregion since the 1990s has demonstrated that 70 percent of the street sellers obtained their supplies on the Italian coast itself (Catanzaro, Nelken, and Belotti 1996). This finding meant that irregular sellers got their supplies from the same sources as the regular local shopkeepers. Therefore, although the research on irregular trade revealed a potential conflict between wholesalers and small-scale shopkeepers, local animosity was only directed toward the irregular street sellers. As the majority of irregular sellers were migrants, one suspects that wholesalers and store keepers preferred a racialized representation of the problem and an ethnic conflict. It is likely that this sort of "new racism" was an unintended consequence of the impact of rescaling processes on the locality (Cole 1997).

Such a state of affairs also affected local policies. Indeed, the local government gradually withdrew from direct involvement with migration, which was considered a hot policy issue that was not politically rewarding, and left all the responsibilities and initiatives to volunteer associations. Migrants' economic and social exclusion produced informal and illegal labor situations that also negatively influenced their right to stay in the country; renewal of the permit to stay in the country (*permesso di soggiorno*) depended on being regularly employed. Thus a vicious cycle has characterized the relationship between migration and socioeconomic change.

Ravenna's history displays a more diverse and pluralistic socioeconomic background. At the beginning of the twentieth century it was mainly an agricultural city. However, the commercialization and manufacturing of agricultural products forged a relationship between the port and the surrounding countryside and stimulated the first processes of development, such as the building of a railway station and a minor financial and administrative center. Between the two world wars, Ravenna strengthened its agricultural production and developed its construction sector. This was a period of dependence on the central authoritarian state that continued after the Second World War. Yet it produced industrialization and the great transformation of the city with a more developed regional institutional connection with the rest of Emilia Romagna. Activities such as the reconstruction of buildings and technical training led to the empowerment of local authorities. The link with the central state became useful because the local authorities were more in tune with national government. As a result, large state enterprises invested in that part of the province where methane fields had been discovered: this was the beginning of Ravenna's industrialization. Between 1951 and 1961 Ravenna emerged as a dynamic industrial center and port, thanks to public enterprise and, to a minor extent, to the cooperatives. The promoter of both the port and the petrochemical industrial center was Enrico Mattei, the manager of ENI (Ente Nazionale Idrocarburi), who introduced the concept of "modernization from outside" (D'Attorre 1994).

It is important to stress here that many economic, social, and political actors were involved in this development. In the 1970s, the national political and economic circumstances changed and with the death of Mattei, the state's entrepreneurial role diminished and the long-standing local social resources reemerged. The local governments became more active by supporting crafts and tourism, and the cooperatives became the main socioeconomic actors throughout the 1980s. During the 1990s Ravenna's public opinion, in contrast to Rimini's, was less hostile toward an interventionist policy that favored migrants. The first initiative included the purchase of and loans for big buildings that were used to provide services for migrants, including information, assistance, housing, and training. The local council and the local branches of the health and social services transferred duties for local immigration policies to a consortium of cooperatives, which ran many different types of social services for migrants, with the declared aim of stimulating their "integration" into the receiving society.

Thus Ravenna serves as a strong center for the entire province and is involved in many different policies, which, unlike Rimini, it has been able to implement efficiently. Furthermore, its institutions communicate well with each other. This may be due to the number of actors affecting the province, which is less dominated by small business associations. However, that does not mean that racism or mistrust toward migrants does not affect Ravenna. For instance, many private landlords and public agencies have been unwilling to rent or sell apartments to migrants (Riccio 2000).

To analyze the contrast between Ravenna and Rimini as immigration societies, it is worth drawing, in a looser illustrative way, on Sandra Wallman's (1986) model of the "ethnic boundaries process." Through a systematic comparison between the structure and organization of two inner-city areas of London (Bow and Battersea), she distinguishes two contrasting types: heterogeneous and homogeneous processes. "Boundaries of the heterogeneous type are...more permeable, more flexible than in the homogeneous case....As the resilience of any system varies with the flexibility of its boundaries, so areas of the first type are relatively more resilient in the face of economic change or population movement" (245). Rimini represents the homogeneous type as an economic structure focused almost entirely on tourism and where the street selling carried out by many Senegalese is easily perceived as threatening the wealth of the community, built mainly by traders and merchants who resent the effects of socioeconomic changes. This difficulty partially explains why, although Rimini was one of the first communities to do something for immigrants in the region, it has taken little action following that first attempt. Ravenna offers a more varied economic structure (industry, agriculture, tourism, and trade), which is able to be more resilient when facing socioeconomic changes. Here, what Grillo (1985) would call an "institutional complex" of linked organizations began to develop in response (reception, information, and accommodation) to the arrival of immigrants. From another point of view, this comparative discussion testifies also to the long-standing reliability of the "strength of weak ties," providing a locality with more flexibility toward social changes (Granovetter 1973).

These are meaningful differences between the two cities in the different levels of migrant work opportunities. As a consequence of Bersani's law (40/1998), which liberalized and regularized self-employment, Senegalese entrepreneurs have found significantly improved business opportunities. It is in the province of Ravenna that Senegalese entrepreneurial activities took off. Indeed, in 2003, with 253 enterprises, the Senegalese ranked first in self-employment among all foreign communities and these enterprises constituted 19 percent of all migrant businesses (Provincia di Ravenna 2003).

Trade and commerce are now run by many of these entrepreneurs who were the former peddlers. However, many attempts to develop a strategy of self-employment in other economic sectors fail because of the lack of training in how to maintain a business activity within a complex and competitive labor market. Furthermore, this labor market is characterized by occasional episodes of discrimination, which makes it more difficult for Senegalese entrepreneurial adventures to survive. In addition, the transnational predispositions of many Senegalese migrants, which facilitate economic activities such as trade and import-export, may be more problematic in other kinds of employment.

Indeed, the possibility of longer holidays, which would permit workers to stay in Senegal for a couple of months, is often the subject of complex negotiations and bitter conflict within the work environment. There are cases in which a migrant worker has left a full-time permanent job to be able to have enough time to travel and visit Senegal. In addition, there are also bosses who ask workers to sign letters of resignation in advance to be used in these cases or who lay them off when they leave for an extended time. These are illegal practices, which substantiate the accusations of exploitation often made by Senegalese workers. Although appreciated as hard workers, Sengalese are sometimes seen with suspicion because of their orientation toward Senegal.

Restructuring and Rescaling: The Collapse of Global and Local Dynamics

To return to the question of superdiversity, which we raised at the beginning of the chapter, migrants in cities and villages of Emilia Romagna comprise a broad range of different groups: Polish or Romanian transnational domestic workers who spend some months in Italy and some months in countries of origin; Senegalese transnational street sellers; Moroccan transnational families; Chinese entrepreneurs; Indian Sikhs working in agriculture; and Albanian and Moroccan nurses, to mention just a few.[3]

Along with the heterogeneity of origins, another important and structural phenomenon of migration in the Emilia Romagna region is the dispersed presence of migrants across the region's landscape: mountains, countryside, smaller cities, and major cities. All of the 341 *comuni* (the smallest administrative unit) in Emilia Romagna have been shaped by a relatively substantial number of migrants. That also means that while in absolute terms bigger cities are home to higher numbers of migrants, the picture may change when we examine the percentage of a locality that is migrant. In 2004, the small village of Luzzara, near Reggio Emilia, saw its migrant population reach 14 percent of the total (1,312 migrants in a total population of 8,890).

The reasons for heterogeneity and also for a wide dispersal of migrants across the region reflect the contours of the productive system, which, as described above, is organized in interconnected districts that are currently experiencing a deep restructuring through the recruitment of cheap and unprotected labor in order to be competitive on a global market. The increasing demand for domestic and care workers in small villages that have been abandoned by the younger local population further explains the dissemination of migrants. Finally, migrants settle in villages because racism and very high rents prevent them from finding accommodations in city. In sum, either they are obliged to rely on their employers' willingness to provide them with accommodations or they end up living in remote villages in the mountains or countryside where prices are more affordable. Recent surveys have verified that in the major provinces where migrants live (Bologna, Modena, Reggio Emilia), families tend to settle in the countryside or in the mountains while singles live in cities.

The case of Sassuolo, referred to at the beginning of the chapter, offers an example of how rescaling processes, affected by neoliberal capitalism, induced a scalar repositioning of a small locality that progressively assumed the features of a global city, impacting on migration dynamics. Sassuolo is a small city near the bigger locality of Modena, where over the course of fifteen years migrants came to represent 10 percent of the total population of forty thousand. This figure is particularly significant if compared with the 6.7 percent growth in the much larger city of Bologna. Sassuolo has historically been a major producer, for both the local and the global market, of ceramics, a sector where the presence of migrant workers became crucial in the course of the nineties. The vast majority are Moroccans, followed by Albanians, Ghanaians, Tunisians, and Turks but also including Romanians, Filipinos, Chinese, and Indians. In this industry they usually work in the semiskilled jobs that the locals have rejected but that offer them the possibility to get a salary through a regular job and therefore to access the regularization process through which, periodically, hundred of thousands illegal migrants have received a resident permit to remain in Italy.

Nonetheless, migrants in Sassuolo are not always lucky enough to find permanent jobs; most often they are employed under very flexible and low-paid working conditions in jobs that involve heavy factory shifts and very long working days, necessitated by the requirements of a globalized local economy. Indeed, a study conducted in Sassuolo showed that migrants' jobs are rarely permanent and are characterized by an extreme flexibility (Marra 2003). The high number of migrants, their employment in a local economy that is increasingly confronted with global challenges, their confinement to marginalized and deprived neighborhoods, and the ensuing stigmatization and discrimination stemming from their spatial segregation have transformed a small locality like Sassuolo into a global city. Rescaling and restructuring are primarily visible in the reorganization of social policies, where voluntary organizations, the Roman Catholic Church, and the third sector deliver most of the social services provided to migrants. The case of Sassuolo gives us a hint of the sense of diffuse insecurity that both locals and migrants experience as a consequence of global economic restructuring, global mobility, and the general crisis of welfare. The result is that in popular discourse migrants are now associated not only with irregular trade but also with petty crime. Recent studies and surveys have shown that fear, distrust, and stigmatization of migrants are now more widespread in the countryside than in cities like Bologna (Città Sicure, 2004).

Sassuolo is now home to second-generation children of first-wave migrants who are getting organized in cultural and religious terms via associations and organizations such as the Giovani Musulmani d'Italia. The association was founded in 2001 at the national level and now has hundreds of members and several branches in different cities and villages in Italy (Salih 2004; Frisina 2005). Its main purpose is to become a frame of reference for young Muslims born or brought up in Italy who want to become active participants in the society in which they live. The organization itself operates simultaneously through local, national, and transnational levels. The same members who operate within the association at the local level in order to bring their concerns to a local audience also take part through their leadership in European interreligious dialogues that promote citizenship and cultural and religious rights. Many young Muslims talk about their dedication to volunteer civic activities such as supporting the elderly and protecting the environment. They stress how important it is that their involvement in the local public sphere should complement their active participation in and identification with the transnational public sphere.

• • •

As Brenner and Theodore (2002a, 375) remind us: "The creative destruction of institutional space at the urban scale does not entail a linear transition from a generic model of the 'welfare city' towards a new model of the 'neoliberal city.' Rather, these multifaceted processes of local institutional change involve a contested, trial-and-error searching process in which neoliberal strategies are being mobilized in place of specific forms and combinations in order to confront some of the many regulatory problems that have afflicted advanced capitalist cities during the post-1970s period" (2002a, 375).

Noting the impact of multifaceted scaling processes in the Emilia Romagna region, we have tried to show the multiple and fragmented implications and outcomes that rescaling has on the various pathways of incorporation into local receiving societies. Economic restructuring, uneven development, and differentiation shape migrants' dispersed settlement, the difficult implementation of housing and migration policies, moral panic, and a growing sense of insecurity. Local economic history and multiple transnational relations are affecting and affected by local migration contexts.

This chapter has paid attention to how a process of scalar repositioning has shifted a traditionally flourishing economy from one based on locally interconnected industrial districts of small and medium industries working in synergy with the local governments toward a fragmented and globalized economic landscape, within a context of welfare rescaling processes. Migrants participants in the labor force became a vital element in the context of this shift in the political economy of the region, upholding the global competition that the local economy began to confront at the end of the eighties. In the context of the Emilia Romagna region, two noteworthy side effects of restructuring and rescaling dynamics have been the erosion of the power of the nation-state in the governance of migration and the simultaneous multiplication of local and regional actors in the management of migration, shaping notions of incorporation and citizenship rights. Indeed, the unfolding of global economic restructuring at the local level and the consequent arrival of substantial numbers of migrants in a relatively short period of time constitute the framework within which the region took an active step in a process of withdrawing from the national governance of the migration phenomenon.

However, even within a region such as Emilia Romagna, which is particularly homogenous in terms of economic development and political culture, there is quite a significant variation with regard to the effects of rescaling policies at the intersection with migrants' incorporation strategies. Rimini and Ravenna, but also smaller cities like Sassuolo, provide different vantage points from which to note the importance of "theorizing locality," allowing us to observe the varying ways that rescaling processes intersect with migrant local and transnational incorporation patterns and strategies. As Glick Schiller and Çağlar suggest in chapter 4 of this book, a scalar perspective allows us "to analyze the dynamics of locality in interaction with power hierarchies. . . . The concept of scale offers us a framework with which to analyze the structures and dynamics of cities or urban zones in close relations to processes of capital accumulation that are not necessarily confined within the states. . . ." As Brenner argues in chapter 2, the notion of scale as developed by political geographers has proven to be a crucial one in order to decipher the ways in which modern capitalism is constituted and operates through "its differentiation among local, regional, national, transnational, and global geographical units." Rescaling processes therefore call attention to how "inherited scalar arrangements are being challenged and reworked." With this in mind, our focus is on the ways in which transnational migrant women and men are incorporated in contexts where global political and economic processes are instituted locally and are affecting local economies.

One of our purposes was to demonstrate that the rescaling processes affecting the cities where migrants live have a significant impact on their local and transnational incorporation strategies and possibilities. One example is the particular way in which the demand for domestic and care workers is framed in the local contexts. Rescaling processes and the subsequent withdrawal of the state from some parts of the welfare state has brought forward a twofold process. On the one hand it has led to the allocation of household and care work to highly transnational, often "irregular" migrant women. These women, whose labor serves to subsidize neoliberal restructuring, are by now a normal presence in small villages and cities in the region's countryside. On the other hand, rescaling has forged the multiplication of local actors who, often through the use of resources acquired from the European Union, are entitled to provide services to an extremely diversified, dispersed, and varied migrant population in the region. Rescaling has also reinforced the regional scale as the most legitimate scale in managing migration.

We have highlighted how, because of the effects of rescaling processes, the tensions typical of global cities are now relocated in relatively thriving small cities or villages in Emilia Romagna, leading to social conflicts and urban and spatial segregation but simultaneously to the emergence of new power and citizenship struggles and discourses by a multiplicity of actors who seek to make transnational identities fit into local strategies of incorporation. This is certainly the case for young Muslims organizing in Sassuolo, who articulate their quest for citizenship at local and transnational levels, but also for Senegalese, who may choose self-employment rather than the precarious jobs offered in Ravenna and Rimini in order to be able to move transnationally.

We have observed the transformations stemming from rescaling processes that affect the region's social, economic, and urban landscape and that convincingly demonstrate that, as Glick Schiller and Çağlar argue (chapter 1, 4, and 10), all cities are global; there exists no nonglobal city.

Notes

1. See, for example, Cole (1997) on North Africans in Sicily and Carter (1997) on Senegalese in Turin.

2. In the United States, Roger Rouse (1995, 366) has defined this new stage in the relations of production as a "reconfiguration of the landscape of socio-economic experience" symbolized by the shift in the strategies of capital accumulation from the multinational corporations, where self-contained processes of production were basically located in different countries, to the era of transnational corporations that distribute a single economic process in various countries and reduce the time of technological communication between the different places and phases of production.

3. Others are North Africans, 25.1 percent; Southeast Asians, 17.8 percent; sub-Saharan Africans, 10.2 percent; and Latin Americans, 4.9 percent. The picture of heterogeneity of migrants' backgrounds is confirmed in the statistics on the country of origin: the biggest "community" is the Moroccan (18 percent), followed by Albanian (13.7 percent), Tunisian (6.4 percent), Romanian (6 percent), Chinese (5.1 percent), Ukrainian (4 percent), Pakistani (3.1 percent), and Indian (2.9 percent). This is followed by a smaller percentage of communities that come from Sri Lanka, Bangladesh, Moldavia, Macedonia, and Montenegro. Following chain migration and job opportunities, moreover, some national groups ended up settling in specific areas, such as Ghanaians in Modena, Equadorian women in Piacenza, and, most notably, Senegalese in Rimini and Ravenna (Regione Emilia Romagna 2005).

Chapter 8

The Campaign for New Immigrants in Urban Regeneration

Imagining Possibilities and Confronting Realities

JUDITH GOODE

In 2001, Philadelphia city councilman James Kenney issued "A Plan to Attract New Philadelphians," a call to welcome immigrants to the city, as a solution to the city's decline. The report, using the material prepared by the Pennsylvania Economy League (hereafter referred to as the Kenney/PEL report) in 1995, was followed by council hearings and media attention. This new initiative was the latest in a series of visions for revitalizing a city hit hard by deindustrialization. Searching for rescaling strategies that would reposition the city in a global urban hierarchy, Philadelphia competed with other cities to "enhance the locational advantages of their territorial jurisdictions as maximally competitive nodes in the world economy" (Brenner 1999b, 440). The campaign for immigrants was one of many moves to "go global" by orienting the city to a global scale of financial and human capital circulation. To do this, they used the same playbook of neoliberal urban projects that other large American cities had used: Jason Hackworth (2007) has identified these as corporate invasion, privatization, gentrification, and public-private revitalization.

Philadelphia, along with its inner-ring suburbs, is experiencing continuing population loss greater than the national trend. The city's population decline over the previous four censuses has steadily lowered its consistent twentieth-century rank as the fourth largest U.S. city to its current sixth position, with a further drop in rank likely by the next census as southwestern metropoles grow. Only one other major U.S. city, Detroit, has more precipitously declined in population. The Philadelphia case also illustrates the significant distinction between mere size and scalar position.

There is a need to disentangle size and scale in discussions not only of global cities, where they are commonly conflated, but also in cities that currently stand outside that classification. Philadelphia's large size is a product of its historical position in earlier world systems. Through the campaign for new immigrants, city leaders are attempting a jumping of scale (Swyngedouw 1992; see also Smith 1991) by increasing the city's economic and social connectedness to key sites in the global power structure. This chapter follows Brenner and Theodore (2002b, 349) in locating the pathways for new immigrant incorporation in the "contextual *embeddedness* of neoliberal restructuring projects...produced within national, regional and local contexts defined by the legacies of inherited institutional frameworks, policy regimes, regulatory practices, and political struggles."

Trying to raise its global and national profile within the processes of neoliberal restructuring, the city has tried to hide one of its number one standings. Philadelphia has the highest proportion of families living below the poverty line among the ten largest U.S. cities, creating both labor force and public safety concerns. This poverty disadvantage is never discussed in venues oriented to investors, tourists, or middle-class consumers and has even receded from recent local political campaigns that celebrate a city on the move. However, in nationally and internationally distributed popular media, Philadelphia is frequently represented through sensationalized media as a dark and criminalized place exemplifying postindustrial decline. This image marks the city as a place of drugs, racial conflict, and danger. In sensationalized news and fictional coverage, angry white working classes engage racial minorities in physically blighted, drug-infested neighborhoods.[1]

The "Turnaround" City: On the Move Again

Philadelphia's size/scale paradox—its large size and low scale effectivity—is a result of its historical scalar trajectory. Philadelphia held a primary global position as the major port and production center in the Atlantic littoral during the mercantile colonial and early federal eras. At that time it was central to the seventeenth- and eighteenth-century triangle trade circuits between England and the Caribbean. Originally the nation's political capital, political centrality and the symbolic and economic capital that accrued was lost to Washington, D.C., in the early federal period. The city became a national and global manufacturing center in the late nineteenth-century industrial capitalist expansion, building on a critical mass of textile mills (Scranton 1983) in the early nineteenth century. Native-born workers, and later the large mid-century wave of Irish immigrants, worked in the mills. By the end of the nineteenth century, the city had been displaced as the dominant U.S. financial center and port by the ascendance of New York.

Capital-intensive heavy manufacturing developed at the time was led by the production of transportation equipment and other capital goods as well as by a larger mass of textile plants.[2] Although the city's industrial plants employed the new wave of 1880–1920 labor immigrants from peripheral eastern and southern Europe (as well as internal rural migrants), Philadelphia was replaced by New York as the major East Coast immigrant gateway city. Deindustrialization in Philadelphia began earlier than in other U.S. cities when manufacturing failed to recover from the Great Depression, and the city experienced a postwar loss of population and scale when naval activities declined. Its diversified industrial base was centered on easily transferable textile production and heavy industries concentrated in old, increasingly obsolete transportation technologies such as railroad cars and trolleys. Rapid deindustrialization followed in the late twentieth century. Today, the city's relatively large size masks a decline in scalar position, which has important implications for immigrant recruitment, retention, and modes of incorporation.

At the same time, the escalation of imagemaking in Philadelphia masks the loss of effectivity and the high rates of economic inequality and poverty. The city is celebrated in national media as the "Next Great City" or as a city of "Great Expectations" in the local press and national magazines, and branded by a striking new skyline and a panoply of luxury hotels, while in popular culture it has an opposing reputation as a destitute war zone. These disjunctive images mirror an increasing wealth gap that is often conflated with depictions of racism, since Philadelphia is one of the few U.S. cities with demographic (and electoral) parity between whites and blacks. The striking absence of popular nativism as a reaction to the official call for immigration is explained by the relatively small number of immigrants, their invisibility prior to the 1990s, and the subtle valorization by whites and middle-class blacks of immigrant work ethics and family structures over those of native-born poor people of color (Goode 1990, 1998). At the same time, black political leaders who need local support to sustain their power see advantages in allying with immigrant people of color (Goode 1998). As a result, with a few exceptions, there is little public anti-immigrant fervor in the city.

The fact that Philadelphia has been a major colonial and industrial city makes it easier to invoke visions for its future as a world-class city. Talk of a global strategy was initiated in the late 1980s and marks a break from earlier campaigns to reverse suburbanization that emphasized bringing back former residents who had moved to the suburbs. Today, city-sponsored campaigns for higher rankings often link cosmopolitan high-end lifestyles to repackaged versions of the city's colonial history as a cosmopolitan political and economic center, as in a 2008 "Ben Franklin in Paris" exhibit. These campaigns use rhetorical slogans to insist that a can-do spirit will restore the city's former glory. A recent hyperbolic op-ed piece in the city's major newspaper, coauthored by the governor, the mayor, and the head of a major foundation, is illustrative: "So move over, Chicago, make way, L.A. and step aside New York—Philadelphia has the vision, enthusiasm and, yes, the attitude to take center stage" (*Philadelphia Inquirer*, May 5, 2006, A19).

Another marketing campaign generates an unofficial public buzz about a new role for the city as the "sixth borough," or an affordable bedroom community for New Yorkers. Beginning as a local realtor campaign to attract New York commuters, the story was picked up by the *New York Times* and generated a local alternative media buzz. Such a strategy, while it might increase the size of the affluent local consuming population, would lower the city's scale or global connectedness, making Philadelphia subordinate to New York's political economy. This serves as a good example of the confusion between achieving population size and rescaling.

Imagining Immigrant Contributions to Philadelphia

Philadelphia's experience with immigrants differs from those of the commonly designated global cities (Sassen 1991) or gateway cities (Waldinger 2001). Today, with its reduced scalar position, the city ranks much lower as an immigrant destination than its former counterparts, which it still considers its peers. In the wake of the 1965 immigration reform, Philadelphia has been experiencing immigrant settlement at a much slower rate than its rank size would indicate. The city population is only 9 percent foreign-born as compared with over 30 percent for Los Angeles, New York, and Chicago—cities with sustained global reach.

Philadelphia's experience with immigrant community formation and processes of incorporation, as shown below, must be understood within the framework of two different phases of the political-economic restructuring processes. In the 1970s and 1980s, newcomers—Southeast Asians (late 1970s) and Soviet refugees (early 1980s), along with Korean, South Asian, Caribbean, and Central and South American merchant capitalists and laborers—came to the city as it attempted to recover from deindustrialization and white suburban flight. Mercantile migrants found opportunities to invest in vacant shopping strips, subcontracting workshops, and abandoned residential spaces of the deindustrializing city. After initial gentrification stalled in the mid-1980s, it revived in the 1990s, bolstered by a more spectacular vision of a cosmopolitan city based on knowledge workers, hyperconsumption, and hypergentrified space. The new vision required a bifurcated labor market composed of the creative classes and flexible contingent low-wage labor to support their lifestyles. New migrants included upscale knowledge workers from Europe, Asia, and Africa as well as working-class migrants, especially from Mexico, Africa, and the Caribbean. Reflecting these experiences, public discourse has tended to avoid the signature representations of immigrants as illegal, criminal, or costly tax and service drains that are embedded in many debates about immigration policy. The mayor, city boosters, and the Kenney/PEL report imagine and valorize immigrants as contributors to or even saviors of the city, in contrast to a native-born underclass. The existence of a racialized native underclass allows newly forming immigrant communities to self-identify in opposition to it.

Discussions of immigrants envision three distinct classed roles for them, each providing solutions for the city's historically developed disadvantages. Immigrants are represented first as a cosmopolitan creative class; second, as developers of inner-city poor neighborhoods—small scale, hardworking mom-and-pop merchants and landlords; and finally as reliable low-wage labor in the new spaces of consumption. The Kenney/PEL report demonstrates that immigrants to Philadelphia have significant cultural capital, possessing higher average years of education than their counterparts in New York, Washington, Boston, San Francisco, and Chicago. This differential, as we see below, is related to the significance of universities and hospitals as engines of growth in the city. In light of a perceived scarcity of highly skilled knowledge workers, a situation often bemoaned when mainstream media such as the *Philadelphia Inquirer* and *Philadelphia Magazine* talk about the future of the city, the immigrant flow to Philadelphia is viewed as desirable.

Immigrants are also imagined (on the basis of the 1970s and 1980s waves) as bringing small-scale merchant capital for mom-and-pop enterprises and are described as working to save crumbling neighborhoods. By buying and rehabilitating abandoned homes and shops, they are seen as providing stabilization by serving as middleman minority merchants and landlords in dangerous low-income neighborhoods. The Kenney/PEL report refers to a correlation study that shows that housing values go up in high immigrant neighborhoods and implicitly employs the widespread assumptions that immigrants' work ethics and family structures are superior to those of the native-born underclass, portrayed as subject to welfare dependence. This view is echoed in the following editorial in the city's upscale booster *Philadelphia Magazine*: "In practically every neighborhood of Philadelphia, you will find thriving Asian small businesses. The men and women who spend 18-hour days in their storefronts are driven by the ethic of hard work; they sustain themselves through close family relationships" (Lipson 1987, 1).

Similarly, the Kenney/PEL report views immigrants as virtuous laborers in an indirect indictment of the native-born, poor people of color who are often blamed for the declining fortunes of the city. This makes them replacements for what Gregory (1998, 135) refers to as workers who have been hyperstratified by being "immobilized or locked up in the underground economy, and the putative cycle of welfare dependency" (and literally locked up in prisons). All of these images and assumptions about immigrants need to be more closely examined against their actual experience within the contingent processes emerging in the city. In this chapter, I will use ethnographic data framed by historical events and processes to look at how immigrants are actually participating in and being affected by the many neoliberal market-privileging projects through which the city strives to rescale itself.

Immigrants within Recent Rescaling Projects

Since the 1990s, Philadelphia's major public-private rescaling projects relate the increased political economic role of universities and related health care institutions that have become central to the city's demography, space, and economy in the absence of large-scale corporate control and command centers. Universities and medical facilities lure global investment, knowledge workers, and the creative classes. Upscale populations, including immigrants, both produce and consume gentrified residential spaces and landscapes for consuming goods and amenities like entertainment and culture. Furthermore, official state-sponsored anti-poverty programs, like enterprise zones in the city, operate to sanitize and beautify spaces adjacent to gentrified areas to mask and contain poor working-class zones.

Other immigrants are becoming incorporated in less officially sponsored ways. Some are operating within local spaces not targeted by public-private ventures, which are driven by the mayor's or ward leader's patron/clientist support or through grassroots place-based community activism.

Using a framework that looks at immigrant social relations and practice from within specific restructuring of geographic spaces and institutions, I argue that migrants are incorporated into the city's rescaling projects in variable ways shaped by the constraints and opportunities of these rescaling strategies. I examine the roles that immigrants play symbolically and materially. Why does the dominant discourse about immigrants position them as saviors of the city—cosmopolitan, respectable, and hard-working—rather than as criminals, undeserving of rights and scapegoated for all social ills, as is often the case in immigration debates? What roles do class and race play in this? What effect do these preexisting structures have on the spatial, social, and political incorporation of immigrants into this rustbelt city? How salient is ethnicity in structuring immigrant incorporation? How do alternative rescaling projects provide different experiences and different possibilities for alliances and action?

Rescaling Regimes: Back to the City versus Going Global

Reversing Suburbanization

During the 1960s and 1970s, before post-1965 immigration was significant in the Philadelphia region (Goode and Schneider 1994), the core city lost status as a corporate control center for both old labor-intensive manufacturing and new capital-intensive industrial sectors such as chemical/pharmaceuticals and finance (banking and insurance). These activities relocated in response to tax incentives offered to them by regional edge cities or other metropolitan areas following mergers and acquisitions often involving transnational corporations.

Prior to the 1980s, before widespread frameworks for understanding global restructuring had developed, Philadelphia's revitalization goals, like those of other deindustrialized rustbelt cities, were expressed in terms of bringing back the financial institutions, corporate headquarters, and suburbanized middle-class workers that had left. In the 1960s Philadelphia began a "back to the city" campaign to revitalize the downtown and bring back suburbanites. The campaign was part of a larger political reform movement, which successfully associated the city's decline with the corruption of the Republican machine. The victorious Democratic coalition was led by white elite reformers, in alliance with an emerging black political leadership and established white working-class ward leaders. The political argument made to justify public investment in gentrification was initially Keynesian—promising that the tax base would be restored to provide social services to the increasingly large number of poor and working-class residents.

We can now identify these projects of the Democratic takeover, spatially realized in the 1960s and 1970s, as early "growth machine" politics in Philadelphia in which the former manufacturing elite leadership was replaced by large-scale financial and real estate development interests linked to local machine politics (Logan and Molotch 1987). Philadelphia's master planner, Edmund Bacon, emphasized redesigning the central business district, gentrification, and transportation projects that better linked suburban commuters to the center. The first major state project, the gentrification of Society Hill in the 1960s and 1970s, utilized federal urban renewal funding, nicknamed "urban removal" by its critics. Neil Smith (1996) has analyzed the project as one of the earliest examples of the use of public subsidies to aid private capital accumulation. In place of a poor black row-house neighborhood, apartment towers designed by IM Pei and fortresslike modernist homes joined newly renovated colonial homes in the area where the city had initially grown up along the Delaware. The development of Society Hill was publicly narrated in terms of restoring the city's historic preeminence and the return to the city of good "old money" families rather than as a move to disrupt the city's conservative image by connecting it to the world. Smith found an absence of a network of local resident institutions to mount a protest. A wave of real estate speculation and upscale housing renovation followed in the 1970s and early 1980s adjacent to Society Hill (Queen Village).

Because these later projects were seen in class terms as benefiting only downtown interests and suburbanites, they did encounter organized neighborhood opposition. Local protests ensued against banks and developers. These protests relied on the same system of block organizations, tactics, and practices used in protests against other state actions, such as the construction of new highways through old neighborhoods that displaced local populations and the city's withdrawal of local education, police, and fire services. Such local actions ultimately became linked in a citywide coalition. One area in which these opposition activities were most successful was in limiting the degree of physical expansion of the two largest universities, the University of Pennsylvania (Penn) and Temple University, in the 1970s (discussed in the next section.)

How did immigrants figure in these processes? Post-1965 immigrants to Philadelphia were not significantly visible in public discourse until the 1990s. The population was small and highly clustered in limited areas that had become available as a result of industrial and residential abandonment. One interesting example was the formation of the Spanish-speaking community as a buffer between whites and blacks in an abandoned industrial edge. Another example was the settlement of Korean merchants in abandoned shopping strips in poor neighborhoods where local organizations subsequently used boycotts to force employment of local residents (Goode and Schneider 1994).

Most of the other immigrants at this time were official refugees from the Soviet Union and Southeast Asia, a category that is overrepresented in Philadelphia, reflecting the nearby Fort Indiantown receiving center. A federal deconcentration policy made Philadelphia with its small immigrant population and abandoned spaces an attractive site for refugee sponsorship and settlement. Since sponsoring organizations place refugees in housing, they tended to create spatial clusters of refugees as well as organizational links. These were built through mandated self-governing mutual assistance associations and designated social service agencies (Schneider 1988). This had the effect of politically organizing immigrants in official state panethnic blocs such as Southeast Asians (Tran 2001) and in panethnic cultural nationalist movements such as Latino and Asian rights initiatives that offered opportunities to protest and voice demands.

The World-Class City: 1990s to Present

By the 1990s, the core city had become progressively poorer. Moreover, many of the institutional bases of the local elites who had spearheaded Society Hill development and had long-term interests in downtown property had disappeared; banks, insurance companies, and department stores had all been incorporated into differently scaled conglomerates that governed from afar and could easily disinvest and relocate. In addition, the city had become more politically isolated from its surrounding region in spite of the many calls for regional metropolitan development strategies. Philadelphia continued to be surrounded by 353 separate political jurisdictions—suburban municipalities—that themselves differed in class and racial composition. Some businesses and residents in inner-ring suburbs remained strongly linked to the city. However, those in edge cities to the west, south, and north could easily link not only to Philadelphia but also to competing metropolitan areas for in-person business and financial services and for the personal consumption of upscale goods and entertainment.

Since the mid-1990s, new forms of state-subsidized gentrification have become rampant, this time in the name of outreach to a global free market and economy. Calls to make Philadelphia a world-class city replaced talk of reversing suburbanization as global competition for transnational capital investment, sister cities, and visitors become dominant. Significant public money from local and state coffers was invested in a convention center and a tourist office whose budget surpassed that for core social services. City boosters gave priority to designing and developing the city's public space to symbolically communicate turnaround, and to create amenities for more cosmopolitan consumers. By the mid-1990s, public space was increasingly privatized and stalled gentrification reenergized through public investment such as a ten-year tax abatement on new condominium construction.

Ideas such as Richard Florida's popular theory that creative classes would revitalize cities meant that any strategy to attract new and "better" laborers or residents could be justified. Simultaneously, the state increasingly withdrew from social provisioning in deference to market mechanisms, placing its schooling, social services, and health care in the private sector and thereby creating a disconnect from concerns with poverty and social justice. New provisioning came in the form of technologies of self-reform for the poor—who would be subject to increased discipline if they failed to succeed.

Recent campaigns to attract upscale populations involve creating a national magazine "buzz" about Philly food or architecture, and well-publicized policing programs to assuage anxiety about public safety. During the administration of Mayor Ed Rendell (1992–2000), downtown projects redesigned the skyline to signal turnaround. This was followed by state investment in landscapes for upscale lifestyle consumption—a downtown Avenue of the Arts, two new stadiums, and several failed attempts at targeting nightlife and luxury living on the two river waterfronts. More privatization of space followed the creation of a center city district, modeled on New York's business improvement districts (BIDs). In this district, local businesses fund and administer their own clean-up and security operations to remove all the jarring "matter out of place," such as dirt, garbage, and homeless people, that might discourage visitor-consumers.

Economic polarization, poverty, and homelessness interfere with the desire for a new global positioning. During the administration of Mayor John Street (2000–2008), campaigns turned to the knowledge industry. Planners and boosters came to view knowledge-producing universities—which trained expert managers and professional experts outside the center—as well as their dispersed health-care facilities and their respective surrounding neighborhoods, as critical spaces to develop. It is in these sites and institutions that many immigrants have played salient roles and become incorporated.

Rescaling through "Meds and Eds"

In the absence of banking and corporate control and command headquarters—leading forces of rescaling in global cities—universities and hospitals play the role of instruments of urban rescaling and global connection in Philadelphia's postindustrial restructured landscape. They become dominant actors in the labor and real estate markets, as well as repositories of symbolic (prestige) and cultural (expertise) capital. In the 1970s, their expansion as part of federal sponsorship of laboratories and scientific projects related to the Cold War led them into conflict with local residents (O'Mara 2005). In the 1990s, as neoliberal partners with the local state, they were engaged in systematic and often co-opting linkages with surrounding local community groups through partnerships. While nonprofit themselves, they attracted corporate capital investment to local spaces, acted as patrons for community projects, and generated jobs and wage taxes.

Institutions of higher education and health care are the most global and cosmopolitan institutions in the city. Today they serve as critical nodes in webs of global connections and are key to the current booster campaign for growing the knowledge industry and creative classes. They also lure high-end national and global retailers to the city by transforming their surrounding areas into destination consumption spaces (Ruben 2003; Shumar 2006). "Meds and eds" thus play an important role in immigrant incorporation for immigrants with high levels of education and expertise as well as for low-wage workers who are either employed by or live within the zones dominated by these institutions. In the 1970s the postwar spatial expansion of the universities was rebuffed by organized neighborhood opposition at the same time that their demographic expansion was limited by the end of the baby boom and the crisis in global capital. Since the 1990s, universities and hospitals have become the central engines in the rescaling of the city, especially since they are anchored by large and specialized physical plants that are not easily transferable. Today, for example, Penn is an active participant in downtown development. The campus, across the Schuykill River from the southwest corner of the downtown, exercises increasing control through its real estate ownership and through its high-end consumers of housing and retail and office space.

Within the general place- and race-based patronage politics (crony capitalism, pay-to-play), in spite of their nontaxable land status the large city universities are clearly positioned to get what they need from the local political machine (space and deregulation) in exchange for symbolic capital. Local residents and largely immigrant vendors were silenced by Mayor Street when they appeared at the city council to protest a bill to create and give the University of Pennsylvania the private, autonomous status of special district, such as the center city district discussed above. This would have created a self-governing entity, which could control its area through autonomous planning, taxation, and administration of its own clean-up and security operations. The mayor, speaking to the protesters, said, "We don't care if you don't like the bill. You're not supposed to like the bill. We have an obligation to the second largest employer in Philadelphia. If you don't think that I and the other members of council are conscious of all the economic benefits that flow from that, you're wrong" (Ruben 2003, 195). Penn succeeded in receiving the special status.

However, Penn's clout comes from much more than its role in providing local jobs. It is its status as a nationally oriented, top-tier Ivy League institution, whose board and alumni represent global corporate capital, that gives it a leading edge in the city's campaign to become a competitive global node. Penn's president, Amy Gutman, played a major role in the city's campaign to host the 2016 Olympics. Penn often promotes the university's international reach and its cosmopolitanism by describing its recent successes in competing with others for globally recruited faculty stars and students. Both national and global corporate leadership serve on the university board and link it to outside wealth.

Universities and Neighborhood Development

Universities are also enlisted to contribute to the blight removal and economic development of the declining neighborhoods in which they are located. They do this by changing the built environment, maintaining order through their private security forces, and replacing the local resident population. Penn contributes to the city's neighborhood development mission in largely black West Philadelphia by replacing blighted structures with the development of an upscale destination shopping zone and developing a mortgage subsidy program for faculty, staff, and students. This program has also been adopted by Temple.

Following the neighborhood opposition of the 1970s, universities made small-scale agreements with the predominantly African American local community groups to hire blue-collar workers for cleaning, maintenance, and landscaping. Those immigrants who participate in low-wage labor activities in universities either are local residents or are working for nonunion subcontractors increasingly used by universities to escape a costly unionized labor force (Ruben 2003). In the latter case, they encounter resentment from the established blue-collar workers fighting to preserve union jobs in the face of subcontracting. In addition, since the troubled 1970s, universities have engaged in outreach and the provision of services to local residents. Local outreach programs are often mislabeled as "reciprocal" or "partnership" processes, which masks the upper hand held by the institutions. Formal partnerships that provide service to the community have divided the local grassroots political leadership into those incorporated into state and market-oriented projects and those in the excluded opposition (Patterson 2006).

Temple University, the city's third largest employer and second largest medical school, is another example. Less wealthy or prestigious than Penn and less connected to conglomerate capital through its board and alumni, Temple University is governed by both the state and private sector and has raised its marketing image from commuter school oriented to local and regional first-generation students to a residential campus with broader class and geographic outreach. Located in a poor black neighborhood, it is engaged in developing its environs with the support of the city and in building well-designed public spaces and bringing social order to the inner city. Temple serves as an anchor for the northward extension of the Avenue of the Arts and related retail expansion. This restructuring was heralded in an article on the front page of the business section of the *New York Times* on May 3, 2006. Headlined "Student Housing Leads an Urban Turnaround," the article linked the university's turnaround to the stimulation of private investment in "one of Philadelphia's most troubled neighborhoods." Temple, along with Penn, was given control of several local schools in the massive privatizing of the system that accompanied a state takeover.

Universities and Immigrants

Universities play a major role in recruiting those "desirable" immigrants discussed in the Kenney report who bring financial and cultural capital from abroad. They are the largest users of H-1 visas that allow foreign professionals to enter and work in the United States and apply for permanent resident status. The hospital staff, particularly the credentialed medical, nursing, and technical staff, is drawn heavily from immigrants and their children. Penn's campaign for recruiting global star faculty has received media attention (*Philadelphia Inquirer,* October 23, 2006, B1). At Temple, more than half the management faculty in the business school is foreign-born, and the same trend exists in biological and information science. The three immigrant populations often cited for their overrepresentation (greater numbers than their national average) in Philadelphia are also groups found in large numbers in university and health-care occupations: East Asians, South Asians, and eastern Europeans. The downtown residential cluster of twelve thousand immigrants near Penn is dominated by East and South Asians (PIUR 2006). This location, within the sphere of influence of Penn and Drexel in the southwestern part of the city reflects the role of universities and medical centers as global magnets. A second non-working-class cluster of immigrants exists in the far northeast section of the city—the heart of Russian refugee resettlement. This cluster is characterized by high levels of education. Interviews in the 1980s with Polish and Russian residents in the northeast indicated large-scale representation in medical and educational institutions (Schneider 1988). Later work in poorer neighborhoods of initial refugee settlement revealed a pattern of relocation in which middle-class Poles and East and South Asian professionals moving upward through attaining stable institutional placements seek more upscale housing (Goode and Schneider 1994).

Universities, hospitals, and biotech firms are settings in which contradictory processes occur vis-à-vis modes of incorporation and ethnic boundaries. Licensing and professionalizing activities minimize the salience of ethnic and national identity by producing a cosmopolitan class. They launch individuals into upwardly mobile careers in which shared class position based on professional privileges, specialized knowledge, collaborative work, mutual identity formation, and intimate sociality (including high rates of cross-national, cross-racial marriages) blurs earlier cultural identity and difference based on nationality and race.

Yet at the same time, universities are centers for representing the city as culturally cosmopolitan. This is accomplished by providing multicultural commodities, especially performances. As universities become the citywide settings for large festivals and celebrations of specific ethnic and religious rituals, a safe form of multiculturalism is provided and embraced in turn by immigrants—professionals-in-training as well as the cosmopolitan native-born. Penn is the site of the largest, most publicized public Hindu celebration in the city. At Temple University, Nigerian faculty created an informal group that provides visa advice as well as festivals for local Yoruba speakers. Students often seek multiculturalism not for understanding but as an applicable life skill in a globalized world (Urciuoli 2003) and as a skill to apply in their professional work. Specific university clinical programs target new populations by providing generic panethnic Asian or Latino services. University cosmopolitanism requires the consumption of diversity and creates the demand for the many new ethnic restaurants dependent on the availability of immigrant capital and labor discussed below.

Moreover, universities incorporate within their leadership a coalition of people of color, both immigrant and native-born, in order to represent themselves as global and multiracial/multicultural. This diverse leadership can be used in many ways. In some instances, their presence legitimates the institutions' role in gentrification and rescaling projects, thereby masking their often devastating economic and political effects on poorer residents of color. At the same time, universities are also sites for promoting universalizing antiracist and social justice movements with national and transnational links. The University of Pennsylvania was an important site in the local "Day without an Immigrant" protests, part of a coordinated national event to protest the Sensenbrenner/King immigration bill. Absence from work and marches through public spaces took place in many U.S. cities during the congressional debates that took place from February to May 2006 to demonstrate the dependence of the nation on immigrant labor. Local Philadelphia events involved a one-day strike and several rallies and marches. They were organized by an educated Mexican labor leader who collaborated with a Filipino activist and reached out to Filipino, Korean, and South Asian workers as well. The central leader had ties to an organized immigration study group at the University of Pennsylvania and a web of Latino and immigrant social service organizations (some organized or staffed by university students), and the Penn campus was used as a site for staging media-oriented activities and recruiting international students as speakers. Television coverage thus both included the usual images of Mexican and Asian unskilled labor and linked them to the legal and bureaucratic difficulties of Penn's diverse international students.

Fig. 5. This mural is located near the special district controlled by the University of Pennsylvania. Profiled as skilled workers and professionals who may be multiracial and multicultural rather than celebrated because of the exotic mix they bring to the city, migrant professionals have been crucial to Philadelphia's efforts to raise the scalar positioning of the city on the basis of the development of its "meds and eds" complex. *The Heart of Baltimore Avenue* (west wall) by David Guinn (Mural Arts Program), 47th and Baltimore Ave., Philadelphia, PA. Photo by Maria Schelle Solano.

One example of the way these contradictions played out can be seen in the case of immigrant food vendors on the Penn and Temple campuses. As both institutions upscaled their surface appearance through design aesthetics (landscaping and architecture), they developed fraught relations with their largely immigrant lunch truck owners whose varied cuisines and convenient locations were important sources of meals and snacks for students, faculty and other staff. Both university administrations considered the trucks to be unsanitary and unsightly and initially outlawed them. Ultimately, both schools set aside a space for vendors under the control of the university after a collaborative political action between students and vendors in the name of social justice presented the vendors as adding a cosmopolitan flavor to the campus (Ruben 2003; *Temple News*, March 16, 2007).

Downscaled Development and Immigrant Incorporation

Shaping Space, Place, Race, Class, and Politics in Philadelphia

The political-economic formation of Philadelphia created a city that became increasingly segregated by race and class. Local spaces were always important political formations in the city, and the ongoing restructuring of the city's economic base and wider economic insertion reshaped these spaces into arenas for past and current immigrant incorporation. There was little class segregation in the colonial and early republican port city (Warner 1987). Class segregation developed in the late industrial capitalist nineteenth century when the elite and middle classes moved to Main Line railroad and streetcar suburbs. Working-class row-house communities solidified around industrial zones. As Catholic immigrants became the dominant working class, parish institutions and schools, as well as settlement houses and mutual aid societies, became the basis of local social life, and sons followed their fathers into the factory and married local women (Yancey, Ericksen, and Juliani, 1976). Moreover, the relatively high rate of home ownership across all classes in the city created both equity and attachment to place.

Places also structured local politics. A local system of place-based, crony clientism developed in working-class electoral wards and still exists as an important local structure. Ward leaders dispensed the resources and political access granted by the Republican machine, which was dominated by privatist industrial and financial elites who turned local affairs over to ward leaders in return for electoral support for tariff and trade issues (Adams et al. 1991; Warner 1987). Race also played a significant role in the city. Philadelphia had a population of locally freed and refugee slaves. Much has been written about how the Irish shared space with blacks in some neighborhoods south of the old city but became channeled separately by political and workplace structures as they moved from being seen as members of a marked racialized category to become accepted as unmarked "whites" in the late nineteenth century (DuBois 1990; Ignatiev 1995; Roediger 1990). In the twentieth century, Philadelphia was a hub in the Great Migration of southern rural blacks, and racial segregation shaped neighborhoods. At the same time, citywide linkages formed under the auspices of Quaker, Jewish, and black religious leaders created some of the earliest fellowship and human relations organizations in the country (Goode and Schneider 1994). Such groups tried to stem the white flight generated by post-World War II suburbanization, but by the 1970s the city had become racially bifurcated into two roughly equal populations—with blacks to the west and whites concentrated in the east.

While it is now clear that disinvestment in local manufacturing, behind-the-scenes financial redlining of working-class neighborhoods, and postwar state-subsidized suburbanization produced the rapid emergence of black-dominated space and landscapes of dilapidation and abandonment that symbolize the city, the behavior and values of racial minorities continue to be the common popular explanation for the decline of the city. At the same time, blacks had become politically active in the city following the civil rights movement and the later black empowerment movements. A black political class began its ascendance in the formal political structures of the city (Countryman 2007). In the postwar years, expanding university and health-care technical needs and requirements for managerial and professional labor helped to produce a growing new black middle class. The increased visibility of this class in politics and service institutions in education and health care masked the parallel escalation of black (as well as Puerto Rican and white) downward mobility produced by plant closings and the loss of unionized jobs. Black movements coupled with later white losses of work opportunities and security ultimately created a corresponding "new ethnicity" movement, which used state-funded museums and parades celebrating Philadelphia's place in the national celebration of the 1976 bicentennial to emphasize the struggles of former European immigrant ethnic groups (Goode 2001; Steinberg 1981).

Given the highly segregated nature of the city (Goldstein 1986), residential space is not readily accessible to immigrants. The small population of immigrants in Philadelphia is highly concentrated in six diverse clusters (PIUR 2006).[3] In two of them, the downtown and northeast cluster discussed above, middle- and upper-middle-class immigrant merchants and professionals live among established whites and are linked to "meds and eds" or the larger-scale merchant development activities discussed below. The remaining four clusters house immigrants from diverse backgrounds who share space with downwardly mobile whites and native-born minorities in spaces outside developing university sites. These neighborhoods are in the sphere of either federal or local economic development projects that displace populations and produce pathways to incorporation through mobilizations or political patronage politics. In other clusters outside current state action, immigrants are producing new commercial and residential spaces.

Federal Economic Development Programs

An example of state-generated economic development that led to organized opposition incorporating immigrants can be found in Kensington, which is adjacent to Northern Liberties, an area just southeast of downtown. Early gentrification first stalled here but was resumed in the 1990s and speeded up to create a millennial focus of residential development for a young creative class.

While post-1970s federal housing and community development programs had created and funded officially recognized local citizen participants through neighborhood action committees (NACs), community development corporations (CDCs), and community trust boards, by the 1990s these local civic structures had become incorporated into the state through a process of auditing and professionalization. They had became more market-oriented and less tolerant of poor residents who saw their space and local social networks in terms of social use value rather than in terms of their exchange value to investors and developers (Goode and O'Brien 2006). Since the 1990s, they have themselves become active in large-scale displacement projects.

Since the city sees Northern Liberties as a magnet for young professional or creative workers, gentrification is encouraged and now encroaches on the neighboring poor area designated as a federal empowerment zone (EZ), where one of the four working-class immigrant clusters is located. EZs formed under President Clinton used participatory structures to involve residents in local development projects. While this specific program has expired, many of the activities have continued through other organizational formats. The American Street EZ was constituted to represent individual residents, enterprises, and organizations of established Puerto Rican, white, and black backgrounds, alongside Latino, Polish, Middle Eastern, and Albanian immigrants through an elected board. Immigrants became incorporated into local fields of social capital through local organizations alongside less formally organized blocks and were linked to CBOs and ward leaders as well as small workplaces where they were workers or customers (Goode 2001).

However, when Mayor John Street merged the resources of the empowerment zone project into his antiblight Neighborhood Transformation Initiative (NTI), projects were redirected to those sectors that attracted large-scale investment capital rather than to opportunities and services for poor households. Under NTI, priority was given to developing green space and redesigning streetscapes, not for resident use but for truck access to serve a planned entertainment, restaurant, and nightlife zone near Northern Liberties. Residents became angry when their aspirations were superseded by the needs of upscale gentrifiers, and the original employment and training goals were deferred. However, it was the use of eminent domain to seize and demolish housing units *owned and occupied* by poor local residents, as well as the ensuing destruction of valuable social capital, that led to the return of oppositional social movements with the potential for linkage to national and international movements.

In these working-class households especially vulnerable to economic downturns, local social relations are essential. These relations are the basis of resource exchange, child care, and safety (through personal surveillance), as well as the point of access to the local party machine or CBO. This social capital helps residents weather economic crises and intense place attachment, both counter to the ethos and practice of development intended to replace current residents with upscaled people. The mobilization against eminent domain abuse began in the EZ centered in one Latino-dominated organization, which reached out to Albanian neighbors and other organized block associations. Many of these had been linked in networks since the activism of the 1970s. These networks held a series of mass community meetings and protest marches and gave testimony to city council. Soon they had linked up with other local immigrants, native-born African Americans, and poor whites. Next they reached out to an activist Indo-Chinese organization from South Philadelphia and two black organizations—one from the West Philadelphia empowerment zone (Caribbean, African, and African American) and one from the North Philadelphia EZ, thus forming class-based coalitions across immigrant and native as well as racial boundaries.

This rapid response soon crossed class lines and became linked to university social justice activists and filmmakers who produced two films and generated more public action and awareness of eminent domain abuse. Moreover, the linking of immigrants, native-born minorities, and poor whites has been sustained for several years and has become part of both national and international networks of antipoverty and peace and social justice activists. The activities of the group have now led it to become affiliated with and draw new tactics and allies from liaisons with the Kensington Welfare Rights Union and the American Friends Service Committee (both internationally oriented social justice movements) as well as with dense university-based social justice activist networks.

Local State Patronage Outreach

Machine politics also remain a key part of the operations of the local state today. Unions and aspiring homegrown developers work within a system of crony capitalism to garner advantages through such mechanisms as no-bid contracts in exchange for campaign contributions and the delivery of votes. Place-based city councilpersons establish local ward electoral bases by developing loyal networks through allocating patronage jobs or city-controlled housing. Frequent scandals and federal investigations of corruption continue to keep this game in the public eye (Maskovsky 2001).

Immigrants in several of the clusters located in poor neighborhoods have also become incorporated through political patronage outreach. Mayor John Street's regime was the first to actively incorporate immigrants into the inner political circle, reaching out to Latinos and to Caribbean and African immigrants. Spanish speakers in one immigrant cluster have created both panethnic Latino networks and cross-ethnic brokerage within the political ward system after using civil rights laws to produce redrawn electoral boundaries and a human relations complaint against their underrepresentation in city government. Mayor Street was the first mayor to incorporate Spanish-speaking leaders as part of his top-level transition and governing administration. While incorporating leaders of the Latino community into the local state symbolizes rising political clout, such participation has also co-opted these leaders and affected the solidarity and common goals of the ethnic community.

During John Street's regime, he and a powerful councilwoman reached out specifically to Caribbean (e.g., Haitian and Jamaican) and African immigrants in heavily black West Philadelphia by forming an office for Caribbean and African affairs in City Hall, and they deploy the practices and rituals of traditional ward organizations based on networks of loyalty and trust. Taking advantage of this outreach, a Liberian-led technocratic development organization has forged relationships with both City Council and the Mayor's office and established itself in a West Philadelphia storefront, where it continues to provide training and social services to African and Caribbean immigrants and native-born blacks, and initiates local development projects.

Immigrant Merchant Capital outside State Projects

Olney and the Italian Market area of South Philadelphia are neighborhoods within two of the working-class immigrant clusters. Neither area is a site of significant city planning or state projects, and it is here that immigrant entrepreneurs are actively contributing to efforts to rescale the city by structuring development in ways that create alternative pathways of collaborative immigrant incorporation. City government welcomes local immigrant capital to declining areas that are not part of downtown hot spots or federal antipoverty programs.

Olney, a former streetcar suburb with a major shopping hub, had been left neglected in the waves of redevelopment that followed deindustrialization. Today it is the residence of downwardly mobile whites and (in descending numerical order) of mixed-nationality Spanish speakers, Vietnamese and Cambodian refugees, Koreans, South Asians, Chinese, and Filipinos. While all groups are represented as merchants in the shopping strip, Koreans are the dominant entrepreneurial group (Goode and Schneider 1994). Olney is both home and investment site for foreign-born realtors, landlords, and merchants, who play a significant role in this space. However, immigrant entrepreneurs vary greatly in the scope of their activities and investments. They include entrepreneurs with single small businesses, or multi-store local chains as well as larger-scale investors in such entities as clandestine sewing factories, malls, banks and insurance agencies, and business brokerages, which often have interurban and transnational reach.

Small proprietors who cater to lower-income neighborhood customers tend to be involved in local civic life through membership in place-based business associations. They are also linked across ethnic groups to multiracial workers and clientele. In the activist 1970s, neighborhood groups formally boycotted Korean merchants who found opportunities in decaying shopping strips until they hired local workers from their customer base. These actions involved both native-born minority populations and other immigrant groups, particularly Spanish speakers. Thus Koreans often hired black and Latino workers and came to see them as buffers between owners and hostile customers. Stable employment and close and trusting relationships resulted (Goode and Schneider 1994). For example, one couple who owned a successful produce business in operation for twenty years first employed a Colombian worker. They then sponsored the green card visas for a brother and cousin whom they eventually hired.

This kind of pan-immigrant solidarity developed in the context of what was mutually perceived as white racism against people of color and the kind of linguistic racialization, a term used by Urciuoli for the systematic social exclusion of Puerto Ricans and other Spanish-speaking immigrants based on imperfect or wrongly accented English rather than skin color (2000). Hiring fellow immigrants went hand in hand with preferring fellow immigrants as a customer base. Without a critical mass of Korean professional and merchant class customers, fellow immigrants are seen as preferable to native-born whites and racial minorities, who are both perceived as biased toward people of color and non-English speakers. However, small entrepreneurs can also be linked to patrons from the larger-scale immigrant investor community that has forged ties to city political machines and national and transnational co-ethnic networks. Such citywide national-origin structures include two Korean associations, the Dominican Grocers Association, and separate Taiwanese, Hong Kong, and ethnic Chinese and Vietnamese networks.

In South Philadelphia, another of the four working-class immigrant clusters is formed in six census tracts surrounding the long-established but declining Italian Market. This area, formerly a warehousing area, was open for investment as retail stores and adjacent small enterprises were abandoned by earlier Italian entrepreneurs. The first foreign-born populations to settle were Vietnamese and Cambodian refugees placed by state-contracted sponsoring agencies. The area was filled with temples, churches, and social service institutions for resident Vietnamese, Cambodian, and Chinese populations. Initially, small-scale enterprises owned by Vietnamese, Chinese, and recently arrived southern Italians replaced the former established Italian owners and incorporated cross-ethnic labor and customers. As Mexican immigration rapidly grew from the 1990s onward, a secondary wave of Mexican chain migrants from Chicago drawn by opportunities in the expanding restaurant industry (Dick 2007) became workers and customers.

When a large public housing project was demolished and no blueprint for future development emerged, larger-scale immigrant investors rapidly transformed the area by constructing markets and restaurants, including national and transnational Asian chains. These outlets now provide food items and cuisine that represent "homeland" to immigrants and "authentic" ethnic cuisine to the growing population of (often university-affiliated) U.S.-born gentry and cosmopolitans. Mexicans continue to migrate and settle in this new area of Asian capital investment and to work here and in new restaurants all over the city.

Larger-scale immigrant developers often bypass local neighborhood organizations and initiate lobbying directly with the entrepreneurial arms of the city, state, and federal government. They work through groups like the Korean American Friendship Society, which reached out to incorporate relevant councilpersons and city government agency representatives as members. They participate in electoral politics by making political contributions to candidates but have been less successful in this domain. Fielding candidates for council positions requires serious multiclass, multiracial alliances. Until the election of 2007, the few Korean candidates, fearing white racism, sought black allies (Goode 1998).

Through these groups, Korean business leaders position themselves both as "transnational citizens" (Ong and Nonini 1997) and as benefactors of the city. As one Korean business leader publicly stated at a Friendship Society meeting, "We have come to make Philadelphia number one again." They look outward to regional, national, and transnational co-ethnic networks and projects. For example, in the 1980s a Philadelphia-based citywide coalition of Korean real estate developers and insurance and business brokers sought to become the regional wholesaler for all Middle Atlantic Korean merchants, such as those from Wilmington, Baltimore, and Pittsburgh.[4] The project to make Olney into a regional Koreatown hub failed because of local resistance but revealed the ways in which the entrepreneurs were embedded in trans-local and transnational Korean networks. This effort also highlighted immigrants' efforts to build networks that reintegrate Philadelphia regionally (Goode 1990, 1998, 2001).

• • •

Philadelphia, relative to other neoliberal cities attempting to find purchase in the rescaling global political economy, is operating from a disadvantaged position that worsened throughout most of the twentieth century. Since the 1970s, city government has relied on neoliberal rescaling projects predicated on a future trickle down of benefits from private wealth accumulation stimulated by public investment. Political leaders have focused on the city's large nonprofit educational and medical institutions and the upscaled populations they attract as their primary strategy for global linkage. The political and corporate leadership looks to immigrants to (1) contribute to the cosmopolitan nature of the city and (2) replace the racialized underclass, who are blamed for most social ills. Their expectations fail to recognize how poverty is produced and how neoliberalism has exacerbated inequality (Goode and Maskovsky eds. 2001).

I have argued that in spite of their overall symbolic valorization, immigrants in actuality become incorporated on both sides of the economic and racial divide—for example, as elite professionals or racialized residents of poor neighborhoods targeted for rescaling. Preexisting race and class formations in Philadelphia influence the choices and actions of immigrants. Civil rights activism forced early Korean entrepreneurs to create jobs for poor local minorities. In this instance, Koreans were seen in class rather than racial terms, as employers who discriminated. Yet, experiencing and fearing white racism, many immigrants of color formed close alliances more easily with the black political class than with white elites. The current black political leadership has reached out to Latino, African, and Caribbean immigrants as part of its patronage-based development team. At the same time, dependence on universities and medical centers as engines of development makes these industries central to both the economics and ideology of the city's rescaling project. With their affiliated medical centers, they have played a major role in the formation of a technical, professional, and managerial black middle class in the city. As market-driven neoliberal institutions, no longer able to serve as gateways to mass class mobility, they are today class-selective.

Multiculturalism is valorized in limited ways on campus, mostly to reinforce class interests. It often represents diversity that in turn symbolizes global cosmopolitanism or an aspect of professional expertise. As universities and medical schools seek to upscale surrounding property values and commercial activity, they welcome class-selected immigrants who join native-born professional/managerial African Americans and the white middle class as participants in institutional gentrification. Through multiracial coalitions and partnerships of university and community agents, they help legitimate the activities that displace racialized working-class residents and immigrant street vendors (until these groups are revalorized as cosmopolitan). They also reduce the clout of blue-collar unions, which oppose lower-paid subcontracted workers who are often immigrants.

On the other hand, a different process develops in the arena of state-sponsored local development projects such as empowerment zones and NTI, where inherited networks and practices of antistate resistance have been mobilized to unite working-class immigrants and native-born in resistance to gentrification through eminent domain. Here boundaries of citizenship, race, national origin, and language are transcended in a movement against the state that eventually links local communities across the city and connects them through the aegis of internationally linked human rights movements. These movements also find support on local university campuses in sites linked to social justice movements critical of increasing global inequality.

I would like to acknowledge support from the Ford Foundation for the Philadelphia Changing Relations Project and the National Science Foundation Program in Cultural Anthropology for the project "Civic Participation in Three Poor Neighborhoods in Philadelphia," as well as support from Temple University. Special thanks go to Michael Katz and Dominic Vitiello, Kathleen Hall, and other colleagues in the Forum on Philadelphia Immigration sponsored by the Penn Institute for Urban Research, as well as to my longtime colleagues and collaborators Jeff Maskovsky, Susan Brin Hyatt, and Jo Anne Schneider and the many talented graduate students in Temple's anthropology program who have contributed.

Notes

1. Such portrayals in print fiction (Steve Lopez's *Third and Indiana*), film (*Rocky, Twelve Monkeys*), and recent TV crime series like *Hack* and *Cold Case* have earned the city a national reputation as "the Badlands." Described as having one of the largest drug supermarkets on the East Coast, Kensington, a Philadelphia neighborhood, was the first site for a recent, heavily publicized police drug cleanup called "Operation Sunrise." An MSNBC documentary entitled "Along Came the Horse" is an especially denigrating depiction that portrays the community as beyond the reach of either police or social service intervention.

2. Jerome Hodos (2002) characterizes Philadelphia from the inception of industrialization (1830s) until the Second World War as a classic "second" city characterized by significant industrial activity, and compares it to Manchester, England.

3. For the purpose of the U.S. census, localities are divided into census tracts. Thirty-three percent of the foreign-born live in fewer than 10 (3 percent) of the city's 365 census tracts. Moreover, a full 90 percent live in a mere 14 percent of the tracts.

4. Interviews with Baltimore merchants confirmed their collaborative participation in this project.

Chapter 9

Rescaling Processes in Two "Global" Cities

Festive Events as Pathways of Migrant Incorporation

MONIKA SALZBRUNN

This chapter presents two empirical examples that address the mutually constituting dynamics between migration and the restructuring and marketing of two global cities, New York and Paris. I focus on festive events as platforms for the negotiation of the inclusion and exclusion of newcomers and the transformation processes experienced by both the migrants and the cities as a result of migration. I use political and cultural events in these two cities as the entry points to understand the different pathways of migrant urban incorporation in these places. This chapter does not take pre-defined ethnic or religious groups as the units of analysis; there is no assumption that people who share a religious or national origin settle as a community. By linking studies of rituals and events in translocal social spaces to an analysis of subjective rescaling processes, this chapter draws attention to the innovative methodological instruments of action theory.

The first case study, the Murid parade in New York, illustrates how the followers of a Sufi group have developed and sought multifaceted relations with local urban institutions and actors. Murids are followers of a Sufi brotherhood founded in the nineteenth century by Sheikh Ahmadou Bamba in Touba (today's Senegal). *Murid* is derived from the Arab term for disciple within a Sufi brotherhood. Murids are members of a *tariqa* (the Arabic word for brotherhood; plural, *turuq*).[1] Paris, New York, and several Italian cities are important nodes in the translocal networks of the Murids. These networks contribute to the outcome of competitive rescaling projects based in both cities. In order to explore the venues of migrant incorporation, I focus on the particular trajectory of a translocal set of networks constituted by the Murids.

Some of the activities of contemporary Murid networks are central to in-corporative events and activities that link migrants to broader social fields within centers of power in Senegal, New York City, Paris, and elsewhere in Europe. Locality is important to members of the worldwide Sufi network. Brotherhoods pay a great deal of attention to places, especially holy places of birth or death of important spiritual leaders. In some cases, the name of a place becomes part of the name of a person.

In particular, this chapter traces the development of a parade celebrat-ing the visits that one of the religious leaders of Murids, Sheikh Mourtada Mbacké, made in order to maintain ties to his pupils in New York City. Al-though based in Senegal for the fifteen years until his death in 2004, Sheikh Mbacké visited religious communities overseas. Certain public events that were not possible in Paris were possible in New York City, and this chapter explores the differences between these two contexts of migrant settlement. Sheikh Mbacké's group embraced particular strategies in its quest to influence local policy decisions (Salzbrunn 2004, 468; Wilson and Rodriguez Cordero 2006, 326). Because religious Sufi transborder networks have developed very local strategies of settlement and incorporation, they are best understood as constituting a transnational field that is shaped by and shapes political pro-cesses in multiple cities and even states (Glick Schiller and Fouron 1999). A strong alliance of these transnational networks contributed to the victory of the Murid Abdoulaye Wade during the Senegalese presidential elections in 2000 (Salzbrunn 2002a, 2004). In both case studies, I apply qualitative meth-ods and embed my results in a broader political, economic, and social context (Petersen-Thumser and Salzbrunn, 1997). I have been following Senegalese migrants' networks since 1994, mainly in France, Senegal, Germany, and the United States.

My second case continues my interest in festive events as political are-nas where inclusion/exclusion and transformation processes are negoti-ated. In the Parisian district of Sainte Marthe, local political struggles are concentrated within festive situations. Through festive events members of a neighborhood are able to resist urban restructuring projects: their collective actions produce a new, geographically defined "we-group," which includes people from various and diverse economic and cultural backgrounds (Salz-brunn 2007a, 2007b). This research is based on ongoing participant observa-tion in the district since 1999: more than 120 observed festive and political events; twenty-three interviews with the presidents and several members of the different associations; and interviews with the local politicians, shop and restaurant owners, and other inhabitants of the district. I demonstrate how through participation in political and cultural events in a city, migrants become actors in both the restructuring and rescaling of the place. It is by taking into account the larger project of restructuring Paris within a globally competitive tourist market that we can understand the different pathways of migrant urban incorporation in a specific gentrifying Parisian neighbor-hood. The second case demonstrates that ethnic origin, which was used as an initial resource within festive events of the district, led to the emergence of a place-based belonging facilitated not by cultural difference but by the efforts to restructure and market urban space.

Focusing on the global cities of New York and Paris allows me to address the following questions. What are the differences in the rescaling processes experienced by both cities and neighborhoods in these cities? What are the different impacts of these processes on the paths and trajectories of migrant transnationalism in these global cities? How do two global cities (Paris and New York) relate to the migrants in different ways? How do the migrants themselves recognize their place in the city vis-a-vis their fellow city dwellers? How do they work out their ties to the city with the other neighborhood dwellers? How do rescaling processes effect the representation of locality and identity in each city? How does the historicity of the neighborhood (the places) shape the ways in which the migrants are being incorporated into the diverse neighborhoods of the urban? Through these research questions I move the study of migrants, global cities, and transnationalism beyond discussions of cultural diversity, cosmopolitanism, and migrants' role in unskilled labor or as ethnic entrepreneurs in the labor economy (Jouve and Gagnon 2006; Kofman 2005a; Lacroix, Sall, and Salzbrunn 2008). In contrast I offer a comparative perspective on migrants as active agents in the restructuring of locality.

"Localizing" Transnational Networks

The field of migration studies has extensively dealt with networks, transnational spaces, and migration fields since the beginning of the 1990s (Glick Schiller, Basch, and Blanc Szanton 1992). More recently, researchers concerned with transnational migration have once again expressed a concern with "the local." However, contained within a shared interest in transnational process and apparently a similar focus on place and space are different perspectives that are worth distinguishing. In addition, by positing a transnational space bounded by a shared national origin or ethnicity, many of the studies have actually reinforced the notion of the naturalness of nation-based identities, reinvigorating methodological nationalism but in a new form (for a critique see Anghel, Gerharz, Rescher, and Salzbrunn 2008; Glick Schiller, Çağlar, and Guldbrandsen 2006). Even when mobility across borders is the central interest of the researchers, it is possible to bound research within national identities in ways that impede an assessment of the relationship between migrants and localities.

Alain Tarrius's work (2002) provides a useful example of the problem. He stresses the primary role of the migration process itself and speaks of the emergence of a "capacity to circulate" (18). By this he means a new capacity of being here and there at the same time and not simply being here or there. While Tarrius's approach allows him to posit that the experience of circulation creates new cosmopolitanisms and the consciousness of a new identity, it leads him to ignore evidence that migrants may remain transnationally connected but simultaneously settle and shape localities of settlement. His focus on circulation leads to a problematic understanding of the migrant experience of localities of settlement. He speaks of a nomadic identity, assuming that these new nomads remain economically dependent exclusively on their place of origin. This assumption is shaped by French migration literature and its engagement with French public policy debates rather than reflecting empirical evidence. Several representatives of French social sciences, namely members of the Migrinter research group [2] have been concerned with independent migrant self-organization. They have facilely assumed that this organization produces a form of empowerment and a political consciousness that is independent of the French nation-state and/or is solely engaged in home-country events and identities (Simon 1996). Tarrius from Toulouse University and other like-minded scholars have failed to examine migrants' multiple ties to and participation in local institutions and social, economic, political, and cultural processes.

Ludger Pries (1996) and Thomas Faist (2000) also identify an emergence of social experiences and identities that goes beyond the sum of the two parts and creates new identities or practices. However, they concentrate not on the process of circulation but on what they posit as transnational space. The term is used to impose a geographic metaphor on the connections, processes, and identities created by people who live across borders. Although space is evoked, the particularity, institutional structures, and history of specific localities are not always a subject of theory or description. Instead, these scholars describe the ways in which cross-border locations are connected through the social networks of migrants. Even though Pries included the importance of elements of the new environment within the transnational social space, the home country seems to be the most important part in the reference system.

Nina Glick Schiller and Ayşe Çağlar (chapter 10; Çağlar 2006; Glick Schiller, Çağlar, and Guldbrandsen 2006) also speak of the local—not to indicate a general sense of multiple rootedness but to call for a specific investigation of the forces that shape specific places. They are concerned with the localities from which migrants and their descendants leave, in which they settle, and to which they are connected by social fields, which often extend across the borders of nation-states. Gildas Simon's concept of polycentered and multi-sited migration spaces that emerge from worldwide networks (1996, 223) is, although not referring to the same literature, close to Glick Schiller's concept of transnational social fields (2005b) but without the stress on the significance of unequal relations of power. Glick Schiller defines a transnational social field as a specific set of networks of ego-centered social relations that are linked to institutions situated within specific places. These fields contain social relations of unequal power constituted by differential access to forms of capital, military force, and means of discursive representation. This approach focuses on social relations and institutions—workplaces, schools, and religious, social, financial, and political organizations that differ in their functions according to their location and that can be empirically studied. Building on this approach, Glick Schiller and Çağlar offer a theorization of locality that brings together a transnational perspective on social relations and the scholarship on the neoliberal rescaling of local urban space.

Translocal Social Spaces: The Importance of Local Living Conditions in the Process of Place-Making

Following Pries's concept of transnational social spaces that takes into consideration the spatialization of the social, and Glick Schiller and Çağlar's work on transnational social fields and localities that emphasizes urban rescaling processes and power relations, I suggest highlighting the importance of specific local living conditions and the process of place-making by adopting the notion of translocal social spaces. This approach allows us to better understand the uneven power within which networks are constituted. Understanding the local context of migration and the way that migrants organize themselves within the new translocal spaces is as important as researching their traditions and customs.

Consequently, I explore the ways in which migrants adapt their strategies of settlement and transnational connection to changing opportunity structures that are available in the specific place of settlement and are a product of the insertion of neighborhoods and cities within larger restructuring processes (Furlong, Biggart, and Cartmel 1996). Understanding the local power relations, the processes and discourses of political lobbying, and the concrete conditions of access to land, property, business, residence permits, etc. is crucial in the implanting of the network within different localities, reaching far beyond a dyadic relation between "home" and "host" countries. The references and contacts of the Murid networks I traced went far beyond their ethnic or national peer group.

If we put aside the use of national states as the "natural" unit of analysis in global contexts and turn from space as a metaphor to an examination of migrants in relationship to specific localities, then we need a new methodological approach. I propose a methodology of actor networks within festive events that facilitates the study of new, inclusive groups within an urban environment. Such groupings may contribute to and be facilitated by transnational social fields. To develop this methodology, I bring together elements of network analysis and event analysis while paying attention to the positioning and restructuring of locality. Once we trace migrants beyond their ethnic connections to other networks present in the locality, we are able to see how networks enable migrants to become rooted in an urban context. Social sciences have produced a vast number of studies focusing on festive events like carnivals (Cohen 1991; Bakhtin 1968; Bausinger 1959; Davis 1975; Ozouf 1976) and on rituals of transgression (Van Gennep 1909; Turner 1982; and the work of Max Gluckman and other members of the Manchester school in the

1940s and the 1950s).[3] The political, social, and economic context determines the evolution of the networks linked to a specific locality. It is particularly useful to trace members of these networks as they negotiate their participation in festive events.

Action theorists have noted that festive events are arenas for local negotiations through which migrants are either included or excluded by institutions and local actors who create, reinforce, change, or block the production of communal feelings; the study of such events makes transformation processes visible. This methodological choice avoids taking a particular ethnic, religious or sociocultural category as an entry point for the study of processes of communitarization. By communitarization, I mean the Weberian approach to group-building processes, *Vergemeinschaftungsprozesse* (Weber 1921, 29). I emphasize here the dynamic character of a group and the emergence of alliances that do not follow ethnic- or religious-based logics.

Inspired by Richard Grathoff's phenomenological perspective on neighborhoods and the interactive creation of space (1994, 52) and Alois Hahn's approach of the construction of the stranger (1994, 140), I focus on the production of the imagined other on the stage that urban festive events provide and concentrate on group-building processes within the social and geographic space of a neighborhood and the new groupings that emerge within reinvented local rituals (Brubaker 2004; Glick Schiller, Çağlar, and Guldbrandsen 2006). Special events like the Murid parade in Harlem, New York City every July 28, and localized Parisian festivals provide rich empirical data for the analysis of the embedding of migrants in local situations in Paris and New York City in ways that are both structured by broader neoliberal political and economic processes and agendas and simultaneously reconfigured by migrants' actions and insertions.

Hence I suggest a definition of translocal social spaces as those that result from new forms of delimitation that consist of but also reach beyond geographic or national boundaries. These spaces become the new sources of identification and action within specific local and global reference systems. However, this does not imply a local determinist position that denies agency to the migrants. It is the migrants who also shape the conditions of the local. They contribute to the upgrading of certain cities and certain urban districts and zones; for example, the African migrants in Harlem in New York City are an important force behind the rehabilitation of housing within the area. An entanglement of various subjective and objective rescaling processes is taking place. As Glick Schiller and Çağlar point out in their introduction to this book, rescaling has led to the reorganization of the relationship between localities, regions, nation-states, and global institutions. Rescaling is the outcome of neoliberal restructuring practices, especially rearrangements of governance, which position cities directly as global competitors.

For example, Manhattan has become one of the centers of the globalized housing markets for Senegalese emigrants. One of the most important real estate agencies is actually selling houses around Dakar directly from its office located in Manhattan rather than from an office in Dakar. Harlem is becoming an important trade platform from which money flows directly to Senegalese localities. The amount of money that arrives through informal self-organized migrants' networks is higher than the amount of development aid that goes through institutions and governmental agencies. These are examples of the consequences of neoliberal restructuring that lead to rescaling processes.

In chapter 1 Glick Schiller and Çağlar provide a concrete operational definition of scale that summarizes the transformation in the objective conditions encapsulated in the literature on scale and rescaling processes: "scaling refers to the ordering of sociospatial units within multiple hierarchies of power. Rescaling refers to a reordering of these relationships. Taken together the terms scaling and rescaling serve as a conceptual shorthand that allows us to speak of the intersection between two processes: restructuring, including movements of various forms of capital, and the reorganization of the relationships of power between specific sociospatial units of governance."

The term scale can be defined as the summary assessment of the differential positioning of cities determined by the flow and control of capital and structures of power as they are constituted within regions, states and the globe (Glick Schiller and Çağlar 2009). However, according to Saskia Sassen (2007, 16), "Existing theory is not enough to map today's multiplication of practices and actors contributing to these rescalings. Included are a variety of nonstate actors and forms of cross-border cooperation and conflict, such as global business networks, the new cosmopolitanism, nongovernmental organisations (NGOs), diasporic networks, and such spaces as global cities and transboundary public spheres." By focusing on festive events in two global cities, I demonstrate that various actors who have differential access to power contribute to rescaling processes.

New York and Paris are both global cities in the sense of Sassen's (1991, 2007) definition. They emerge as one territorial or scalar moment in a transurban dynamic, and each is a complex structure that can articulate a variety of cross-boundary processes and reconstitute them as a part of their version of urbanity. Paris, while marketed as quintessentially French, is not representative of France. Similarly, while New York serves as a cultural reference for the United States, it differs from other big American cities in multiple ways, including the tremendous diversity of its migrant population and its long history of encouraging the identity politics of its newcomers. Both contain not only diverse migrant populations but also significant concentrations of West African migrants. New York (and the U.S. East Coast more generally) contains the greatest proportion of West African migrants to the United States (Stoller 2002).

First Case Study: The Murid Parade in New York

In the period between 1980 and 2005, Senegalese migration destinations, including Murid networks, shifted first from West African cities to France, next from France to its neighboring countries, and finally toward the United States. From New York City, New York State, Connecticut, and New Jersey, these migrants have spread over the whole country, building several regional centers, including that in Atlanta. In New York City, a group of several hundred Murids set up their first *dahira* in 1986. *Dahira* is a term in Wolof (the national language spoken in Senegal), which is derived from the Arabic word for circle. In Senegal and in places in which Senegalese reside abroad, a dahira is a group of followers of the same brotherhood who help each other and pray together. Especially among Murids, this solidarity fosters commercial networks.

During the 1980s the Murids met regularly in Brooklyn, at Keur Serigne Touba house. After beginning to make annual visits to New York and becoming aware of the growing number of Senegalese and African American *talibes*[4] (followers) there, Sheikh Mourtalla, a Senegalese religious leader of the Murid Brotherhood, set up a nonprofit organization whose aim was to create a permanent center for the Murids in that city. The Murid Islamic Community of America Inc. (MICA) was founded as a 501(c)(3) charitable organization, which allows donors to deduct the amount of their contributions from their income taxes. Sheikh Balozi, known as "the first American talibe," became the president of MICA.

In 1991, three years after his first visit to New York, Sheikh Mourtalla asked MICA to buy a house there in order to create a House of Islam. While it proved difficult to find the space to expand in Brooklyn, it was possible for the organization to find sufficient space in Manhattan, the heart of New York City, by buying property in Harlem. Because of racialization and racial segregation, Harlem at the time remained a rare place of abandoned or undervalued property in Manhattan. Sheikh Mourtalla gave $55,000 to support the project. In eight years, the Murids managed to raise $500,000 through gatherings and assemblies in order to rehabilitate the building. First, a mosque and a school "for the teaching of Muslim religion" were installed on the first floor. A residence for Mourtalla was constructed on the second floor, which eliminated hotel costs during his visits. According to official sources, the rest of the space was reserved for welcoming other Murid dignitaries who visited the city (*Mouride* 2001, 14, and www.toubamica.org). My informants reproduced the discourse of Murid hospitality, declaring that "anybody who arrives and who is looking for an apartment can go to the House of Islam and reside a couple of days there" (interviews with Murid followers in Harlem, September 3, 4, 6, 2002). In the talibes' discourse, the House of Islam is a symbol of Murids' hospitality and openness.

Across the translocal spaces that they construct, the Murid migrants, notably the political and religious activists, follow various strategies of connection to their localities of settlement. In the following paragraph, I give concrete examples when I speak about New York City. These strategies take into consideration the cultural and political differences between their various places of residence. In New York City, West African Muslim groups have successfully promoted their specific Islamic practices by connecting them to common American discourses on minorities. Making use of the available religious discursive resources in the United States and their prominence within the identity politics of New York City, Murid organizations and movements have developed in a particularly successful form of incorporation in New York.

Murid organizations pay attention to the different inhabitants of Harlem and its local geographical setting, to the representatives of the state and their politics of immigration, as well as to the mayor and his political program. These actors are part of specific opportunity structures that interest groups can exploit when pursuing their goals in New York (Furlong, Biggart, and Cartmel 1996; Wilson and Rodriguez Cordero 2006). Senegalese brotherhoods need connections to key persons in the religious communities in New York and to the local administration in order to build up their commercial, social, political, and religious structures.

These migrants' establishment of religious and political structures in New York requires a keen appreciation of the configuration of existing institutions and opportunities and a profound local knowledge of law, customs, and administration (Salzbrunn 2004). In turn, the available structures, resources, and institutional and discursive opportunities have influenced and modified the experiences and strategies of the Murids and led to new hybrid practices that take into consideration the very specific local situation in Harlem.

The positive response by the political authorities to the opening of the House of Islam in Harlem was one indication of how deeply the Murids have become rooted in that neighborhood. The symbolic presence of Senegalese religious leaders within the public space provides a feeling of recognition and intimacy among brotherhood members. In contrast to those in New York, Paris Murid houses are far from the city center: Keur Serigne Touba, named after the founder of the Murids, is located in a northern suburb; another important place with a large Senegalese population is in Mantes-La-Jolie, at the border between the Parisian region and Normandy. Both French sites are invisible in the public space, and almost no events are celebrated publicly.

The Visits of Sheikh Mourtada Mbacké to New York

By the end of the 1990s, the two-week-long annual visit of the Murid sheikh Mourtada Mbacké had become an important event, not only within the Murid transnational networks and in Harlem but also within New York City. The Senegalese and New York press, as well as radio stations, regularly reported the news. Video producers filmed the whole event in order to market the tapes through retailers in the United States, Europe and Senegal.

The sheikh's arrival in New York in 1999 unfolded as follows. A crowd of hundreds of talibe wearing large *boubous* (clothing composed of trousers and a dress that covers the legs) welcomed him at JFK Airport with *khassaides* (religious songs and prayers). Serigne Mbacké Ndiaye, a Murid representative, and Adja Aram Adji, president of the female dahira Sokhna

Diarra, directed the organization of the visit: women are important contributors to the Murid brotherhood and are always part of the main events.
El Haj Mohammad Balozi, the first African American convert to the Murid
brotherhood, was the first person to salute Sheikh Mourtada on American
soil. He led the sheikh toward a huge white limousine, where the sheikh,
accompanied by *khassaides,* left the airport with an escort of New York Port
Authority police.

In the eyes of the participants, the significant engagement of the police,
who provided a motorcade, was a sign of prestige rather than a hostile act.
Whereas events organized by Muslim minorities in European cities are sometimes accompanied by large numbers of police to prevent conflict and aggres-
sive acts by members of the crowd, the engagement of the local New York
police in this specific religious event was seen as a way of officially honoring
the arrival of a religious authority who deserved protection and respect. As
early as 1988, the president of the borough of Manhattan had signed an official declaration of welcome, reflecting a tradition, in New York as well as
other U.S. cities, of recognizing ethnic groups as legitimate political interest
groups.[5] In France, the republican idea of equality and universalism would
not be compatible with this kind of official declaration favoring a group on
the basis of their religious affiliation and belonging.

On his arrival at the Pennsylvania Hotel (the House of Islam had not been
opened yet), Sheikh Mourtada was once more saluted by a huge crowd, comprised primarily of women and children. On that occasion dozens of post-
ers, mostly in English but also in Arabic, proudly celebrated "blackness" or
stated "Allah the Creator of the Universe." Children wore T-shirts especially
printed for this event; some showed Senegalese and American flags. Several
messages on the banners targeted potential converts: "You young people.
Get the achievement of peace and justice as your ultimate goal while striving
for knowledge and enlightenment."

On Sheikh Mourtada's 2001 visit, the ambassador of Senegal and his son
welcomed him at the salon d'honneur reception room at JFK. This manifes-
tation of official honor was reported in the bimonthly francophone *Muride*
magazine distributed around the different migration platforms. Obtaining
Senegalese and American official proclamations or symbolic honors is part
of the Murid strategy of keeping a presence in public space. Although the
Senegalese constitution is based on a radical separation of religious and
political affairs, Senegalese citizens do not see their religious presence in
public spaces as contradicting the secular constitution of Senegal. The cul-
minating point of the annual visit was the Murid parade, a march through
the streets of Harlem that ended with several speeches delivered in Wolof,
Arabic, and English[6] at a corner of Central Park, the southern boundary of
Harlem. The videotapes of the 1999 Murid parade contain interviews with
several participants and speakers during the march. The common point of
most of their comments was that the event celebrated African unity and the
desire to bring together "Africans born in America and Africans born in
Senegal."

During the parade the speakers issued an invitation to the African American population to reinvent Africanness. Clear allusions were made to the Black Muslim movement and Afrocentric philosophy: "We want to thank Sheikh Mourtada for coming here to spread Islam among the African American community.... We would like to thank Sheikh Mourtada for his dedication, his hard work, his support for the last ten years to the Murid Islamic community here in America. Insh'Allah, next year, the Murid Islamic community will be continuing to propagate Islam, propagating and letting the world know that the Senegalese, that the African American community have come together to do something great. That something has been prophesied by Sheikh Ahmadou Bamba, one day we will come together and be one." After the public speeches, several Senegalese and African Americans responded with emphatic accolades to demonstrate their unity.

The women, who marched at the end of the parade, were also interviewed and expressed in Wolof or French their great satisfaction with their participation in this event. Fewer women than men participate in religious or political events in Senegal. Moreover women do not play a major roles in these events, although they frequently attend them. During official meetings with religious or political authorities in New York, women are well represented and participated in debates. For this reason, the participation of the female dahira Mame Diarra in the 2001 Murid parade, and in the community activities in general, was reported in the *Mouride* (2001, 14) as an "immense oeuvre." The article summarizing the parade and related activities in New York stated, "Behind every great man, a great woman is hidden" (ibid.). Indeed, the women controlled the financial affairs and occupied a predominant place in the leadership of the event, though men were more publicly visible.

The Murid parade in New York City has become an annual religious event organized by the Murids as part of a larger strategy of recruiting converts to support the religious network based in Senegal; some of the richest contributors reside outside West Africa. The economic success by Murid traders and entrepreneurs (shop and restaurant owners, bank managers, etc.) makes them attractive to converts from other Muslim brotherhoods and from other religions. Financial support from members of the networks, trade relationships, and spiritual help are still the most important motives for both non-Muslims and Senegalese members of other brotherhoods converting and entering Murid networks. At the same time, Senegalese migrants have become a significant financial force in New York and abroad. The petty traders (small business owners, merchants, or street sellers) and taxi drivers who were a majority in the beginning of this migration are now being joined by very rich investors who more fully commit themselves and their businesses to their new places of residence rather than to their home villages.

I have met Senegalese migrants who, once they succeeded economically, tried to escape from the duty of sending important financial contributions to their Marabout, which is their personal religious authority (each Marabout in Senegal has his or her own group of followers). None the less, the remittances sent by the Murids to Touba, the central Murid town in Senegal, are much higher than the budget of the municipality and recently supported the construction of a hospital there.

At the same time, the reasons for both the growth of Murid networks and their positive reception in New York are the expanding networks themselves and their increasing political character. This process became accentuated and more visible when a politician (and member of the Murid network) became the president of Senegal. The weekly "House of Islam" lunch at a Senegalese restaurant in Harlem owned by members of a Sufi order and the annual political and religious events have become important places of sociability, which transcend belonging to a religiously defined network. They can be analyzed as the "landscapes of confluence" of different kinds of local and global networks.

The easy access to public space—e.g., the possibility of organizing religious events on the street—both reinforces Senegalese migrants' notion of belonging and contributes to their efforts to build their transnational social field. Footage of the Murid parade in New York and of the Murid religious events celebrated in the Senegalese town of Touba are sold in Senegalese shops all over the world and contribute to an impression of ubiquity of that network, which is particularly deeply rooted in New York. New York has become an important powerful node within Murid transnational migration fields, as well as in the field of Senegalese political power: for example, a large number of Senegalese real estate transactions are coordinated from New York. The Senegalese election campaign was organized partly from Paris, but New York played an essential role (Salzbrunn 2002a; 2004). The webmaster of the winning party directed the Internet campaign from New York.

The Senegalese who participate in these activities are becoming part of the landscape of Harlem through their religious expression and its visibility in public space. Instead of feeling marginalized in a predominantly Christian country, through their religious organizations and presence in the public sphere Senegalese migrants in New York City have become more and more incorporated into the city in the eyes of other residents, including black and white Americans. In return, this acceptance allows the Senegalese to identify more with American values and political practices. Examples of this ongoing identification process are the increasing use of the English language and the decreasing use of French and the presence of American flags, especially on T-shirts, during religious demonstrations like the Murid parade.

Crisscrossing Alliances in Harlem

Another part of the Murids' strategy of becoming firmly rooted in the public space in Harlem is the translation of their values into a language and a social discourse understood by Americans. The representation of Murid economic and moral practices plays an important role in how they locate themselves vis-à-vis the other inhabitants of Harlem. The ideology of very hard work and the ideal of a certain form of piety are welcomed by a section of American society, as represented by the mainstream press. In his 1988 proclamation of Sheikh Ahmadou Bamba Day, David N. Dinkins, then the president of the borough of Manhattan, connected African roots and Sufism with a reference to "African personality and culture." Such connections enable the African American Muslims, searching for their African roots, to identify themselves with this spiritual leader. In the context of city officials' open battle against drugs and alcohol, the promotion of an ascetic lifestyle by the Murids was considered a helpful initiative. The authorities trusted the new migrants because of their Muslim ethics. Murids, in turn, underscored these social values in the course of their political lobbying and in public events such as the annual Murid parade. This positive response contributed to the success of attracting these migrants to New York.

In this context, it is important to note that the local Murid networks in Harlem have contributed to the transformation of the urban landscape of New York City and paved the way for the current gentrification of Harlem. Since the arrival of the first Senegalese migrants in the 1980s, the real estate within that area has considerably changed. The specific local discourse of the Murids in New York reflects their awareness of the opportunities provided by the local context. In their own discourse, Murids declare that they have reconstructed large parts of Harlem, fought crime, and stopped the disintegration of the area. They see themselves contributing economically and morally by helping to upgrade a decaying neighborhood. The administrative and economic support and encouragement provided to them by the state and city of New York and its borough of Manhattan facilitate Murid incorporation into economic networks and the administrative structures of daily life. The visibility of religious practices within public space infuses Senegalese Muslims, and particularly the members of the Murid brotherhood, with a feeling of positive recognition and acceptance by the United States.

While their positive roles in the neighborhood, public recognition, and success in making converts give the Africans in the Murid networks self-esteem in their place of settlement, this self-perception is being built at the expense of other groups in Harlem, especially African Americans. Murids have adopted the more general U.S. negative prejudices against African Americans, particularly about their putative work attitudes and loose morals. However, this view has not gone unchallenged, and the apparent unity celebrated in the Murid parade seems to be in contrast with everyday tensions between African Americans and Africans in Harlem. African Americans working in shops and restaurants recently opened by Murids view their new immigrant employers as exploitative. They also argue that Africans fail to show solidarity and that they even adopt a hostile attitude toward the native blacks that inhabit Harlem.

Almost every person I interviewed from both groups gave a concrete example of a negative experience with the other group. It is clear that Murids underestimate the degree of racial discrimination still faced by African

Americans. Yet Muridism continues to be attractive to African Americans because of the economic and political power of Murid networks and the related benefits they bring to their members, and because of the spirituality and sense of authenticity that the brotherhood offers. Despite the tension-ridden everyday relations between the African American citizens and Africans, the Murids have succeeded in emphasizing a common black background by references to their shared experiences of racialization. They have linked the two populations within lobbying campaigns for particular rights and recognition. The demonstration of religious ethics such as piety and hard work can easily be translated into American Protestant thinking, and this has helped with the Murids' public recognition and esteem. This strategy is directly shaped by the institutional and discursive opportunities that this particular local context offered. The outcome of such a strategy is the hybridization of their religious, political, and social practices.

Like Pentecostalism, which "has become a transnational phenomenon that, in its modern form, is locally expressed through a highly accelerated circulation of goods, ideas and people" (Van Dijk 2002b, 178), Muridism has also developed its own transnational social field. On the one hand, the local expression of Muridism changes according to the specific context and influences of the religious network as a whole. On the other hand, this expression contributes to the restructuring of a local territory including its social, economic, and political practices. I have shown how the Murids make use of the available administrative opportunities to have access to public space as a religious community and of the specific symbols of belonging to America (through the proclamation of Sheikh Ahmadou Bamba day, etc.) in order to become part of Harlem.

In the context of the questions raised by this chapter and this book, it is important to note that Muridism has contributed to the restructuring of Harlem, and with it, New York City. The wealth and power of the city are manifest in the transformations of its various neighborhoods, but this restructuring is part of the positioning of New York within more global fields of social and economic relations. Migrant flows such as those constructed by the Murid transnational social fields are a product of and contribute to the global restructuring of local urban space.

Although the flow of financial resources within transnational Murid networks is part of their insertion in many places in the world, it is rarely transparent. Murids do not usually seek visibility in public space, but in the case of New York, public visibility and the construction of a peaceful, tolerant, and even workaholic image of themselves were helpful to both the Murids and David Dinkins, the African American president of the borough of Manhattan. This representation also shaped the Murid evaluation of New York. They repositioned New York City so that it was placed in a higher position within their subjective scalar positioning of cities than Paris.

The occupation of public space was not an aim in itself, but it could be considered an instrument of the efficient local rooting of a translocal network. In any case, we have seen that the Senegalese residing in New York do not exclusively refer to the national or religious network but are connected to a multitude of frames of reference that are concentrated in political and religious events. For the actors, nationality is only one of various existing resources. However, converting local people is one of the missions of the Murids all over the world. By converting a rich entrepreneur in New York who has become the key person of the local network, they have made that city one of the most important places within their frame of references. This is due to their success in converting the kinds of followers who allow the community to increase their reputation and financial power. This changing balance of the relative regional centers, which finds its expression in public demonstrations, is closely related to the broader dynamics that are part of the restructuring of the locality and are one of the many forces that globally position New York.

The success of New York, as I mentioned before, is also due to the Murids' experience of exclusion in Europe and particularly in France. Abdoulaye Gueye (2001) points out that the Senegalese in general have "downgraded" France after having felt downgraded by the French. His French expression "déclassement" captures the migrants' subjective process of reranking localities. (In this case the demotion covers not only Paris as a node of the religious and political networks but also France and Europe in general as an immigration option.) This process is closely related to the French hostility toward displays of religious symbols within the public space. During the 2007 French presidential election campaign, politicians both from left- and right-wing parties were denouncing communitarianism, which, according to them, threatened republican unity and equality. Nicolas Sarkozy (member of the right-wing party UMP [Union pour la Majorité Présidentielle, Union for the Presidential Majority] and winner of the election) and José Bové (from the leftist altermondialist [alter-globalization] movement) were among the politicians denouncing communitarianism. They failed to note that the republican ideal of equality wasn't working in practice and that immigrants were increasingly aware of their exclusion from the job market and various spheres of social life. This subjective process of repositioning cities, states, and regions is influenced by objective rescaling processes. The different ways in which New York and Paris try to maintain their positioning as global cities have an impact on ongoing rescaling processes.

Second Case Study: Urban Belonging in Paris

In my second example, I move from examining migration through an ethnic or religious lens and concentrate on the insertion of migrants from multiple backgrounds within a particular neighborhood in the throes of gentrification processes. These processes were intensified by efforts of the city leadership to increase its competitiveness within the global tourist market. I examine an event as entry point into the local dynamics of the Parisian district of Sainte

Marthe in order to show how groups emerge or evolve in a migratory context (Çağlar 1997, Salzbrunn 2002b, 2008).

In 2001 the global competition among cities contributed to the electoral victory of a Socialist mayor, Bertrand Delanoë, and his allies from the Green Party in Paris. This victory was the culmination of pressures to recognize, celebrate, and market the diversity of the city. Efforts to highlight Parisian diversity had begun in 1995, with leftist parties' victory in municipal elections in the multiethnic neighborhoods. In addition, a global marketing trend that highlighted cultural and geographical diversity, as seen in several carnivals initiated in European cities such as Berlin and London (Knecht and Soysal 2005), stimulated efforts to market Paris as a capital of international recreation. The introduction of arts and crafts villages (such as a street of fashion in Barbès) and several festive events supported by the city of Paris—such as the Chinese New Year in 2007—were all products of this commitment to highlight diverse cultures (Raulin 2004) in order to reposition the city within the global tourist industry.

Sainte Marthe is named after one of the two parallel streets in the district. Many of the current buildings in the area were built in the 1860s in a former Parisian suburb (Faubourg) by the Comte de Madre, an entrepreneur whose utopian ideas led to the invention of a new architecture for workers' homes, known today as *le style Madre*. These tiny two- and four-story houses were constructed with cheap material and no foundation. A workshop or boutique was installed on the ground floor, while on the upper floors the workers' living quarters consisted of one- or two-room apartments without sanitation. The building complex still has the form of an H on the map: two parallel streets were joined in the middle by a small perpendicular street. These were closed by gates because at the end of the nineteenth century the whole district was private property.

By the 1980s the buildings were in danger of collapsing because of their poor quality, and at the beginning of 1991 the mayor wanted to destroy the whole quarter in order to construct huge buildings like the ones located north and east of Sainte Marthe. The inhabitants, afraid of being expelled, developed a variety of resistance strategies. The association, Village Saint Louis Sainte Marthe, organized banquets and festivals through an extensive public relations campaign in order to win public and political support. The association's name alluded to a territorial identity within a big city. In the festivals and activities organized by the association, the architectural and aesthetic value of the houses and the cultural richness of the inhabitants were emphasized. The history of the place and the inhabitants' struggle against their common enemy of right-wing politicians and real estate speculators strengthened a sense of belonging to this particular neighborhood.

In 1994 the notion of rehabilitation figured for the first time in the new urban projects in Paris. During the municipal election campaign in 1995, the local left-wing agenda focused on opposition to real estate speculation (which would have lead to destruction of the neighborhood) and support for restoration of this quarter. Thanks to mobilizations against the destruction of the neighborhood complexes in 1995, the Left won district elections. Subsequently, in 2001, the whole city of Paris was conquered by the Left for the first time. However, it was not until 2003 that the restoration project of the quarter was approved and the home owners were offered financial support.

A central point of interest in Sainte Marthe is the celebration of cultural diversity. Today the population includes working migrants from North Africa and the former Yugoslavia who arrived in the 1960s, artists and musicians who have occupied the deserted ateliers of the artisans, and a middle-class population attracted by the diversity and villagelike ambience of the place. Since the 1990s festive events have been organized on Sainte Marthe square in which participants are called on to disguise themselves and paint their faces in order to change their identity but are also asked to display their cultural background through on-stage performances.

The events are organized by Four Horizons, an association created in 1997. Its founder and president, Kheira, is a French woman of Algerian origin who has sought to provide activities to the inhabitants (especially the youth) of the quarter, create links between different people, and establish a meeting venue for the Algerian women who suffer from isolation. She works as a housekeeper in the district and serves as a mediator between people searching for housing and for sites for shops, and she is known as an informal real estate agent. Because of her involvement in real estate transactions in the district, she has been criticized by several inhabitants, even though she is engaged in saving the neighborhood from destruction. Four Horizons organizes cultural events such as outdoor balls, as well as public couscous banquets and carnivals, which have made Sainte Marthe more and more popular in the eyes of tourists, potential investors in real estate, and local political representatives. The organization of festive events also has played a central role in shaping the inhabitants' identification with the quarter.

The association receives public funding from the state secretary of urban affairs for its social work and from the district mayor for participating in the organization of the annual multi-sited nationwide Fête de la Musique on the square Sainte Marthe. It also gets money from members fees (thirty to forty members) and from the banquets and food sold during the festivals. In the course of building and conducting these events, the association interacts with various key persons in the district: the mayor and elected deputies and the presidents of other associations (especially the association for local history). Others, such as local artists and craftswomen, participate in and benefit from these festive events.

In 2001 the small picturesque central square at the upper end of Sainte Marthe Street, which had been abandoned by the inhabitants because of the petty crime that occurred there, was symbolically inaugurated as one of the representative streets of Paris and was officially named *Place Sainte Marthe.* The act of putting plates with that name on different house facades of the square was a kind of a political victory for the mobilized residents

Fig. 6. This outdoor banquet in the Place Sainte Marthe is one instance of the organized resistance to efforts to replace the multiethnic Parisian district with urban redevelopment. A place-based movement emerged that was facilitated not by cultural difference but by common efforts to preserve urban space. Photo by Monika Salzbrunn.

of the neighborhood. During the Fête de la Rentrée in 2005 (celebrating the end of school vacation), the organizers interviewed the local inhabitants in order to collect their impressions. All those interviewed seemed to be appreciative of the solidarity between the neighbors and of the beautiful and rare architecture of the district. Those interviewed testified to the strong sense of belonging experienced by the inhabitants of the neighborhood. The presentation of this audio self-portrait during a festive event was itself instrumental in shaping a place-based identification among the residents of Sainte Marthe.

In this quarter, feasts called "carnivals" have been celebrated in three different forms. One is a summer carnival organized by a theater company and supported by the city. Local artists from the rue Sainte Marthe and the president of Four Horizons have enlivened this event by helping the children create masks and costumes. Second, beginning in 2003, several inhabitants of the quarter participated in a new type of summer carnival inspired by the London Notting Hill carnival. They named it Barbès Tour in reference to a popular quarter in the northern Paris (Barbès) where migrants from sub-Saharan Africa and North Africa have settled. The year 2003 was declared the official year of Algeria in France; the president of Four Horizons and its other members acknowledged this in the festival by wearing Berber costumes in front of a banner with "Algeria my love" written in Arabic. In 2004 the Barbès

Fig. 7. Kheira (left) is founder and president of the local Parisian organization that successfully resisted efforts to redevelop Sainte Marthe. The organization used food and music to rebrand the neighborhood as culturally diverse, a strategy that resonated with the city's efforts to compete within a global tourist market by promoting multiculturalism. Photo by Monika Salzbrunn.

Tour took place in Barbès and Sainte Marthe, where a concert with different musical styles was given.

The third type of carnival is one based on the Roman Catholic calendar. On Mardi Gras, one day before Ash Wednesday, the Four Horizons offers crêpes to the children of Sainte Marthe and prepares a Moroccan dish (*tajine*) in a local restaurant run by an association. There is also reference to a Catholic feast day (*la Chandeleur*), which has become only a pretext for consuming crêpes together. Similarly, in 2004 Four Horizons celebrated both Halloween and the beginning of Ramadan at a restaurant. All these references and the activities exemplify the cultural bricolage that marks the neighborhood. By consciously mixing Catholic and Muslim references during the festive events, as well as combining food and music from various origins, Four Horizons and the inhabitants of the neighborhood draw attention to the inhabitants' place-based sense of belonging. Despite the power asymmetries within this field of identification, the local political identity construed through festive events has led to the emergence of a we-group and created a sense of belonging that extends beyond ethnic and religious origin and identity.

One important consequence of these activities was that the new left-wing mayor realized the cultural and economic potential of the quarter. He launched a district-wide festival called "Ensemble, nous sommes le Xe" (together, we are the tenth district of Paris), during which the local associations presented their activities and their particular cultural identities (through food, music, clothes), which led in some cases to a reinvention of these identities.

The local governance structures thus contributed to the development of place-based identities. The district mayor followed the program of Mayor Bertrand Delanoë, who had based his activities on four principles: "solidarity; quality of life; openness to the world; citizenship." Although different neighborhood groups presented and sold their so-called traditional craft objects and/or food, the display of cultural heritage was only one aspect of the residents' activities. These gatherings and festive events also provided local entertainment and opportunities for the negotiation of local power relations and for influencing the ongoing urban restructuring processes by repositioning the neighborhood anew within the global tourist industry. They provided venues for publicly pressuring the politicians taking part in these events to revisit their image of the neighborhood and the urban redevelopment plans they advocated.

It is important to note that if I had focused on the members of the district who were of Algerian descent, I could have told a story of an ethnic or transnational network: there are indeed connections between the president of Four Horizons, her nephew in Great Britain, and her uncles in Algeria. To begin instead with neighborhood ties and the evolving sense of local community does not deny the fact that this "communitas" evolves with the political context faced by North Africans. Living within transnational social fields, North Africans in Paris are very sensitive to France's colonial history. They also face increasing daily restriction of access to public space, especially around Belleville and Sainte Marthe, because of growing identity controls, which the government justifies by concerns about illegal migration.

However, in Sainte Marthe the response to the surveillance of migrants has been local rather than solely ethnic or religious. Surveillance has led to the development of solidarity networks for the protection of political and economic refugees. Several individuals were supported by a network that extends beyond persons of Algerian descent. Inhabitants of Sainte Marthe include these forms of solidarity among the reasons to be proud of their neighborhood. Consequently, I argue that cultural practices and alliances can best be analyzed in the context of specific local political, social, and economic conditions, which are manifested with a specific time and space (Barth 1969; Cohen 1993). Actors' identities are "partial, multiple and fractured by crosscutting alliances" (Werbner 1997, 265).

The local dynamics of Sainte Marthe were shaped by the struggle to restructure the neighborhood as part of broader globe-spanning forces that are repositioning cities. The residents resisting the gentrification of the neighborhood were able to find support for their cause from the district authorities because of the increasing value of cultural diversity (displayed within the neighborhood) in marketing cities within the global tourist industry. The appropriation of urban space by the migrants in this case and its repositioning locally and globally were partly the outcomes of the subjective rescaling of the place from the local inhabitants' perspective (both migrant and native) and of local politicians' recognition of this neighborhood's value in repositioning Paris. As Bodaar and Rath (2005, 4) point out, the city "boosters increasingly acknowledge that urban diversity is a vital resource for the prosperity of cities and a potential catalyst for socio-economic development, particularly since business investors consider this diversity as one of the factors determining the location of businesses. The commodification and marketing of diversity, through the commercial use of the presence of the ethnic 'others' or their symbols, fits in well with this process, and this helps explain the growing enthusiasm for 'interesting' landscapes that have the potential to draw tourists."

• • •

Several processes of structural and migrant subjective rescaling can be observed within and between New York and Paris. It is also possible to observe the processes through which the subjective scaling has a direct impact on the institutional structures of urban life in ways that reposition the entire city in relationship to flows of people, capital, and relations of power. In the eyes of many West African migrants, New York is a more desirable location than Paris because of their growing awareness of discrimination and exclusion from the Parisian job market. After September 11, 2001, identity controls were expanded from national borders to public space in Europe and have increasingly become an appearance-based form of racial profiling. This form of surveillance produces new feelings of exclusion and denies practices of belonging, particularly among those of sub-Saharan origin, despite their European citizenship. In contrast to Europe, the image of the United States in the eyes of African migrants resonates strongly with the opinion expressed by Senegalese president Abdoulaye Wade. According to him, "It is difficult to enter, but once you are in, you are in peace."[7]

These nationwide or continent-wide administrative and executive practices are part of the uneven distribution of power within social fields and contribute to the subjective rescaling of places by migrants. The official website of Murid headquarters clearly describes this subjective positioning of places within migrant transnational social fields: "The industrialized Western Europe plunged into a deep economic crisis. And African immigrants in Europe faced a powerful xenophobic push. This was especially true for the Senegalese in France. The xenophobia culminated in what became finally the anti-immigrant legislation known as the Pasqua Law, named for the former French minister of Interior, Charles Pasqua. The Pasqua Law sent many Murid immigrants back home but a few of them landed in New York" (www. toubamica.org).

As migrants experience these exclusion and inclusion processes in the two global cities, their cultural, political, and financial activities contribute directly to the rescaling of districts within these cities. For example, Parisian Barbès and New York's Harlem have become very important sites from which to send remittances to Africa. This makes them important places for particular kinds of global financial flows that avoid most of the official banks and state-controlled fluxes. They become nodes in migrants' transnational fields of communication, as well as sites for social and political mobilizations. It is no coincidence that both the religious Murid parade and the Senegalese election campaign took place within public space in Harlem (Salzbrunn 2004). All these activities reflect the emergence of New York as a crucial node within the Murid transnational social field, where financial, spiritual, and political power is concentrated.

Although New York and Paris show common points in their marketing of cultural and spatial dynamics, there are still important differences between these two global cities. Paris is not only the biggest French city but also the capital of France, whereas New York City is not a political center. The role, positioning, and possibilities for the incorporation of migrants and their transnational connections are different in the two cities. I have illustrated this different positioning by using festive events as entry points for my analysis: the Murid parade in New York and a set of neighborhood festivals in Paris. In both cases the city political leaders transgressed national discourses that portrayed immigrants as a threat to the coherence of the national cultural and social fabric. It is noteworthy that while the mayor of Paris chose to send a positive message of belonging to the African residents of Paris by sponsoring a concert with the best-known African musicians on Bastille Day (a French national holiday held on July 14), the president of the country chose a French singer of popular but old-fashioned chansons for the same occasion. This choice, as well as the choice of an old-fashioned star to sing the national anthem on the evening of Election Day, was interpreted by several journalists as an illustration of his political program on migration and his wish that migrants should think of themselves as French nationals with a particular identity.

As local leaders who must constantly assure the continuing successful regional and global connectedness of their cities, mayors of global cities support and celebrate the diversity of their urban space. They strive to facilitate continued global flows of capital, investments, and a highly skilled (migrant) labor force, as well as tourists. Placing our analysis on the local rather than the national level allows us to note the situations in which urban discourses and policies may differ from those formulated by national leaders. It is noteworthy that the perspectives of the mayor of Paris and the borough president of New York, as well as other local leaders in these cities, were closer to the sociological reality of immigrants and migrant incorporation than the views espoused by the leaders of France and the United States, who acted within national frameworks. The borough president of Manhattan and the district mayors in the northeastern quarters of Paris generated responses to migration that reflected an awareness of competitive marketing of both cities and the contributions of migrants to both the restructuring and the marketing.

However, the short-term success of the rescaling process both in New York and Paris can lead to midterm social problems and increase inequalities in the city. The gentrification process in Harlem that has been undertaken by Senegalese highly skilled and middle-class immigrants is to a certain extent built on the exclusion of the poorer African American population from this area, as the latter can no longer afford the real estate prices. In Paris, the gentrification process as mediated through neighborhood interventions and struggles reinforced the notion of belonging. The Parisian and district mayors were able to retain their positions within this dynamic, at least as long as they maintained a certain balance between different interest groups in the voters' eyes.

In the analysis of the interplay between urban and migrant settlement dynamics in New York and Paris, it is important not to follow the common pattern in which social scientists build their nationwide models on specific urban examples like Paris or New York. New York's ethnic politics have been a product of New York and its particular relationship to national and global relationships of power. Conclusions drawn from studying New York are not reflective of the United States in general. Similarly, Paris's recognition of urban diversity was a product of the local context of Paris, including its specific electoral politics, which was shaped in interface with the global and regional pressures asserted on that city and the way its leaders sought to reposition the city and themselves in urban politics and governance structures. Paris can fruitfully be compared to London as a capital and global city with specific local policies under Mayor Livingstone, although Great Britain is organized differently in national political terms than France.

Although migrants' subjective ranking of places within transnational social fields may follow a logic different from the rescaling of cities within neoliberal restructuring, the New York case demonstrates that both processes are entangled with each other. In New York, Harlem has become a global platform for the Murid brotherhood and acquired a central position in the imagination of highly skilled Senegalese and Murids who reside in Europe, but desire to migrate from Europe. In Paris, rescaling processes within the city realized partly by migrants' activities and festive events place the city on a different scale for an emerging type of tourist who travels in search of sociologically dynamic quarters like Notting Hill in London or Kreuzberg in Berlin. Nevertheless, it should be noted that perceptions of France and its restrictive immigration laws make New York a more attractive place for highly skilled Senegalese migrants and potential Murid investors.

Both New York and Paris share intensive gentrification processes where spaces are globally marketed in ways that reflect the struggle of both cities to retain their dominant global positioning. Examining the relationship between urban rescaling processes and migration allowed us to reposition urban political economy within more global fields of capital, tourism, investment, and transnational social fields. It also placed the restructuring of neighborhoods and gentrification processes within globally extending markets in interaction with migrants' transnational social fields and settlement dynamics. Using festivals as entry points to analyze the interplay between migrant dynamics, transnational networks, global restructuring, and questions of political representation, this chapter illustrated how local political discourses on immigration may diverge from homogenized narratives of national policy.

Furthermore, focusing on localities rather than on specific groups based on national, ethnic, or religious criteria allowed us to go beyond methodological nationalism and to follow the actor's social practices, which extend beyond national frameworks. It became clear in this multi-sited fieldwork on one specific group of migrants that a systematic comparison of the rescaling and restructuring of localities was indispensable. I suggest that a focus on events can avoid taking a defined ethnic, religious, or sociocultural category as a key issue in the processes of communitarization. This epistemological perspective with its comparative design reveals some surprising crosscutting local alliances that go beyond predefined categories.

I thank Nina Glick Schiller, Ayşe Çağlar, and Gudrun Lachenmann for their helpful comments on this chapter and the German Research Foundation for its support of my research in Paris through an Emmy Noether grant.

Notes

1. The other important *tariqa* in Senegal is the Tijâniyya, founded by Sheikh Ahmad Ibn Muhammad Ibn al-Mukhtar Ibn Salim at-Tidjâni (1727–1815).

2. Migrinter means "Migrations, espaces, sociétés (Migration, Spaces, Societies) and is a French research group founded by the geographer Gildas Simon and based in Poitiers."

3. See Evens and Handelman (2006) for an overview of the Manchester School.

4. The word *talibe*, used in Wolof, comes originally from the Arab word *talibe*, tullab (pl.), meaning pupil or follower.

5. This tradition of valorizing minorities is now part of the politics of U.S. gateway cities. In Atlanta in 1997 the Murids were also welcomed with an official declaration.

6. They wanted to show their integration into the American society by speaking English rather than French.

7. Source: Official videotape distributed during the 2000 Senegalese election campaign by Abdoulaye Wade's party, PDS (Parti Démocratique Sénégalais, Senegalese Democratic Party), and sent to Senegalese migrants residing in France. Translated from the French by M.S.

Chapter 10

Downscaled Cities and Migrant Pathways

Locality and Agency without an Ethnic Lens

NINA GLICK SCHILLER AND AYŞE ÇAĞLAR

Beginning in the 1990s, a conjunction of several forces in both Europe and the United States, including refugee resettlement policies, led to an increased dispersal of migrants beyond global or gateway cities. However, as we noted in chapter 4, most migration theory continues to be built on research conducted in cities that are thought to be global, world, or gateway, where researchers focus on well-established immigrant neighborhoods and ethnic institutions. The ethnic pathways of settlement and transnational connection followed by migrants in those cities have commonly been assumed to be representative of migrant experiences and their place-making practices, wherever they may live. Researchers who deploy an ethnic lens have failed to examine the different types of relations that develop between migrants and cities and may reflect and contribute to the differential positioning of cities within global hierarchies of economic, political, and cultural power.

In this chapter we argue that studies of migrant pathways of incorporation in cities that find themselves disempowered and relatively impoverished within neoliberal restructuring and rescaling processes can contribute to an analysis of the relationship between migrants and cities. We define "incorporation" as a process of building or maintaining ongoing social, economic, political, and religious relations so that an individual or organized group becomes a participant in multiple and diverse social fields of uneven power composed of networks of networks (Epstein 1967). Although beginning on the level of observable interaction, this approach to incorporation traces the linkages between individuals and institutions that are situated within multiple scales, configurations, and layers of governance (Esser 2004; Portes 1995; Schmitter Heisler 1998). We recognize the significance of state-based

regulatory and symbolic systems without confining the processes of incorporation to a single state-based system.

The term "pathways" signals our understanding that there is no single
organizational form for migrant incorporation. The pathways of incorporation are multiple and may include simultaneous local and global embeddedness (Levitt and Glick Schiller 2004). We are not arguing that non-ethnic
pathways of local and transnational incorporation occur only in downscaled
cities; rather, we are suggesting that in these cities non-ethnic pathways of
incorporation are more visible because other organizational possibilities are
less feasible or not at all possible.

Downscaled cities are those that are disadvantaged in terms of their insertions within the global hierarchies that have emerged through the neoliberal restructuring of urban economies and the concurrent rearrangement
of governance on national and global scales. Hence the term "downscaled"
refers not to the absolute size of a city in terms of its population or physical space but to its relative positioning within emerging national, regional,
and global hierarchical configurations of power. It is our contention that
while migrants live in cities with varying positions in regional, national, and
global hierarchies of power, the relationship between migrants and a locality with limited opportunity structures and local narratives of the disempowerment of place has its own trajectories. These trajectories merit study
and theorization. The mutual constitution of cities and migrants within processes of restructuring and rescaling is found in such "forgotten cities" as
well more powerful cities. However the relationship between migrants and
cities in downscaled cities is different from that found in cities whose structural positioning reflects greater access to economic, political, and cultural
capital (Markusen 2004).

Our approach to the scalar positioning of a city puts aside the concept
of scale as a fixed and territorially based nesting of relations of governance.
Instead, scalar position and the term "city scale" are used as summary terms
that refer to a dynamic continuum of multiple forms of relations of power—economic, political, cultural—within which cities come to be positioned
(Brenner 1998; Glick Schiller and Çağlar chapter 4; M. P. Smith 2002). Some
cities are upscaled and others are downscaled in the competitive processes of
repositioning that are global in their reach. However these processes are always the product of the territorial grounding of organizations of production,
consumption, control, and status. As Janet Abu-Lughod (1999) has argued in
her critique of the global cities literature, these rescaling processes are much
older than the current moment of neoliberalism. However, the contemporary
global penetration of neoliberal capitalism and the rearrangement of governance have made cities everywhere active agents competing for global flows
of capital and global reputations. These struggles to improve the positioning
of cities within hierarchies of power affects the pathways of incorporation
for all residents of a city, including migrants. In cities that have been unsuc-
cessfully struggling for capital, political clout, and representation, migrants

may provide flows of capital and labor that would otherwise be unavailable. They may act as signification agents of revitalization. Their restructuring of neighborhoods, business districts, and the workforce can contribute to the resurgence of the city and its competitive position. Alternatively, migrants' settlement in an impoverished city may reflect and contribute to the city's decline. Furthermore, migrants' subjective assessments of a city in terms of its desirability as a place to settle are part of the narrative of a particular city that contribute to, as well as reflect, its trajectory of disempowerment or re-development (Lee and Yeoh 2005).

Depending on the historical conjuncture, the city's history and institutional structure, and the educational and transnational assets of the migration, migrants may or may not play the role of scale makers in downscaled cities or depressed neighborhoods within cities (see chapters 8, 9, and 11). To make the case for the study of migration in downscaled cities, we examine data from our ethnographic study of the local and transnational pathways of incorporation of new migrants in Manchester, New Hampshire, a downscaled city in northern New England, and in Halle/Saale, a downscaled city in Saxony-Anhalt in Germany. Beginning in the 1990s, Manchester, with a metropolitan region of 200,000, began to experience a small but highly visible influx of migrants from all over the world (City of Manchester n.d.). The city in particular, and southern New Hampshire in general, experienced a manufacturing effervescence at the end of the 1990s, and during this period both international and internal migrants settled in Manchester, with some of the influx initiated by refugee resettlement agencies. After German unification in 1989, which marked the end of the German Democratic Republic and its socialist economy, Halle experienced a dramatic deindustrialization, and the population shrank to approximately 232,000 (Halle die Stadt, 2004a). Yet some internal and international migrants sought to settle in the city despite very high levels of unemployment. Among these were refugees, students, and migrant business people.

While Manchester and Halle are significantly different in terms of their history and employment opportunities, we argue that a comparative scalar perspective on locality allows us to note important similarities in the global positioning of these two cities that have shaped the pathways, possibilities, and limitations of the incorporative and transnational strategy of migrants. As Charles Tilly (1984, 82–83) has noted, comparative historical methods can follow various strategies, each of which has its own productivity for social theory. By suggesting "variation finding," as a globally encompassing comparative approach our goal is to investigate whether the differential positioning of cities engenders alternative pathways of migrant incorporation and transnational connection (82–83). This perspective allows us to compare downscaled cities, including their claims to have been regenerated as centers of knowledge and advanced technology within the global economy. At the same time, it is possible, using this variation finding comparative approach, to note that local people's understanding of the causes of the downscaled positioning of their city is mediated by the distinctiveness of each city's history. Halle's deindustrialized postsocialist local narrative, which has been accompanied by substantial investment from the European Union, differs from Manchester's discourse of urban decline through deindustrialization and suburbanization that can be overcome through neoliberal public-private partnerships.

We use the term "neoliberal restructuring" to refer to the conjuncture of several discrete aspects of state policy and capitalist investment (Brenner and Theodore 2002; Glick Schiller and Çağlar, chapter 4). As scholars of the neoliberal global restructuring of urban governance have noted, local officials have found themselves competing to attract foreign capital and market their cities by recasting their localities as centers of knowledge, finance, and tourism (Henry, McEwan, and Pollard 2002; Holland et al. 2006; MacLeod and Goodwin 1999; Zukin 1991).

In both Manchester and Halle, we explored the relationship between the scalar positioning of the city, the opportunity structures that the city offered its residents of migrant and native background, and the pathways of incorporation taken by migrants. Between 2001 and 2005, members of our research team interviewed officials, service providers, and religious officials and attended public meetings, religious services, and events that concerned migrants. In Manchester, 115 migrants were interviewed.[1] In addition to this research we conducted ongoing participant observation in Vietnamese, Bosnian, Congolese, Nigerian, Iraqi, Sudanese, Pakistani, and Colombian households or workplaces. In Halle, we interviewed sixty-five migrants from the Congo, Nigeria, Russia, Bosnia, Vietnam, Iraq, and Syria; these interviews were accompanied by more intensive fieldwork.

Downscaled Cities within Neoliberal Globalization: Manchester and Halle/Saale

Both Halle/Saale in Saxony-Anhalt, Germany, and Manchester in New Hampshire, United States, are marginalized cities, on the peripheries of more successful urban centers. In spite of the efforts by each city to project a high-technology profile, both cities have found themselves in a relatively weak competitive position within national and global hierarchies of cities. At this point, we can only begin to outline the similarities of scale, but the evidence we have assembled provides useful perspectives on what might otherwise seem puzzling aspects of the relationship between these cities and their migrants. Our analysis does not deny the path-determined historical differences between the two cities, and we will highlight those elements that affect positioning of migrants and natives within the city. However, given the clear differences between the histories of German and U.S. national policies on migration and social welfare, as well as the postsocialist history of Halle, it is interesting to encounter similarities.

Although it is one of the largest cities in northern New England, Manchester is a downscaled city. It has relatively little political or economical importance globally, nationally, or regionally, although, like most cities today, it has global connections. Although it was only after 2000 that Manchester's political and institutional officials began to discuss the growth of immigration to the city, renewed migration following decades of decline had actually begun in the 1960s, when primarily but not exclusively Spanish-speaking immigrants began to settle there. This wave of migration was followed in the 1980s by the settlement of Vietnamese refugees, who were generally assisted by local churches. By the 1990s a diverse migration of primary and secondary immigrants and refugees from all over the world began settling in Manchester, providing some of the low-wage labor that contributed to the city's short-lived resurgence as a manufacturing center (Houston, 2004). Next, refugee resettlement agencies identified Manchester as a location with affordable housing and available low-wage, low-skilled jobs. Both refugees and immigrants who resettled in Manchester after first living elsewhere in the United States brought relatives directly to Manchester from abroad through U.S. immigration laws that allow for marriage and family reunion. The 2000 census reported that 9.4 percent of the population of Manchester was foreign-born. However, many of these were elderly French Canadians, English, Greek, and Irish immigrants who had lived for over fifty years in the United States. Approximately 4 percent of the foreign-born were recent immigrants (U.S. Census 2003, 2008).

Manchester is a city founded on textile mills that in the nineteenth and early twentieth century attracted a largely immigrant labor force. During its period of intensive industrialization, it considered itself a city of immigrants, but the newcomers faced heavy assimilationist pressure. Beginning in the 1930s and continuing through the 1960s, Manchester lost most of its textile industry and related industrial base. In the 1970s the growth of suburban malls led to the demise of the central and retail business district just as a new wave of industrial downsizing and outsourcing led to a further decline of local industries, such as the machine-tool shops that had previously remained viable in the region. Since the 1980s, the local economy has been marked by a roller coaster of expansion and subsequent contraction that has made it difficult for city leaders to undertake restructuring to establish Manchester as a player in the highly competitive postindustrial urban landscape.

For a short period in the 1990s, small nonunion industrial factories, which stood at the end of complicated flexible supply chains, flourished in the greater Manchester area (Gittell 2001). These small shops responded to global competition by offering relatively low-cost production on the basis of low-wage labor. Manchester promoted its "durable goods production, especially metal products, electrical products and machinery, and plastics" (City of Manchester 2005). Many of these workplaces were owned by large corporations whose headquarters and primary investment centers were located elsewhere, including Europe. At the same time, Manchester increasingly became a bedroom community for persons working in the belt of high-tech "knowledge-oriented" industries that ringed Boston. Perhaps as a consequence, a short-lived mini-high-tech boom developed in Manchester during this period. The new computer industries hired college-educated immigrants, and a local university attracted an increasing number of foreign students who sought to settle in the Manchester area and obtain work in these industries. In the short term the low-wage factories and high-tech industries brought growth, jobs, and both international and internal migrants to Manchester; however, the trajectory of growth could not be sustained. A new reversal of fortunes began with the high-tech crash in 2000, and in the following years manufacturing declined. The ever-increasing global competition sharply reduced the viability of the small-shop production strategy, and the migrant-dependent workplaces were forced to either shut down or lay off workers. In New Hampshire, 13.4 percent of the workforce was employed in manufacturing in 1998, and in 2004 only 9.5 percent held manufacturing jobs. This downward trend continued.

Meanwhile, by the first few years of the twenty-first century, a group of Manchester's political and business leaders had united to put in place an infrastructure development plan that was again geared toward reconfiguring the city, this time as a center of financial and medical services, recreation, and tourism. The new infrastructure included a sports arena complete with hockey team, a minor league baseball stadium, a new medical center, a business park, and investment in the public schools, all supported by increased city taxes. Efforts were made to attract investment in the downtown city area with expensive high-rise housing, rehabilitated office buildings, and a hotel complex bordering the ballpark. However, despite the gentrification of the city that had been fueled by public-private investment in the city center and the subprime mortgage industry in the city's neighborhoods, Manchester was unable to make a qualitative leap from its downscale positioning, and the opportunity structure for both natives and migrants did not expand. The official unemployment rate of 2.4 percent in 2000 had climbed to 4.3 percent in 2004 (U.S. Department of Labor 2005).

Although there were no local statistics about migrant incorporation in the labor force, our interviews with migrants and local officials indicated that most migrants continued to be employed in the shrinking number of industrial plants, while some obtained service industry jobs, such as working with the disabled, sick, and elderly. Many were employed below their educational levels, including those that had obtained higher education or retraining in New Hampshire. Migrants with poor English skills were unable to find a sufficient supply of service-sector jobs in office or hotel cleaning, restaurant work, or health care, as they might have done in global cities. The downtown development was not sufficient to provide adequate professional employment for educated natives or migrants.

During this same period, 1990–2005, Halle similarly attempted to reinvent itself from the deindustrialization that accompanied German unification.

When socialism ended, more than thirty thousand people lost their jobs after a majority of factories were closed or downsized. Despite the subsequent modernization of its chemical plants by international investors such as Dow Chemical and extensive German and EU investment in gentrification of the city center, Halle has been positioned as a downscale city characterized by low-wage jobs and a high rate of unemployment. The type of investment that was made in industry created higher productivity while employing far fewer workers (Barjak 2000). In 2004, the unemployment rate stood at just under 20 percent of the population. Competing with the neighboring city of Leipzig (located one hundred miles from Berlin, the nearest globally prominent city), Halle has had trouble attracting adequate investments in high-tech industries or financial services. The capital that was invested in Halle did not generate profits for local companies and often didn't provide employment for local people. Most of the people who have benefited from the efforts to build a financial sector in the city have come from western Germany. The limited size of this sector has left few professional jobs for natives of the east and almost none for local migrants, as construction and supply contracts often went to firms from western Germany.

Because of the factors that discourage migrant settlement, the figures for foreigners in Halle were rather low, especially in comparison with German cities of different scalar positioning. Although the size of the migrant population doubled in the fifteen years following German unification, it was only 4 percent of the population of Halle in 2005, with the largest number of migrants coming from the European Union. Within this population African migrants made up a small but visible minority. In contrast to the situation in Manchester in the late 1990s, few migrants came to Halle voluntarily, and those who did often chose to leave and settle in western Germany, where there were much greater possibilities for employment. The narrative of Halle as a shrinking city that was unfriendly to migrants contributed to their outward flow. Those who remained included asylum seekers whose mobility in Germany was legally limited; migrants who were married to, or had had children with, Germans who had ties to the city; the elderly who came as refugees, as Jewish settlers, or as "ethnic Germans" and who didn't believe they would be employable elsewhere in Germany; and students. Although city leaders often portrayed the migrants as uneducated rather than desirable technologically skilled newcomers who could help rebuild the city, relatively most migrants had some education. The migrant population included some people who arrived with professional degrees and others who had come as students and wanted to settle in Halle after graduation.

The city leadership of Halle spoke of developing the city as a center of technology and knowledge, based on its nineteenth-century history as a center of science, its historic university, and the location since 1990 of several research institutions. However, although Halle was the largest city of the new state of Saxony-Anhalt, it did not become the capital of the state following German reunification in 1989. Without this power, Halle was unable to command the resources it needed to reinvigorate its economy. For example, an initiative to build a critical mass of educational and research institutions was derailed when crucial departments of its medical school and university were downsized or closed. The much-touted city-region knowledge and business networks, which supported the petrochemical industrial sector and broader development in Saxony-Anhalt, generally were not linked to the leadership of the locality or to its inhabitants.

In 2004, Halle officials described the city as "the nucleus of a wide area constituting an economic metropolis, in which service industries and technology centers predominate" (Halle Die Stadt 2004b). Yet the same website reported that the "best known local products are Hallorenkugel chocolates, Kathi cake mix, and railway rolling stock built at Ammendorf," ignoring the fact that chocolate and cake mixes were not examples of advanced technology and that the railway car factory was closing. In 2005, the biggest news was the opening of a call center, and though several hundred jobs were assured, most were neither high-tech nor high-salaried.

Consequently, there was stiff competition, even for unskilled and illegal work. Migrants with legal permission to work found few opportunities for employment and even less for occupational mobility, with the exception of becoming small entrepreneurs. In the 1990s, migrants and natives found themselves in a postsocialist city without a multitude of small shops. As we will show, migrants found places for themselves within this niche, not by forming an ethnic enclave of entrepreneurs who employed and served migrants of the same ethnic background but by contributing to businesses that served all the residents. The legal system provided an incentive: migrant professionals and workers who had come during the socialist period could get permission to stay only if they could document the self-sufficiency that a small business provided.

Neither Manchester nor Halle were able to fund ethnic organizations as a pathway to immigration, social mobility, and local leadership. Public and charitable funding was generally made available to a population defined in terms of a "special need" rather than on the basis of cultural difference. In Manchester, a small number of public or charitable agencies served the poor, the homeless, people with AIDS, severely disabled children, and persons defined by the general category of "minority" rather than by specific cultural heritage.[2] The few ethnic organizations initiated by migrants lacked the political clout to obtain federal grants and did not have the networks and professionalism to attract local charitable sources. In Halle, mainstream Christian organizations such as Caritas, which receive tax support, provided some minimal free services, including German lessons for asylum seekers. Halle's Eine Welt Haus (One World House), a nongovernmental organization with public funding, won government contracts to provide some social services but focused primarily on cultural programming about foreigners, or for foreigners, throughout the year. The city also funded a community center that was dedicated to foreign-native interaction, consisting primarily of cultural events. The few organizations begun by migrants had no public or charitable support and few members or activities.

This situation is very different from that in global or gateway cities, where, despite neoliberal policies that reduce public funding, the city's political leadership and local institutions may continue to support immigrant ethnic organizations. Ethnic concentrations provide economies of cultural difference that can increase the competitive edge of the city, as well as provide economic niches for investment in industries such as media that reach transnationally (for a German example, see Çağlar 2005). In some gateway cities in the United States, ethnic concentrations continue to provide a political base for rising politicians, who then redistribute city funds to ethnic organizations. However, in downscale cities in the current global and national context, ethnic communities would seem to be a much less viable pathway of incorporation. This is not only because these cities may not contain ethnic concentrations but also because they cannot afford ethnically organized social services.[3] There are not the political constituencies, the available funds, or the interest in local charities necessary to sustain ethnic organizations.

Even though in Manchester and Halle funding and activities organized around the public representation of cultural diversity were relatively sparse, there were occasions in both cities when city leaders celebrated diversity or devoted public space to the promotion of immigrant organizations. City developers sometimes used celebrations of diversity in order to promote their cities as culturally diverse as part of the effort to repackage and market them. In a ten-minute video available in 2004 on Manchester's official website, the government explicitly marketed the city and its workforce as diverse. The video, which was aimed at inviting investment and entrepreneurial capital and enticing highly paid professionals to settle in the city, mentioned the multiplicity of cultures several times.

As part of their aspirations to attract new economy industries, Halle's leadership also positively referred to the presence of migrants in their city. However, city developers in Halle approached the migrant presence within a very different context. City leaders understood that in order to attract increased flows of capital and global talent, they must counter Halle's particularly negative reputation in Germany not only as polluted and bleak but also as racist (interviews with mayor and city council representatives 2000–2001). This reputation reflected media coverage of violent attacks on African migrants by a handful of unemployed neo-Nazi youth in Halle and Dresden. These eastern cities had been branded through these images, despite the fact that the attacks were not representative of popular opinion and that western German cities had likewise experienced murderous attacks on homes for asylum seekers.

In terms of their position on migration, both Manchester and Halle were pulled in different directions by competing interests that reflected their similar positioning as downscale cities. On the one hand, some of the media, politicians, and service providers in both cities saw foreigners as a new and criminal factor in urban life. Others argue that migrants seriously exhausted local services. There was actually little evidence of this so they referred to the large number of languages spoken in the schools. Halle public schools reported that there were more than fifty languages being spoken by their students, and Manchester schools observed approximately forty student languages (but the press sometimes provided a much higher number).

Economic and Religious Non-ethnic Incorporation: Scalar Considerations

Whether they examined local settlement or transnational connection, by ignoring questions of city scale, researchers on migrant incorporation have taken descriptions of migrants' ethnic activities, such as businesses and religious organizations, to typify the relationship between migrants and cities. Because ethnic pathways of incorporation often are so plentiful in cities labeled global or gateway, researchers may focus on them to the exclusion of non-ethnic modes of incorporation, which have been understudied and undertheorized. By briefly reviewing forms of migrant economic and religious non-ethnic incorporation in Manchester and Halle, we highlight the importance of tracing variant pathways of incorporation.

In the "new geographies of governance," where the cities are under increasing pressure to generate local capital, both Halle and Manchester had reduced access to public monies and resources. Both had a shrinking tax base, little money for city services, and little or no money for services for migrants. Unlike larger-scale cities, such as Berlin or New York, very few public or private agencies provided migrants with opportunities to develop careers as culture brokers who represented the needs or interests of particular ethnicities. The few well-established migrants who over the past few decades have achieved political or public prominence were able to do so not as ethnic leaders but on the basis of a broader constituency. If their foreignness was at all publicly marked, it was on occasions when they played the role of public foreigners—persons called on to be general representatives and spokespeople for all foreigners in the city—rather than serving as representatives of a particular ethnic group.

There has been significant scholarship that describes immigrant businesses and entrepreneurialism (Bonacich and Modell 1980; Light 1972; Portes and Böröcz 1989; Waldinger 1986b; Wilson and Portes 1980). However, as Jan Rath and Robert Kloosterman (2000) have pointed out, in many cases the study of migrant economic activity and business practices very quickly becomes the study of ethnic economy and ethnic business. In Manchester as well as Halle migrant businesses must be understood as part of the overall urban economy rather than as indicators of ethnic enclaves. Migrants in both cities built networks that linked them to natives in various ways, including through migrant entrepreneurship. Most migrant businesses in both cities served the local population and/or migrants from various regions of the world. Their national and transnational supply networks both built on cross-cutting ethnic affiliations.

Migrant incorporation in many factories in Manchester took place through a form of paternalistic labor management practices. Workplace relationships between migrants and native coworkers or employers contributed to building social fields that extended beyond the factory and into migrants' family life in Manchester and transnationally. Small factories often worked through personalized systems that extended favors to migrants in return for their acceptance of exploitative and dangerous working conditions. There seemed to be a sense, particularly within a network of factories in the same industry, that "everybody knows each other." While this may have contributed to quiescent workers because a reputation as a troublemaker was hard to conceal, it also meant that networks extended across hierarchies of worker, supervisor, and manager and crosscut ethnic lines. For example, a white native New Englander with a job as a plant supervisor helped find jobs for migrants from various backgrounds whom he considered born-again Christians. This supervisor was married to a Filipino woman who was a factory worker. A supervisor who was native to New Hampshire helped a Vietnamese worker sponsor the migration of his family, and another supervisor assisted a Vietnamese worker to obtain a college degree and a better position in the factory.

Therefore, at the beginning of the twenty-first century Manchester presented a context for migrants that combined the patriarchal features of nineteenth-century industrialization with the contemporary neoliberal profile of a downscaled city with few social services or resources to assist in migrant settlement. While similar pathways of incorporation may be basic to migration settlement in cities of different scalar positions, it is clear that in downscaled Manchester they were a central aspect of migrant incorporation.

This is not to say that there were no businesses in these cities that highlighted the ethnic background of their owners. When the Manchester city leaders needed to revitalize the small-business sector of the city center that had been virtually abandoned for several decades after the advent of a large shopping mall built on the outskirts of the city, they looked to migrants to jump-start this development. Assisted by certain tax advantages, a number of migrant businesses opened on the main street of the city between 2000 and 2005. These included a Hungarian pastry shop, a Vietnamese restaurant, a Vietnamese travel agent, a Columbian-owned upscale coffee shop, and Chinese and Mexican restaurants. The staff from the Manchester city planning office believed that this form of cultural diversity was an important urban asset in their campaign to make the city center more attractive to highly paid professionals and tourists. Part of the planned restructuring assumed that the newly rebuilt city center would attract high-tech workers, both native and foreign, who required a cosmopolitan lifestyle. However, the businesses were valued primarily because they brought life to the previously moribund street, replacing secondhand clothing stores and abandoned store-fronts with bright new facades. What mattered most was main street gentrification rather than the marketing of a particular ethnicity or any ethnicity. Thus the upscale coffee shop developed by migrant business capital was as valued as the Mexican restaurant developed by an Ecuadorian businessman who had accumulated capital in the office-cleaning business.

In Halle legal migrants—even those from EU countries—faced difficulties in obtaining employment. High unemployment rates and national policies prioritized the hiring of people of German nationality, followed by EU migrants, effectively keeping other migrants from working in industrial, service, or public sectors. Even the networks that linked migrants to natives were ineffective as a means of helping people find jobs, because so many natives were unemployed. Most migrants in the workforce were employed as unskilled labor through short-term work contracts that were imposed on people who received social welfare benefits from the state.

However, migrant businesses have flourished in Halle, and they have done so to a greater degree than in Manchester. The local opportunity structure in the 1990s—an absence of local businesses and inexpensive storefronts, rather than previous business experience—led both Vietnamese professionals and Kurdish farmers to become small merchants. Some migrants, primarily North Vietnamese, were working or studying in Halle at the time of unification. They faced expulsion unless they could prove independent sources of support, such as owning a business. In Halle they provided vitally needed products and services for the native population, offering affordable clothing and food for a substantial portion of the German population who had been forced to subsist on low-wage jobs or social welfare. In the city center area we surveyed in 2001, up to 12 percent of the shops on the central arteries were migrant businesses, although only 4 percent of the population were migrants.

Scholars of migration have also looked at religion as a pathway of migrant incorporation. In U.S. migration studies, immigrant churches have long been seen as playing dual roles of providing social and emotional support for migrants within a familiar culturally bounded religious community while simultaneously acting as agents of assimilation (Schermerhorn 1949; Warner 1998). More recently the focus has been on migrants participating in transnational religious organizations and networks. However, apart from research on Islam, this scholarship has focused primarily on culturally delineated religious communities; it has ranged from studies of Hindu nationalists to a growing literature on African Christianity in Europe (van Dijk 2004; Haar 2000). In this research, as in the studies of ethnic entrepreneurs, there has been a general failure to examine the variations in religious practice that may reflect or be accentuated by localities of settlement or transnational connection.

Again, ethnographies of migrant religious pathways of incorporation in Manchester and Halle prove useful in reconfiguring current perspectives on migration and urban life. In both cities we found non-ethnic religious

Fig. 8. A fruit and vegetable stand owned by a Vietnamese entrepreneur was among the businesses located in the rebuilt central train station of Halle/Saale. Between 2000 and 2008 migrant entrepreneurs were disproportionately represented in central urban spaces, which had been rehabilitated in an effort to rebuild the city and attract new-economy industries. Photo by Nina Glick Schiller.

pathways of local and globe-spanning connections. While such pathways exist in cities of different scalar positioning, in downscale cities such as Halle and Manchester they were more readily apparent because ethnic options were fewer. Moreover, in such cities migrants provided pathways of local and global connections that were otherwise difficult for local residents to forge or maintain. For this reason, these non-ethnic religious pathways may well have taken on a greater significance for migrants and natives alike. Migrants in both cities found that they not only had been welcomed into religious organizations with global religious identification but also were able to play leading roles in them. These organizations provided venues for participation within local social life as well as for becoming part of global religious communities. Given the limited possibilities for economic incorporation and social mobility for both migrants and natives, such organizations played incorporative roles for both sectors of the local population.

In Manchester we followed the organizing efforts of a Nigerian preacher, Heaven's Gift;[4] a small group of religious organizers including a woman of Puerto Rican descent; a white native of New Hampshire and his Filipino wife;

and several other white natives of New Hampshire. They succeeded in building the Resurrection Crusade, a network of more than fifteen area churches.
Heaven's Gift had come to Manchester via born-again Christian networks
as an Ogoni refugee from the Rivers State of Nigeria, a center of struggle
for control over the country's oil resources. The Resurrection Crusade promised "spiritual reformation in Manchester" with a "revitalization strategy"
designed "to equip and empower communities." In forming the Crusade,
Heaven's Gift and his organizers linked local residents, both natives and migrants, within a globe-spanning network of born-again churches. Heaven's
Gift's networks included prominent Nigerian pastors such as Reverend Madugba, who was based in Port Harcourt, Nigeria, and London. However,
Heaven's Gift's Nigerian connections did not reflect his embedding in a
transnational ethnic community. Instead they situated the Crusade within
a fundamentalist Christian set of linkages. Reverend Madugba was part of
the Harvest Ministries based in Melbourne, Florida, and had links to Tikkun International, a "network of emissaries in Israel and around the world,
working toward the restoration of Israel and the unity of Jew and Gentile in
the Body of Messiah" (Tikkun International Ministries 2008). The Crusade
networks intersected with the Christian Broadcast Network and Regent University, a Christian university founded by Pat Robertson. The university had
John Ashcroft, former attorney general in the George W. Bush administration,
as a member of its faculty, and it contributed more than 150 of its graduates
to that administration. Heaven's Gift was also linked to U.S.-based global
ministries whose preachers spoke to gatherings of thousands in far-flung locations that included India, Indonesia, and South Korea.

The Crusade drew from the global/local discourse of Pentecostal Christianity, which joins migrants and natives to claim specific cities as battlegrounds
in which to wage "spiritual warfare." According to Alice Smith (1999, 6), a
white American pastor and leader of the U.S. Prayer Center based in Texas
and a frequent speaker at Crusade conferences in Manchester, spiritual warfare is the "cosmic conflict that rages between the Kingdom of God and the
Kingdom of Satan." The Crusade trained "prayer intercessors" in "strategic
or city level spiritual warfare" against "the Devil" who assigns his "territorial
spirit...to rule geographical territories and social networks" (23).

The discourse of spiritual warfare to oust disruptive spirits that destroyed
community resonated with both local New Hampshire residents and newly
arrived migrants. They looked to theological explanations to understand the
marked disparities of fortunes and opportunities, which they observed globally and experienced locally within the restructured landscape of new high-
rent apartments and offices in the city center; the gentrified restaurants and
shops of the main street; the rise in real estate values that were brought by
high-tech professionals settling in Manchester but employed in the Greater
Boston area; and a general lack of social mobility for the locally college educated residents, whatever their birthplace and cultural heritage. Consequently,
although Nigerian connections played a central role in bringing Heaven's

Gift and African preachers in his network to Manchester, the discourse of demons and devils that the Manchester Resurrection Crusade members used to speak about the problems that faced their city and themselves cannot be attributed to an ethnically differentiated African Christianity.

The dividing line of identity drawn by these churches reflected not ethnic differences but a moral separation between those who stood with the Lord and those who worked for the Devil. We should note that two of the churches in the Crusade network, a Spanish-language church and an African American church, seemed at first glance to minister to an ethnic constituency and therefore have a somewhat different mission. However, the Spanish-language church conducted bilingual services that were open to all, and its leadership insisted that the goal of the church was not to build a separate ethnic congregation but to win the city for the Lord. The members of the African American congregation shared this goal.

By first founding the Crusade and then opening a prayer center in the newly gentrified city center, Heaven's Gift's network brought not only the current globally circulating discourses of born-again Christianity but also significant political and social capital to Manchester. Heaven's Gift and his core organizers helped introduce those who attended the Resurrection Crusade and Prayer Center's events to a vision of the local that participated in, and contributed to, the global constitution of spiritual forces and circuits of influence. Claiming Manchester for God meant reaching into the political life of the city, and this was achieved in several ways.

First of all, the mayor of Manchester, Robert Baines, and the governor of the New Hampshire, Craig Benson, were invited to endorse and attend prayer conferences and breakfasts. During our field research Mayor Baines, who was a member of the Democratic Party and a Catholic, attended two prayer breakfasts and sent messages of greeting to the prayer conferences. Craig Benson, the Republican governor attended one of the breakfasts. The prayer breakfast held in the fall of 2003 included seventy people who were affiliated with more than ten different churches. In 2004 more than one hundred people attended the spring breakfast, and not all who wished to could be accommodated.

In addition to these breakfasts, the Crusade used the ties it had forged with the mayor to position its activities in central public locations in the city. On the National Day of Prayer, which was established by Congress in 1952 and popularized by born-again Christian churches, Heaven's Gift led prayer services in the aldermanic chambers of city hall and a large public prayer meeting in city parks. In 2005 Mayor Baines provided free access to a public park, complete with a band shell and a free speaker system. Members of the Manchester fire department attended the outdoor meetings. At the breakfasts and open-air prayer meetings, approximately two-thirds of those who attended were natives of New Hampshire, predominantly white. The rest were recent migrants from a wide range of countries of Latin America, Asia, and Africa.

Migrants and natives said that they came to the events sponsored by the Crusade because of their concerns for religious unity, stronger families and churches, and the need to insure that Manchester was a Christian city. The occupations of the white natives ranged from manual labor to business ownership. Many had developed personal networks with migrants through shared activities as prayer intercessors or through other Christian projects in the city. The Crusade was more than an organizational nexus; it also comprised individual activists who drew members of their own personal networks into an expanding field of Christian activity and connection. This network of Christian believers was the primary social field of core activists, migrants and natives alike. At the same time, migrant core activists built weak but significant bridging ties into other spheres of urban life, including the political domain.

While the ties to political actors provided by the Crusade's networks were not based on multiple mutual or dense connections, migrants did obtain social capital. They became connected to people who could, and did, provide resources: for example, a shop foreman helped believers find factory jobs, middle-class white women furnished the apartments of African newcomers and provided clothing and baby furniture for newborn babies, and public officials provided prestige, social acceptance, and access to public resources. Heaven's Gift succeeded in buying a two-family house with the assistance of his religious network. Migrants who were not activists in the Crusade but who attended churches, breakfasts, prayer conferences, and days of prayer linked to it were able to enter this social field in a city where they had few other opportunities to obtain social or economic capital. At the same time, because the Crusade was part of a global network, those who participated in Crusade events in Manchester found themselves in personal contact with visiting pastors from other parts of the country and world. The width and depth of the Crusade's network lent credence to its local organizing efforts and reinforced the claims of migrants to a rightful place in the city and the sense of all local members that they had joined a nationally and globally powerful network.

The churches in this network were not alone in efforts to intensively evangelize migrants by offering them supportive prayer sessions and healing, as well as social support, companionship, and assistance in finding jobs, establishing households, and purchasing automobiles, which were essential in Manchester to commute to work or to shop. Several evangelizing churches convinced migrants who came to Manchester as Catholics to convert to Protestantism as part of their incorporation into the city.

When we began looking at churches in Halle, Germany, the situation at first seemed dramatically different from that in Manchester. We found two Pentecostal congregations made up primarily of migrants: the Miracle Healing Church, an English-speaking congregation, most of whose members were from Nigeria; and God's Gospel Church, a French- and Lingalla-speaking congregation, which was mostly Congolese. It was not until we began systematically attending church services and prayer meetings and met with the pastors and congregants that we began to see that representing these churches as ethnic congregations obscured the complexity of the incorporative pathway they were forging in Halle and transnationally.

The pastors of both congregations, although they led churches that were composed primarily of migrants, stressed not ethnicity but a Christian identity in ways that resembled the self-representation of Heaven's Gift and the Crusade. As did Heaven's Gift, the migrant pastors divided the world and the people of their new city into those who accepted Jesus into their lives and those who needed to find the light. They saw themselves and their migrant congregants as sent by God to evangelize in the city; both pastors and several of their core activists told us it was not by accident that they had come to this city. They insisted that their churches were not Nigerian or Congolese but were churches "of Jesus."

While the migrants in Manchester who followed a born-again pathway of incorporation found that in the United States their form of religious belief was accepted as a legitimate means of achieving political connection and legitimating political position, the migrants in Halle who pursued a similar pathway confronted a different situation. In Germany, Pentecostal churches, which were outside the mainstream, were viewed by many people as sects—even though they were legally recognized and affiliated with a German federation of Pentecostal churches (Bund freikirchlicher Pfingstgemeinden). The situation was more complex in eastern German cities such as Halle, where most people were distant to and distrustful of all churches. However, a minority turned to the church to replace the social and spiritual support they had found in socialist institutions, and some of these people proved open to the missionary efforts of the African migrants.

Consequently, migrants in Halle were able to use their religious networks to build a social field that offered to both migrants and natives incorporative possibilities in Halle, Germany, and transnationally. The fact that Halle was a city of nonbelievers legitimated the born-again division between "persons of God and the Devil" and strengthened the migrants' belief that they were sent by God to evangelize. The migrant members of both the Miracle Healing and God's Gospel churches claimed that their presence in Halle and in Germany fulfilled the biblical prophecies that had promised the land to true believers. According to Pastor Mpenza, the Congolese pastor of God's Gospel Church, the message of the Bible was clear: "Every place whereon the soles of your feet shall tread shall be yours" (Deut. 11:24, King James Version).

The two congregations differed in their size, the networks of their pastors, the particular talents of their leaders, and the legal status of their members. Most of the members of God's Gospel Church were asylum seekers and quite poor, although the pastor and his wife had been granted refugee status with permanent residency. The congregation of approximately thirty members was not exclusively African; there were also a few German women. Only a few of the African members could speak passable German. In contrast, the

Miracle Church had approximately 150 members, and many of the migrants in the congregation had permanent legal status, obtained primarily through marrying Germans. Pastor Joshua could speak German, and by 2005 about 15 percent of the membership was German.

In that year, the Miracle Church posted on the homepage of its website two photos, one of the church building and one of Pastor Joshua praying with a young, blonde white woman. The caption proclaimed that the church was "the place of miracles, signs, and wonders. There is Power in God's Word!! Here…the sick get healed, the blind see, and many are delivered from bondage of sin." By 2005, the Miracle Healing Church had recruited between six and ten white German women and men as part of their core of church activists. Significantly, while many of the German members of the general congregation were women who were married to or had had children with African men, most of the German activists did not have such relationships. A female activist who served as a translator for most events was a student who came from a small local village, while another woman who did occasional translation had worked in Asia as a missionary. The German woman in the choir traveled to Halle every weekend from another city, where she was a children's librarian. She had been a Christian for almost twenty years but found Pastor Joshua to be more "a man of God" than other pastors. In assessing the social and cultural aspects of these local contacts, it is important to note that those who joined the church worked to bring partners and family members with them, and each of these conversions or memberships increased the density of migrants' networks, which in turn facilitated their access to social, economic, and legal resources. Attendance at Sunday services ranged from 75 to 150 people.

Initially the Miracle Church received support from a Protestant youth organization in Halle, which provided the congregation with access to buildings for prayer services and other activities. By 2004 the congregation had a sufficient income from its own tithes and donations to rent and renovate its own building. In 2005 the Miracle Church, supported by several other missionary churches and organizations in Halle—including a U.S.-based Mennonite mission with members primarily based in Germany and a congregation based in a Vietnamese family network—rented a local ice hockey arena and organized a five-day "healing conference." Most of the two to three hundred people who attended each day's activities were native German. Most of the natives, including teachers, counselors, and the unemployed who attended and sought healing, were already members of local churches in surrounding villages. Almost all of those who attended had more economic resources than the migrants. Ranging in age from teenagers to pensioners, they sought a more intense spiritual life, which the migrants promised to help them obtain. Pastor Joshua and spiritual warriors of the Miracle Church preached to the natives that the Holy Spirit would force the demons of illness and failure from their body and "the door of power" would be opened (field notes, Healing Conference 2005).

Fig. 9. In Halle/Saale, in eastern Germany, Germans increasingly joined Africans in building a Pentecostal church based not on ethnic ties but on Christian missionizing. The church provided one of the few possibilities in this downscaled city for newcomers or natives to obtain community, respect, or transnational networks. Photo by Nina Glick Schiller.

As had been the case with Heaven's Gift and his network of visiting pastors, "healing miracles" were the main form of evangelism employed by Pastor Joshua and the international and German missionaries who visited the congregation in Halle. In Halle, as in Manchester, natives and migrants came up to be healed during regular prayer services and special healing services and "conferences," sometimes falling into a trance. The migrant members of the Miracle Church found themselves increasingly participating in a local religious social field to which they gave, as well as received, emotional support and special forms of knowledge. This was particularly evident at the healing conferences held in both cities. Several members of the Miracle Healing Church attended a pan-European Pentecostal conference in a Berlin stadium in June 2003 that was called to arrange a European-wide organization of Pentecostal Churches and bring religious revival to Germany. Pastor Joshua joined the circuit of pastors, not only ministering to his own congregation but also performing healing in other cities. By 2005, he had preached in India and Korea, as well as in other German cities.

The transnational religious connections developed by the pastors were important for locating them within multiscalar networks, as well as providing legitimacy and social ties for individual migrants. In Halle, as in Manchester, weak ties were significant in several different ways. Through their pastors, the congregants were exposed to, and experienced themselves as part of, overlapping Christian globe-spanning networks that validated their faith and their presence in Halle. These types of indirect connections and organizational ties overlapped with the personal friendships that migrants made with visiting pastors and missionaries.

Some material resources also become available to migrants through their participation in the churches and the broader social fields. Both congregations used some of the money they collected to directly assist members who had personal or family crises. In addition, the insistence of the church on marriage facilitated the ever-increasing number of marriages between migrants and Germans. The desire of the African partner to marry was removed from its utilitarian context, despite the fact that such marriages made the spouse eligible for permanent residence in Germany. Instead, migrants who married within the church community were able to legitimate their marriages as a covenant with God that ensured the health, prosperity, and fulfillment of both partners. Nonetheless, these unions brought migrants legal status, increased social benefits, and a German family network that provided local knowledge and social support. In addition to this, a German spouse could make it easier to open up a business or provide a legal basis to begin a transnational trading network rooted in Germany.

• • •

Understanding the contradictory pressures that confront both migrants and downscaling cities as they influence each other can provide scholars with insights into the broad spectrum of pathways of migrant incorporation, many of which have not been sufficiently addressed within the migration literature. It is in the context of an economic environment that cannot sustain sufficient small businesses to constitute a vibrant city center that the relationship of migrants to the economy of the two cities can be understood. Halle and Manchester (except for its brief industrial resurgence at the turn of the twenty-first century) did not need migrant labor, but both cities needed to fill vacant storefronts and attract people to the city center. In global or gateway cities migrant businesses often cater to the general population or an ethnically diverse migrant population, and persons of migrant background may open stores that market cultural difference and thereby give the city a more diverse profile. Sometimes they adopt ethnic identities different from their own. In downscale cities such as Manchester and Halle, not only are these aspects of entrepreneurship more visible because of the restricted economic and social opportunities for ethnic pathways of incorporation, but also migrant businesses that serve consumers in the city center may play an important role in the local economy. In Halle, these businesses provided inexpensive food and goods for the German population and filled shops in the newly renovated city center, while in Manchester the immigrant businesses contributed to the gentrification of the city center.

At the same time, the migrant business niche was too small in Manchester and Halle to provide a sufficient base for the incorporation of most migrants. It was within these constrained opportunity structures that the church congregations and pastors embedded in global Christian networks found their place. Such congregations certainly exist in global cities or more relatively upscale cities, but they appear to play a larger role in cities such as Manchester and Halle. In these two cities born-again Pentecostal Christian congregations offered desirable social networks to local residents, ranging from interactions with preachers who belonged to powerful transnational religious social fields to political leaders who were important in local, national, and global arenas. The social and symbolic capital these networks provided were certainly visible in both cities, although the relationship of migrants and natives to Christianity as a local pathway of incorporation varied in ways that reflected historical differences between the cities.

Manchester's Christian religious climate made politicians eager to gain religious endorsements from religious leaders. Moreover, in Manchester the societal pressure toward church affiliation made it difficult not to belong to a religious group. Church-based social services were promoted by government policy, and religious activity was officially encouraged, as the example of the mayor's support for the celebration of the National Day of Prayer in the aldermanic chambers and public parks made clear. In Halle, where there were few active churches, the link between politics and religion was weaker, but the postsocialist, deindustrialized, and marginalized context of the city provided migrant preachers with an opportunity to play leading roles in Christian recruitment and the provision of venues for global connections. In both cities, migrants who joined churches that could not be easily designated as ethnic were looking for a setting that did not publicly highlight cultural difference. The universalistic Christian messages of these churches were welcoming on many levels. Christian born-again churches, such as those in the Resurrection Crusade network or the Pentecostal churches of Halle, divided the world between the saved and unsaved. This categorization gave migrants legitimacy by allowing them to be among both the saved and the saviors.

While our data is only suggestive, our research does indicate that in both downscaled cities global Christian churches offered some migrants a pathway of incorporation into the life of the city, the country, and the world that few other institutions in those cities were able to provide. In both Halle and Manchester migrants were cast as simultaneously dangerous and useful contributors to efforts to market the city as a global actor. By choosing to emphasize a Christian universalism rather than an ethnic particularism, some migrants responded to this positioning by seeking different ways to become incorporated as local and global actors on their own terms. The non-ethnic

Christianity we have been examining offered migrants in downscaled cities incorporation into social relations with access to various kinds of social, economic, political, and symbolic resources locally and globally.

What does the study of migrant settlement in downscale cities like Manchester and Halle teach us about the pathways of migrant incorporation that have marked the period of neoliberal restructuring? First of all, pathways of migrant incorporation that have historically been the basis of migrant survival—small businesses and a religious community—continue to be significant in settings that are as culturally and historically diverse as Manchester and Halle. In cities that have not been able to successfully restructure their economies and reposition themselves within hierarchies of power, migrant pathways may prove to be more widespread than ethnic community. Second, these pathways have both local and transnational aspects because migrant social fields reflect and contribute to the contemporary globality of all cities.

At the same time, in a downscale city migrants may have easier access to natives who are willing to offer them assistance in finding a job or to provide an array of supports on the basis of religious bonds. These weak ties provided migrants in Manchester and Halle with various kinds of incorporative possibilities that otherwise would have been much more difficult for them to achieve. Moreover, although migrants may make up only a small percentage of the population, they may be significant actors in neoliberal processes in cities that experience downscaling. They may contribute to the restructuring and rebranding of such cities as well as to the efforts of local people to react to the dehumanizing effects of these processes through establishing alternative and transnational forms of community. Seeking social support and transnational connection in the face of the pressures of neoliberal restructuring, both migrants and natives in Manchester and Halle turned to the religious networks that were mutually constituted by local and transnational actors. Migrant entrepreneurs responded to the need of city planners and developers to revitalize the city center and became part of the efforts to resist and reverse the downscaling process confronting both cities. Through the locally based transnational social fields they create within a downscaled city, migrants may prove to be active agents of the reconstitution of urban life.

The implementation of a neoliberal agenda worldwide has had wide-ranging implications for social welfare institutions, refugee regimes, and the provision of public services in states throughout the world. However, while the effect of unequal economic and political restructuring on urban life is being documented everywhere, scholars know very little about how this rescaling has affected migrant settlement and incorporation. How much the scalar repositioning of a city affects pathways of migrant incorporation is an empirical question that requires broad and cross-national comparisons. We argue that if cities differ in their relationships to flows of capital, goods, people, and power, this variation should be examined in terms of the roles migrants play within neoliberal urban restructuring and rescaling. It is our hope that the data provided in this chapter, while illuminating aspects of life in two downscaled cities, will also prove useful in stimulating new theorization of the relationship between varying pathways of migrant incorporation and the different ways in which urban life is being reconstituted.

Notes

1. We use the word "migrant" to include both immigrants and refugees, despite the fact that they have different entitlements and refugees have a faster track to citizenship. In Manchester, many people who arrived with permanent resident or student visas came from war-torn countries. People with various entry statuses often are members of the same networks, organizations, or families, share workplaces and places of worship, and are served by many of the same organizations.

2. The only significant exception was the Latin American Center. It provided elementary English as an Other Language (EOL) and translation services to Spanish-speaking migrants. In 2005 it had a staff that was in part composed of volunteers, was underfunded, and faced significant cuts in its public funding.

3. In fact, ethnic concentrations may be rarer in downscale cities because of refugee resettlement policies and the limitations of local opportunity structures. However, even when there are such clusters, the resources necessary to foster a viable ethnic constituency or an ethnic social service agency generally are limited.

4. We have used pseudonyms for the names of migrants and churches in Halle and Manchester in accordance with commitments we made to protect the confidentiality of persons interviewed. The names of transnational religious organizations and public figures have not been changed.

Chapter 11

Remaking Locality

Uneven Globalization and Transmigrants' Unequal
Incorporation

BELA FELDMAN-BIANCO

The photograph below was taken by Marcus Halevi, a professional photographer who documented the making of my visual ethnography *Saudade*.
The documentary portrays the ways in which Portuguese immigrants have
re-created their homeland's past in their everyday lives in an industrial
American city (Feldman-Bianco 1991).[1] The photograph depicts an Azorean
rural ritual—a Holy Ghost procession—juxtaposed against the landscape of
a rather antiseptic American highway in New England. It evokes memories
of my own astonishment at suddenly encountering a similar, albeit smaller,
procession in 1987 during my preliminary fieldwork excursions into the
streets of the small, historic city of New Bedford, Massachusetts. I was struck
by the apparent incompatibility of Holy Ghost cows with the city's industrial setting, compelling me to further explore the question of who and what
constitute appropriateness in place. My research was extensively inspired
by the multiple and contradictory allegorical images of Portuguese temporalities and spatialities imposed upon and contrasting with an American industrial setting. In a way, these metaphors of "Portugueseness" appeared to
draw symbolic borders around a series of ethnic enclaves spread throughout
small New England cities. While my research also considered the parallel
and simultaneous processes of immigrants' incorporation into New Bedford,
I centered my attention on cultural constructions of *saudade* (nostalgia) in the
diaspora.

It is worth remembering that by 1990 a combination of factors had stimulated the reconstitution of Portuguese culture and identity. Between the 1960s
and 1980s American policies fostering chain migration enabled new contingents from the Azores and continental Portugal to settle in New England

Fig. 10. Scene in industrial New England from an Azorean rural ritual known as a Holy Ghost procession. Photo by Marcus Halevi.

and continue its tradition of incorporating immigrants as unskilled labor. In the 1970s the U.S turn to multiculturalism further stimulated the politics of difference and consequently the flourishing of ethnicity. Subsequently, a 1985 Portuguese nationality law favoring those who could claim ties of blood and descent facilitated the incorporation of the diaspora into Portugal's repositioning as a postcolonial nation. This further renewed Portuguese transnational identity as emigrants and descendants became entitled to dual nationality and citizenship rights. Therefore, it was not a coincidence that the "ethnographic present" I encountered in New Bedford in the 1990s led me to examine the dynamic field of the reconfigurations of Portugueseness in the diaspora and, from that viewpoint, the transnational social fields and incorporative processes linking emigrants to their country of origin.

At that time most scholars who analyzed transnational migration to the United States focused on the newly arrived Caribbean and Asian immigrants settling in gateway cities. Yet I encountered a situation in the New Bedford area in which the newest immigrants hailed from the Azores, continental Portugal, Cape Verde, and (to a smaller degree) Madeira; these migrants followed a long tradition of movement from these sites to small cities and towns in New England. Given these repeated migrations to New Bedford and surrounding towns, I was able to address whether transnationalism was an old or a recent phenomenon. Relying on analyses of migration genealogies, domestic structures, and grassroots research, I indicated that in the past, as in the present, through their experiences Portuguese migrants have connected localities in which they have lived in continental Portugal, the Azores, and Madeira regions and the localities to which they migrated in New England (Feldman-Bianco 1992, 1995, 1995a, 1996, 1999). I also acknowledged the intensification of old as well as the emergence of new forms of connection and identification with Portugal since the 1970s. My analysis enabled me to map contemporary events against a longer history of migration and to identify an exacerbation of localism among the Portuguese in ethnic enclaves. These patterns turned out to be constitutive of the dynamic interplay between globalization and localisms in this particular juncture of global capitalism.

While my earlier research focused on the relations between Portuguese transmigrants and Portugal, I turn now to an examination of the incorporation of these migrants as active protagonists in New Bedford's social life. This chapter offers an analysis of the interplay between global and local processes that highlights the context of contemporary global capitalism in light of the changes in the world political economy over the last twenty years. These dynamics are once again restructuring New Bedford and the incorporative processes that link migrants to this gateway locality, as well as reinforcing migrants' transatlantic connections and instigating new transnational initiatives to reinvent the city both economically and culturally. Considering these developments, I attempt to discern the ways in which transmigrants have confronted, mobilized against, negotiated with, or conformed to changing historical forms and circumstances of capital formation and efforts to control and subordinate labor. I am particularly interested in unveiling the seeming paradoxes that underlie current neoliberal projects, which are driven by specific ideologies of cultural diversity and sustained by the flexible organization of labor, increasingly restrictive immigrant policies of national security, and the criminalization of immigrants.

As I turn to examine the synergy between the global processes that are restructuring New Bedford and the incorporative processes linking migrants to this locality in neo-liberal times (Glick Schiller, Nina, and Ayşe Çağlar, 2006), I will once again rely on my ethnohistorical data. While the "city scale approach" tends to refer predominantly to contemporary globalization, questions regarding the "restructuring and reinventing of urban life through transnational processes" and "the role played by migrants and their local and transnational practices of incorporation in the rescaling and restructuring of cities" (Glick Schiller and Çaglar 2006, 6), call for an understanding of historical processes underlying (and constraining) the making and remaking of localities and regions. Instead of centering on the Portuguese as a unit of analysis, I focus here on New Bedford and local politics to explain the relationship between globalization, city scale, and the incorporation of immigrants.

As Saulo Cwerner (2000, 335) has rightly pointed out, while scholars have tended to focus on the spatial configurations of cosmopolitanism and globalization, the historical dimension of global society has been largely forgotten. In accordance with his call for a sensitivity to both the temporal and spatial dimensions of globalization,[2] I delineate the continuities and changes in the positioning and role of Portuguese transmigrants, as well as their local and transnational practices of incorporation throughout the rescaling and restructuring of New Bedford. My analysis also takes into account the repositioning of the regions and country of origin of these transmigrants; I trace the impact of Portugal's repositioning in the global economy as a result of European Community membership and concomitant changes in living conditions within Portuguese regions and localities. Since the mid-1980s, while Portugal benefited from European Community investments, the South Coast of Massachusetts, including the cities of New Bedford and Fall River, has experienced disinvestment and economic decline. These processes, resulting in a drastic reduction of Portuguese migration to New England in the last decade, have led to a reversal of positions between the South Coast of Massachusetts localities and the Azores. This realignment has manifested itself in cultural, educational, and economic partnerships between actors in New Bedford and Portugal, which have been forged by influential bicultural and bilingual brokers.

These processes also demonstrate how Fordist and neoliberal practices are superposed on each other in old manufacturing centers, such as New Bedford and Fall River. They further clarify the ways in which these two cities, which are part of the South Coast region, have continued to be interlinked to Portuguese regions and localities through immigrants' social fields and bicultural brokers' incorporative practices. These processes illuminate how the remodeling and transnational practices of Portugal's postcolonial state itself have made inroads in the South Coast, including in the channeling of Portuguese grants and donations to U.S. local and regional institutions.

The Cutting Edge of Global Capitalism

Once upon a time New Bedford was at the forefront of the global whaling (1815–60) and textile industry (1880–1925). Since the early twentieth century, however, New Bedford has been striving to attract manufacturing and service industries and, more recently, tourism. When I first arrived in the whaling city in the late 1980s, the imposing structures of the textile mills—symbols of an era when the city was at the cutting edge of global capitalism—were occupied by labor-intensive factories employing immigrants, mostly from the Azores and continental Portugal. However, as I noted repeatedly in my fieldwork diaries, these factories were closing down or leaving town one after the other, mostly as a direct result of outsourcing. The production previously performed in New Bedford was being relocated to other countries. Concomitantly, as part of an interrelated trend in the global economy, the local fish-processing houses began to be incorporated by larger businesses, resulting in a similar relocation of labor. During the same period, repeated attempts by workers to save Morse Cutting Tools, the remaining tool-and-die enterprise in town, were unsuccessful; ultimately, this business was also closed. In short, the last two decades of the twentieth century in New Bedford were marked by another phase of deindustrialization in the wake of a short-lived "Massachusetts economic miracle."

In making the film *Saudade,* noting that Portuguese laborers were facing yet another wave of local plant closures, salary cuts, and unemployment, I chose to juxtapose memories and images of the six-month-long strike in 1928 with scenes of a 1988 Carol Cable strike organized by the United Electric Union. In doing so, I sought to signal the long-term incorporation of Portuguese immigrant workers into the American labor force, including through union mobilization. However, I have come to understand that the strikes were a part not only of the story of Portuguese migration or of the history of New Bedford's labor movements but also of the restructuring and repositioning of the city. These two strikes symbolically marked the shifting positioning, or rescaling, of New Bedford in the global economy at different historical junctures. In fact, together with the Great Depression, the 1928 six-month strike is remembered by local inhabitants in connection with New Bedford's downfall as a leading city in the textile era after its recovery from the demise of the whaling industry. New Bedford has confronted deindustrialization ever since the 1920s, when local mills lost out in competition with the American South. Yet in the context of the Massachusetts economic and fiscal crisis, the decline of manufacture and fishing during the past few decades reflects a new downscaling of New Bedford. The city is now situated in a historical juncture marked by the flexibility of capital and labor, outsourcing, and the ongoing neoliberal restructuring of cities.

In this chapter, by paying attention to both the global processes restructuring New Bedford and migrants' political mobilization and transnational practices, I highlight the underlying rescaling of New Bedford and the shifting positions of the Portuguese in the city's economy, politics, and culture. I do so by examining two events. The first event, the 1928 strike, allows me to revisit the formation, apogee, and downfall of the local textile manufacturing center and its repercussions on the city. Although the labor force of the textile industries was composed mostly of European workers of different nationalities, the 1928 strike exposed existing cleavages among skilled and unskilled workers at a time when immigrants' mobilization was expressed mostly in terms of their participation as members of the working class. Moreover, it foregrounds how, as a result of the prevailing politics of race, the Portuguese were located at the bottom of the labor force hierarchy because of their association with immigrants from Cape Verde (which was until the 1970s a colony of Portugal).

The second event, the 1988 strike and its aftermath, proved pivotal to the ways in which the Portuguese subsequently shifted their image and position in New Bedford. Portuguese history and folklore were made a part of the local intangible heritage, a valuable cultural asset in contemporary processes of urban renewal marked by the politics and marketing of culture. Both episodes further illuminate the changing understanding of the Portuguese as a group at different historical junctures. The historical analysis I adopt also draws attention to the danger of using the category of "ethnic group" (in this case, the Portuguese) as if it were self-evident and immanent.

The Formation of a Textile Manufacturing Center (1880–1925), the 1928 Strike, and the Rescaling of the Gateway City for Immigrants

In the eighteenth and part of the nineteenth century (1815–60), New Bedford was the most important whaling port in the United States. Upon the discovery of petroleum, whaling expeditions, based on Azorean and Cape Verdean crews, started to decline. As whaling became less profitable, New Bedford merchants shifted their capital from whaling to cotton but nevertheless continued to control economic and political power in the locality. At a time when the neighboring textile towns were involved with the production of coarse cloth, New Bedford mills decided instead to specialize in fine cloth. They thereby avoided competition with mills in the American South, which after the end of the Civil War (1865) were able to use cheaper labor, the absence of state labor laws, and more advanced machinery to offer lower prices for coarse cloth than New England-based mills could. Therefore, at the beginning of the twentieth century and during a second wave of displacement following World War II, many textile mills left New England and moved to the South.

New England textile manufacturers, including those of New Bedford, recruited a labor force composed predominantly of European immigrants who were sometimes categorized by their nationalities in rather generic ways and differentiated according to their skills. They included skilled English and Irish workers and the unskilled Portuguese (continental Portuguese, Azoreans, and Madeireans), Cape Verdeans (who were then Portuguese subjects), the "Polish" (a designation referring to immigrants from Eastern Europe), "Syrians" (referring to immigrants from the Middle East), French Canadians, and Italian workers. But it was only at the turn of the twentieth century that the Portuguese, along with other southern and eastern European unskilled workers, began arriving in large numbers as cheap labor in the cotton economy. By 1910, the Portuguese already represented 40 percent of that labor force. Estimates further suggest that by 1930, 80 percent of the Portuguese were cotton mill workers, while 15 percent were professionals and businesspeople.[3] These immigrants were fleeing poverty in a period of Portugal's major economic decline; finding that hard times prevailed in New Bedford, many moved to other U.S. regions or returned to their homeland. Those who remained in the region were deeply affected—as were other local residents—by the decline of the textile industry and the thirty-year-long depression of the New Bedford economy that was to follow.

By the turn of the twentieth century, New Bedford, already the largest producer of fine cloth in the United States, was a manufacturing city "with large mill complexes and vibrant working class neighborhoods" (Georgeanna and Aaronson 1993, 11). Textile manufacturing led to the formation of two multiethnic neighborhoods around the mills at the city's south and north ends. While life in the neighborhoods entailed everyday interaction among immigrants from different nationalities, the English and the Lancaster Irish, and to a certain degree the French Canadian, were at the top of the ethnic hierarchy in the workplace. Even after the Portuguese became the largest labor force in the mills, the English maintained control over union leadership and skilled jobs. The French Canadians were able to secure the remaining skilled jobs and succeed in local politics. In contrast, by 1926, the Portuguese and Cape Verdeans held among them fewer than 10 percent of the skilled jobs and were alienated from the craft unions and politics. Moreover, stigmatized since the whaling era as "Black Portuguese," they were given the worst jobs, as bobbin boys, doffers, carders, combers, sweepers, and spoolers, and jobs that required only brief training (Reeve 1997b, 231). The Cape Verdeans tended to be confined to the card room, known as the "slavery department of a cotton mill." According to an oral history,

> The slavery department of a cotton mill was the card room. You never sat down. You always had plenty of work to do and were never paid much money. Mostly Portuguese and CapeVerdean people worked there. They would never hire a colored guy and put him in the spinning room. They would never make a weaver out of him. Not that the white guys wouldn't work with him. We'd have been glad to. It was management's way of doing things. The management kept us apart. The management kept the colored people in the card room. You saw very few white people in there, except for the boss.[4]

The English and the Lancaster Irish formed their own craft unions and did not encourage or welcome unskilled workers in their Textile Council. The conservative leadership of the Textile Council was firmly in power by 1901, when New Bedford's textile unions joined other unions to form the United Textile Workers, an affiliate of the American Federation of Labor (AFL). Beginning in the twentieth century, members of the Textile Council were often elected to city and state positions, and they eventually formed the Labor Party in 1918. Moreover, their relations with management were friendly following 1893, the year in which they organized a major strike. In contrast, the majority of the mill workers of other nationalities were not union members. This unskilled labor force was composed of underpaid men, women, and children confronting difficult labor conditions and monotonous tasks with long hours of work (six-day workweeks with ten- to twelve-hour shifts). Yet the union leaders relied on these masses of unskilled workers when they mobilized against management (Georgeanna and Aaronson 1993, 29; Reeve 1997a).

Although New Bedford mills had found a niche in the production of fine cloth, upon the outbreak of the First World War, the local textile industry decided to switch to coarsely woven products for the military. The industry profited greatly from the wartime boom. Sales more than quadrupled, and profits increased sixfold, while the local population reached one hundred thousand (Wolfbein 1944). However, after the end of the war, "the mills began accumulating unsold cloth rather than profits...and mill owners began withdrawing from textile production" (Georgeanna and Aaronson 1993, 44–45). Even though most of their machinery was old and outdated, they opted not to invest in new textile equipment. Some moved their investment and production to the South. After the cloth market collapsed in the early 1920s, mill owners decided to lay off thousands of mill workers and stopped production. When they reopened the mills, wages were drastically cut. The following years were even harsher, and in 1928 the mill owners announced a further 10 percent wage cut.

The announcement angered workers. Moreover, it violated a pact with the Textile Council to let the union leaders know in advance about plans to cut wages. The workers started the six-month-long strike of 1928. From the beginning of the strike, the council counted on the support of the clergy, business community, and media. The masses of unskilled workers who did not belong to the craft unions became "the main force of the strike" for "[t]hey were fed up with the wage cuts and the speedups, and it was almost as if everything was organized beforehand, but it wasn't. When the Textile Council rejected the ten percent cut and announced that they were gonna strike, all the unskilled people that they paid no attention to got out there. And they became the main force of the strike."[5] However, these lower-paid, mostly Portuguese, Cape Verdean, and Polish unskilled workers sided instead with the leftist Textile Mill Committees (TMC), whose representatives came to New Bedford to challenge the Textile Council. A few Portuguese who had been union organizers in Portugal and had fought fascism in their homeland helped the TMC newcomers to distribute leaflets and introduced them to the Portuguese workers. According to Daniel Georgeanna and Roberta Hazen Aaronson's careful research on the strike,

> The TMC quickly took the alienation and frustration of the unskilled, lower-paid workers, who had been excluded from the craft unions, and turned it into an enthusiasm unrivaled in previous New Bedford strikes. Daily picketing, meetings, rallies and soup kitchens created excitement, purpose and unity behind the strike in the Portuguese and Polish communities. Thousands walked the picket lines and attended rallies organized to educate and entertain. The TMC concentrated its efforts in the immigrant neighborhoods located around the mills in the North and South ends of the city and left the center of town, where the mill owners lived and commerce reigned, to the Textile Council.

Organizers went to people's homes to encourage participation. Families pick-
eted as groups—women with babies in their arms, young children, and young
children walking. (1993, 83–84)

Under the leadership of the TMC, the strikers demanded a 20 percent wage
increase, a forty-hour week, equal pay for equal work, an end to speedups,
no discrimination against union members, and an end to child labor. Eula
Mendes, a Portuguese labor activist, remembered, "We wanted a union that
would take in all of the textile workers. We called for an industrial type of
union instead of a craft union, and that was progressive at that time because
most of the unions in the United States at that time were craft unions. The
whole idea was to get all the textile workers in one mill to belong to one union
and all of the textile workers to belong to a single textile union" (83).

In oral histories I collected, former workers invariably recalled how the
agricultural background of Portuguese textile workers, the gardens they
grew, and the social support of Portuguese dairy farmers, bakers, and fishermen who donated milk, bread, and fish to be distributed at the TMC headquarters helped them to confront the hard times. Even if their actions and
interactions were informed by prior experiences in Portugal and continuing
ties to the homeland, these strikers were mobilizing as workers rather than
along ethnic lines. After six months, mill owners tried to end the strike on
their own terms and reopened the mills with the 10 percent cut in effect. At
this juncture, the Textile Council leaders and the mill owners reached a settlement and attempted to eliminate the TMC. Many workers were arrested, and
a few were even deported; one of these was Augusto Pinto, who had been
arrested on the picket lines and convicted twenty-two times. Even though he
was released by the superior court, the U.S. Immigration Service placed him
on a ship to Lisbon. After he arrived, the Portuguese dictatorship sent him to
Cape Verde to be imprisoned. He reportedly died during the voyage. While
most textile workers got their jobs back after the strike, they were confronted
one year later with the Great Depression, unemployment, and increasing
poverty. Between 1929 and 1934, sixteen out of the thirty-five mills operating
in the city closed their gates permanently. Economic conditions deteriorated
further, not only in New Bedford but also throughout the United States.

The strike and the Great Depression concentrated the processes that led
to the downfall and repositioning of New Bedford regionally and nationally.
As was the case with many other mill towns, New Bedford did not recover
its position of importance within the United States or even in the state of
Massachusetts. The strike also marked the Portuguese workers' fuller incorporation into the local and U.S. labor movement, even as the restructuring
of the New Bedford economy began to make it difficult for these workers to
earn a living in the city. During the decline of the cotton industry and later,
during the Great Depression, return migration from New Bedford and other
New England cities to Portuguese regions was relatively high. Some immigrants returned to their homeland with their entire families, which in many

cases included American-born children; others left their married offspring in the United States, returning to Portugal with their younger (American and Portuguese-born) children.

To a certain extent—even during the 1930s and 1950s, when restrictive American immigration quotas allowed only five hundred Portuguese to enter the United States annually[6]—American-born Portuguese continued to move between their homeland and the United States, sometimes bringing along their Portuguese mates. In the same fashion, as a result of the decline of New England's mill economy, some Portuguese offspring who had been left in the United States eventually returned to Portugal. Others, while remaining settled in the United States, went to Portugal to find mates. Still others moved from New England to other American regions, particularly California and New Jersey, where there seemed to be more possibilities of employment. Those who remained in New Bedford continued to cope with hard times, both in New England and back home. Many remained in touch with their relatives in the homeland, and, when they could, sent remittances. For many, the symbolic representations and social practices associated with the past prior to immigration provided an outlet for self-expression. Alongside the proliferation of regional voluntary associations and mutual aid societies, in the 1920s and 1930s immigrants established Portuguese schools. Radio programs and six Portuguese theater groups were formed. The most radical of these groups, the Popular Dramatic Group (linked to the antifascist Liberal Alliance in Portugal), was an offspring of Portuguese involvement in both the 1928 six-month-long strike and the fight against fascism in Portugal.

In those times, given the prevalence of territorialized nationalisms, immigrants and descendants continuously confronted the choice between remaining Portuguese or assimilating and becoming American. On the one hand, Portuguese nationalism stressed the exclusive maintenance of Portuguese culture, language, nationality, and the supremacy of the Portuguese "race."[7] On the other hand, as oral histories suggest, the pressures of the Americanization campaigns had a potent effect on the descendants of immigrants. Furthermore, Americanization allowed individuals to distance themselves from a Portuguese identity, which racialized them as nonwhite. Rejection of a classification as Portuguese avoided the issue of race. In order to avoid discrimination, particularly the stigma of "Black Portuguese," Portuguese Americans tended to "pass" within the mainstream culture, even though in many cases they retained the Portuguese language and traditions. Some, but not all, intermarried into other immigrant groups. At the same time, Americanization provided the possibility of gaining access to political, social, and economic mobility within the United States. Overall, those who stayed in the city underwent a gradual process of incorporation into New Bedford, and some Portuguese Americans ultimately gained positions of influence both in the locality and within labor unions.

Immigration was resumed in 1958 with the Azorean Refugee Act.[8] At a time when the United States was attracting new immigrants from Asia and the Caribbean, contingents of immigrant workers (mostly from the Azores, mainland Portugal, and Cape Verde) continued to settle in the city. These newcomers found a new industrial regime of labor-intensive factories that began to develop in the partially abandoned industrial sites of New Bedford. The continuous arrival of those contingents to the United States was facilitated, between the 1960s and the 1980s, by American governmental policies fostering chain migration. In fact, these policies enabled many families to reunite in New England and simultaneously reinforced the common family strategy of choosing mates for daughters and sons in the homeland. Moreover, the tendency of the local factories to engage in the paternalistic labor strategy of hiring family members of "docile" workers contributed to the formation of a labor force mainly composed of Portuguese male and female workers. In fact, until the late 1980s, when many corporations began once again to close their local plants, it was not unusual to find immigrants who had worked together with their relatives in the same factory for fifteen or twenty years. But within the factory, promotion was possible only for those with knowledge of the English language. While many immigrant workers spoke only Portuguese, supervisors as well as union representatives were bilingual.

As had previous older generations of workers, immigrants from rural backgrounds reconstructed social practices associated with their agricultural past—such as gardening, wine making, sewing, embroidery, and folk festivals—as a way of dealing with monotonous industrial work. While during their work shift they were proletarians, in their free time they continued to be peasants and artisans. Most tried as soon as they could to buy houses in New Bedford with backyards, where they could cultivate gardens and raise animals. While through their symbols and social practices, these migrants reconstituted Portugueseness in the ethnic neighborhood, they were also redeveloping the city. The migrants were acting as agents of urban revitalization by keeping the city alive not only through their labor but also through their investments in neighborhoods and small businesses. They were aware of their role in renewing dilapidated housing and rejuvenating local commerce, including through the opening of ethnic stores and restaurants. These post-1950s migrants maintained transnational family ties; some planned to return to the homeland after retirement in the United States, which would afford them full access to pensions and the U.S. Social Security and Medicare systems to which they had contributed through their taxes.

However, the arrival of these new contingents led to cleavages between Portuguese Americans and the new immigrants, further accentuating regional divisions. Moreover, these new arrivals increased the prevailing discrimination against the Portuguese. In this context, a 1983 gang rape, known as the Big Dan, in which a third-generation Portuguese American woman was attacked by a handful of unemployed Azorean immigrant workers, exposed the different cultural codes in operation and the existing prejudice and xenophobia against the new immigrants. Sensationalized by the media, this internationally infamous rape case involved and divided all sectors of the local population in an apparent confrontation between an emerging consciousness of sexual abuse and the growing militancy of ethnically organized populations. The Big Dan rape became a point of struggle in an environment in which multiculturalism was increasingly becoming a hegemonic U.S. discourse that emphasized the politics of the everyday rather than the politics of class. Media coined New Bedford the "Portuguese gang rape city of America," and the city and Portuguese immigrants were portrayed equally pejoratively by the national and even international media. The case foregrounded New Bedford's shifting positioning in the global political economy from the richest whaling city in the world to a decaying and depressed gateway city for bizarre and dangerous immigrants. The incipient revitalization of the city by Portuguese immigrants, which would lead to a reclamation of the Portuguese identity, was not yet recognized. That change did not occur until both Portugal and New Bedford were once more transformed by the global restructuring of capital and migration (Feldman-Bianco 2007a).

The Rescaling of New Bedford and the Shifting Position of Portuguese Americans in Neoliberal Times

Since the late 1950s, the renewal of immigration from continental Portugal, the Azorean Islands, and Cape Verde has ensured that the majority of the New Bedford working class has remained of Portuguese origin. The Carol Cable labor force was not an exception. Carol Cable had been built on the new immigration but subsequently had to confront the fact that the very forces that had brought the industry to New Bedford were poised to relocate it to other sites where the conditions of profitability for operating such a plant were greater. In their meetings, the Carol Cable workers were aware of this global trend. At the same time, only five years after the Big Dan gang rape that brought to the fore their anger against long-standing anti-Portuguese prejudice and xenophobia, the workers perceived the company's attempt to impose wage cuts and cancel workers' health insurance as discrimination against the Portuguese. Transforming their demands as workers into an ethnic mobilization, they also claimed that their salaries were already lower than those of the workers at other Carol Cable plants. In the end, the workers won the strike, but one year later Carol Cable closed its plant in New Bedford. Since then, and particularly after the signing of the North American Free Trade Agreement (NAFTA) in 1993, numerous other plants have closed their operations in the city.

The processes of economic restructuring experienced by New Bedford were statewide in scope. Both individual cities and the state of Massachusetts as a whole were strongly affected by NAFTA. Between 1993 and 2000 Massachusetts lost an estimated total of 17,000 jobs. The apparel industries were dramatically affected by the NAFTA protocol throughout the 1990s; local manufacturing employment fell drastically by 55.1 percent from 20,528 jobs in 1985 to 9,212 in 1999 (Barrow and Borges 2001). If the twenty-year period from 1985 to 2005 is considered, the overall loss of manufacturing jobs was even greater, reaching a total of 61 percent (Sá and Borges 2009). However, whereas other regions within the state were able to cope with the global structural changes of the 1980s by diversifying their local economies or attracting new-technology industries, New Bedford and neighboring Fall River continued to depend heavily on older forms of industrial production and fishing. In the 1990s, commercial fishing shrank because of changing laws, and as a result the local fishing workforce was reduced (Georgeanna and Schrader 2008, 188).

Consequently, in 1995 the state designated New Bedford an economically distressed area after a Department of Housing and Urban Development report characterized the city as being "double burned" by population loss and high unemployment and poverty rates. Total employment rates decreased from 65 percent in 1985 to 50 percent in 2001. In that same year, the locality was ranked the 348th lowest-income community among the 351 municipalities in Massachusetts (Barrow and Borges 2001, 2). These were the clear signs of New Bedford's downscaling. Like laborers around the world, New Bedford's working class had to cope with the restructuring of global capitalism and the reorganization of workforces as "flexible labor" without long-term job security, benefits, unions, or grievance procedures. In this situation, many local citizens started to look for alternatives elsewhere. Accordingly, the city's population dropped from 99,222 inhabitants in 1990 to 93,768 in 2000. While some Portuguese decided to migrate to other regions of the United States—especially Florida, where they believed the cost of living was lower[9]—others opted to return to the homeland, where economic conditions had improved after Portugal joined the European Community. For those who remained in New Bedford, the growing services sector and the declining manufacturing industry were the major employers in the city. Those who lost their factory employment because of NAFTA were forced to learn new skills, including the English language. Most began looking for employment in the services sector in the city and surrounding region. The majority of the men went into blue-collar trades, especially construction work, while women tended to move into pink-collar occupations like office work, child care, elderly care and social work (Sá, 2008).

Thus, Portuguese laborers, like their counterparts elsewhere, were exposed to even greater economic vulnerability as they entered flexible labor employment, which does not offer either job stability or social benefits. However, in what seems like a paradoxical development, they have concurrently advanced their position within the local working class. Upon the drastic decrease of immigration from the Azores and continental Portugal to New England, new contingents from Latin America and the Caribbean have settled in the city and taken unskilled jobs in the remaining factories and fish-processing plants. Since most of these new immigrants—from Guatemala, Mexico and Nicaragua, and, to a lesser degree, Brazil—are undocumented migrants, they have became the local underclass, exploited by their employers and exposed to stringent post-9/11 immigration policies that make them victims of workplace raids by officers of the Homeland Security Department. The ferocity of raids in New Bedford, which were accompanied by deportations without due process or appeal, gained national attention in the United States in 2004 and 2007.

Harsh legislation implicating immigrants as a threat to national security began to be implemented in the United States in 1996, five years before 9/11. Besides restricting the rights of immigrants to access to most forms of federal assistance, the 1996 legislation made minor offenses a basis for deportation even for individuals married to American citizens and those with American-born children. The leadership of the New Bedford Immigrants' Assistance Center (formed by the Portuguese in the 1970 with U.S. federal funds) responded by establishing programs with U.S. and Portuguese funds to provide services to the deportees (mostly from the St. Michael Islands) and their families and to strengthen cooperation and informational exchanges between local New Bedford and Azorean officials. With the aim of counteracting the restrictive immigration law of the previous year, in 1997 bicultural community leaders began an extensive "naturalization" campaign to ensure that immigrants living in the United States had a political voice and access to U.S. social benefits. The naturalization campaigns resonated with the politics of dual nationality and citizenship promoted by the postcolonial Portuguese state. Accordingly, the motto, "to be a good Portuguese, it is necessary to be a good American," used by leading Portuguese Americans in the 1930s to persuade immigrants to apply for U.S. citizenship and assimilate into American society, was redefined by former president Mario Soares during a 1987 visit to New England to stimulate biculturalism. He advocated a new politics emphasizing the incorporation of diasporic Portuguese into their respective localities of settlement to enable them to act as representatives of Portugal.

Toward this end, the Luso-American Development Foundation (or FLAD), a private, financially independent institution created by the Portuguese government in 1985 "to contribute towards Portugal's development by providing financial and strategic support for innovative projects by fostering cooperation between Portuguese and American civil society,"[10] joined the ongoing naturalization campaign." In 1999 it launched a Portuguese American citizenship project to promote citizenship and civic involvement in Portuguese American communities. According to a leading cultural broker, the FLAD's project has helped to structure the campaign across different American regions. As an outcome of these joint undertakings, citizens of Portuguese descent have been better represented in public office in New Bedford as well as in the New England region more broadly. In 2009, seven of the eleven town councilors of New Bedford are of Portuguese descent, and an eighth is the widow of a deceased Portuguese councilor who still retains her husband's Portuguese surname. Portuguese immigrants are further represented on the school committee and on the board of elections committee. However, these representatives do not necessarily play ethnic politics but rather contribute to efforts to improve the competitive position of the city.

In this regard, it is important to consider that while most migrants from continental Portugal and the islands to the New Bedford area in the late 1950s originally worked as fishermen or in factories, they experienced a gradual process of differential social mobility and unequal incorporation. Many managed to retire in the United States and thus gain access to the American structure of retirement benefits.[11] Their sons and daughters were able, at least from the 1970s, to pursue a U.S. education. Some offspring who earned a college degree began to serve as cultural brokers between immigrants and American institutions. They benefited from the prevailing celebration of multiculturalism and from their bilingual and bicultural skills by entering occupations within the local government structure and the bilingual educational system, as well as in the New Bedford Portuguese institutions that were created in the 1970s with the aid of American grants (Feldman-Bianco 1992). Others managed to open their own businesses or became professionals in different fields. And, though their numbers are small, it is also possible to find Portuguese immigrants and descendants who are now millionaires (Sá 2008).

Against this background, the Portuguese, who had been characterized in the early 1970s as an invisible minority (Smith 1974), seem to have enhanced their structural location as an ethnic group in New Bedford, including within the realm of local politics. This improvement is the result of the interplay of a number of factors, including the drastic reduction of immigration from continental Portugal and the archipelagos of the Azores and Madeira, the gradual process of unequal incorporation of immigrants and their descendants in the locality and region, and the corollary processes of upward mobility and suburbanization. The most important factors, however, have been the positioning of the Portuguese state in the global economy and the role played by Portuguese American bicultural and bilingual brokers in changing the image of Portugal and its islands in New England. This is a process that began with the entrance of the Portuguese postcolonial state into the European communitarian space in 1985.

Acknowledging that the diaspora remains a part of the nation, the Portuguese state now provides emigrants and their descendants with dual nationality and citizenship rights and encourages leading citizens of the diaspora "to represent Portugal in the world." This became an asset in places like New Bedford. Relying on the brokerage of diasporic associations to reach the dispersed migrant population, the Portuguese government eventually formed a World Council of Portuguese Community in 1996. On the basis of both the incorporation of Portuguese emigrants into the nation and the redefined relations with former colonies, Portuguese officials and intellectuals have further reinvented Portugal's "Atlantic and universal vocation" as a way of reconstituting its earlier role as a broker in the global economy and thus negotiating its position within the European Community (Feldman-Bianco 1995b, 2001). Through combined actions of the ministries of Foreign Affairs,

Culture, and Economy, the government has built a solid information industry tying the promotion of the Portuguese cultural patrimony to the ongoing
politics of expansion in markets, tourists, and investments. In this endeavor,
it has progressively shifted its focus toward strengthening its relations with
the affluent and influential leadership of the diaspora, who are capable of
both occupying positions of power in their localities and countries of settlement and playing brokerage roles for Portugal's interrelated politics of culture and investments. In the same spirit, the Portuguese state has established
the Camões Cultural Institute in charge of disseminating Portugal's ancestral
universal culture across the world, including via traveling exhibits (Feldman-
Bianco 2001, 2007b). Consequently, the FLAD Portuguese American citizenship project should also be seen in conjunction with both the Portuguese
state's long-distance nationalism and concerted efforts by affluent and influential Portuguese and Portuguese Americans to increase the political power
of the Portuguese as an ethnic group in U.S. mainstream politics.[12]

As I have noted, Portuguese Americans and immigrants who have
achieved upward social mobility have repeatedly attempted to become part
of the main political, economic, and social streams of society in the United
States. In the past, they were continuously confronted with the choice of
either continuing to be a stigmatized and racialized Portuguese minority
in New Bedford or publicly assuming an American identity, even while in
many cases retaining the Portuguese language and traditions. Later, in the
1970s, as part of their efforts to establish themselves as part of the majority—rather than as a minority—affluent and influential Luso-Americans
decided not to make use of affirmative action initiatives. They maintained
this position even when confronted with the choice between becoming as-
similates or bicultural and bilingual immigrants (formulated as mutually
exclusive categories). Thus they distanced themselves from the issue of race
at a time when Cape Verdeans, already independent from Portugal, had
chosen the "minority path." However, since the 1990s, newer generations
of upwardly mobile immigrants and descendants have joined an already
established stratum of Luso-Americans, some of whom had even reclaimed
their Portuguese American identities after U.S. policies shifted from assimilation to multiculturalist ideologies.

While in the past the possibility of attaining upward mobility and political power required the rejection or invisibility of Portuguese identity and
ancestry, since the 1980s an inverse process has been taking place. On the
one hand, the Portuguese state, by strengthening its relationships with the
leading citizens of the Portuguese communities abroad, has been trying to
establish "the presence of Portugal in the world." On the other hand, in their
attempts to establish themselves as part of the mainstream of American society, those leaders have been using reinvented tradition (using Eric Hobsbawm's definition of the term) to improve their positioning within the realm
of American multiethnic politics (Hobsbawm and Ranger 1983). This may be
illustrated by the formation of organizations like the Prince Henry Society in

New Bedford. This club, composed mostly of English-speaking Portuguese Americans and immigrant professionals and businesspeople, was named in honor of Prince Henry the Navigator. It was one of the few associations that succeeded in reuniting Azoreans, Madeireans, mainlanders, and Portuguese Americans in the locality. Since its formation, the Prince Henry Society has aimed at playing a political, economic, and social role in the New Bedford region. Toward these goals, it has revived the historical memory of the Portuguese age of exploration and promoted Portuguese high culture by honoring leading citizens of New Bedford and organizing classical music concerts, art exhibits, and conferences. Rather than reflecting an obsession with Portugal's historical and cultural past, these activities enhance the members' own class position as representatives of Portugal in New Bedford and simultaneously challenge the stereotype of the Portuguese as peasants engaging in folk-religious festivals.

Along with the politics of high culture of the postcolonial state, a Center for Portuguese Studies and Culture was formed in the mid-1990s at the University of Massachusetts Dartmouth. This center has played a major role in changing the image of Portugal and of the Portuguese in the region through a multiplicity of educational and cultural programs and activities, including summer language programs, the establishment of a Department of Portuguese, the publication of English translations of Portuguese literary and scholarly work, the organization of seminars and conferences with renowned scholars and writers, the creation of an endowed chair, the formation of Portuguese American archives to document the history of the Portuguese in the United States, and the launching of a new graduate program in Luso-Afro-Brazilian Studies. As a corollary of the transnational social fields and practices of these faculty members, the center has received financial support and grants both from the state of Massachusetts and the Luso-American Development Foundation. Through fund-raising, it has also received the support of affluent immigrants and Portuguese Americans of New England for its endeavors, including the creation of an endowed chair and the formation of Portuguese American archives aimed at documenting the history of Portuguese immigration. Working in tandem with the political leadership of the Portuguese postcolonial state, as well as with the Portuguese American citizenship project, the center and the new Ph.D. program have provided new venues for students from the United States and abroad, regardless of their national and ethnic backgrounds. While the University of Massachusetts Dartmouth has been one of the main academic institutions in the southeastern Massachusetts region to enable the higher education of successive generations of Portuguese immigrants and descendants, these programs in turn have enhanced the image of the university itself.

In Janus-like manner, leading Portuguese and Portuguese-American professionals and businessmen have made use of their transnational reach in order to act as intermediaries for both their homeland and their localities of settlement in New England. Some of those transnational brokers have also become involved in "the concerted efforts by local governance in partnership with state and federal governments, citizens and business organizations, non-profit agencies and institutions of higher education regarding the implementation of economic development policy" to address, in the words of the incumbent mayor of New Bedford, "the 21st century challenges" (Lang 2005). In 1995, the very year the municipality was named an economically distressed area, the New Bedford Economic Development Council—a public and private partnership—was formed to provide leadership and coordination of economic development initiatives, to serve as a business liaison to city hall, and to provide financing and educational opportunities to create and strengthen economic development opportunities in Greater New Bedford. Also, like other towns, cities, and even nation-states (like Portugal) in this era of flexible capitalism and neoliberal projects, the local government started to invest in both a free trade zone and tourism to promote economic recovery. Efforts to attract tourists included the creation in 1996 of a long-desired national heritage park and a museum that displayed the material cultural heritage of the whaling past. In 1998, the city became one of the sixteen showcase communities under the Brownfields National Partnership, a program set up by Vice President Gore to promote local cleanup and rehabilitation of abandoned, idle, or underused commercial and industrial properties. This designation provided access to the necessary resources for implementing three new master plans, which aimed at economic development, job creation, open protection, recreation enhancement, and increased environmental protection.

By 1997, the repositioning efforts of the Portuguese state and the New Bedford initiatives at urban reinvention through attracting international investment had borne fruit. Encouraged by leading Azoreans from New Bedford, Portugal's Ministry of Foreign Affairs (then headed by an Azorean), provided a $500,000 grant to the Whaling Museum for the construction of a special wing to portray the cultural heritage of the Azorean whalers of the city. This donation ensured that the whalers would finally be incorporated into the historical heritage of the city's elite. In light of the changing image of Portugal and its islands in the region, the New Bedford Economic Council also attempted to attract Portuguese enterprises to the city's business park and free trade zone. As a result of these efforts, a few Portuguese banks started operations in the city. Former directors of that council paid a visit to Portugal in search of investments, and in 2008 a delegation of fifty government, education, and business leaders, assisted by a leading Azorean businessman of Fall River, went to the Azores on a trade mission. This mission was designed to strengthen educational, cultural, and economic ties between the Massachusetts South Coast region (a new regional designation dating from the 1990s) and the islands. There is great interest on the part of those South Coast business delegates to gain access to markets throughout the Azores.

In 2006, in an attempt to attract manufacturing, offices, and service industries, the council had begun promoting the city as a cost-effective location with an ample supply of experienced labor with much lower wage rates than those in Greater Boston. Following the pattern that began in the Great Depression, the local government is most concerned with the creation of jobs by new businesses. Consequently, the city has exempted local industries from paying taxes in order to prevent their relocation.[13] As part of the effort to market and repackage the city, the council has drawn attention to the availability of cheaper housing and cheaper rental space in New Bedford, as well as to the ecology and geographical location of the city. Since the inclusion of the city in the Brownfields Partnership, there has been an attempt to bring artists to the renovated structures of the old mills. Yet New Bedford confronts a major handicap—the lack of a railroad connection to either Boston or Providence, the two nearest major cities. While plans for such construction exist, the city seems to lack the power to implement them. In the spring of 2008, the mayor opened a bus line between the campus of the University of Massachusetts Dartmouth and the city in order to attract students to its downtown area. In reality, however, the students still prefer to visit Providence.

In order to promote tourism, New Bedford, the gateway city for immigrants, has been advertised as a multicultural and multiethnic city. And the Portuguese identity, which had previously been racialized and was then linked to the moniker "Rape Capital of America," has become a component of the cultural heritage of the city. As part of the city's Office of Marketing and Tourism strategy to attract tourists, Portuguese restaurants, bakeries, and summer Festivals—including the Day of Portugal, which was at the time of my research essentially a celebration by and for the Portuguese and their descendants—have been promoted as "A Taste of Portugal" and have become a part of the city's intangible yet highly marketable cultural diversity.

The ongoing interplay between the politics of culture·and the politics of investments seems to mask the current stringent American immigration policies and the continuing raids by Homeland Security officers against undocumented workers. In 2004 and 2007, New Bedford attracted national news coverage because of these raids. Thirteen undocumented immigrants working at a fish-processing plant were detained in 2004. In 2007, Homeland Security agents arrested three hundred women and men, mostly from Guatemala, Nicaragua, and Mexico. Although in smaller numbers, Brazilians, and Azoreans were also among the detained. Yet, since the "Mayans" have become the new scapegoats, the media largely ignored the Azoreans under arrest. As a considerable number of mothers were separated from their small children when they were arrested, their drama caught the attention and sympathy of local and state authorities including senators Ted Kennedy and John Kerry. This incident also mobilized the citizens of New Bedford, including the leaders of labor unions and other community leaders. This local and state support also acknowledged the significant role of unskilled labor in maintaining the economic base of even the reinvented and restructured city of New Bedford. It also made apparent that among the New Bedford residents who were subject to these raids and were deported there were people who had permanently settled in the area and were contributing to the revitalization of neighborhoods and commerce in the city. However, despite the considerable social solidarity displayed and the reliance of the city on its immigrants, the stringent federal immigration laws did not leave room for appeal.

· · ·

This chapter brings to the fore the importance of a historical perspective and the utility of long-term ethnographic research in mapping the interplay of global and local processes. A historical perspective has enabled me to relate the recent renewal of Portugueseness in New Bedford and Portuguese migrants' incorporation into their country of origin, which I noticed during my initial fieldwork in the late 1980s, to a simultaneous process of rescaling that was once again transforming the city. The migrants' transnational incorporation into their home country was entangled with their concurrent incorporation as active social agents in their locality of settlement. Looking back further in time and focusing on the apogee and decline of New Bedford, my analysis has ultimately disclosed a story whose main protagonist is a predatory industrial capitalism, nourished on the control and exploitation of immigrant labor.

During the textile era, competition between New England mill towns and the American South forced local mills to close or move to the American South, where labor was cheaper and social legislation not enforced. Since the 1980s, flexible capital and the process of increasing outsourcing, together with NAFTA, have led again and again to the closing or relocation of factories across the globe in the search for cheaper labor. As part of the same process, regulatory policies have also resulted in the reduction of the local fishing industry. The persistent decline in manufacturing and the destruction of and subsequent failure to replace the former railroad system were among several variables that prevented the diversification of the local economy and led to the recurrent downscaling of the once-celebrated whaling city within the global political economy.

Yet any examination of the history and political economy of New Bedford forces us to take into account the city's positioning as a gateway city for immigrants. By doing so, we can better understand the transformations and mobilizations that are occurring today as well as the active role played by the city's transmigrant populations and their social networks in shaping these processes. The story begins with Azorean and Cape Verdean sailors whose labor in eighteenth- and nineteenth-century whaling expeditions created the capital invested in the early New Bedford textile mills. The destruction of the mills' international position in the beginning of the twentieth century and the labor struggles of that period paradoxically marked the full incorporation of Portuguese migrants into the local class structure.

Meanwhile, return migration deepened and strengthened the transnational social fields that linked the city to continental Portugal and the Azores and Cape Verde. Portuguese migrants have more recently proved to be central actors in the efforts of New Bedford and neighboring localities to reposition themselves regionally as the South Coast and internationally as a location for investment, trade, and tourism in relationship to Portugal and the European Union.

These revitalization efforts have been marked by a new valuation of the role of the Portuguese in the region as a result of dramatic decreases of migration from the Azores and continental Portugal, the arrival of immigrants from Latin America and the Caribbean who now occupy the lower ranks of the immigrant labor force, the "whitening" of the Portuguese within the United States racialized hierarchy of migrant populations, and the efforts at local universities to promote Portuguese high culture. The intensified connections of Portuguese Americans and Portuguese immigrants with their original homeland and the increased presence of the Portuguese state within the political and cultural economy of this declining region have significantly contributed to the new and more positive image of Portugal and the Portuguese. This revaluation has reversed the old negative image of Portuguese immigrants that had been pervasive in the city and that was reinforced through the 1983 gang-rape drama.

The more public identification of New Bedford with Portuguese immigration and Portugal ironically became an asset in the city's struggle to become more competitive regionally and globally. Migrants were able to play a crucial role in securing the transnational reach of the city. The entrance of Portugal into the European Community was crucial to the new positioning of Portuguese migrants in New Bedford as social, economic, and political actors both within their place of settlement and vis-à-vis the Portuguese state. Exactly because of the deterioration of the regional and global positioning of New Bedford, the transnational reach of Portuguese migrants, especially their reach to the European Community, is especially significant for both the migrants and the city. Their connections position them more centrally in the political and economic landscape of the South Coast as they facilitate educational and economic partnerships in their homeland, particularly with the Azores. They also are brokers who channel much-desired Portuguese funds to New Bedford and the region. They have become part of the repositioning efforts of both New Bedford and the Portuguese state within the neoliberal global order. However, while the restructuring has brought improvements in social position and cultural capital of these migrants in New Bedford and in their homelands, it has meant significant losses in the quality of life and future aspirations of those who labor, lost their jobs. and must migrate to seek work. The neoliberal regime of flexible capital and labor, together with stringent immigration policies that criminalize undocumented migrants and approach them from the perspective of national security has meant not only

the end of safe and secure working conditions won by the labor mobilizations of the early twentieth century but also increased exploitation and economic vulnerability.

Notes

1. The Holy Ghost procession was organized by immigrants from the Azorean Island of
Santa Maria who settled in east Providence, Rhode Island. Scenes of this procession appear
in the documentary *Saudade,* directed by Bela Feldman-Bianco, Peter O'Neill, and Michael
Majoros (1991, 58 minutes) and distributed by DER—Documentary Educational Resources,
Watertown, MA.

2. In this regard, Cwerner (2000, 331) suggests the concept of "chronopolitanism," which
according to him, "is developed as a theoretical and ethical opening that reconfigures the
search of a world political community in time and history. It is a move that has the explicit aim
of extending social and political responsibilities to past, present, and future generations, as
well as to the diversity of histories and rhythms that coexist in the global present."

3. Data come from Montepio Luso-Americano, *Os Portugueses de New Bedford* (*The Portuguese of New Bedford*) (New Bedford: Montepio Luso-Americano, 1932), a book published by
the immigrants themselves as part of the celebration of the fifth centenary of the discovery of
the Azores.

4. Extract of Pete Fauteux's oral history in Georgeanna and Aaronson (1993, 40).

5. Joe Figueiredo's testimony in Georgeanna and Aaronson (1993, 58).

6. In the years preceding these hard times, the United States instituted a series of restrictive immigration laws (between 1917 and 1924). The most controversial provision was the
exclusion of all "aliens over sixteen years of age who could not read the English language."
The 1924 act established the "national origins quota system," which severely restricted the
entrance of migrants from most southern and eastern European countries, who since the 1890s
had settled in large numbers in the United States. The law also continued the earlier prohibi-
tions against the immigration of East Asians and Asian Indians.

7. At that time the term "race" was used instead of the terms "people" or "community."

8. This act was issued on the occasion of a volcanic eruption in the island of Fayal to enable the dislocated population of that island to settle in the United States.

9. I thank Onésimo de Almeida for this information.

10. According to the mission statement at FLAD's website, http://www.flad.pt.

11. This strategy is less possible within the neoliberal restructuring of work because temporary employment leads to no employment-based pensions and reduced accumulation of
Social Security retirement benefits. Faced with the new flexible labor strategy, migrants may
return to their homeland, aiming to find a more favorable Portuguese economic situation.

12. For a definition and exploration of state-based long-distance nationalism, see Glick
Schiller and Fouron (2001).

13. One plant that benefited from this policy was the Bianco factory, the locus of the 2007
Homeland Security raids that arrested three hundred undocumented immigrants, mostly
from Guatemala and Nicaragua.

Afterword

An Ethnographic View of Size, Scale, and Locality

GÜNTHER SCHLEE

According to the editors of this book (introduction and chapter 4), city scale is rarely a variable in migration research. One wonders why. One of the reasons might be the fact that scale is a rather complex measure of recent theorization, comprising population size, economic importance, and global connectedness. The situation with size (no matter how it is burdened by the problems of defining group boundaries) as a simple measure of the population of cities and immigrants is no different. There are not many studies exploring the relationship between size and forms of migrant incorporation either, even though this relationship should be more obvious. The idea of size is closer to our everyday thinking than the complex concept of scale. It should not be difficult to anticipate that the size of a migrant community in a given area will have an impact both on the forms of migrant inclusion and on the structure and organization of migrant communities. We can easily observe this relationship in our daily experience.

For example, in the small rural town in Westphalia where my family lives, the odd Eritrean, the Lebanese, the one Somali, and some Kurds are aware of each other and socialize with each other in many ways. There seems to be a community composed of all non-European migrants. Any ethnicity-based designation will fail to encompass the scope of this community. Although they all have a Muslim background, this seems to be of secondary importance. A Kenyan Christian, who was our guest for an extended period, for example, was also part of this circle.

If we contrast that with a city like Berlin, obviously a gateway city, we would find larger populations of many migrant groups. The migrant community in Berlin is divided along ethnic and religious lines, and communities are substructured by region of origin and other criteria. There are many criteria of every kind, and therefore groups defined by relatively narrow criteria can be large enough to be self-sufficient in many ways. However, size comes with a high degree of closure. A setting of this kind may be described in terms of John Furnivall's classic chapter "The Plural Society" (1948, 303–12). Groups are largely self-sufficient and form closed spheres of communication articulating only at certain points with the wider society. Often it is the men who provide the points of contact. Men interact on the labor market with the wider society and are often fluent in German, while women communicate almost exclusively within the community or a certain segment of it—German has little functional value for them. Such a pattern is possible only if there are large populations of migrants in the place of settlement.

The argument that larger communities can afford to have a higher internal complexity, that they tend to divide more clearly into subunits that have a higher degree of self-sufficiency for a larger number of activities, and that smaller communities have a weaker form of substructuring and a stronger tendency toward interaction is a familiar one. It goes back to an old discussion that was not about city scale as defined in this book but was about "small-scale societies."[1] In order to assess how many of the arguments about city scale and migration presented in this book are really specific to cities and migrants, one may look at very similar arguments that are not about cities at all but about different kinds of villages in rural India, where the divisions are between the castes rather than between the natives and migrants.

Gerald Berreman (1978, 56–61) groups the villages of north-central India into two types: mountain villages and the villages of the plains. The latter are populous and close to each other. They have a diverse caste composition. Interaction between castes is formal and contractual and takes place to the degree necessitated by economic specialization. Other spheres of life are separate. Intense and frequent interaction takes place within castes, not between them. Higher castes can live up to their standards of ritual purity by avoiding contact with lower castes or untouchables.

This is not possible in the mountain villages, which are scattered and much smaller. Often the number of members of a given caste is so small that interaction must be between castes. There might only be one source of water and one shop, making mutual avoidance almost impossible. Correspondingly, plains people do not regard members of their own castes who come from mountain villages as their equals. They consider that mountain villagers of the same caste have failed to meet their standards of ritual purity. Group size is a crucial factor for the functioning of full-fledged caste system.

It is important to consider the arguments this book makes about cities, scale, and migrants together with the above-mentioned examples about villages, size, and castes. The rural example here is particularly useful when we examine the notions of scale and city scale and the convergences as well as the tensions between the concepts of scale and size.

Experiences from different parts of the world with different migrant groups could be useful in exploring the entanglements between size and scale. The examples below illustrate how the sheer increase in size sets in motion particular dynamics in the institutions of the society of settlement vis-à-vis the newcomers, which in turn initiate further changes in the categories of newcomers and their modes of incorporation into their places of settlement. For example, as Boris Nieswand's work (2008) illustrates, with the strengthening of the visa regime in Germany, newcomers from Ghana saw refugee status as a possible gate to legal residency. However, the sharp increase in the number of asylum seekers in Germany (exceeding one hundred thousand a year) in the late eighties initiated the debates about the "abuse" of the asylum laws, which in turn resulted in legal changes which made these laws more restrictive. The number of asylum seekers was simply considered too high by large segments of the media and the public. The restrictive laws made marriage to a German one of the few paths by which Ghanaian migrants could obtain legal residency. The patterns of incorporation open to migrants, asylum seekers, and those married to Germans differed substantially. It was the increase in the numbers of the incoming migrants and then the asylum seekers that paved the way for the Ghanaian migrants' different modes of incorporation into Germany.

Similarly, Günther Schlee and Isir Schlee (n.d.), show that the steady numbers of Somalian refugees that had been coming to Germany since 1969 suddenly rose after 1991, and this increase coincided with the tightening of the asylum laws in Germany. The institutional, legal, and social opportunity structures open to the refugees after 1990 differed substantially from those available to the pre-1990 refugees. The later arrivals often had to confront a very precarious residence status. Even if they were allowed to stay, most often they were not allowed to work. Their residency permits just entitled them to some form of welfare. Eventually many of them moved on, mostly illegally, to England or other countries, where a secure residence permit and ultimately citizenship are easier to acquire (Abdulkadir 2001). A secure legal status seems to be a more important factor than welfare in directing migrant flows.[2] For the post-1991 Somalian refugees, not only did Germany cease to be an attractive place, but many of the post-1991 migrants with no prospects of a secure future made little effort toward local integration. Unlike pre-1991 Somalian refugees, post-1991 arrivals made little effort to learn the language and showed strong tendencies toward seclusion and self-sufficiency because they were a large group and could afford to remain isolated and cohesive.

It is important to note that it is not only size but also density that plays an important role in determining the self-sufficiency of the groups and consequently their relationships to other groups. Clustering in big cities is not a necessity for self-sufficiency. The Somalian refugees are allocated living quarters in widely dispersed places, often smaller towns. In medium-sized cities of 200,000 or 300,000 inhabitants, a Somali community has a chance to develop and reach the desired density (in terms of numbers and spatial closeness of in-group contacts). For example, Münster (270,000 inhabitants plus a large temporary student population) has this kind of small but socially "large" self-sufficient community.

Population size is an important factor not only in migrant and "host society" relations but also in shaping relations within and between migrant groups. There are two groups of Ghanaians in Germany, "students" (comprising former students) and (often illegal) labor migrants. These define themselves in opposition to each other and with reference to the differences in their standing in the country of origin and their relationship to German society. Relations between the pre- and post-1991 Somalian refugees are also marked by prejudice and tension.

These examples make it clear that city scale is not the only factor that influences forms of migrant inclusion. Often, migrant incorporation is more directly affected by group size. This brings us to the question of group size in the context of conflict studies.

Identification Politics, Group Size, and the Nuer in Iowa

According to the dominant constructivist perspective in social sciences, social identities are not immutable but are subject to continuing identification processes, which I refer as identification work. With every change of identity, group size is affected. Group size, just like scale, is a variable, the importance of which is so obvious that one wonders why it has not been studied more systematically. Ever since the work of Fredrik Barth (1969), no one doubts that social identities and differences are constructed in contradistinction to other identities. They are situational and can change (though within certain limits) in relation to the groups faced and opportunities in hand. It is obvious that migrants faced with new groups in the context of migration develop new definitions of group boundaries and new ethnicities.

A key factor in these processes of identification and re-identification is, as stated, group size. However, this is not only the actual group size but also the group size that results from the identification process. If one is rich in resources and does not help to defend these resources, one is likely to adopt a rather narrow identity definition reaching out to few people. However, if one needs the solidarity of a wider group, broader identification processes are set in motion. The resulting group sizes are thus an important variable veiling different dynamics of identification processes. Consequently, they entail inclusionist and exclusionist mechanisms for drawing identity boundaries.

Let me illustrate the effect of migration on group identities and group sizes with just one example, taken from Falge's study (Falge 2006). The Nuer, Nilotic cattle pastoralists of the Sudan, who are one of the paradigmatic cases of anthropology, define a narrow range of agnates as closely related to themselves. It is these close relatives who will engage in certain joint activities like contributing to someone's bridewealth. Many of the Nuer who went to the United States ended up settling in Iowa as a result of American refugee resettlement policies, and they often work in the meat-packing industry. They mostly live in smaller cities with large slaughterhouses. They do not identify with African Americans, who after all are descendants of slaves. Rather, they identify with conservative, Christian middle-class whites who actively engage in church life, including missionary activities and humanitarian projects like help for refugees. However, most of their social contacts are limited to other Nuer, and they are more interested in Sudanese than in local politics.

When they marry, they still need bridewealth, and for a host of other activities they need relatives as well. Being fewer in numbers in the country of settlement, they widen the boundary of those belonging to the category of close relatives to include more kin types. This more comprehensive category is guided by considerations of group size and is in direct response to the context of migration.

Furthermore, there are wider identifications of a truly global nature. The Nuer see themselves as crusaders against Islam and thus on the side of the "good people" in the "War on Terror." To belong to the same group as George W. Bush, U.S. president at the time of Falge's study, gave them a feeling of strength. They felt close to the American Right, perceived by the Nuer as fellow crusaders against Islam. We have to leave open whether this feeling of strength and this designation of closeness was reciprocated. City size is a factor here as well. A Christian identity is claimed by all Nuer in the United States (while the Christians among the Sudanese Nuer are only a large minority). In a small town, however, they will have to affiliate with whatever Christian church exists, while in a big city they can choose among many denominations. In such situations they have the option of splitting along clan lines. In other words, group size and city size are closely enmeshed.

Scale and Size

Now I would like to review the preceding chapters in this book through the lens of size and then raise some questions about the relationship between size and scale. It is obvious that there is a connection among city scale, the size of the groups, and their relationships. It is hard to imagine that city scale should have nothing to do with the inclusivity or exclusivity of people's claimed or ascribed social identities and with the size of the groups defined by these identities. This book provides new insights into the relationships between scale and size, even though a single, coherent theory is still to be developed.

In the introduction, Ayşe Çağlar and Nina Glick Schiller explain, with reference to Neil Brenner in chapter 2, that urban scale operates "as a localized node within globally organized circuits of capital accumulation and is related to power hierarchies, which situates cities unevenly in terms of their global reach and power. Indicators of city scale include the size and strength of the banking sectors, the relative success in attracting flows of capital as well as educational and other development indicators. The size of the population of the city is useful not as an absolute measure but as a possible indicator of regional, national, and global relationships."

Thus scale is something clearly distinct from but not completely independent of size. It seems that the genealogy of this concept shows a close relation to size, where it has gradually moved away from size. It used to be size plus something else. According to Barth (1978, 253), "it should serve us as a concept to capture fundamental aspects of both 'size' *and* 'complexity.'" From being size plus something, in this case complexity, scale has become a positionality different from size but interacting with it.

Michael Samers (chapter 3) explains that "'city scale' might refer to the size of cities," especially to "large cities and world' or global cities." He contrasts this understanding with another meaning of the term, which has "emerged in the late 1980s" referring to scales below and above the national scale.

Without mentioning the term "group size," Caroline Brettell (chapter 5) makes an interesting observation about how group size and scale interact. Dallas has a lower scalar position than the Silicon Valley in terms of information technology networks and headquarters, and consequently it fails to attract sufficient numbers of Indian migrants from different schools to form separate alumni groups, despite a large Indian migrant population. As a result, several alumni groups are combined in a single organization.

Similarly, Rijk van Dijk's analysis of Ghanaians in Amsterdam and The Hague (chapter 6) as part of a global Pentecostal network could be read as a discussion beyond scale. In fact the global dimension might also be called transnational because of the preponderance of the U.S. element.[3] Couldn't we, then, consider this transnational quality of the networks also a question of size? What does this mean in terms of taxonomic levels? Shifting the identification from Christian to Pentecostal Christian is a movement from the general to the specific, from a higher to a lower taxonomic level. It may, however, be the global connections provided by this narrower, more exclusive identification that represent a special value.

Judith Goode (chapter 8) describes "confusion between achieving population size and rescaling," not in the minds of scholars but in the minds of some social actors she observed. Those campaigning to attract New York commuters to Philadelphia were unaware that, while increasing the population of Philadelphia, this effort would give the city a lower scalar position, making it even clearer than before that New York was where the action was while Philadelphia would be the affordable sleeping place.

Also with reference to Philadelphia, Goode describes a form of solidarity that has developed among all immigrants whose English still shows traces of recent acquisition. This is a response to "linguistic racialization." "Without a critical mass of Korean professional and merchant class customers, fellow immigrants are seen as preferable to native-born whites and racial minorities, who are both perceived as biased toward people of color and non-English speakers." There are two arguments here, one about size and the other about identification. If there were enough Korean customers, Korean merchants would not need to bother about other people. Because of the insufficient size of their own community, they have to include others in their we-group, and they prefer to identify with newcomers of other ethnic groups rather than with longer-established residents.

Monika Salzbrunn's chapter (chapter 9) demonstrates that Murids, in order to increase their appeal in New York, do things they would never have done at home in Senegal. They involve women in their activities, even in public debates, and they play the African card for attracting African Americans. They clearly engage in politics of size by trying to broaden their base, by expanding first across the gender divide and second along ethnic lines.

In their comparison between two small-scale cities, Halle/Saale (Germany), and Manchester (New Hampshire), Nina Glick Schiller and Ayşe Çağlar (chapter 10) conclude that ethnic communities are a less viable pathway of incorporation. This is so not only because there are not enough co-ethnics to form networks but, in an interesting twist to the argument, because the cities cannot afford to provide services for ethnic groups comprising only a minimal number of people. The ways that group size and city or settlement scale interact in Halle and Manchester echo Berreman's conclusions about Indian villagers in India, Brettell's arguments about the alumni of South Asian educational institutions in Dallas, and Goode's observations about the professional migrants in Philadelphia.

· · ·

I have been interested in group size for a decade or so,[4] and much of the work carried out by others in my department also considers group size an important variable. Nina Glick Schiller and I have repeatedly, and rather inconclusively, discussed whether we should speak of size or scale. My conclusion is that the two are not the same. Size is certainly one of the factors that contributes to city scale, and there are many other interrelations between size and scale. In order to study these interrelations, we have to keep the two concepts analytically separate; otherwise, the relationships between them are no longer visible.

The contributions to this book have focused specifically on scale. We also need to consider size, taxonomic levels, and levels of inclusivity along different conceptual dimensions, between which people move up and down in their identity discourses. Scale is just one of the conceptual tools we need in order to structure our mental representations of our social world. In itself it is a complex notion. It is a special tool for special tasks, not a *passe-partout* or multipurpose tool. As Berreman (1978, 75) warned more than thirty years ago, "If 'scale' is to be used in social analysis, its referent must be clearly spelled out, and the manner in which its constituent dimensions are to be operationalized and weighted must be specified."

Notes

1. Berreman (1978, 46–48) links the distinction between "small scale" and "large scale" to other dichotomies like folk/urban, *Gemeinschaft/Gesellschaft*, status/contract, and sixty-nine other pairs of concepts. In a way, most sociological and anthropological concepts can be subsumed under this distinction.

2. Somewhat cynically, one can apply a market model to this situation, in which the "buyers," the recipient countries of migrants, are not necessarily aware of what they are buying. Some countries have liberal immigration policies, and in these cases the influx of migrants can be regarded as intended. In other cases, the migration flow might be the unintended consequence of an action or omission. Some countries have restrictive policies but are unable to implement them. An example for this is Great Britain, a popular destination for many reasons. The absence of registration at one's place of residence and the ease with which one can adopt multiple personal identities make it easy to draw more than one welfare check and to benefit from community housing schemes in more than one place. In addition, phony or faked education certificates are usually recognized there without much difficulty. This helps migrants to acquire more degrees of all descriptions from the British educational system, which is geared toward numerical output. Some Somalis jokingly say they now exploit Britain in revenge for former colonial exploitation by the British. Compared to Britain, the only thing Somalis really appreciate in Germany is the medical care.

3. There may be Pentecostal communities in Ghana, Peru, Kyrgyzstan, and many other places. In analyses of power, the links of these communities to counterparts in the United States are generally more important than the links they have to each other. Many Pentecostal networks are U.S.-centered.

4. For the most recent synthesis and references to earlier work, see Schlee (2008).

Bibliography

Abdulkadir, M. Alim. 2001. "The Changing Nature of the Global Refugee and Immigration Movement: The Case of Somali People." PhD diss., University of Bielefeld.

Abraham, Margaret. 2000. *Speaking the Unspeakable: Marital Violence among South Asian Immigrants in the United States.* New Brunswick, NJ: Rutgers University Press.

Abrahamson, Mark. 2004. *Global Cities.* New York: Oxford University Press.

Abu-Lughod, Janet. 1995. "Comparing Chicago, New York and Los Angeles: Testing Some World City Hypotheses." In *World Cities in a World System,* edited by Paul L. Knox and Peter J. Taylor, 171–91. Cambridge: Cambridge University Press.

——. 1999. *New York, Chicago, Los Angeles: America's Global Cities.* Minneapolis: University of Minnesota Press.

Abu-Lughod, Lila. 1991. "Writing against Culture." In *Recapturing Anthropology: Working in the Present,* edited by Richard Fox, 132–67. Santa Fe: School of American Research Press.

Achor, Shirley. 1978. *Mexican Americans in a Dallas Barrio.* Tucson: University of Arizona Press.

Adams, Carolyn, David Bartlett, David Elesh, Ira Goldstein, Nancy Kleniewski, and William Yancey. 1991. *Philadelphia: Neighborhoods, Division, and Conflict in a Postindustrial City.* Philadelphia: Temple University Press.

Agarwal, Priya. 1991. *Passage from India: Post 1965 Indian Immigrants and their Children: Conflicts, Concerns & Solutions.* Palos Verdes, CA: Yuvati Publications.

Agnew, John. 1997. "The Dramaturgy of Horizons: Geographical Scale in the 'Reconstruction of Italy' by the New Italian Political Parties, 1992–1995." *Political Geography* 16 (2): 99–121.

Albrow, Martin. 1996. *The Global Age: State and Society beyond Modernity.* Cambridge: Polity Press.

Alemani, Claudia. 1994. "La Fabbrica Delle Donne." In *Le Mani Invisibili. La Vita e il Lavoro Delle Donne Immigrate,* edited by G. Vicarelli, 51–65. Rome: Ediesse.

Allen, John. 2004. *Lost Geographies of Power.* Oxford: RGS/Blackwell.

Ambrosini, Maurizio. 2001. *La Fatica di Integrarsi. Immigrazione e Lavoro in Italia*. Bologne: Il Mulino.

Amin, Ash. 2002. "Spatialities of Globalization." *Environment and Planning* A 34:385–99.

———. 2003. "Regions Unbound: Towards a New Politics of Place." *Geografiska Annaler* 86:33–44.

Amin, Ash, and Stephen Graham. 1997. "The Ordinary City." *Transactions of the Institute of British Geographers* 22 (4): 411–29.

Amiraux, Valerie. 2001. *Acteurs de l'Islam entre Allemagne et Turquie. Parcours Militants et Expériences Religieuses*. Paris: L'Harmattan.

Andall, Jacqueline. 2000. *Gender, Migration and Domestic Service. The Politics of Black Women in Italy*. Ashgate, UK: Aldershot.

Andall, Jacqueline, and Raffaella Sarti. 2004. "Servizio Domestico, Migrazioni e Identità di Genere in Italia dall'Ottocento a Oggi." *Polis: Ricerche e Studi su Società e Politica in Italia* 18 (1): 5–46.

Anderson, Bridget, and Ben Rogaly. 2005. "Forced Labor and Migration to the UK." Study prepared by the Centre on Migration, Policy and Society (COMPAS) in collaboration with the Trades Union Congress. http://www.tuc.org.uk/international/tuc-9317-f0.cfm.

Anderson, Bridget, and Martin Ruhs. 2006. "Changing Status, Changing Lives: The Socio-Economic Impact of EU Accession on Low Wage Migrant Labor in the UK." Paper delivered at the annual international conference ("Irregular Migration—Research, Policy, and Practice") of the Centre on Migration, Policy and Society (COMPAS), Oxford University, 7–8 July.

Anghel, Remus Gabriel, Eva Gerharz, Gilberto Rescher, and Monika Salzbrunn, eds. 2008. *The Making of World Society. Perspectives from Transnational Research*. New Brunswick, NJ: Transaction Press.

Appadurai, Arjun. 1996. *Modernity at Large: Cultural Dimensions of Globalization*. Minneapolis: University of Minnesota Press.

Atkinson, Rowland, and Gary Bridge. 2005. "Introduction." In *Gentrification in a Global Context: The New Urban Colonialism*, edited by Rowland Atkinson and Gary Bridge, 1–17. Milton Park, UK: Routledge.

Bakhtin, Mikhail. 1968. *Rabelais and His World*. Cambridge, MA: MIT Press.

Balibar, Etienne, and Immanuel Wallerstein. 1991. *Race, Nation, Class*. London: Verso.

Barbagli, Marzio, and Asher Daniel Colombo. 2004. *Partecipazione Civica, Società e Cultura in Emilia-Romagna*. Milan: Franco Angeli.

Barjak, Franz. 2000. "Differences in the Economic Capability of Regions—A Typology of East Germany and Poland." *Working Papers, Halle Institute for Economic Research*, http://www.iwh-halle.de/asp/pubsearchresults.asp?Scope=Pub&lang=e&Desk1=182&ACTION=Search&Order=Autoren.

Barrow, Clyde W., and David Borges. 2001. "Greater New Bedford Economic Base Analysis: Critical and Emerging Industries and Work Force Development Target." Economic Research Series No. 29, Center for Policy Analyses, University of Massachusetts, Dartmouth.

Barth, Fredrik. 1969. *Ethnic Groups and Boundaries: The Social Organization of Cultural Difference*. Boston: Little Brown.

———. 1978. Conclusion to *Scale and Social Organisation*, edited by Fredrik Barth, 253–73. Oslo: Universitetsforlaget.

Basch, Linda, Nina Glick Schiller, and Cristina Szanton Blanc. 1994. *Nations Unbound: Transnational Projects, Postcolonial Predicaments, and Deterritorialized Nation-States*. New York: Gordon and Breach.

Bauder, Harald. 2006. *Labor Movement: How Migration Shapes Labor Markets*. Oxford: Basil Blackwell.

Baumann, Gerd, Steven Vertovec, Werner Schiffauer, and Riva Kastroyano, eds. 2004. *Civil Enculturation: Nation-State, School and Ethnic Difference in the Netherlands, Britain, Germany and France.* New York: Berghahn.

Bausinger, Herrmann, ed. 1959. *Schwäbische Weihnachtsspiele. Mit Beiträgen von Willi Müller, Josef Lanz und Wilhelm Kutter.* Stuttgart: Silberburg.

Beaverstock, Jonathan, Richard Smith, and Peter Taylor. 1999. "A Roster of World Cities." *Cities* 16 (6): 445–58.

Beck, Ulrich. 2000a. *The Brave New World of Work.* Cambridge: Polity Press.

Beck, Ulrich. 2000b. "The Cosmopolitan Perspective: Sociology of the Second Age of Modernity." *British Journal of Sociology* 51 (1): 79–105.

Benton-Short, Lisa, Marie D. Price, and Samantha Friedman. 2005. "Globalization from Below: The Ranking of Global Immigrant Cities." *International Journal of Urban and Regional Research* 29 (4): 945–59.

Bernardotti, María Adriana, ed. 2001. *Con la Valigia Accanto al Letto. Migranti e casa a Bologna.* Milan: Franco Angeli.

Berndt, Christian. 2000. "The Rescaling of Labour Regulation in Germany: From National and Regional Corporatism to Intrafirm Welfare?" *Environment and* Planning A 32 (9): 1569–92.

Berreman, Gerald D. 1978. "Scale and Social Relations: Thoughts and Three Examples." In *Scale and Social Organisation,* edited by Fredrik Barth, 41–77. Oslo: Universitetsforlaget.

Betz, Fritz. 1996. "Cultural Production and the Politics of Identity: On the Strategic Use of 'Multiculturalism' in Two Austrian Cities." *Innovation: The European Journal of Social Sciences* 9 (1): 105–17.

Bhalla, Vibha. 2006. "The New Indians: Reconstructing Indian Identity in the United States." *American Behavioral Scientist* 50:118–36.

Bodaar, Annemarie, and Jan Rath. 2005. "Cities, Diversity and Public Space." *Metropolis World Bulletin* 5 (September): 3–5.

Bommes, Michael, and Frank-Olaf Radtke. 1996. "Migration into Big Cities and Small Towns—An Uneven Process with Limited Need for Multiculturalism." *Innovation: The European Journal of Social Sciences* 9 (1): 75–86.

Bonacich, Edna, and John Modell. 1980. *The Economic Basis of Ethnic Solidarity.* Berkeley: University of California Press.

Boyer, Robert, and J. Rogers Hollingsworth. 1997. "From National Embeddedness to Spatial and Institutional Nestedness." In *Contemporary Capitalism: The Embeddedness of Institutions,* edited by J. Rogers Hollingsworth and Robert Boyer, 433–84. New York: Cambridge University Press.

Brenner, Neil. 1997. "Global, Fragmented, Hierarchical. Henri Lefebvre's Geographies of Globalization." *Public Culture* 10 (1): 135–67.

——. 1998. "Between Fixity and Motion: Accumulation, Territorial Organization and the Historical Geography of Spatial Scales." *Environment and Planning D: Society and Space* 16 (4): 459–81.

——. 1999a. "Beyond State-Centrism? Space, Territoriality and Geographical Scale in Globalization Studies." *Theory and Society* 28 (1): 39–78.

——. 1999b. "Globalization as Reterritorialisation: The Re-scaling of Urban Governance in the European Union." *Urban Studies* 36:431–51.

——. 2000. "The Urban Question as a Scale Question: Reflections on Henri Lefebvre, Urban Theory and the Politics of Scale." *International Journal of Urban and Regional Research* 24 (2): 361–79.

——. 2001. "The Limits to Scale? Methodological Reflections on Scalar Structuration." *Progress in Human Geography* 25 (4): 591–614.

——. 2004. *New State Spaces: Urban Governance and the Rescaling of Statehood.* Oxford: Oxford University Press.

——. 2009a. "Is There a Politics of 'Urban' Development? Reflections on the US Case." In *The City in American Political Development,* edited by Richard Dillworth, 121–40. New York: Routledge.

——. 2009b. "A Thousand Leaves: Notes on the Geographies of Uneven Spatial Development." In *A New Leviathan? The New Political Economy of Scale,* edited by Roger Keil and Rianne Mahon. Vancouver: University of British Columbia Press.

Brenner, Neil, Bob Jessop, Martin Jones, and Gordon MacLeod. 2003. "Introduction: State Space in Question." In *State/Space: A Reader,* edited by Neil Brenner, Bob Jessop, Martin Jones, and Gordon MacLeod, 1–26. Oxford: Blackwell.

Brenner, Neil, and Nik Theodore. 2002a. "Cities and Geographies of 'Actually Existing Neoliberalism.'" *Antipode* 34 (3): 348–79.

——. eds., 2002b. *Spaces of Neoliberalism: Urban Restructuring in North America and Western Europe.* Oxford: Blackwell.

Brettell, Caroline B. 2003. "Bringing the City Back In: Cities as Contexts for Immigrant Incorporation." In *American Arrivals: Anthropology Engages the New Immigration,* edited by Nancy Foner, 163–96. Santa Fe: School of American Research Press.

——. 2005a. "The Spatial, Social, and Political Incorporation of Asian Indian Immigrants in Dallas." *Urban Anthropology* 34: 247–80.

——. 2005b. "Voluntary Organizations, Social Capital, and the Social Incorporation of Asian Indian Immigrants in the Dallas-Fort Worth Metroplex." *Anthropological Quarterly* 78:821–51.

——. 2007. "Theorizing Migration in Anthropology: The Social Construction of Networks, Identities, Communities, and Globalscapes." In *Migration Theory: Talking across Disciplines,* 2nd. ed., edited by Caroline B. Bretell and James F. Hollifield, 97–136. New York: Routledge.

——. 2008. "Meet Me at the Chat Corner: The Cultural Embeddedness of Immigrant Entrepreneurs." In *From Arrival to Incorporation: Migrants to the US in a Global Era,* edited by Elliott Barkan, Hasia Diner, and Allen M. Kraut, 121–42. New York: New York University Press.

Brettell, Caroline B., and Deborah Reed-Danahay. 2008. "Communities of Practice for Civic and Political Engagement: Asian Indian and Vietnamese Immigrant Organizations in a Southwest Metropolis." In *Civic Hopes and Political Realities,* edited by S. Karthick Ramakrishnan and Irene Bloemraad, 195–221. New York: Russell Sage Foundation.

Brubaker, Rogers. 2004. *Ethnicity without Groups.* Cambridge, MA: Harvard University Press.

Bulkeley, Harriet. 2005. "Reconfiguring Environmental Governance: Towards a Politics of Scales and Networks." *Political Geography* 24:875–902.

Buzar, Stefan, Philip Ogden, and Ray Hall. 2005. "Households Matter: The Quiet Demography of Urban Transformation." *Progress in Human Geography* 29 (4): 413–36.

çağlar, Ayşe. 1995. "German Turks in Berlin: Social Exclusion and Strategies for Social Mobility." *New Community* 21 (3): 309–23.

——. 1997. "Hyphenated Identities and the Limits of 'Culture.'" In *The Politics of Multiculturalism in the New Europe. Racism, Identity and Community,* edited by T. Modood, P. Werbner, 169–85. London: Zed/The Postcolonial Encounter.

——. 2001. "Constraining Metaphors and the Transnationalisation of Spaces in Berlin." *Journal of Ethnic and Migration Studies* 27 (4): 601–13.

——. 2005. "Mediascapes, Advertisement Industries: Turkish Immigrants in Europe and the European Union." *New German Critique* 92:39–62.

———. 2006. "Hometown Associations, the Rescaling of State Spatiality and Migrant Grassroots Transnationalism." *Global Networks* 6 (1): 1–22.

Caponio, Tiziana. 2002. "Policy Networks e Immigrazione: Le Politiche Sociali a Milano e a Napoli." In *Assimilati ed Esclusi. Stranieri in Italia,* edited by A. Colombo and G. Sciortino, 253–82. Boulogne: Il Mulino.

Caritas Migrantes. 2004. *Immigrazione, Dossier Statistico 2004.* Rome: Anterem.

Caritas Migrantes. 2005. *Immigrazione, Dossier Statistico 2005.* Rome: Anterem.

Carter, Donald Martin. 1997. *States of Grace: Senegalese in Italy and the New European Immigration.* Minneapolis: University of Minnesota Press.

Castells, Manuel. 1976. "Is There an Urban Sociology?" In *Urban Sociology: Critical Essays,* edited by Chris Pickvance, 33–59. New York: St. Martin's.

———. 1977. *The Urban Question.* Cambridge, MA: MIT Press. First published in French as *La question urbaine.* Paris: Maspero, 1972.

Castles, Steven, and Mark J. Miller. 2003. *The Age of Migration: International Population Movements in the Modern World.* 3rd ed. New York: Guilford.

Castree, Noel. 2000. "Geographic Scale and Grass-Roots Internationalism: The Liverpool Dock Dispute, 1995–1998." *Economic Geography* 76 (3): 272–92.

Catanzaro, Raimondo, David Nelken, and Valerio Belotti, 1996. "Un Posto per Vendere. I Commercianti Ambulanti Irregolari Sulla Riviera Emiliano-Romagnola." *Sociologia del lavoro* 64:85–119.

Choenni, Chan. 2002. *Ghanezen in Nederland. Een profiel.* Den Haag: Ministerie van Binnenlandse Zaken en Koninkrijkszaken.

Città Sicure. 2004. "Politiche e Problemi Della Sicurezza in Emilia Romagna: 1994–2004." *Decimo Rapporto Annuale* 30:279–336. http://www.regione.emilia-romagna.it/sicurezza.

City of Manchester. 2005. "Economic Information for Businesses." http://www.manchesternh.gov/CityGov/MED/EconInfo/Home.html

———. 2010. "Quick Facts: 'Population.'" http://www.yourmanchesternh.com/quick-facts.aspx.

———. n.d. "Mid-Year Status of Planning Projects and Programs." http://www.manchesternh.gov/CityGov/.

Clark, William. 2004. "Race, Class, and Segregation Patterns in U.S. Immigrant Gateway Cities." *Urban Affairs Review* 39 (6): 667–88.

CNEL (Consiglio Nazionale dell'Economia e del Lavoro). 1995. *Tempi e Modi di Esodo. Il Rapporto sull'Immigrazione Nelle Città Italiane.* Rome: Documenti Cnel, 65.

Cohen, Abner. 1991. "Drama and Politics in the Development of a London Carnival." In *Black and Ethnic Leaderships in Britain: The Cultural Dimensions of Political Action,* edited by Pnina Werbner and Muhammad Anwar, 170–202. London: Routledge.

Cohen, Abner. 1993. *Masquerade Politic Explorations in the Structure of Urban Cultural Movements.* Berkeley: University of California Press.

Cole, Jeffrey. 1997. *The New Racism in Europe: A Sicilian Ethnography.* Cambridge: Cambridge University Press.

Collinge, Chris. 1999. "Self-Organization of Society by Scale: A Spatial Reworking of Regulation Theory." *Environment and Planning D: Society and Space* 17:557–74.

Collinge, Chris. 2006. "Flat Ontology and the Deconstruction of Scale." *Transactions, Institute of British Geographers* 31:244–51.

Council of Europe/Parliamentary Assembly (Assemblée Parlementaire). 2003. "Migrants in Irregular Employment in the Agricultural Sector of Southern European Countries." Document 9883, July 18.

Countryman, Matthew. 2007. *Up South: Civil Rights and Black Power in Philadelphia.* Philadelphia: University of Pennsylvania Press.

Cox, Kevin. 1997. "Introduction: Globalization and Its Politics in Question." In *Spaces of Globalization: Reasserting the Power of the Local,* edited by Kevin Cox, 1–18. New York: Guilford.

Cwerner, Saulo. 2000. "Research Note. The Chronopolitan Ideal: Time, Belonging and Globalization. *Time & Society* 9 (2/3): 331–45.

D'Attorre, Pier Paolo, ed. 1994. *Il "Miracolo Economico" a Ravenna. Industrializzazione e Cooperazione.* Ravenna: Longo Editore.

Davis, Nathalie Zemon. 1975. *Society and Culture in Early Modern France.* Stanford: Stanford University Press.

De Bruijn, Mirjam, Han van Dijk, and Rijk van Dijk. 2001. "Cultures of Travel: Fulbe Pastoralists in Central Mali and Pentecostalism in Ghana." In *Mobile Africa: Changing Patterns of Movement in Africa and Beyond,* edited by Mirjam de Bruijn, Rijk van Dijk, and Dick Foeken, African Dynamics Series 1, 63–88. Leiden: Brill.

De Bruijn, Mirjam, Rijk van Dijk, and Jan-Bart Gewald, eds. 2007. *Strength beyond Structure: Social and Historical Trajectories of Agency in Africa.* African Dynamics Series 6. Leiden: Brill.

De Fillippo, Eduardo. 1994. "Le Lavoratrici 'Giorno e Notte.'" In *Le Mani invisibili. La Vita e il Lavoro Delle Donne Immigrate,* edited by G. Vicarelli, 65–72. Rome: Ediesse.

Delaney, David, and Helga Leitner. 1997. "The Political Construction of Scale." *Political Geography* 16 (2): 93–97.

De Witte, Marleen. 2005. "The Spectacular and the Spirits: Charismatics and Neo-Traditionalists on Ghanaian Television." *Material Religion* 1 (13): 314–35.

DiCicco-Bloom, Barbara. 2004. "The Racial and Gendered Experiences of Immigrant Nurses from Kerala, India." *Journal of Transcultural Nursing* 15:26–33.

Dick, Hilary Parsons. 2007. "Patterns of Mexican Migration to Three Sites in Pennsylvania: Philadelphia, Kennett Square and Norristown." Paper delivered at the University of Pennsylvania Institute for Urban Research Forum on Race and Migration, January 19.

DuBois, William Edward Burghardt. 1990. *The Philadelphia Negro.* Philadelphia: University of Pennsylvania Press.

Eade, John, ed. 1997. *Living the Global City: Globalization as Local Process.* London: Routledge.

Edin, Per-Anders, Peter Fredriksson, and Olof Åslund. 2004. "Settlement Policies and the Economic Success of Immigrants." *Journal of Population Economics* 17 (1): 133–35.

Edwards, Richard. 1979. *Contested Terrain: The Transformation of the Workplace in the Twentieth Century.* New York: Basic Books.

Ellis, Mark. 2001. "A Tale of Five Cities? Trends in Immigrant and Native-Born Wages." In *Strangers at the Gates: New Immigrants in Urban America,* edited by Roger Waldinger, 117–58. Berkeley: University of California Press.

——. 2006. "Unsettling Immigrant Geographies: US Immigration and the Politics of Scale." *Tijdschrift voor Economische en Sociale Geografie* 97:49–56.

Ellis, Mark, Richard Wright, and Virginia Parks. 2007. "Geography and the Immigrant Division of Labor." *Economic Geography* 83 (3): 255–81.

England, Kim, and Kevin Ward, eds. 2007. *Neoliberalization: States, Networks, People.* Oxford: Blackwell.

Epstein, Arnold Leonard, ed. 1967. *The Craft of Social Anthropology.* London: Tavistock.

Escobar, Arturo. 2007. "The 'Ontological Turn' in Social Theory." *Transactions, Institute of British Geographers* 32 (1): 106–11.

Esser, Helmut. 2004. "Does the New Immigration Require a New Theory of Intergenerational Integration." *International Migration Review* 38 (3): 1126–59.

Evens, T. M. S., and Don Handelman, eds. 2006. *The Manchester School. Practice and Ethnographic Praxis in Anthropology.* Oxford: Berghahn.

Fainsten, Susan, and Scott Campbell. 2002. *Readings in Urban Theory.* New York: Blackwell.

Faist, Thomas, 2000. *The Volume and Dynamics of International Migration and Transnational Social Spaces.* Oxford: Oxford University Press.

Falge, Christiane. 2006. "The Global Nuer: Modes of Transnational Livelihoods." PhD diss., University of Halle-Wittenberg.

Feldman-Bianco, Bela. 1991. *Saudade* (ethnographic video documentary), 58 min., Watertown, MA: D.E.R.

———. 1992. "Multiple Layers of Time and Space: The Construction of Class, Ethnicity and Nationalism among Portuguese Immigrants." In *Transnational Perspectives on Migration: Race, Class, Ethnicity, and Nationalism Reconsidered,* edited by Nina Glick Schiller, Linda Basch, and Cristina Blanc-Szanton, 145–74. New York: New York Academy of Sciences.

———. 1995a. "A Reconstrução da Nação Portuguesa e a Transnacionalização." *Cadernos CERU, USP* 2 (6): 89–104.

———. 1995b. *Saudade, Immigration and the Politics of Reterritorialization and Deterritorialization.* Oficina do CES. Coimbra: Centro de Estudos Sociais, University of Coimbra. Working paper 46: 1–33.

———. 1996. "A Saudade Portuguesa na América: Artefatps Culturais, Histórias Orais e a Tradução de Culturas." *Revista Crítica de Ciências Sociais,* no. 45: Coimbra: Centro de Estudos Sociais (CES). University of Coimbra, 113–26.

———. 1999/2000. "Immigration, Cultural Contestations and the Reconfigurations of Identities: The Case of Female Cultural Brokers," *Journal of Latin American Anthropology,* Special Issue on Brazil, vol. 4 (1 and 2), 126–41.

———. 2001. "Brazilians in Portugal, Portuguese in Brazil: Constructions of Sameness and Difference." In *Colonialism as a Continuing Project: The Portuguese Experience,* a special issue of *Identities: Global Studies in Politics and Culture,* edited by Bela Feldman-Bianco, 4(4): 607–50.

———. 2007a. "The Aftermath of a Rape Case: The Politics of Migrants Unequal Incorporation in Neo-Liberal Times." Paper presented at the 106th annual meeting of the American Anthropological Association, Washington, DC.

———. 2007b. "Empire, Postcoloniality, and Diasporas (Feature)." *Hispanic Research Journal* 8 (3): 267–78.

Foner, Nancy. 1987. "Introduction: New Immigrants and Changing Patterns in New York City." In *New Immigrants in New York,* edited by Nancy Foner, 1–33. New York: Columbia University Press.

———. 2000. *From Ellis Island to JFK: New York's Two Great Waves of Immigration.* New Haven: Yale University Press and Russell Sage Foundation.

Frey, William H. 2001. *Melting Pot Suburbs: A Census 2000 Study of Suburban Diversity.* Washington, DC: Brookings Institution, Center on Urban and Metropolitan Policy.

Friedman, Andrew L. 1977. *Industry and Labour: Class Struggle at Work and Monopoly Capitalism.* London: Macmillan.

Friedman, L. Thomas. 2000. *The Lexus and the Olive Tree.* New York: Anchor Books.

Friedmann, John. 1986. "The World City Hypotheses." *Development and Change* 17 (1): 69–84.

———. 1995. "Where We Stand: A Decade of World City Research." In *World Cities in a World System,* edited by Paul L. Knox and Peter J. Taylor, 21–47. Cambridge: Cambridge University Press.

Friedmann, John, and Goetz Wolf. 1982. "World City Formation: An Agenda for Research and Action." *International Journal of Urban and Regional Research* 6 (2): 309–39.

Friesen, Wardlow, Laurence Murphy, and Robin Kerns. 2005. "Spiced-Up Sandringham: Indian Transnationalism and New Suburban Spaces in Auckland, New Zealand." *Journal of Ethnic and Migration Studies* 31:385–401.

Frisina, Annalisa. 2005. "Giovani Musulmani d'Italia. Trasformazioni Socio-Culturali e Domande di Cittadinanza." In *Musulmani in Europa*, edited by Jocelyne Cesari, Andrea Pacini, and Agnelli Giovanni. Turin: Edizioni della Fondazione Agnelli.

Furlong, Andy, Andy Biggart, and Fred Cartmel. 1996. "Neighborhoods, Opportunity Structures and Occupational Aspiration." *Sociology* 30 (3): 551–65.

Furnivall, John Sydenham. 1948. *Colonial Policy and Practice. A Comparative Study of Burma and the Netherlands India*. Cambridge: Cambridge University Press.

Garbaye, Romain. 2005. *Getting into Local Power*. London: Blackwell.

George, Sheba Mariam. 2005. *When Women Come First: Gender and Class in Transnational Migration*. Berkeley: University of California Press.

Georgeanna, Daniel, with Roberta Hazen Aaronson. 1993. *The Strike of '28*. New Bedford, MA: Spinner Publications.

Georgeanna, Daniel, and Debra Shrader. 2008. "The Effects of Days at Sea on Employment, Income and Hours of Work: Some Preliminary Evidence." *Human Ecology Review* 15 (2): 185–93.

Gibson-Graham, J. K. 1996. *The End of Capitalism as We Knew It*. Oxford: Basil Blackwell.

——. 2002. "Beyond Global vs. Local: Economic Politics outside the Binary Frame." In *Geographies of Power: Placing Scale*, edited by Andrew Herod and Melissa W. Wright, 25–60. Oxford: Basil Blackwell.

Gifford, Paul. 1998. *African Christianity: Its Public Role*. London: Hurst.

——. 2004. *Ghana's New Christianity: Pentecostalism in a Globalising African Economy*. London, Hurst.

Gittell, Ross. 2001. *Manufacturing: New Hampshire's Secret Strength Building on Our Advantage*. Durham, NH: New Hampshire Small Business Development Center.

Glick Schiller, Nina. 1977. "Ethnic Groups Are Made Not Born." In *Ethnic Encounters: Identities and Contexts*, edited by George Hicks and Philip Leis, 23–35. North Scituate, MA: Duxbury Press.

——. 2005a. "Transborder Citizenship: Legal Pluralism within a Transnational Social Field." In *Mobile People, Mobile Law: Expanding Legal Relations in a Contracting World*, edited by Franz von Benda-Beckmann, Keebet von Benda-Beckmann and A. Griffiths, 27–50. London: Ashgate.

——. 2005b. "Transnational Social Fields and Imperialism: Bringing a Theory of Power to Transnational Studies." *Anthropological Theory* 5 (4): 439–61.

——. 2009. "'There Is No Power except for God': Locality, Global Christianity, and Immigrant Transnational Incorporation." In *Permutations of Order*, edited by Burtrand Turner and Thomas Kirsch, 125–47. London: Ashgate.

Glick Schiller, Nina, and Ayşe Çağlar. 2006. "Towards a Theory of Locality in Migration Studies: Migrant Incorporation and City Scale." Paper delivered at Migrinter Colloque 1985–2005, Poitiers, July 7.

——. 2008a. "'And Ye Shall Possess It, and Dwell Therein': Social Citizenship, Global Christianity, and Non-Ethnic Immigrant Incorporation." In *Immigration and Citizenship in Europe and the United States: Anthropological Perspectives*, edited by Deborah Reed-Danahay and Caroline Brettell, 201–25. New Brunswick, NJ: Rutgers University Press.

——. 2008b. "Beyond Methodological Ethnicity and Towards the City Scale: An Alternative Approach to Local and Transnational Pathways of Migrant Incorporation." In *Rethinking Transnationalism: The Meso-link of Organisations*, edited by Ludger Pries, 40–61. London: Routledge.

——. 2009. "Towards a Comparative Theory of Locality in Migration Studies: Migrant Incorporation and City Scale." *Journal of Ethnic and Migration Studies* 35 (2): 177–202.

Glick Schiller, Nina, Ayşe Çağlar, and Thaddeus Guldbrandsen 2006. "Beyond the Ethnic Lens: Locality, Globality, and Born-Again Incorporation." *American Ethnologist* 33 (4): 612–33.

Glick Schiller, Nina, and Georges Fouron. 1999. "Terrains of Blood and Nation: Haitian Transnational Social Fields." *Ethnic and Racial Studies* 22 (2): 340–66.

———. 2001. *Georges Woke Up Laughing: Long Distance Nationalism and the Search for Home.* Durham, NC: Duke University Press.

Goldstein, Ira. 1986. "The Wrong Side of the Tracts: A Study of Residential Segregation in Philadelphia." PhD diss., Temple University.

Gonzalez, Nancie. 1988. *Sojourners of the Caribbean: Ethnogenesis and Ethnohistory of the Garifuna.* Urbana: University of Illinois Press.

Goode, Judith. 1990. "A Wary Welcome to the Neighborhood: Community Responses to the New Immigration." *Urban Anthropology.* 19 (1):125–53.

———. 1998. "The Contingent Construction of Local Identities: Koreans and Puerto Ricans in Philadelphia." *Identities* 5 (1): 33–64.

———. 2001. "Let's Get Our Act Together: How Racial Discourses Disrupt Neighborhood Activism." In *The New Poverty Studies: The Ethnography of Power, Politics and Impoverished People in the United States,* edited by Judith Goode and Jeff Maskovsky, 364–98. New York: New York University Press.

Goode, Judith, and Robert T. O'Brien. 2006. "Whose Social Capital? How Economic Development Projects Disrupt Local Social Relations." In *Social Capital in Philadelphia,* edited by Richard Dilworth III, 159–76. Philadelphia: Temple University Press.

Goode, Judith, and Jo Anne Schneider. 1994. *Reshaping Ethnic and Racial Relations in Philadelphia: Immigrants in a Divided City.* Philadelphia: Temple University Press.

Gordon, Milton. 1964. *Assimilation in American Life: The Role of Race, Religion and National Origins.* New York: Oxford University Press.

Gottdiener, Mark. 1985. *The Social Production of Urban Space.* Austin: University of Texas Press.

Gozdziak, Elzbieta M., and Susan F. Martin. 2005. *Beyond the Gateway: Immigrants in a Changing America.* Lanham, MD: Lexington Books.

Graham, Stephen. 1997. "Cities in the Real-Time Age: The Paradigm Challenge of Telecommunications to the Conception and Planning of Urban Space." *Environment and Planning A* 29:105–27.

Granovetter, Mark S. 1973. "The Strength of Weak Ties." *American Journal of Sociology* 78:1360–80.

Grathoff, Richard. 1994. "Von der Phänomenologie der Nachbarschaft zur Soziologie des Nachbarn." In *Die Objektivität der Ordnungen und ihre kommunikative Konstruktion,* edited by W. M. Sprondel, 29–55. Frankfurt-au-Main: Suhrkamp.

Greater Dallas Chamber. 2006. "22 DFW Companies Make Fortune 500 List—Up Five from 2005." http://www.wliinc2.com/cgi/foxweb.dll/wlx/cs/wlxenews?cc=DCCC TX&action=DISPLIST.

Gregory, Steven. 1998. *Black Corona.* Princeton: Princeton University Press.

Grillo, Ralph. D. 1985. *Ideologies and Institutions in Urban France: The Representation of Immigrants.* Cambridge: Cambridge University Press.

———. 2000. "Plural Cities in Comparative Perspective." *Ethnic and Racial Studies* 23 (6): 957–81.

Grzymala-Kazlowska, Aleksandra. 2005. "From Ethnic Cooperation to In-Group Competition: Undocumented Polish Workers in Brussels." *Journal of Ethnic and Migration Studies* 31 (4): 675–97.

Gueye, Abdoulaye. 2001. "Quand les Sénégalais s'organisent aux Etats-Unis: Le Déclassement de la France." *Sociétés Africaines et Diaspora* 12:121–37.

Haar, Gerrie Ter. 2000. "Halfway to Paradise: African Christians in Europe." *Journal of Religion in Africa* 30 (4): 506–8.

Hackworth Jason. 2007. *Neoliberal City: Governance, Ideology and Development in American Urbanism.* Ithaca: Cornell University Press.

Hahn, Alois. 1994. "Die Soziale Konstruktion des Fremden." In *Die Objektivität der Ordnungen und ihre kommunikative Konstruktion,* edited by W. M. Sprondel, 140–63. Frankfurt/Main: Suhrkamp.

Halle Die Stadt. 2004a. http://www.halle.de/index.asp?MenuID=17&Sotierung.

Halle Die Stadt. 2004b. http://www.halle.de/index.asp?MenuID=912.

Hammar, T. 1990. *Democracy and the Nation State: Aliens, Denizens, and Citizens in a World of International Migration.* Aldershot: Avebury.

Hamnett, C. 1994. "Social Polarisation in Global Cities: Theory and Evidence." *Urban Studies* 31(3): 401–24.

———. 1996. "Social Polarisation, Economic Restructuring and Welfare State Regimes." *Urban Studies* 33(8): 1407–30.

Hannerz, Ulf. 1992. *Cultural Complexities. Studies in the Social Organisation of Meaning.* New York: Columbia University Press.

Hanson, Susan, and Geraldine Pratt. 1991. "Time, Space, and the Occupational Segregation of Women—A Critique of Human-Capital Theory." *Geoforum* 22 (2): 149–57.

Hanson, Susan, and Geraldine Pratt. 1995. *Gender, Work, and Space.* New York: Routledge.

Harding, Alan. 2007. "Taking City Regions Seriously? Response to Debate on 'City-Regions: New Geographies of Governance, Democracy and Social Reproduction.'" *International Journal of Urban and Regional Research* 31(2): 443–58.

Hardwick, Susan W. 2006. "Nodal Heterolocalism and Transnationalism at the United States-Canadian Border." *Geographical Review* 96:212–28.

Harvey, David. 1982. *The Limits to Capital.* Chicago: University of Chicago Press.

———. 1985. "The Geopolitics of Capitalism." In *Social Relations and Spatial Structures,* edited by John Urry and Derek Gregory, 128–63. London: Macmillan.

———. 1989. *The Urban Experience.* Baltimore: Johns Hopkins University Press.

———. 2001. *Spaces of Capital: Towards a Critical Geography.* Edinburgh: University of Edinburgh Press.

———. 2003. *The New Imperialism.* Oxford: Oxford University Press.

———. 2005. *Brief History of Neoliberalism.* New York: Oxford University Press.

———. 2006. *Spaces of Global Capitalism: Towards a Theory of Uneven Geographical Development.* London: Verso.

———. 2008. "The Right to the City." *New Left Review* 53:23–40.

Heckmann, Frederik. 2003. "From Ethnic Nation to Universalistic Immigrant Integration: Germany." In *The Integration of Immigrants in European Societies: National Differences and Trends of Convergence,* edited by Frederik Heckmann and Dominique Schnapper, 45–78. Stuttgart: Lucius und Lucius.

Henry, Nick, Cheryl McEwan, and Jane S. Pollard. 2002. "Globalization from Below: Birmingham—Postcolonial Workshop of the World?" *Area* 34 (2): 117–27.

Herod, Andrew. 1991. "The Production of Scale in US Labor Relations." *Area* 23:82–88.

———. 1997. "Labor's Spatial Praxis and the Geography of Contract Bargaining in the US East Coast Longshore Industry, 1953–1989." *Political Geography* 16 (2): 145–69.

———. 2001. *Labor Geographies.* New York: Guilford.

Herod, Andrew, and Melissa W. Wright. 2002. "Placing Scale: An Introduction." In *Geographies of Power: Placing Scale,* edited by Andrew Herod and Melissa W. Wright, 1–14. Oxford: Blackwell.

Hiebert, Daniel. 1999. "Immigration and the Changing Social Geography of Greater Vancouver." *British Columbia Studies* 121:35–81.

———. 2002. "The Spatial Limits to Entrepreneurship: Immigrant Entrepreneurs in Canada." *Tijdschrift voor Economische en Sociale Geographie* 93 (2): 173–90.

Hill, Jonathan. 1989. "Introduction: Indigenous Peoples and Nation-States." *Latin American Anthropology Review* 1 (2): 34–35.

Hill, Richard. 2004. "Cities and Nested Hierarchies." *International Social Science Journal* 56 (181): 373–84.

Hirschman, Albert. 1970. *Exit, Voice, and Loyalty.* Cambridge: Harvard University Press.

Hobsbawm, Eric, and Terence Ranger, eds. 1983. *The Invention of Tradition.* Cambridge: Cambridge University Press.

Hodos, Jerome. 2002. "Philadelphia and Manchester as Secondary Industrial Centers." PhD diss.: University of Pennsylvania.

Hoefle, Scott William. 2006. "Eliminating Scale and Killing the Goose That Laid the Golden Egg?" *Transactions of the Institute of British Geographers* 31 (2): 238–43.

Holgate, Jane. 2005. "Organizing Migrant Workers: A Case Study of Working Conditions and Unionization in a London Sandwich Factory." *Work, Employment and Society* 19 (3): 463–80.

Holland, Dorothy, Catherine Lutz, Donald Nonini, Lesley Bartlett, Thaddeus C. Guldbrandsen, and Marla Enrique Murillo. 2006. *If This Is Democracy . . . Public Lives and Private Politics in an Age of Neoliberalism.* New York: New York University Press.

Holton, Kimberly DaCosta. 2005. *Performing Folklore: Ranchos Folclóricos from Lisbon to Newark.* Bloomington: Indiana University Press.

Holtzmann, Jon D. 2000. *Nuer Journeys, Nuer Lives: Sudanese Refugees in Minnesota.* Boston: Allyn and Bacon.

Houston, Gail. 2004. *Insight into New Hampshire's Manufacturing Employment.* Economic and Labor Market Bureau. Concord: New Hampshire Employment Security Office, State of New Hampshire.

Howitt, Richard. 1998. "Scale as Relation: Musical Metaphors of Geographical Scale." *Area* 30 (1): 49–58.

Hudson, Kenneth. 2007. "The New Labor Market Segmentation: Labor Market Dualism in the New Economy." *Social Science Research* 36:286–312.

Ignatiev, Noel. 1995. *How the Irish Became White.* New York: Routledge.

Ires Piemonte. 1994. *Le Chiavi Della Città. Politiche per gli Immigrati a Torino e Lione.* Turin: Rosemberg & Sellier.

Itzigsohn, Jose. 2000. "Immigration and the Boundaries of Citizenship: The Institutions of Immigrants' Political Transnationalism." *International Migration Review* 34(4): 1126–55.

Itzigsohn, Jose, and Silvia Giorguli Saucedo. 2002. "Immigrant Incorporation and Sociocultural Transnationalism." *International Migration Review* 36 (3): 766–99.

Jacobs, Dirk, Karen Phalet, and Marc Swyngedouw. 2004. "Associational Membership and Political Involvement among Ethnic Minority Groups in Brussels." *Journal of Ethnic and Migration Studies* 30 (3): 543–59.

James, Paul. 2005. "Arguing Globalizations: Propositions towards an Investigation of Global Formation." *Globalizations* 2:193–209.

Jessop, Bob. 2000. "The Crisis of the National Spatio-Temporal Fix and the Ecological Dominance of Globalizing Capitalism." *International Journal of Urban and Regional Research* 24 (2): 323–60.

——. 2001. "Globalisation, Entrepreneurial Cities, and the Social Economy." In *Urban Movements in a Globalizing World,* edited by Pierre Hamel, Henri Lustiger-Thaler, and Margit Mayer, 81–100. London: Routledge.

——. 2002. *The Future of the Capitalist State.* London: Polity.

Jessop, Bob, Neil Brenner, and Martin Jones. 2008. "Theorizing Socio-Spatial Relations." *Environment and Planning* D: *Society and Space* 26:389–401.

Jones, Andrew. 2002. "The 'Global City' Misconceived: The Myth of 'Global Management' in Transnational Service Firms." *Geoforum* 33 (3): 335–50.

Jonas, Andrew. 2006. "Pro Scale: Further Reflections on the 'Scale Debate' in Human Geography." *Transactions of the Institute of British Geographers* 31:399–406.

Jones, Katherine T. 1998. "Scale as Epistemology." *Political Geography* 17:25–8.

Jouin, Nicolas. 2006. "Les Travailleurs Immigrés du Bâtiment entre Discrimination et Precarité. L'exemple d'une Activité Externalisée: Le Ferraillage." *Revue de l'IRES* 50 (1): 3–25.

Jouve, Bernard, and Alain-G. Gagnon, eds. 2006. *Les Métropoles au défi de la Diversité Culturelle.* Grenoble: Presses Universitaires de Grenoble.

Kastoryano, Riva. 2002. *Negotiating Identities. States and Immigrants in France and Germany.* Princeton: Princeton University Press.

Katznelson, Ira. 1993. *Marxism and the City.* New York: Oxford.

Kaya, Ayhan. 2002. *Sicher in Kreuzberg: Constructing Diasporas: Turkish Hip-Hop Youth in Berlin.* Bielefeld: Verlag.

Kearney, Michael. 1986. "From the Invisible Hand to Visible Feet: Anthropological Studies of Migration and Development." *Annual Review of Anthropology* 15: 331–61.

Keil, Roger, and Rianne Mahon, eds. 2009. *The New Political Economy of Scale.* Vancouver: University of British Columbia Press.

King, Anthony, ed. 1991. *Global Cities: Post-Imperialism and the Internationalization of London.* London: Routledge.

Knecht, Michi, and Levent Soysal, eds. 2005. *Plausible Vielfalt. Wie der Karneval der Kulturen denkt, lernt und Kultur macht.* Berlin: Panama.

Knox, Paul L., and Peter J. Taylor, eds. 1995. *World Cities in a World System.* Cambridge: Cambridge University Press.

Kofman, Eleonore. 2005a. "Citizenship, Migration and the Reassertion of National Identity." *Citizenship Studies* 9 (5): 453–67.

——. 2005b. "Gender and Skilled Migrants: Into and Beyond the Work Place." *Geoforum* 36:149–54.

Kogan, Irena. 2004. "Last Hired, First Fired? The Unemployment Dynamics of Male Immigrants in Germany." *European Sociological Review* 20 (5):445–61.

Koltyk, Jo Ann. 1997. *New Pioneers in the Heartland: Hmong Life in Wisconsin.* Boston: Allyn and Bacon.

Koopmans, Ruud, and Paul Stratham. 1999. "Challenging the Liberal State? Postnationalism, Multiculturalism, and the Collective Claims of Migrants and Ethnic Minorities in Britain and Germany." *American Journal of Sociology* 105:652–96.

——. 2000. "Migrant Mobilization and Political Opportunities: An Empirical Assessment of Local and National Variations." Paper presented at the International Conference Explaining Changes in Migration Policy, Geneva, October 27–28.

Koser, Khalid. 2007. "Refugees, Transnationalism, and the State." *Journal of Ethnic and Migration Studies* 33 (2): 233–54.

Krabbenborg, Mirjam. 1995. "De religieuze beleving van enkele Afrikanen in Zuid-Nederland en in de door Afrikanen geleide Acts Revival Church in Den Haag. Een godsdienstwetenschappelijke terreinverkenning." PhD diss., Tilburg University.

Krause, Linda, and Patrice Petro, eds. 2003. *Global Cities: Cinema, Architecture, and Urbanism in a Digital Age.* New Brunswick, NJ: Rutgers University Press.

Kyriakides, Christopher, and Satnam Virdee. 2003. "Migrant Labor, Racism and the British National Health Service." *Ethnicity and Health* 8 (4): 283–305.

Kwong, Peter. 1996. *The New Chinatown.* New York: Hill and Wang.

Lacroix, Thomas, Leyla Sall, and Monika Salzbrunn. 2008. "Les Marocains et Sénégalais de France, Permanences et évolution des Relations Transnationales." *Revue Européenne des Migrations Internationales* 24 (2): 23–43.

Lamanthe, Annie. 2005. "Les Transformations du Marché du Travail: Un Éclairage à partir de l'Analyse des Décalages entre Offre et Demande dans un Système Productif Localize." *Sociologie du Travail* 47 (1): 37–56.

Lamphere, Louise, ed. 1992. *Structuring Diversity: Ethnographic Perspectives on the New Immigrants.* Chicago: University of Chicago Press.

Lang, Scott W., 2005 "State of the City Address." City of New Bedford, March 1.

Lee, Yong-Sook, and Brenda S.A. Yeoh. 2005. *Globalisation and the Politics of Forgetting.* New York: Routledge.

Leeds, Anthony. 1994. The Anthropology of Cities: Some Methodological Issues." In *Cities, Classes and the Social Order,* edited by Anthony Leeds and Roger Sanjek, 233–46. Ithaca: Cornell University Press.

Lefebvre, Henri. 1991. *The Production of Space.* Cambridge, MA: Blackwell.

——. 1996. *Writings on Cities.* Oxford: Blackwell.

——. 2006. *Writings on Cities.* Translated by Eleonore Kofman and Elizabeth Lebas. Malden, MA: Blackwell.

Lefresne, Florence. 2002. "Vers un Renouvellement de l'Analyse Segmentationniste." *Economie et Sociétes: Series Travail* 22:1421–67.

Leitner, Helga, and Bryon Miller. 2007. "Scale and the Limitations of Ontological Debate: A Commentary on Marston, Jones and Woodward." *Transactions of the Institute of British Geographers* 32 (1): 116–25.

Leitner, Helga, Jamie Peck, and Eric S. Sheppard, eds. 2007. *Contesting Neoliberalism: Urban Futures.* New York: Guilford.

Leitner, Helga, Eric Sheppard, and Kristin Sziarto. 2008. "The Spatialities of Contentious Politics." *Royal Geographical Society* 33:157–72.

Leitner, Helga, Eric Sheppard, Kristin Sziarto, and Anant Maringanti. 2007. "Contesting Urban Futures. Decentering Neoliberalism." In *Contesting Neoliberalism. Urban Frontiers,* edited by Helga Leitner, Jamie Peck, and Eric Sheppard, 1–25. New York: Guilford Press.

Leonard, Karen Isaksen. 1997. *The South Asian Americans.* Westport, CT: Greenwood.

——. 2004. "American Muslims. Race, Religion and the Nation." *ISIM-Newsletter* 14:16.

Levitt, Peggy, and Nina Glick Schiller. 2004. "Transnational Perspectives on Migration: Conceptualizing Simultaneity." *International Migration Review* 38 (3): 1002–39.

Ley, David. 2003. "Offsetting Immigration and Domestic Migration in Gateway Cities: Canadian and Australian Reflections on an American Dilemma." Working Paper 03–01, Vancouver Centre of Excellence for Research on Immigration and Integration in the Metropolis.

——. 2004. "Transnational Spaces and Everyday Lives." *Transactions of the Institute of British Geographers* 29:151–64.

Li, Wei. 1998. "Anatomy of a New Ethnic Settlement: The Chinese Ethnoburb in Los Angeles." *Urban Studies* 35:479–501.

Light, Ivan. 1972. *Ethnic Enterprise in America.* Berkeley: University of California Press.

——. 2004. "Immigration and Ethnic Economies in Giant Cities." *International Social Science Journal* 56 (3): 385–98.

Light, Ivan, Richard B. Bernard, and Rebecca Kim. 1999. "Immigrant Incorporation in the Garment Industry of Los Angeles." *International Migration Review* 33 (1): 5–25.

Lipson, Herbert. 1987. "Off the Cuff." *Philadelphia Magazine,* September.

Logan, John, Richard D. Alba, Michael Dill, and Min Zhou. 2000. "Ethnic Segmentation in the American Metropolis: Increasing Divergence in Economic Incorporation, 1980–1990." *International Migration Review* 34 (1): 98–132.

Logan, John, and Harvey Molotch. 1987. *Urban Fortunes: The Political Economy of Place.* Berkeley: University of California Press.

Lopes de Souza, Marcelo. 2001. "The Brazilian Way of Conquering the 'Right to the City.'" *DISP* 147:25–31.

Low, Setha M. 1996. "The Anthropology of Cities: Imagining and Theorizing the City." *Annual Review of Anthropology* 25:383–409.

——. 1997. "Theorizing the City: Ethnicity, Gender, and Globalization." *Critique of Anthropology* 17:403–9.

Luce, Stephanie, and Kate Bronfenbrenner. 2005. "Capital Mobility and Job Loss in Massachusetts: A Look at Corporate Restructuring, Production Shifts, and Outsourcing." Paper presented at Future of Work Conference, University of Massachusetts-Boston, April 28.

MacLeod, Gordon, and Mark Goodwin. 1999. "Space, Scale, and State Strategy: Rethinking Urban and Regional Governance." *Progress in Human Geography* 23 (4): 503–27.

Mahler, Sarah. 1995. *American Dreaming: Immigrant Life on the Margins.* Princeton: Princeton University Press.

Malik, Jamal, and John Hinnells, eds. 2007. *Sufism in the West.* London: Routledge.

Malkki, Liisa. 1995. "Refugees and Exile: From 'Refugee Studies' to the National Order of Things." *Annual Review of Anthropology* 24:495–523.

——. 1997. "National Geographic: The Rooting of Peoples and the Territorialization of National Identity among Scholars and Refugees." In *Culture, Power, Place,* edited by Akhil Gupta and James Ferguson, 52–74. Durham, NC: Duke University Press.

Mandel, Ruth. 1990. "Shifting Centers and Emergent Identities: Turkey and Germany in the Lives of Turkish Gastarbeiter." In *Muslim Travelers: Pilgrimage, Migration and the Religious Imagination,* edited by Dale F. Eickelman and James P. Piscatori, 153–71. London: Routledge.

Mansfield, Becky. 2005. "Beyond Rescaling: Reintegrating the 'National' as a Dimension of Scalar Relations." *Progress in Human Geography* 29 (4): 458–73.

Marcuse, Peter, and Ronald van Kempen. 2000. *Globalizing Cities: A New Spatial Order?* Malden, MA: Blackwell.

Markusen, Anne. 2004. "The Work of Forgetting and Remembering Places," *Urban Studies* 41 (12): 2303–2313.

Marra, Claudio. 2003. "Immigrazione e Politiche Urbane nei Distretti Industriali. Uno Studio di Caso." Università degli Studi di Modena, http://www.oasimmigrazione.net/index.html.

Marston, Sallie A. 2000. "The Social Construction of Scale." *Progress in Human Geography* 24 (2): 219–42.

Marston, Sallie A., John Paul Jones, and Keith Woodward. 2005. "Human Geography without Scale." *Transactions of the Institute of British Geographers* 30 (4): 16–432.

Martins, Herminio. 1974. "Time and Theory in Sociology." In *Approaches to Sociology. An Introduction to Major Trends in British Sociology,* edited by John Rex, 248–94. London: Routledge.

Maskovsky, Jeff. 2001. "The Other War at Home: The Geopolitics of U.S. Poverty." *Urban Anthropology* 30 (2–3): 215–28.

Massey, Doreen. 1985. *Spatial Divisions of Labour.* London: Macmillan.

——. 2005. *For Space.* London: Sage.

Mattingly, Doreen J. 1999. "Job Search, Social Networks, and Local Labor Market Dynamics: The Case of Paid Household Work in San Diego, California." *Urban Geography* 20:46–74.

May, Jon, Jane Wills, Kavita Datta, Yara Evans, Joanna Herbert, and Cathy McIlwaine. 2007. "Keeping London Working: Global Cities, the British State and London's New Migrant Division of Labor." *Transactions of the Institute of British Geographers* 32:151–67.

Mayer, Margit. 2007. "Contesting the Neoliberalization of Urban Governance." In *Contesting Neoliberalism: Urban Frontiers,* edited by Helga Leitner, Jamie Peck, and Eric Sheppard, 90–115. New York: Guilford.

McCann, Eugene J. 2004. "Urban Political Economy beyond the 'Global City.'" *Urban Studies* 41 (12): 2315–33.

McDowell, Linda, Adina Batnitsky, and Sarah Dyer, 2007. "Division, Segmentation, and Interpellation: The Embodied Labors of Migrant Workers in a Greater London Hotel." *Economic Geography* 83 (1): 1–25.

McMaster, Robert B., and Eric Sheppard 2004. "Introduction: Scale and Geographic Inquiry." In *Scale and Geographic Inquiry,* edited by Eric Sheppard and Robert B. McMaster. Oxford: Basil Blackwell.

McNevin, Anne. 2006. "Political Belonging in a Neoliberal Era: The Struggle of the Sans-Papiers." *Citizenship Studies* 10 (2): 131–51.

Mendoza, Cristóbal. 2001. "The Role of the State in Influencing African Labor Outcomes in Spain and Portugal." *Geoforum* 32:167–80.

Merrifield, Andy. 2002a. *Dialectical Urbanism.* New York: Monthly Review Press.

———. 2002b. *Metromarxism.* New York: Routledge.

Meyer, Birgit. 1995. "Translating the Devil. An African Appropriation of Pietist Protestantism: The Case of the Peki Ewe in South-eastern Ghana, 1847–1992." PhD diss., University of Amsterdam.

———. 1998. "'Make a Complete Break with the Past': Time and Modernity in Ghanaian Pentecostalist Discourse." In *Memory and the Postcolony,* edited by Richard Werbner. London: Zed Books.

———. 2004. "'Praise the Lord ...' Popular Cinema and Pentecostalite Style in Ghana's New Public Sphere." *American Ethnologist* 31 (1): 92–110.

———. 2007. "Religious Revelation, Secrecy and the Limits of Visual Representation." *Anthropological Theory* 6:431–52.

Min, Pyong Gap. 1996. *Caught in the Middle: Korean Communities in New York and Los Angeles.* Berkeley: University of California Press.

Mitchell, Don. 2003. *The Right to the City: Social Justice and the Right for Public Space.* New York: Guliford.

Mitchell, Katharyne. 2003. *Crossing the Neoliberal Line: Pacific Rim Migration and the Metropolis.* Philadelphia: Temple University Press.

Montepio Luso-Americano. 1932. *Os Portugueses de New Bedford.* New Bedford, MA: Montepio Luso-Americano.

Moody, Kim. 1997. *Workers in a Lean World: Unions in the International Economy.* London: Verso.

Morrison, Philip. 1990. "Segmentation Theory Applied to Local, Regional and Spatial Labor Markets." *Progress in Human Geography* 14 (4): 488–528.

Mottura, Giovanni. 2000. "Immigrati e sindacato." In *Rapporto Immigrazione. Lavoro, sindacato, società,* edited by E. Pugliese. Rome: Ediesse.

Mouride (official magazine of the Mourids in the United States). 2001. No. 14.

Nash, June, and Patricia Fernandez Kelly. 1983. *Women, Men, and the International Division of Labor.* Albany: SUNY Press.

Nieswand, Boris 2008. "Ghanaian Migrants in Germany and the Status Paradox of Migration: A Multi-Sited Ethnography of Pathways of Migrant Inclusion." PhD diss., University of Halle-Wittenberg.

Nimako, Kwame. 1993. "Nieuwkomers in een "gevestigde" samenleving: Een analyse van de Ghanese gemeenschap in Zuidoost (Amsterdam)." [Nimako 1993: Publication by City-council Amsterdam, report to Southeast City-area council].

——. 2000. *De Ghanese Gemeenschap in Amsterdam. Emancipatie op Eigen Kracht.* [2000: The Hague, Report published by Netherlands Ministry of Home Affairs].

Nyers, Peter. 2003. "Abject Cosmopolitanism: The Politics of Protection in the Anti-Deportation Movement." *Third World Quarterly* 24 (6): 1069–93.

O'Mara, Margaret. 2005. *Cities of Knowledge: Cold War Science and the Search for the Next Silicon Valley.* Princeton: Princeton University Press.

Ong, Aihwa. 2006. *Neoliberalism as Exception: Mutations in Citizenship and Sovereignty.* Durham, NC: Duke University Press.

——. 2007. "Boundary Crossings. Neoliberalism as a Mobile Technology." *Royal Geographical Society,* n.s., 32:3–8.

Ong, Aihwa, and Stephen J. Collier. 2004. *Global Assemblages: Technology, Politics, and Ethics as Anthropological Problems.* Malden, MA: Blackwell.

Ong, Aihwa, and Don Nonini, eds. 1997. *The Cultural Politics of Modern Chinese Transnationalism.* New York: Routledge.

Oomen, Mar, and Jos Palm. 1994. *Geloven in de Bijlmer. Over de rol van religieuze groeperingen.* Amsterdam: Het Spinhuis.

Østergaard-Nielsen, Eva. 2003. *Transnational Politics: Turks and Kurds in Germany.* London: Routledge.

Ozouf, Mona. 1976. *La Fête Révolutionnaire 1789–1799.* Paris: Gallimard.

Patterson, Melina. 2006. "The West Philadelphia Partnership: Is the Playing Field Level?" In *Social Capital in Philadelphia,* edited by Richard Dilworth III. Philadelphia: Temple University Press.

Pattillo, Mary. 2003. "Extending the Boundaries and Definition of the Ghetto." *Ethnic and Racial Studies* 26 (6): 1046–57.

Payne, Darwin. 2000. *Big D: Triumphs and Troubles of an American Supercity in the 20th Century.* Dallas: Three Forks Press.

Peck, Jamie. 1996. *Workplace: The Social Regulation of Labor Markets.* New York: Guilford.

Pécoud, Antoine. 2000. "Thinking and Rethinking Ethnic Economies." *Diaspora* 9:439–61.

Peil, Margaret. 1995. "Ghanaians Abroad." *African Affairs* 94 (376): 345–67.

Petersen-Thumser, Jens, and Monika Salzbrunn, eds. 1997. *Libérer le Potentiel d'Auto-Promotion en Décentralisant les Mesures de Politique Sociale.* Berlin: Deutsche Stiftung für Internationale Entwicklung.

Piore, Michael. 1979. *Birds of Passage.* Cambridge: Cambridge University Press.

Portes, Alejandro. 1995. *The Economic Sociology of Immigration: Essays on Networks, Ethnicity, and Entrepreneurship.* New York: Russell Sage Foundation.

Portes, Alejandro, and József Böröcz. 1989. "Contemporary Immigration: Theoretical Perspectives on Its Determinants and Modes of Incorporation." *International Migration Review* 87 (23): 606–30.

Portes, Alejandro, and Alex Stepick. 1993. *City on the Edge: The Transformation of Miami.* Berkeley: University of California Press.

Pratt, Jeff. 2002. "Italy: Political Unity and Cultural Diversity." In *The Politics of Recognising Difference: Multiculturalism Italian-Style,* edited by Ralph Grillo and Jeff Pratt, 25–41. Aldershot, UK: Ashgate.

Pries, Ludger. 1996. "Transnationale Soziale Räume. Theoretisch-empirische Skizze am Beispiel der Arbeitswanderungen Mexico-USA." *Zeitschrift für Soziologie* 25 (6): 456–72.

Provincia di Ravenna. *Osservatorio Immigrazione.* Ravenna.

Pugliese, Enrico, ed. 2000. *Rapporto Immigrazione. Lavoro, Sindacato, Società.* Rome: Ediesse.

Purcell, Mark. 2003a. "Citizenship and the Right to the Global City: Reimagining the Capitalist World Order." *International Journal of Urban and Regional Research* 27 (3): 564–90.

——. 2003b. "Islands of Practice and the Marston/Brenner Debate. Toward a More Synthetic Critical Human Geography." *Progress in Human Geography* 27 (3): 317–33.

Raghuram, Parvati, and Eleonore Kofman. 2002. "The State, Skilled Labour Markets, and Immigration: The Case of Doctors in England." *Environment and Planning* A 34(11): 2071–89.

Rajan, Gita, and Shailja Sharma. 2006. *New Cosmopolitanisms: South Asians in the US*. Stanford: Stanford University Press.

Ranci, Costanzo, 2005. "Local Welfare. Systemic Actions, Territories and Governance." *Italian Journal of Social Policy* 2 (April–June): 3–23.

Rankin, Katharine N. 2003. "Anthropologies and Geographies of Globalization." *Progress in Human Geography* 27:708–34.

Rath, Jan. 2000. *Immigrant Businesses: The Economic, Political and Social Environment*. New York: St. Martin's.

Rath, Jan, and Robert Kloosterman. 2000. "Outsiders' Business: A Critical Review of Research on Immigrant Entrepreneurship." *International Migration Review* 34 (3): 657–81.

Raulin, Anne. 2004. *Anthropologie Urbaine*. Paris: Armand Colin.

Reeve, Penn. 1997a. "The Portuguese Worker." In *Portuguese Spinner: An American Story*, edited by M. L. MaCabbe and J. D. Thomas, 230–35. New Bedford, MA: Spinner Publications.

——. 1997b. "Three Lives for Labor: Eula Mendes, Manny Fernandes and Tina Ponte." In *Portuguese Spinner: An American Story*, edited by M. L. MaCabbe and J. D. Thomas, 236–45. New Bedford, MA: Spinner Publications.

Regione Emilia Romagna, 2005. "Domanda di Care Domiciliare e Donne Migranti. Indagine sul Fenomeno Delle badanti in Emilia Romagna." *Dossier 110/2005*, 1–90, http://asr.regione.emilia-romagna.it/wcm/asr/collana_dossier/doss110.htm

Reich, Michael, David Gordon, and Richard Edwards. 1973. "A Theory of Labor Segmentation." *American Economic Review* 63:359–65.

Rex, John, ed. 1996. *Multiculturalism and Political Integration in European Cities*. Special issue of *Innovation: European Journal of Social Sciences* 9 (1).

Rex, John, and Yunas Samad. 1996. "Multiculturalism and Political Integration in Birmingham and Bradford." Special issue, *Innovation: European Journal of Social Sciences* 9 (1): 11–31.

Reyneri, Emilio. 2001. "Migrants' Involvement in the Underground Economy in the Mediterranean Countries of the European Union." ILO—International Migration Working Paper 41, International Labor Organization.

Riccio, Bruno. 1999. "Senegalese Street-Sellers, Racism and the Discourse on 'Irregular Trade' in Rimini." *Modern Italy* 4 (2): 225–40.

——. 2000. "The Italian Construction of Immigration: Sedentarist and Corporatist Narratives Facing Transnational Migration in Emilia-Romagna." *Anthropological Journal on European Cultures* 9 (2): 53–74.

——. 2001. "From 'Ethnic Group' to 'Transnational Community'? Senegalese Migrants' Ambivalent Experiences and Multiple Trajectories." *Journal of Ethnic and Migration Studies* 27 (4): 583–600.

Robinson, Jennifer. 2002. "Global and World Cities: A View from off the Map." *International Journal of Urban and Regional Research* 26 (3): 531–54.

——. 2006. *Ordinary Cities: Between Modernity and Development*. New York: Routledge.

Roediger, David. 1990. *The Wages of Whiteness: Race and the Making of the American Working Class*. London: Verso.

Rouse, Roger. 1995. "Thinking through Transnationalism: Notes on the Cultural Politics of Class Relations in the Contemporary United States." *Public Culture* 7 (2): 353–402.

Ruben, Matthew. 2003. "Penn and Inc.: Incorporating the University of Pennsylvania." In *Campus Inc.: Corporate Power in the Ivory Tower*, edited by Geoffrey D. White and Flannery C. Hauck. Amherst, NY: Prometheus Books.

Ruhs, Martin, and Bridget Anderson. 2006. "Semi-Compliance in the Migrant Labour Market." Working Paper 30, Centre on Migration, Policy and Society (COMPAS), Oxford University.

Rutherford, Tod. 2006. "Requiem or Re-birth? Internal Labour Markets and Labour Market Restructuring in the Kitchener and Sault Ste. Marie Regions." *Canadian Geographer* 50 (2): 197–216.

Sá, M. Gloria de 2008. "The Azorean Community on the East Coast." In *Capelinhos: A Volcano of Synergies—Azorean Emigration to America*, edited by Tony Goulart, 159–70. San Jose: Portuguese Heritage Publications of California.

Sá, M. Gloria de, and David Borges. 2009. "Context of Culture: Portuguese-Americans and Social Mobility." In *Community, Culture, and the Makings of Identity: Portuguese-Americans along the Eastern Seaboard*, edited by Kimberly DaCosta Holton and Andrea Klimt, 265–90, Portuguese in the Americas Series. Dartmouth: University of Massachusetts Center for Portuguese Studies and Culture.

Sadler, David. 2000. "Organising European Labor, Governance, Production, Trade Unions, and the Question of Scale." *Transactions of the Institute of British Geographers* 25:135–52.

Salih, Ruba. 2002. "Recognising Difference, Reinforcing Exclusion. The Case of a Family Planning Centre for Migrant Women and Their Children in Emilia Romagna." In *The Politics of Recognizing Difference. Multiculturalism Italian-Style*, edited by Ralph D. Grillo and Jeff Pratt, 139–59. Aldershot, UK: Ashgate.

——. 2003. *Gender in Transnationalism. Home, Longing and Belonging among Moroccan Migrant Women*. London: Routledge.

——. 2004. "The Backward and the New: National, Transnational and Post-national Islam in Europe." *Journal of Ethnic and Migration Studies* 30 (5): 995–1014.

Salzbrunn, Monika. 2002a. "La Campagne Présidentielle Sénégalaise en France." *Hommes et Migrations* 1239 (September–October): 49–53.

——. 2002b. "Hybridisation of Religious Practices amongst West African Migrants in France and Germany." In *The Transnational Family. New European Frontiers and Global Networks*, edited by Deborah Bryceson and Ulla Vuorela, 217–29. Oxford: Berg.

——. 2004. "The Occupation of Public Space through Religious and Political Events: How Senegalese Migrants Became a Part of Harlem, New York." *Journal of Religion in Africa* 32 (2): 468–92.

Salzbrunn, Monika. 2007a. "Enjeux de Construction des Rôles Communautaires dans l'Espace Urbain: Le Cas du Quartier de Belleville à Paris." In *Esprit Critique*, edited by Jean Louis Laville, Ivan Sainsaulieu and Monika Salzbrunn, 10(1), http://www.esprit critique.fr/Dossiers/article.asp?t03code=65&varticle=esp1001article05&vrep=1001.

——. 2007b. "Lokale und Globale Produktion von Alteritäten im Rahmen von Ereignissen—Wie ein heterogenes Pariser Stadtviertel seine Identität Konstruiert." In *Beziehungsgeschichten. Minderheiten—Mehrheiten in europäischer Perspektive*, edited by Elka Tschernokoshewa and Volker Gransow, 151–68. Bautzen, Ger.: Domowina.

——. 2008. "The Feast as Marginal Politics: Carnival as a Mode of Expression in Migration." In *Rituals in an Unstable World. Contingency—Hybridity—Embodiment*, edited by Alexander Henn and Klaus-Peter Koepping, 151–70. Frankfurt: Peter Lang.

Samers, Michael. 2002. "Immigration and the Global City Hypothesis: Towards an Alternative Research Agenda." *International Journal of Urban and Regional Research* 26 (2): 389–402.

——. 2008. "At The Heart of Migration Management: Immigration and Labour Markets in the European Union." In *Governing International Labor Migration*, edited by Christina Gabriel and Hélène Pellerin. London: Routledge.

Sanchez, Mary. 2006. "States Are Taking Immigration into Their Own Hands." *Dallas Morning News*, March 13, 17A.

Olivier de Sardan, Jean-Pierre and Thomas Bierschenk. 1993. "Les Courtiers Locaux du Développement." *APAD Bulletin* 5:71–76.

Sassen, Saskia. 1988. *The Mobility of Labor and Capital*. Cambridge: Cambridge University Press.

——. 1991. *The Global City: New York, London, Tokyo*. Princeton: Princeton University Press.

——. 1996. "New Employment Regimes in Cities: The Impact on Immigrant Workers." *New Community* 22 (4): 579–94.

——. 1998. *Globalization and Its Discontents*. New York: New Press.

——. 2000a. *Cities in a World Economy*. 2nd ed. Thousand Oaks, CA: Pine Forge Press.

——. 2000b. "New Frontiers Facing Urban Sociology at the Millennium." *British Journal of Sociology* 51 (1): 143–59.

——. 2000c. "Spatialities and Temporalities of the Global: Elements for a Theorization." *Public Culture* 12 (1): 215–32.

——. 2007. *A Sociology of Globalization*. New York: Norton.

Sassen-Koob, Saskia. 1984. "The New Labor Demand in Global Cities." In *Cities in Transformation, Urban Affairs Annual 26*, edited by Michael P. Smith, 139–71. Beverly Hills, CA: Sage.

Saunders, Peter. 1986. *Social Theory and the Urban Question*. 2nd ed. New York: Holmes & Meier.

Sayer, Andrew. 1992. *Method in Social Science*. 2nd ed. London: Routledge.

——. 2004. "Seeking the Geographies of Power" (review of John Allen's *Lost Geographies of Power*). *Economy and Society* 33 (2): 255–70.

Sayre, Nathan. 2005. "Ecological and Geographical Scale: Parallels and Potential for Integration." *Progress in Human Geography* 29 (3): 276–90.

——. 2008. "Scale." In *A Companion to Environmental Geography*, edited by Noel Castree, David Demeritt, and Bruce Rhoads. Cambridge: Blackwell.

Schermerhorn, Richard Alonzo. 1949. *These Our People: Minorities in American Culture*. Boston: D.C. Heath.

——. 2008. *How Enemies Are Made*. Oxford: Berghahn.

Schlee, Günther, and Isir Schlee. N.d. "Ghanaische und Somali-Migranten im Vergleich." Unpublished manuscript.

Schmitter Heisler, Barbara. 1998. "Immigration and German Cities: Exploring National Policies and Local Outcomes." *German Politics and Society* 16:18–41.

Schneider, Jo Anne. 1988. "In the Big Village: Eastern European Immigrants in Philadelphia." PhD diss., Temple University.

Schrover, Marlou, Joanne van der Leun, and Chris Quispel. 2007. "Niches, Labour Market Segregation, Ethnicity and Gender." *Journal of Ethnic and Migration Studies* 33 (4): 529–40.

Schuster, Liza. 2005. "The Continuing Mobility of Migrants in Italy: Shifting Between places and Statuses." *Journal of Ethnic and Migration Studies* 31 (4): 757–74.

Schütz, Alfred, and Thomas Luckmann. [1975]1984. *Strukturen der Lebenswelt*. Neuwied, Darmstadt/Frankfurt am Mein.

Scott, Allen J. 1980. *The Urban Land Nexus and the State*. London: Pion.

——. 1998. *Regions and the World Economy*. New York: Oxford University Press.

Scott, Allen, and Edward Soja. 1996. *The City: Los Angeles and Urban Theory at the End of the Twentieth Century*. Berkeley: University of California Press.

Scott, James. 1998. *Seeing Like a State: How Certain Schemes to Improve the Human Condition Have Failed*. New Haven: Yale University Press.

Scranton, Philip. 1983. *Proprietary Capitalism: Textile Manufacture in Philadelphia: 1880–95*. New York: Cambridge University Press.

Sgrignuoli, Adina, ed., 2002. *Donne Migranti dall'Accoglienza alla Formazione*. Milan: Franco Angeli.

Sheppard, Eric. 2002. "The Spaces and Times of Globalization: Place, Scale, Networks and Positionality." *Economic Geography* 78:307–30.

Sheppard, Eric, and Robert McMaster. 2004. "Introduction: Scale and Geographic Enquiry. In *Scale and Geographic Inquiry*, edited by Eric Sheppard and Robert McMaster. Oxford: Basil Blackwell.

Short, John, and Yeong-Hyun Kim. 1999. *Globalization and the City*. New York: Addison Wesley Longman.

Shumar, Wesley. 2006. "Universities as Landscapes of Consumption." Paper delivered at the sixth annual meeting of the Society for the Anthropology of North America, April.

Simon, Gildas. 1996. "La France, Le Système Migratoire Européen et la Mondialisation." *Revue Européenne de Migrations Internationales* 12 (2): 261–73.

Singer, Audrey. 2004. *The Rise of the New Immigrant Gateways*. Washington, DC: Brookings Institution, Center on Urban and Metropolitan Policy.

Singer, Audrey, Susan Hardwick, and Caroline Brettell, eds. 2008. *Twenty-First Century Gateways: Immigration and Incorporation in Suburban America*. Washington, DC: Brookings Institution.

Skop, Emily H. 2002. "Saffron Suburbs: Indian Immigrant Community Formation in Metropolitan Phoenix." PhD diss., Arizona State University.

Skop, Emily H., and Wei Li. 2003. "From the Ghetto to the Invisiburb: Shifting Patterns of Immigrant Settlement in Contemporary America." In *Multicultural Geographies: Persistence and Change in U.S. Racial/Ethnic Patterns*, edited by John W. Frazier and Florence Margai, 113–24. New York: Academic.

Smith, Alice. 1999. *Dispelling the Darkness: How to Deal with Demonic Rulers*. Houston: U.S. Prayer Center.

Smith, Anthony. 1983. "Nationalism and Social Theory." *British Journal of Sociology* 34:19–38.

Smith, Estellie M. 1974. "Portuguese Enclaves: The Invisible Minority." In *Social and Cultural Identity: Problems of Persistence and Change*, edited by T. Fitzgerald, 81–91. Athens: University of Georgia Press.

Smith, Lothar. 2007. *Tied to Migrants: Transnational Influences on the Economy of Accra, Ghana*. African Studies Collection series 5. Leiden: African Studies Centre.

Smith, Michael Peter. 2001. *Transnational Urbanism: Locating Globalization*. Malden, MA: Blackwell.

——. 2005. "Transnational Urbanism Revisited." *Journal of Ethnic and Migration Studies* 31 (2): 235–44.

Smith, Michael Peter, and Joe Feagin. 1987. *The Capitalist City*. Oxford: Oxford University Press.

Smith, Neil. 1991. *Uneven Development: Nature, Capital, and the Production of Space*. 2nd. ed. Oxford: Blackwell.

——. 1992. "Geography, Difference and the Politics of Scale." In *Postmodernism and the Social Sciences*, edited by Joe Doherty, Elspeth Graham, and Mo Malek, 57–79. New York: St. Martin's.

——. 1993. "Homeless/Global: Scaling Places." In *Mapping the Futures. Local Cultures, Global Change,* edited by Jon Bird, 87–119. New York: Routledge.

——. 1995. "Remaking Scale: Competition and Cooperation in Pre-National and Post-National Europe." In *Competitive European Peripheries,* edited by Heikki Eskelinen and Folke Snickars, 59–74. Berlin: Springer Verlag.

——. 1996. *The New Urban Frontier: Gentrification and the Revanchist City.* London: Routledge.

——. 2002. "New Globalism, New Urbanism: Gentrification as Global Urban Strategy." *Antipode* 34(3): 427–50.

——. 2003. "Remaking Scale: Competition and Cooperation in Pre-national and Post-national Europe." *State/Space: A Reader,* edited by Neil Brenner, Bob Jessop, Martin Jones, and Gordon Macleod, 227–38. Malden, MA: Blackwell.

Smith, Neil, and Ward Dennis, 1987. "The Restructuring of Geographical Scale: Co-alescence and Fragmentation of the Northern Core Region." *Economic Geography* 63:160–82.

——. 1989. *Postmodern Geographies.* New York: Verso.

——. 1992. "The Stimulus of a Little Confusion: A Contemporary Comparison of Amsterdam and Los Angeles." In *After Modernism: Global Restructuring and the Changing Boundaries of City Life,* edited by Michael P. Smith, 17–38. New Brunswick, NJ: Transaction Books.

——. 2000. *Postmetropolis.* Cambridge, MA: Blackwell.

Sollors, Werner, ed. 1989. *The Invention of Ethnicity.* New York: Oxford University Press.

Soysal, Levent. 2001. "Diversity of Experience, Experience of Diversity: Turkish Migrant Youth Culture in Berlin." *Cultural Dynamics* 13 (1): 5–28.

Soysal, Yasemin. 2000. "Citizenship and Identity: Living in Diasporas in Post-war Europe?" *Ethnic and Racial Studies* 23 (1): 1–15.

Steinberg, Stephen. 1981. *The Ethnic Myth: Race, Ethnicity and Class in America.* New York: Atheneum.

Storper, Michael, and Richard Walker. 1989. *The Capitalist Imperative: Territory, Technology and Industrial Growth.* Cambridge, MA: Blackwell.

Straßburger, Gabriele, Horst Unbehaun, and Lale Yalçin-Heckmann. 2000. "Die türkischen Kolonien in Bamberg und Colmar: Ein deutsch-französischer Vergleich sozialer Netzwerke von Migranten im interkulturellen Kontext, Forschungsbericht," Universität Bamberg: Elektronische Hochschulschriften, http://elib.uni-bamberg.de/volltexte/2000/2.html.

Swyngedouw, Erik. 1989. "The Heart of the Place: The Resurrection of Locality in an Age of Hyperspace." *Human Geography* 71:31–42.

——. 1992. "The Mammon Quest: 'Glocalisation,' Interspatial Competition and the Monetary Order: The Construction of New Scales." In *Cities and Regions in the New Europe,* edited by Mick Dunford and Grigoris Kafkalas, 39–68. London: Belhaven.

——. 1997a. "Excluding the Other: The Production of Scale and Scaled Politics." In *Geographies of Economies,* edited by R. Lee and J. Wills. London: Arnold.

——. 1997b. "Neither Global nor Local: 'Glocalization' and the Politics of Scale." In *Spaces of Globalization: Reasserting the Power of the Local,* edited by Kevin Cox, 137–66. New York: Guilford.

Tarrius, Alain. 2002. *La Mondialisation par le Bas. Les Nouveaux Nomades de l'Économie Souterraine.* Paris: Balland.

Tarrow, Sidney. 2005. *The New Transnational Activism.* Cambridge: Cambridge University Press.

Taylor, Peter J. 1995. "World Cities and Territorial States: The Rise and Fall of their Mutuality." In *World Cities in a World-System,* edited by Paul Knox and Peter Taylor, 48–62. New York: Cambridge University Press.

——. 2004. *World City Network: A Global Urban Analysis.* London: Routledge.

Taylor, Peter J., and Robert E. Lang. 2005. "U.S. Cities in the 'World City Network.'" Brookings Institution, 26 July 2007. http://www.transcomm.ox.ac.uk/working_papers.ht.

Ter Haar, Gerrie. 1998. *Halfway to Paradise: African Christians in Europe.* Cardiff: Cardiff Academic Press.

Tikkun International Ministries. 2008. "Partnering for the Full Restoration of Israel and the Church." http://www.tikkunministries.org/

Tilly, Charles. 1984. *Big Structures, Large Processes, Huge Comparisons.* New York: Russell Sage Foundation.

Tomasetti, Fabio. 1983. "La Storia Urbana di una Città Turistica; Gli Ultimi Studi su Rimini." *Storia urbana* 24:163–82.

Torpey, John. 1998. "Aller et Venir: Le Monopole Étatique des 'Moyens Légitimes de Circulation.'" *Cultures et Conflits* 31–32:1–16.

Tran, Hoa. 2001. "Structuring Vietnamese Life in Philadelphia: Contesting Leadership and History." PhD diss., Temple University.

Turner, Victor. 1982. *From Ritual to Theatre: The Human Seriousness of Play.* New York: PAJ Publications.

U.S. Census. 2003. "The Foreign-Born Population: 2000." http://www.census.gov/prod/2003pubs/c2kbr-34.pd.

——. 2008. "Manchester (city) QuickFacts from the U.S. Census Bureau." http://quickfacts.census.gov/qfd/states/33/3345140.html.

U.S. Department of Labor. 2005. Bureau of Labor Statistics data. http://data.bls.gov/PDQ/servlet/SurveyOutputServlet?series_id=LNS14000000.

UNESCO-UN-Habitat-ISS. 2005. Habitat International Coalition, "Urban Policies and Right to the City." Discussion paper, March. http://www.hic-net.org/articles.asp?PID=299.

Urciuoli, Bonnie. 2000. *Exposing Prejudice: Puerto Rican Experiences of Language, Race and Class Boulder.* Colorado: Westview Press.

——. 2003. "Excellence, Leadership, Skills, Diversity: Marketing Liberal Arts Education." *Language & Communication* 23 (3–4): 385–408.

Valenzuela, Abel. 2001. "Day Laborers as Entrepreneurs?" *Journal of Ethnic and Migration Studies* 27 (2): 335–52.

Van der Sar, Jap, and Roos Visser. 2006. *Gratis en Waardevol: Rol, Positie en Maatschappelijk Rendement van Migrantenkerken in Den Haag.* Utrecht: Stichting Oikos.

Van Dijk, Rijk. 1997. "From Camp to Encompassment: Discourses of Transsubjectivity in the Ghanaian Pentecostal Diaspora." *Journal of Religion in Africa* 27 (2): 135–69.

——. 2001. "Time and Transcultural Technologies of the Self in the Ghanaian Pentecostal Diaspora." In *Between Babel and Pentecost Transnational Pentecostalism in Africa and Latin America,* edited by Andre Corten and Ruth Marshall-Fratani. London: Hurst.

——. 2002a. "Ghanaian Churches in the Netherlands: Religion Mediating a Tense Relationship." In *Merchants, Missionaries & Migrants: 300 years of Dutch-Ghanaian Relations,* edited by Ineke Van Kessel. Amsterdam: KIT.

——. 2002b. "Religion, Reciprocity and Restructuring Family Responsibility in the Ghanaian Pentecostal Diaspora." In *The Transnational Family: New European Frontiers and Global Networks,* edited by Deborah Bryceson and Ulla Vuorela. Oxford: Berg.

——. 2002c. "The Soul Is the Stranger: Ghanaian Pentecostalism and the Diaspora Contestation of 'Flow' and 'Individuality.'" *Culture and Religion* 3 (1): 49–67.

——. 2003. "Pentecostalism and the Politics of Prophetic Power: Religious Modernity in Ghana." In *Scriptural Politics: The Bible and the Koran as Political Models in the Middle East and Africa,* edited by Niels Kastfelt. London: Hurst.

——. 2004. "Negotiating Marriage: Questions of Morality and Legitimacy in the Ghanaian Pentecostal Diaspora," *Journal of Religion in Africa* 34(4): 438–67.

——. 2005a. "The Moral Life of the Gift in Ghanaian Pentecostal Churches in the Diaspora. Questions of (in-)dividuality and (in-)alienability in Transcultural Reciprocal Relations." In *Commodification, Things, Agency, and Identities: The Social Life of Things Revisited,* edited by Wim van Binsbergen and Peter Geschiere. Münster: Lit-Verlag.

——. 2005b. "Transculturele Rligie Versus Integratie: Ghanese Pinkstergemeenten en Deconstructie van Kosmopolitische Identiteiten in Nederland." In *Veranderingen van het alledaagse 1950–2000,* edited by Isabel Hoving, Hester Dibbits, and M. Schrover. The Hague: SDU.

Van Gennep, Arnold. [1909] 1981. *Rites de Passage.* Paris: A. et J. Picard.

Varsanyi, Monica. 2006. "Interrogating 'Urban Citizenship' vis-à-vis Undocumented Migration." *Citizenship Studies* 10 (2): 229–49.

Vertovec, Steven. 2006. The Emergence of Super-diversity in Britain. Working Paper 26, *Centre on Migration, Policy and Society (COMPAS),* Oxford University.

——. 2007. "Super-diversity and Its Implications." *Ethnic and Racial Studies.* 30, 6: 1024–54.

Vicarelli, Giovanni, ed. 1994. *Le Mani invisibili. La Vita e il Lavoro Delle Donne Immigrate.* Rome: Ediesse.

Von Benda-Beckmann, Franz, and Keebet von Benda-Beckmann. 2000. "Coping with Insecurity." In *Coping with Insecurity,* edited by Franz and Keebet von Benda-Beckmann, 7–24. Hans Marks: Foocal.

Waldinger, Roger. 1986a. "Immigrant Enterprise: A Critique and Reformulation." *Theory and Society* 15:249–285.

——. 1986b. *Through the Eye of a Needle. Immigrants and Enterprise in New York's Garment Trade.* New York: City University Press.

——. 1996a. "From Ellis Island to LAX. Immigrant Prospects in the American City." *International Migration Review* 30:1078–85.

——. 1996b. *Still the Promised City? New Immigrants and African-Americans in Post-Industrial New York.* Cambridge, MA: Harvard University Press.

——, ed. 2001. *Strangers at the Gates: New Immigrants in Urban America.* Berkeley: University of California Press.

Waldinger, Roger, and Mehdi Bozorgmehr. 1996. *Ethnic Los Angeles.* New York: Russell Sage Foundation.

Waldinger, Roger, and Michael I. Lichter. 2003. *How the Other Half Works: Immigration and the Social Organization of Labor.* Berkeley: University of California Press.

Wallman, Sandra. 1986. "Ethnicity and the Boundary Process in Context." In *Theories of Race and Ethnic Relations,* edited by John Rex and David Mason, 226–45. Cambridge: Cambridge University Press.

Walzer, Michael. 1996. *What it Means to Be an American: Essays on the American Experience.* New York: Marsilio Publishers.

Warner, R. Stephen. 1998. "Immigration and Religious Communities in the United States." In *Gatherings in Diaspora: Religious Communities and the New Immigration,* edited by Stephen R. Warner and Judith Wittner, 3–34. Philadelphia: Temple University Press.

Warner, Sam Bass. 1987. *The Private City: Philadelphia in Three Periods of Development.* Philadelphia: University of Pennsylvania Press.

Wastl-Walter, Doris, Lynn Staeheli and Lorraine Dowler, eds. 2005. *Rights to the City.* Rome: Societa Geografica Italiana.

Weber, Max. 1921. *Wirtschaft und Gesellschaft.* Tübingen, Ger.: Mohr, 2006.

Werbner, Pnina. 1990. *Imagined Diasporas among Manchester Muslims: The Public Performance of Pakistani Transnational Identity Politics.* Oxford: James Currey.

——. 1997. "Afterword: Writing Multiculturalism and Politics in the New Europe." In *The Politics of Multiculturalism in the New Europe. Racism, Identity and Community*, edited by Tariq Modood and Pnina Werbner, 261–67. London: Zed/The Postcolonial Encounter.

——. 2002. *The Migration Process: Capital, Gifts and Offerings among British Pakistanis.* 2nd ed. Oxford: Berg.

White, James W. 1998. "Old Wine, Cracked Bottle? Tokyo, Paris and the Global City Hypothesis." *Urban Affairs Quarterly* 33:451–77.

White, Jenny. 1999. "Turks in the New Germany." *American Anthropologist* 99 (4): 754–67.

Wills, Jane. 2000. "Uneven Geographies of Capital and Labor: The Lessons of European Work Councils." *Antipode* 33 (3): 484–509.

Wilson, Bruce M., and Juan Carlos Rodriguez Cordero. 2006. "Legal Opportunity Structures and Social Movements. The Effects of Institutional Change on Costa Rican Politics." *Comparative Political Studies* 39 (3): 325–51.

Wilson, Kenneth, and Alejandro Portes. 1980. "Immigrant Enclaves: An Analysis of the Labor Market Experiences of Cubans in Miami." *American Journal of Sociology* 86 (2): 295–319.

Wimmer, Andreas, and Nina Glick Schiller. 2002. "Methodological Nationalism and Beyond: Nation-State Building, Migration and the Social Sciences." *Global Networks* 2 (4): 301–34.

——. 2003. "Methodological Nationalism, the Social Sciences, and the Study of Migration: An Essay in Historical Epistemology." *International Migration Review* 37 (3): 576–610.

Wright, Richard, Adrian Bailey, Ines Miyares, and Alison Mountz. 2000. "Legal Status, Gender and Employment among Salvadorans in the US." *International Journal of Population Geography* 6 (4): 273–86.

Wright, Richard, and Mark Ellis. 2000a. "The Ethnic and Gender Division of Labor Compared among Immigrants to Los Angeles." *International Journal of Urban and Regional Research* 24 (3): 583–600.

——. 2000b. "Race, Region, and the Territorial Politics of Immigration in the US." *International Journal of Population Geography* 6: 197–211.

Xiang Biao. 2007. *Global "Body Shopping": An Indian International Labor System in the Information Technology Industry.* Princeton: Princeton University Press, 2007.

Yalçin-Heckmann, Lale. 1997. "The Perils of Ethnic Associational Life in Europe: Turkish Migrants in Germany and France." In *The Politics of Multiculturalism in the New Europe: Racism, Identity, and Community*, edited by Tariq Modood and Pnina Werbner, 95–110. London: Zed Books.

Yancey, William, Eugene P. Ericksen, and Richard N. Juliani. 1976. "Emergent Ethnicity: How Work and Space Shape Identity." *American Journal of Sociology* 41 (3): 391–402.

Yeates, Nicola. 2004. "A Dialogue with 'Global Care Chain' Analysis: Nurse Migration in the Irish Context." *Feminist Review* 77:79–95.

Yeoh, Brenda S. A. 1999. "Global/Globalizing Cities." *Progress in Human Geography* 23 (4): 607–16.

Zelinsky, Wilbur. 2001. *The Enigma of Ethnicity: Another American Dilemma.* Iowa City: University of Iowa Press.

Zelinsky, Wilbur, and Bruce Lee. 1998. "Heterolocalism: An Alternative Model of the Sociospatial Behavior of Immigrant Ethnic Communities." *International Journal of Population Geography* 4:281–98.

Zukin, Sharon. 1991. *Landscapes of Power: From Detroit to Disney World.* Berkeley: University of California Press.

——. 1995. *The Cultures of Cities.* Oxford: Blackwell.

Biographical Notes

NEIL BRENNER is professor of sociology and metropolitan studies at New York University. He is the author of *New State Spaces: Urban Governance and the Rescaling of Statehood* (Oxford: Oxford University Press, 2004) and coeditor (with Nik Theodore) of *Spaces of Neoliberalism: Urban Restructuring in North America and Western Europe* (Oxford: Blackwell, 2002) and (with Roger Keil) of *The Global Cities Reader* (New York: Routledge, 2006). His research interests include critical urban theory, sociospatial theory, state theory, and comparative geopolitical economy.

CAROLINE BRETTELL is Dedman Family Distinguished Professor in the Department of Anthropology and University Distinguished Professor at Southern Methodist University. She has written extensively on problems of international migration in general and on aspects of Portuguese and Asian Indian migration in particular. Her most recent books are edited volumes: *Citizenship, Political Engagement, and Belonging: Immigrants in Europe and the United States* (with Deborah Reed-Danahay) (New Brunswick, NJ: Rutgers University Press, 2008); *Twenty-First Century Gateways: Immigration and Incorporation in Suburban America* (with Audrey Singer and Susan W. Hardwick) (Washington, DC: Brookings Institution, 2008); *Crossing Borders/Constructing Boundaries: Race, Ethnicity and Immigration* (Lanham, MD: Lexington Books, 2007); and *Migration Theory: Talking across Disciplines*, 2nd ed. (with James F. Hollifield) (New York: Routledge, 2007).

AYŞE ÇAĞLAR is professor of sociology and social anthropology at the Central European University in Budapest and Research Group Leader at the Max Planck Institute for the Study of Religious and Ethnic Diversity, Göttingen,

Germany. She is the coeditor (with Levent Soysal) of "Forty Years of Turkish Migration to Germany: Issues, Reflections, and Futures," a special issue of the journal *New Perspectives on Turkey* (2003). Her articles on globalization and transnationalization processes, international migration, urban processes and migration, nationalist discourses and popular culture, and theories of popular and consumer culture have appeared in various journals, including *American Ethnology, Journal of Ethnic and Migration Studies, Ethnic and Race Studies, Global Networks, Cultural Dynamics, Material Culture,* and *Sociologus and Historische Anthropologie.*

BELA FELDMAN-BIANCO teaches social anthropology at the State University of Campinas (UNICAMP) in Brazil, where she also directs the Center for the Study of International Migration (CEMI). She has extensive research experience in small towns of both Brazil and the United States as well as in the major cities of Brazil and Portugal. In addition to directing the 1991 documentary film *Saudade (Nostalgia)* about the experience of seven Portuguese Americans in New Bedford, Massachusetts, she has edited several books and special issues of journals. Among them are *Trânsitos Coloniais: Diálogos Críticos Luso-Brasileiros (Colonial Transits: Luso-Brazilian Critical Dialogues)* (with Cristiana Bastos and Miguel Vale de Almeida) (Campinas, Brazil: Editora da Unicamp, 2007); "Colonialism as a Continuing Project: The Portuguese Experience," a special issue of *Identities: Global Studies in Culture and Power* (2001), and "Globalization and Circulation" (with Carmen Rial and Gustavo Lins Ribeiro), a special issue of *Vibrant: Virtual Brazilian Anthropology* (2009).

NINA GLICK SCHILLER is professor of social anthropology and director of the Research Institute for Cosmopolitan Cultures at the University of Manchester, England. Her research employs a comparative and historical perspective on migration, transnational processes and social relations, diasporic connection, long-distance nationalism, and cosmopolitanism. She is the founding editor of the journal *Identities: Global Studies in Culture and Power.* Her books include the co-authored books *Nations Unbound: Transnational Projects, Postcolonial Predicaments, and Deterritorialized Nation-States* (Routledge, 1994) (with Linda Basch and Cristina Blanc-Szanton); *Georges Woke Up Laughing: Long Distance Nationalism and the Search for Home* (Durham, NC: Duke University Press, 2001) (with Georges Eugene Fouron); and *Towards a Transnational Perspective on Migration: Race, Class, Ethnicity and Nationalism Reconsidered* (New York Academy of Sciences, 1992) (co-edited with Basch and Blanc-Szanton). She has conducted research in Haiti, the United States, and Germany and has worked with migrants from all regions of the globe.

JUDITH GOODE is professor of anthropology at Temple University, where she has served as the director of Urban Studies and as chairperson of the Anthropology Department. After early fieldwork in cities in Colombia, she has spent several decades doing urban ethnography in Philadelphia. She is a past president of the Society for Urban, National and Transnational Anthropology and the Society for the Anthropology of North America (SANA). Winner of the SANA Prize in the Critical Anthropology of North America in 2000, she served as one of the first chairs of the Committee on Public Policy of the American Anthropological Association. Among her publications, she co-authored (with Jo Anne Schneider) *Reshaping Ethnic and Racial Relations in Philadelphia: Immigrants in a Divided City* (Philadelphia: Temple University Press, 1994) and co-edited (with Jeff Maskovsky) *The New Poverty Studies: The Ethnography of Power, Politics, Policy and Impoverished People in the United States* (New York: New York University Press, 2001).

BRUNO RICCIO is researcher and lecturer in cultural anthropology and anthropology of migration at the University of Bologna (Italy). His research interests include West African transnational migration, codevelopment, citizenship, Italian multiculturalism, and racism. He has published numerous articles in journals, is the editor of six books, and has authored two monographs: *"Toubab" and "vu cumrprà": Transnationalism and Representation in the Senegalese Migration to Italy* (in Italian) (Advoa: Cleup, 2007) and *Politics, Associations, and Urban Interactions* (in Italian) (Rimini: Guaraldi, 2008).

RUBA SALIH is a social anthropologist and a senior lecturer at the University of Exeter (UK). She is the author of two monographs: *Gender in Transnationalism. Home, Longing and Belonging among Moroccan Migrant Women* (London: Routledge, 2003) and *Muslim Women Revealed: Women, Islam, Modernity* (in Italian) (Rome: Carocci, 2008). She has published extensively on the broad areas of Islam and modernity, transnational migration and gender across the Mediterranean, multiculturalism and citizenship, and gender and Islam in Europe.

MONIKA SALZBRUNN holds a full professorship in religion, migration, and diaspora at Lausanne University and leads the French team on Policymaking, Gender, and Migration (GEMMA) at Ecole des Hautes Etudes en Sciences Sociales, Paris. Her main research areas are the political anthropology of festive events, religious networks in Europe and the United States, and gender issues. Her latest co-edited publications include *Faire communauté en société* (Rennes: Presses Universitaires de Rennes, 2010) and *The Making of World Society. Perspectives from Transnational Research* (New Brunswick: Transaction Publishers, 2008).

MICHAEL SAMERS is associate professor in the Department of Geography at the University of Kentucky, having previously held positions at the University of Liverpool and the University of Nottingham. His research interests include the economic and urban dimensions of immigration and alternative forms of economic activity, including Islamic banking and finance. He is coauthor (with Noel Castree, Neil Coe, and Kevin Ward) of *Spaces of Work: Global Capitalism and Geographies of Labour* (London: Sage, 2004) and author of *Migration* (New York: Routledge, 2010).

GÜNTHER SCHLEE is director of the Integration and Conflict Department (focusing on Africa, Central Asia, and Europe) at the Max Planck Institute for

Social Anthropology, Halle. From 1986 to 1999 he was professor of social anthropology at Bielefeld University. His books include *Identities on the Move: Clanship and Pastoralism in Northern Kenya* (Manchester, UK: University of Manchester Press, 1989), *How Enemies Are Made: Towards a Theory of Ethnic and Religious Conflict* (Oxford: Berghahn, 2008), and (with Elizabeth Watson) *Changing Identifications and Alliances in North-East Africa,* 2 vols. (Oxford: Berghahn 2009).

RIJK VAN DIJK is a senior researcher and anthropologist at the African Studies Centre at Leiden University. His research and publications focus on the rise of new religious movements in Africa, particularly Pentecostalism, in relation to globalization and transnational connections. He has done extensive research on the emergence of Pentecostal movements in Malawi and the way these have involved youth, politics, and societal transformation. Van Dijk is the editor in chief of *African Diaspora: The Journal of Transnational Africa in a Global World* and has co-edited seven books, including *Situating Globality: African Agency in the Appropriation of Global Culture* (with Wim Van Binsbergen) (2005), *Strength beyond Structure: Social and Historical Trajectories of Agency in Africa* (with Mirjam De Bruijn and Jan-Bart Gewald) (2007), and *Mobile Africa: Changing Patterns of Movement in Africa and Beyond* (with Mirjam De Bruijn and Dick Foeken) (2008), all published by Brill in Leiden.

Index